ADempiere 3.6 Cookbook

Over 100 recipes for extending and customizing
ADempiere beyond its standard capabilities

Ajit Kumar

[PACKT] open source
PUBLISHING   community experience distilled

BIRMINGHAM - MUMBAI

ADempiere 3.6 Cookbook

First published: March 2011

Production Reference: 1040311

Published by Packt Publishing Ltd.
32 Lincoln Road
Olton
Birmingham, B27 6PA, UK.

ISBN 978-1-849513-38-8

www.packtpub.com

Cover Image by Asher Wishkerman (a.wishkerman@mpic.de)

Credits

Author
Ajit Kumar

Reviewers
Anuj Agarwal
Bahman Movaqar

Acquisition Editor
Steven Wilding

Development Editor
Susmita Panda

Technical Editor
Prashant Macha

Indexer
Hemangini Bari

Editorial Team Leader
Mithun Sehgal

Project Team Leader
Lata Basantani

Project Coordinator
Vishal Bodwani

Proofreader
Lisa Brady

Graphics
Nilesh R Mohite

Production Coordinator
Melwyn D'Sa

Cover Work
Melwyn D'Sa

About the Author

Ajit Kumar started his IT career with Honeywell, Bangalore in embedded systems area and moved on to enterprise business applications (such as ERP) in the 11 years of his career. From day one, he was a staunch supporter and promoter of Open Source and believes, strongly, that Open Source is the way for a liberal, diversified, and democratic setup like India.

He dreams and continuously endeavors that the architecture, frameworks, and tools must facilitate the software development – at the speed of thought.

Ajit holds a B.E. degree in Computer Science and Engineering from Bihar Institute of Technology and has co-founded Walking Tree, which is based out of Hyderabad, India. This is the place where he plays the role of a CTO, and works on fulfilling his vision.

I would like to thank my wife, Priti, my 4 year old son, Pratyush, and the new born who was very patient and supportive; my work colleague, Suman, whom I've had the pleasure to learn from; my business partners, Alok and Pradeep who relentlessly talk about the book; friends who always encouraged me; the reviewers, and all the people behind the ADempiere project and other Open Source projects.

About the Reviewers

Anuj Agarwal has a passion for providing easy solutions to complex business problems using information technology as a key tool.

Anuj started his career in merchant banking/investment banking and worked for a while in general management functions including finance, legal, and investor relations.

Anuj's passion to create smart solutions for business problems led him to consulting on large projects. He consulted for companies in the public sector and the private sector on solutions relating to finance, accounts, inventory, corporate loan management, housing loan management, treasury, personnel, and HR management.

Anuj has been involved in ERP implementation for the last 10 years.

Anuj is currently the Director of Aditi Business Solution, a startup providing smart business solutions to the corporate sector, public sector, and government sector in the areas of ERP, CRM, Hospital Management, IT Trainings, Mobile APPS, and Scanning and Digitization of documents and maps.

> I would like to dedicate my work to Mr. B.K. Seth, my teacher, friend, and philosopher, and would like to thank my wife Siddhi for all the support she extended to me, while I spent extra hours on this book.

Bahman Movaqar is an ERP and Information Systems consultant specializing in Open Source solutions. He has been working on ADempiere and Compiere projects for more than 5 years and has made several contributions to the ADempiere project, most notable among them is finding and patching a major security hole. He is currently working with the Iranian National Tax Administration Bureau as the CTO of an ERP project. He sometimes blogs on `http://BahmanM.com`.

I'd like to thank my lovely wife Nahid for her patience during all those nights I spent working on this book and my dear friend Timo for opening the gateway to free Internet for me.

www.PacktPub.com

Support files, eBooks, discount offers, and more

You might want to visit www.PacktPub.com for support files and downloads related to your book.

Did you know that Packt offers eBook versions of every book published, with PDF and ePub files available? You can upgrade to the eBook version at www.PacktPub.com and as a print book customer, you are entitled to a discount on the eBook copy. Get in touch with us at service@packtpub.com for more details.

At www.PacktPub.com, you can also read a collection of free technical articles, sign up for a range of free newsletters, and receive exclusive discounts and offers on Packt books and eBooks.

http://PacktLib.PacktPub.com

Do you need instant solutions to your IT questions? PacktLib is Packt's online digital book library. Here, you can access, read, and search across Packt's entire library of books.

Why Subscribe?

- Fully searchable across every book published by Packt
- Copy and paste, print and bookmark content
- On demand and accessible via web browser

Free Access for Packt account holders

If you have an account with Packt at www.PacktPub.com, you can use this to access PacktLib today and view nine entirely free books. Simply use your login credentials for immediate access.

Table of Contents

Preface

ADempiere is one of the leading open source ERP products in today's business market. ADempiere offers everything you need to make your business successful. Efficient data management, streamlining business processes, reduction in costs, and minimal complexity.

What this book covers

Chapter 1, Preparing the Ground: This is the starting point. The chapter prepares us for the journey ahead. In this chapter, we would learn how to set up a typical development as well as deployment environment. This chapter introduces the different tools and teaches us how to make use of them in the development.

Chapter 2, ADempiere Customization – Part I: In this chapter, we are going to look at the overall customization capability of ADempiere, mainly through the Application Dictionary configuration. The chapter covers topics such as creating a new window, how to customize an existing one, how to create multiple tabs in a window, the search widget, zoom option, and menu tree. A case study-based approach has been taken to explain the practical relevance of each of the topics.

Chapter 3, ADempiere Customization – Part II: In this chapter, we will look into the advanced configuration options of ADempiere and topics such as data filtration, using display and default logics, lookup record, dynamic validation, customizing print format, working with the models, callouts, processes, and toolbars.

Chapter 4, Web Services: This chapter covers the recipes and the steps required to get the Web services capability built into the ADempiere. The chapter explains the different types of ADempiere Web services and how to make use of them.

Chapter 5, VirtueMart Integration: This chapter introduces Joomla!'s VirtueMart shopping cart component and its integration with ADempiere. The recipes try to provide the required information using which we shall be able to use VirtueMart as the web store.

Chapter 6, JasperReports with ADempiere: JasperReports is at the heart of ADempiere's reporting framework. In this chapter, you learn how to set up the environment, how to develop a new report with/without a database view, how to make use of ADempiere's context in a report, using sub-reports, and how to use a custom report for printing.

Chapter 7, PayPal Integration: This chapter is dedicated to the integration of PayPal with ADempiere. The recipes include setting up the environment, making use of the PayPal APIs, and the specific use cases, like, making payment to a PayPal account, receiving payment from a PayPal account, and the Instant Payment Notification.

Chapter 8, Equifax Integration: Equifax is a popular credit reporting agency, which is used to find out the information pertaining to the customers to evaluate his/her credit status and validity about information provided by the customer. In this chapter, we would discuss about integrating ADempiere with Equifax. The chapter covers the different services offered by Equifax, such as, the address matching service, bank validation service, company matching service, consumer bureau service, and the password change service.

Chapter 9, Mondrian Integration for Analysis: In this chapter, we will learn about the Open Source OLAP engine – Mondrian, and understand how to use it and integrate it with ADempiere to provide the analysis capability on top of the existing ADempiere schema. The chapter covers the concepts such as cube, slicing, dicing, and the provided recipes show how to build them using Mondrian.

Chapter 10, E-mail Integration with Mozilla Thunderbird: This chapter contains the recipes demonstrating the steps required to integrate Mozilla Thunderbird (an e-mail client) with ADempiere. It takes us through the steps needed to build a Thunderbird add-on for ADempiere, using which the user can import the e-mail IDs of the contact, setup in ADempiere, and use them to compose mails.

What you need for this book

- Eclipse Galileo (Eclipse for JEE development)
- JBoss 4.2.3 GA
- JDK 1.6
- PostgreSQL Database 8.x
- SVN client (for example, TortoiseSVN)
- soapUI for Web services, VirtueMart, Thunderbird, and so on

Who this book is for

If you want to easily implement ADempiere in your organization, this book is for you. This book will also be beneficial to system users and administrators who wish to implement an ERP system. Only basic knowledge of ADempiere is required. This cookbook will build on that basic knowledge equipping you with the intermediate and advanced skills required to fully maximize ADempiere. A basic knowledge of accounting and the standard business workflow would be beneficial.

Conventions

In this book, you will find a number of styles of text that distinguish between different kinds of information. Here are some examples of these styles, and an explanation of their meaning.

Code words in text are shown as follows: "In this recipe, we saw how we can use the Ant build file `build.xml` to compile the code and create the installation packages (`.zip` and `.tar.gz` files)."

A block of code is set as follows:

```
SELECT ad_client_id,c_momstatus_id,name,isdefault,value FROM
c_momstatus;
```

Any command-line input or output is written as follows:

```
java mondrian.test.loader.MondrianFoodMartLoader -verbose -tables
-data -indexes -jdbcDrivers="org.postgresql.Driver,sun.jdbc.odbc.
JdbcOdbcDriver" -inputFile=C:\mondrian\demo\FoodMartCreateData.
sql -outputJdbcURL="jdbc:postgresql://localhost/foodmart"
-outputJdbcUser=adempiere360 -outputJdbcPassword=adempiere
```

New terms and **important words** are shown in bold. Words that you see on the screen, in menus or dialog boxes for example, appear in the text like this: "Click on the **Product** link, uncheck **Patio Table** and click on the **OK** button".

[Warnings or important notes appear in a box like this.]

[Tips and tricks appear like this.]

Reader feedback

Feedback from our readers is always welcome. Let us know what you think about this book—what you liked or may have disliked. Reader feedback is important for us to develop titles that you really get the most out of.

To send us general feedback, simply send an e-mail to feedback@packtpub.com, and mention the book title via the subject of your message.

If there is a book that you need and would like to see us publish, please send us a note in the **SUGGEST A TITLE** form on www.packtpub.com or e-mail suggest@packtpub.com.

If there is a topic that you have expertise in and you are interested in either writing or contributing to a book, see our author guide on www.packtpub.com/authors.

Customer support

Now that you are the proud owner of a Packt book, we have a number of things to help you to get the most from your purchase.

> **Downloading the example code for this book**
>
> You can download the example code files for all Packt books you have purchased from your account at http://www.PacktPub.com. If you purchased this book elsewhere, you can visit http://www.PacktPub.com/support and register to have the files e-mailed directly to you.

Errata

Although we have taken every care to ensure the accuracy of our content, mistakes do happen. If you find a mistake in one of our books—maybe a mistake in the text or the code—we would be grateful if you would report this to us. By doing so, you can save other readers from frustration and help us improve subsequent versions of this book. If you find any errata, please report them by visiting http://www.packtpub.com/support, selecting your book, clicking on the **errata submission form** link, and entering the details of your errata. Once your errata are verified, your submission will be accepted and the errata will be uploaded on our website, or added to any list of existing errata, under the Errata section of that title. Any existing errata can be viewed by selecting your title from http://www.packtpub.com/support.

Piracy

Piracy of copyright material on the Internet is an ongoing problem across all media. At Packt, we take the protection of our copyright and licenses very seriously. If you come across any illegal copies of our works, in any form, on the Internet, please provide us with the location address or website name immediately so that we can pursue a remedy.

Please contact us at copyright@packtpub.com with a link to the suspected pirated material.

We appreciate your help in protecting our authors, and our ability to bring you valuable content.

Questions

You can contact us at questions@packtpub.com if you are having a problem with any aspect of the book, and we will do our best to address it.

Preparing the Ground

1

In this chapter, we will cover:

- ▶ Creating the installer from the source code
- ▶ Installing ADempiere
- ▶ Debugging the ADempiere client application (Desktop version)
- ▶ Debugging the ADempiere server application (Web version)
- ▶ Running multiple instances on a single machine
- ▶ Giving ADempiere your identity

Introduction

Before we get started with the real customization work in ADempiere, it is very important that we set up the right environment for the development and equip ourselves with the tools required for the customization. Most important among them is the ability to debug the existing code, so that when we make changes to the existing code or add a new functionality, we would have a way to find out the source of the problem, identify the cause, and make the necessary change to resolve it.

With this goal in perspective, in this chapter, we will understand how to setup ADempiere development environment and the different deployment mechanism which can be applied to the operational aspect of ADempiere. The chapter starts with the focus on the development environment where we will see how to check out the code from the ADempiere SVN repository, build it, create an installer from it, use the installer to install ADempiere on your system, debug the client version of ADempiere, and debug the server version. Subsequently, we will move on to the operational aspect where we will understand what it takes to run multiple instances of the ADempiere server on a single machine. As part of this, we will cover different deployment topologies, keeping the database and the application server in perspective and understand the topology-wise differences.

With most of the Open Source applications, it is more likely that you will customize or enhance ADempiere to suit yours or your customers' needs and you would like to give it your identity. You may want to give it a different name, use a different logo, or a different look-and-feel. We will cover this aspect in the last recipe of this chapter.

Software requirement

Like any other software application, ADempiere also requires certain software to be installed and configured on your system. In order to be able to customize or enhance ADempiere, you need a few more tools/applications and we have to have them properly configured before we start on our goal. Though not mandated by ADempiere, throughout this book, we will use the following list of software on the MS Windows platform:

- ▸ Eclipse Galileo (Eclipse for JEE development)
- ▸ JBoss 4.2.3 GA
- ▸ JDK 1.6
- ▸ PostgreSQL Database 8.x
- ▸ SVN client (for example, TortoiseSVN)

> Though ADempiere supports Oracle and Oracle XE databases, for this book, we will use PostgreSQL database to keep these things simple and light.

The steps to install and configure the previously listed software are out of this book's scope. You may refer to `http://wiki.postgresql.org/wiki/Detailed_installation_guides` for the installation steps. Each one of these software come along with their own installation and setup manual. Kindly refer to them for installation and configuration. There is no specific configuration requirement for using this software with ADempiere. So, if you follow the respective installation manuals, you will be fine. However, at the end of the installation of all the software, ensure that the following environment variables are set and they are valid:

- ▸ JAVA_HOME

For ease of reference, let us assume that the following is the installation path for the previously listed software on your system and the corresponding name that we will use to refer to those paths:

- ▸ **Eclipse Galileo**—C:\EclipseGalileo – ECLIPSE_HOME
- ▸ **JBoss 4.2.3 GA**—C:\JBoss_423_GA – JBOSS_HOME
- ▸ **JDK 1.6 or above**—C:\Java\jdk1.6_X – JAVA_HOME
- ▸ **PostgreSQL Database 8.x**—C:\postgresql8.x – POSTGRES_HOME

At this point, we are all set to get started on our tour of ADempiere customization and enhancement.

> JBoss 4.2 version has been used throughout this book as it is closer to the version which ADempiere 3.4 uses. Though the steps are not too different in JBoss 5.0, I would refrain from making it a rule.

Creating the installer from the source code

The recipe describes the steps involved in building the ADempiere source code and creating an installer out of it, which is ready for you to install on your own system or any other system. These installer images are installable on MS Windows as well as Linux systems.

This is the basic recipe and a pre-requisite for any other recipe mentioned in this book.

How to do it...

1. Check out the ADempiere code from the following SVN URL:

   `https://adempiere.svn.sourceforge.net/svnroot/adempiere/tags/adempiere360lts`.

   Say, we have checked out the ADempiere code in the `C:\adempiere_svn\ tags\adempiere360lts` folder. We'll refer to the `C:\adempiere_svn` folder by name, say, `ADEMPIERE_SVN`

2. Start Eclipse.

3. Click on **File menu** and select **Import...**

4. Select the **Existing Projects into Workspace** option under the **General** category and click on the **Next** button. Dialog with the title **Import Projects** appears with the **Select root directory** radio button.

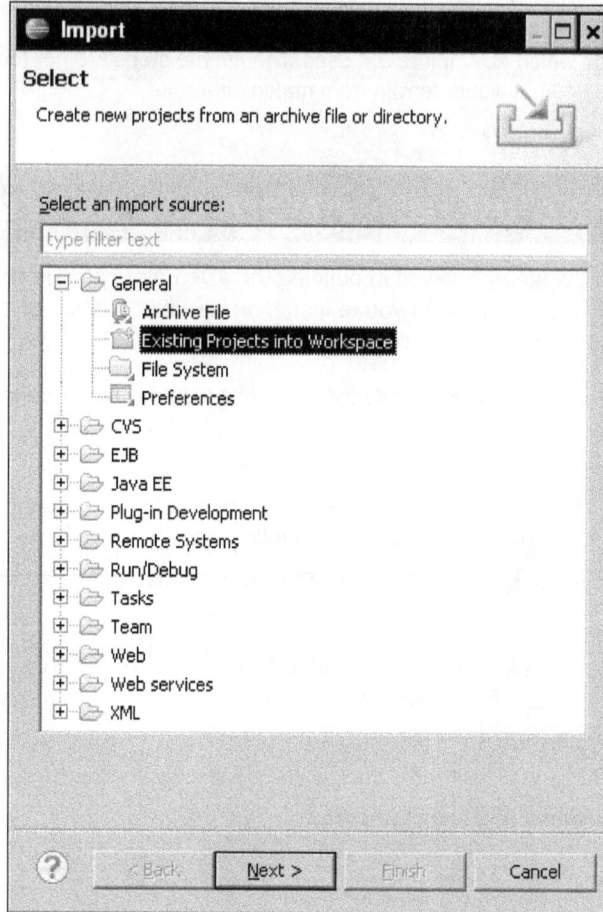

5. Click on the **Browse** button next to the **Select root directory** radio button and select the `adempiere360lts` folder under the `<ADEMPIERE_SVN>\tags` folder. This will add `adempiere_360` to the Projects list.

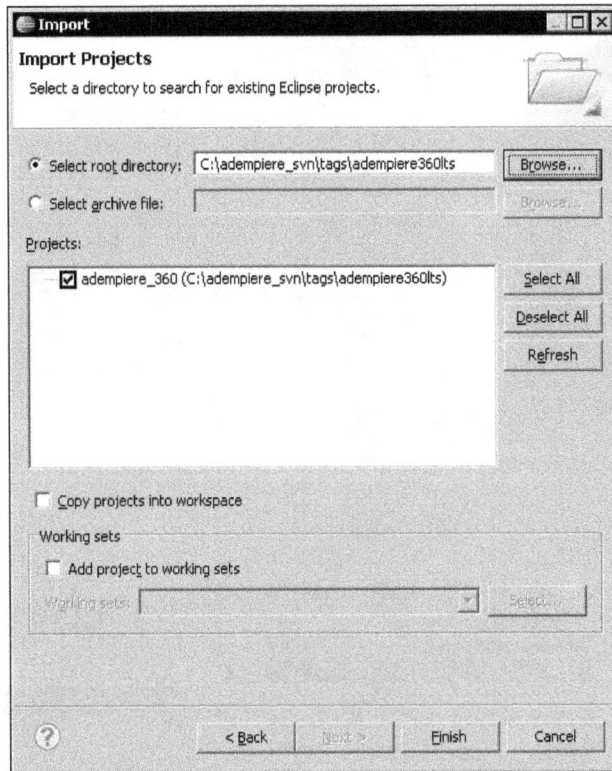

6. Click on the **Finish** button. This will import the project `adempiere_360` into your Eclipse Workspace and build it, if the **Build Automatically** option is set in your Eclipse. If not, build the project.

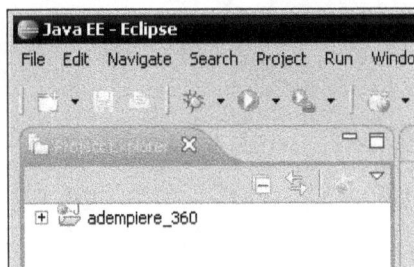

7. Expand the `adempiere_360` project in Eclipse. You will see the **utils_dev** folder.

8. Expand the **utils_dev** folder and you will find **build.xml**. This is the Ant build script to compile the ADempiere source code and create the installable binaries.

9. Right click on **build.xml** and select **Run As | Ant Build**. This will start the build process.

The following message appears in the console at the end of the build:

A successful build will create the **adempiere** folder under the project folder and the following binary installers are created, which can be used to install ADempiere on MS Windows or Linux:

- `Adempiere_360LTS.zip`

- `Adempiere_360LTS.tar.gz`

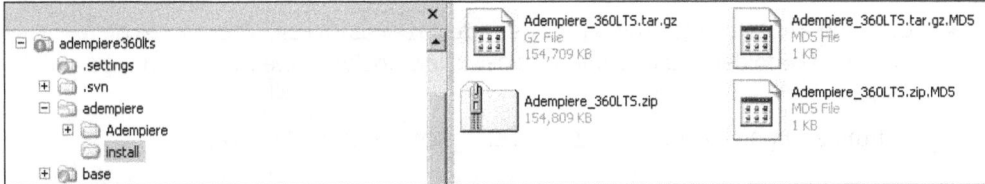

How it works...

In step 1, we first get the ADempiere code from its SVN repository. In steps 2 through to 6, we compile the code. In steps 7 through to 9, we create the distributions (Linux as well as MS Windows) by running the default Ant target inside the `build.xml` file, present under the `utils_dev` folder

There's more...

In this recipe, we saw how we can use the Ant build file `build.xml` to compile the code and create the installation packages (`.zip` and `.tar.gz` files). The same can be achieved by running a batch file.

Using RUN_Build.bat to create the installer

If you like working with command prompt, then you can use the `<ADEMPIERE_SVN>\ tags\ adempiere360lts\utils_dev\RUN_Build.bat` script from the command prompt. This script, after a successful build, will create the installers.

 For the Linux users, there is an equivalent script with the extension `.sh`. For all the `.bat` script for MS Windows, there is a corresponding `.sh` shell script available.

Installing ADempiere

Now that we have created the installers in the previous recipe, here we will make use of it to install an instance of ADempiere for our use. This recipe describes the steps involved in installing and setting up the ADempiere instance to make it usable.

Getting ready

1. Create a new database in PostgreSQL by name, say, **adempiere360**.

2. Add the **adempiere** user in the PostgreSQL database with **adempiere** as the password.

3. Stop and restart PostgreSQL.

4. Copy the `<ADEMPIERE_SVN>\ tags\adempiere360lts \adempiere\ Adempiere` folder and its content to `C:\`. Now, you will have the `C:\Adempiere` folder.

5. Set the environment variable `ADEMPIERE_HOME` to `C:\Adempiere`.

How to do it...

1. Open a command prompt by selecting `Start Button | Run | Open` and enter `cmd`.

2. Change the directory to `<ADEMPIERE_HOME>\data`.

3. Run the following commands to set up the ADempiere schema:

```
psql -U adempiere -d adempiere360 -c "drop schema sqlj cascade"
psql -U adempiere -d adempiere360 -f Adempiere_pg.dmp >> dump_
errors.log.
```

When prompted, enter `adempiere` as the password.

4. Change the directory to `<ADEMPIERE_HOME>`.

5. Run `RUN_setup.bat`. This will bring up a window to enter various details.

6. Enter the valid values.

Database Server	localhost/127.0.0.1
Database Type	postgresql
Database Name	adempieredb
Database User	adempiere
Database Password	adempiere
System Password	<your PostgreSQL database admin user password>

7. Click on the **Test** button. First time setup will pop up the **Key Store Dialog**. Enter the relevant details, as shown in the following screenshot, and click on the tick button:

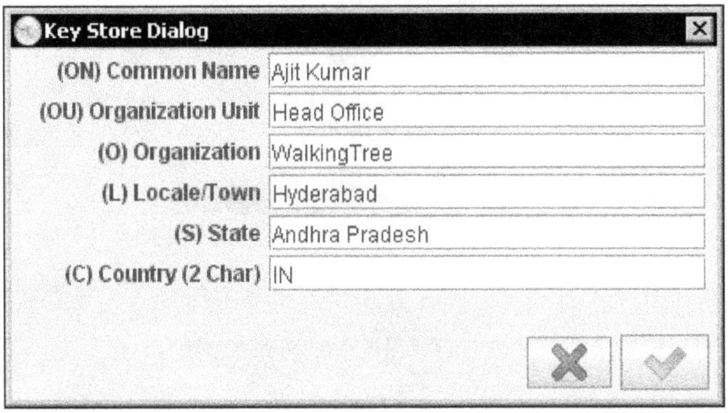

8. Click on the **Test** button and verify that all the tests have been passed (a tick mark appear next to the fields, as shown in the following screen shot):

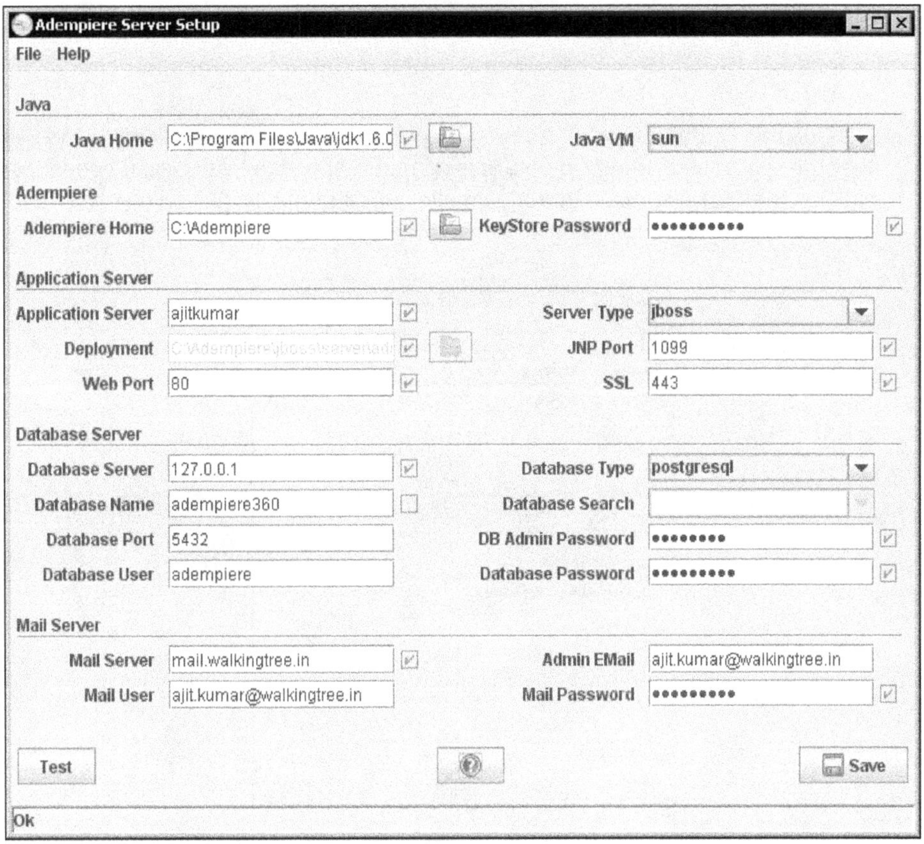

9. Click on the **Save** button to save the settings.

10. Accept the license term, when prompted. This will create an `Adempiere.properties` file in the <ADEMPIERE_HOME> folder.

11. When setup is complete, change directory to <ADEMPIERE_HOME>.

12. Run `RUN_Adempiere.bat`. This will start the client version of ADempiere and will show you the following login screen.

13. Click on the button, which is on the right-hand side of the Server field, and verify that the database connection details is correct. Change the settings, if needed, and click on the **Test Database** button to make sure that the cross icon changes to a tick icon, as shown in the following screen shot:

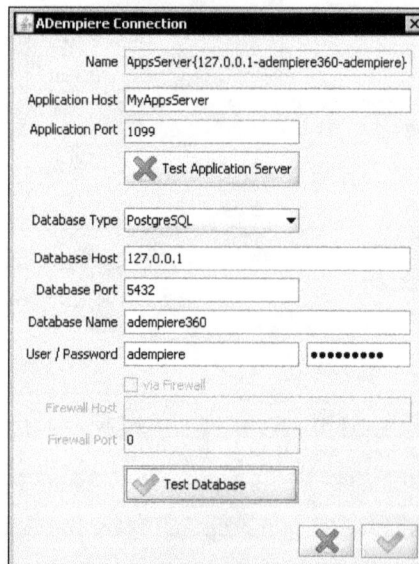

14. If you want to run the server version of ADempiere, then change the directory to <ADEMPIERE_HOME>\utils and run RUN_Server2.bat. This will deploy ADempiere in JBoss, which is distributed along with it, and start the JBoss server. After the server has been started, you may verify your ADempiere installation by accessing the following URL from the browser of your choice —http://localhost:8080/webui—8080 is the default JBoss port. If it is different in your case, replace 8080 with your JBoss' port number. This needs to be done to ensure that the port that you are using for your JBoss server instance is free; otherwise the server will not run.

   To stop the server, you shall run RUN_Server2Stop.bat.

How it works...

First, we create the database and import the ADempiere data dump using steps 1 through to 3. In steps 4 through to 10, we complete the initial setup of our ADempiere instance with details such as database detail, mail server detail, and so on, so that it is ready to run. Steps 11 through to 13 helps us to run the desktop as the well as web version of ADempiere.

There's more...

Alternatively, to import ADempiere schema and the initial (GardenWorld) data, you may go to the <ADEMPIERE_HOME>\utils folder and run the RUN_ImportAdempiere.bat file.

See also

> Creating installer from the source code

Debugging the ADempiere client application (Desktop version)

Debugging the client version is pretty straightforward and quick. In this recipe, we will see how to configure the project in Eclipse so that we can debug ADempiere when we run it as a client application (the Swing version).

Getting ready

Before we can run ADempiere, there are properties, specific to ADempiere, which need to be configured properly for example, JDK location detail, application server detail, database detail, SMTP detail (for e-mails), and so on. The following steps must be completed to ensure that these properties are set up correctly:

1. In Eclipse, open the **Open Resource** window and select the Setup.java file. It is available under the install\src\org\compiere\install package of your adempiere360lts project.

2. Right-click on the `Setup.java` file in the **Project Explorer** and select the option `Run As | Java Application`. This will launch an ADempiere setup screen.

For the client version, we need to set the fields in the following sections of the screen:

▸ **Java**

▸ **Adempiere**

▸ **Database Server**

▸ **Mail Server** (Optional)

Click on the **Test** button and if everything was set correctly, you will see the **Ok** message at the bottom of the setup screen. In case you get errors, verify the values you have entered. Correct them and **Test** until you get the **Ok** message. Any errors during the testing are also shown on this window.

> In case any errors occur during your practice and it is not described in the book, you may refer to the ADempiere Wiki and forums for more information.

3. Click on the **Save** button. This will create the `Adempiere.properties` file in the **Adempiere Home** directory. After creating the property file, the program tries to build the code base but fails with a build error. Do not worry! Our intention was to only get the `Adempiere.properties` file created, which we will use in our subsequent setups.

How to do it...

Now that we have got the `Adempiere.properties` file out, it is a trivial task to be able to debug the application. Here are the steps:

1. In Eclipse, open the **Open Resource** window and select the `Adempiere.java` file. It is available under the `base\src\org\compiere` folder of your `adempiere_360` project. This class is the entry point class for the client version.

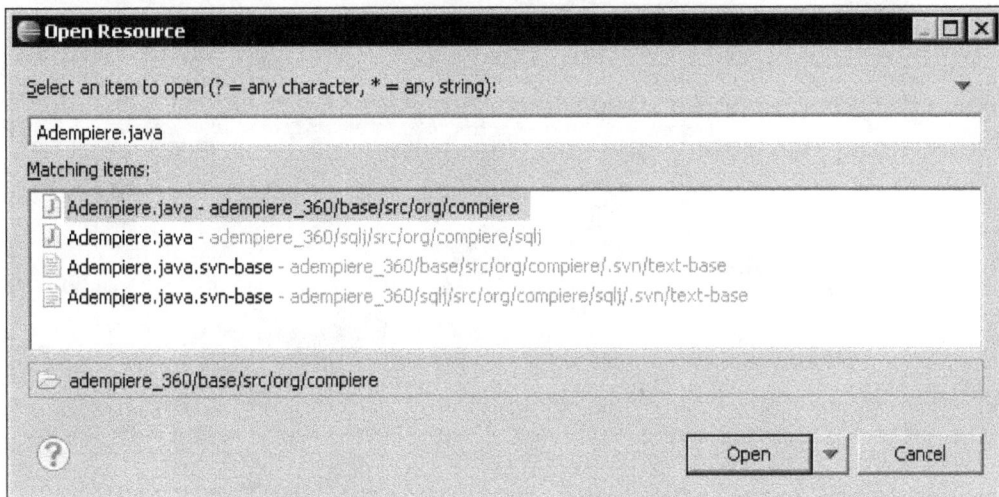

2. Add a break-point at Line 594 inside the main method.

3. Right-click on the `Adempiere.java` file and select **Debug As | Debug Configuration**. This will bring up the **Debug Configurations** window.

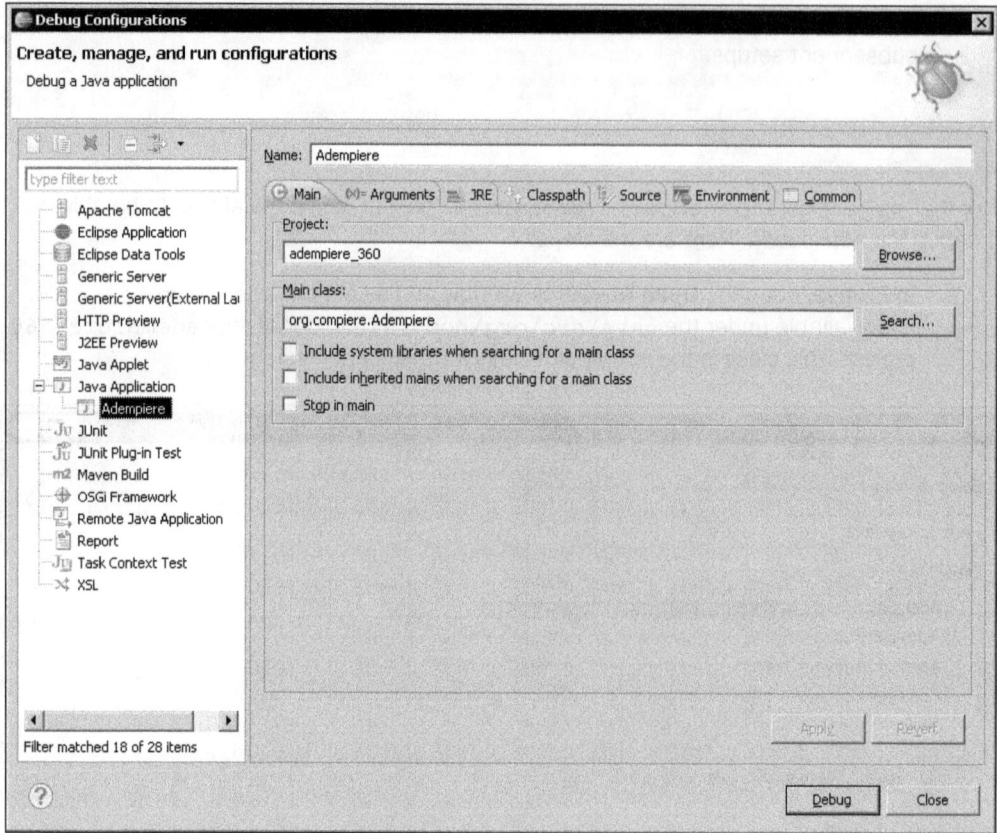

4. Click on the **Arguments** tab and specify the following **VM arguments**:

```
DPropertyFile="C:\adempiere_svn\tags\adempiere360lts\ADempiere.
properties" -
DADEMPIERE_HOME="C:\ tags\adempiere360lts"
```

   ❑ `PropertyFile`: Points to the `Adempiere.properties` file, which we had created earlier

   ❑ `ADEMPIERE_HOME`: Points to the **Adempiere** folder

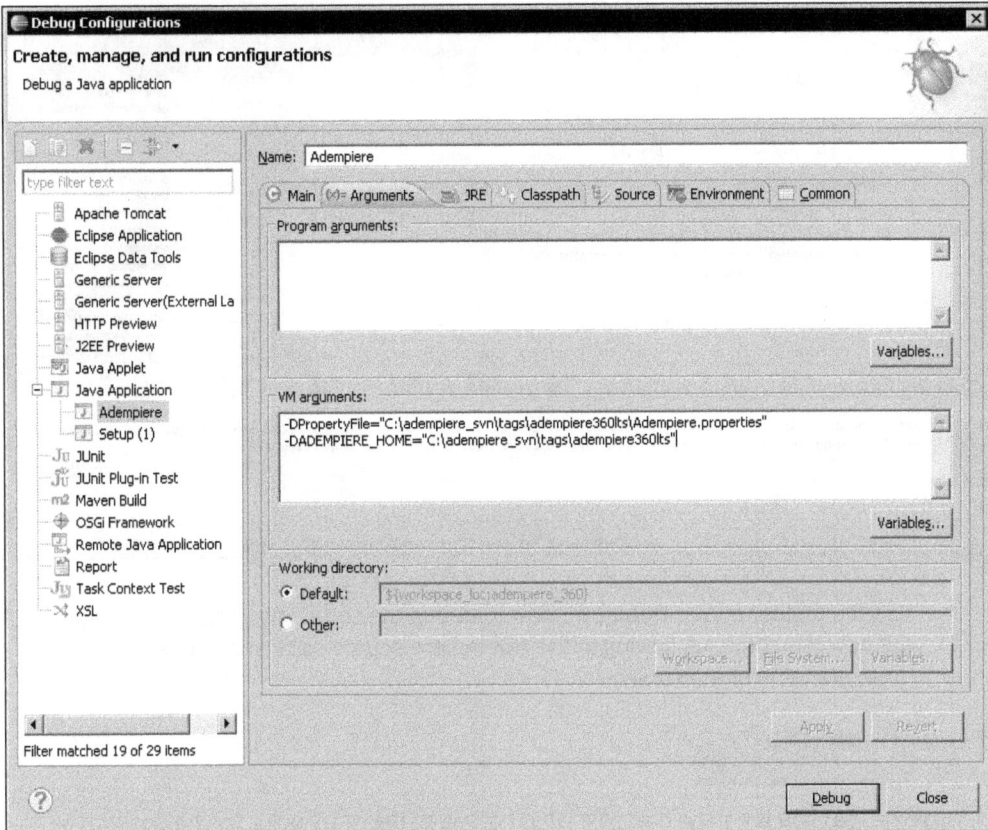

5. Click on the **Debug** button to start the debugging.

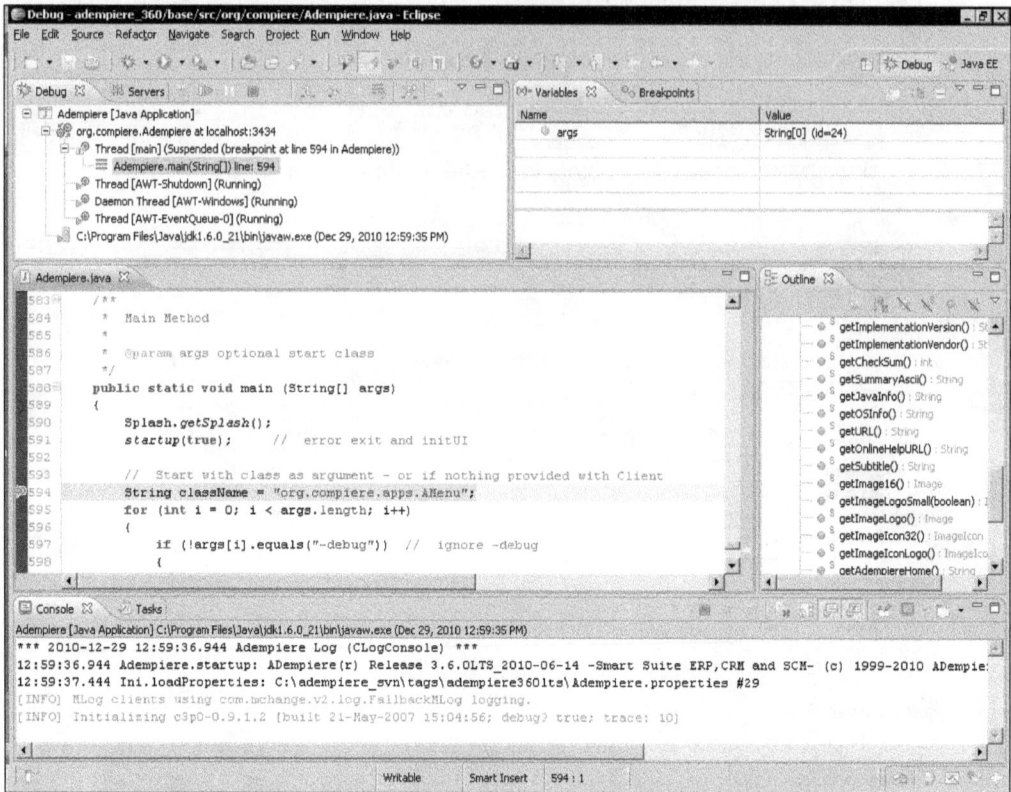

6. Use the toolbar on the **Debug** window to debug the code. This way, you can figure out how the control is flowing in the ADempiere source code and gain a better understanding of the subject.

How it works...

`Adempiere.java` is the main class file which provides the entry point for the desktop version of ADempiere. This is the class where you will find the `main` method. To this class, the two important properties—`PropertyFile` and `ADEMPIERE_HOME` must be passed so that it can read the setup information (database, mail server, JRE path, and so on) and run the application.

See also

▸ Creating an installer from the source code

▸ Installing Adempiere

Debugging the ADempiere server application (web version)

Working with the web/server version of ADempiere is equally practical and required as compared to the client/desktop version. The server version runs inside a J2EE container, like JBoss. In this recipe, we will see how to configure ADempiere and JBoss to be able to debug the code when it is deployed as a server. Though ADempiere comes along with a JBoss distribution, to have a better understanding of the subject matter, we will use the external JBoss installation.

Getting ready

▸ Verify that JBoss is installed on your system and set up correctly

How to do it...

1. In Eclipse, go to the **Servers** view.

2. Right-click and select **New | Server**. You will see the **New Server** window.

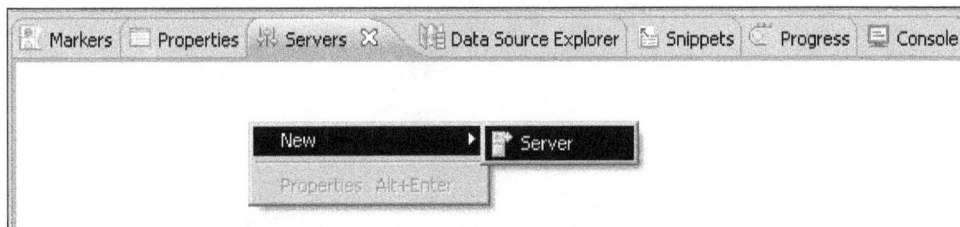

3. On the **New Server** window, select the **JBoss V4.2** and click the **Next** button. This will take you to the **New JBoss V4.2 Runtime** window.

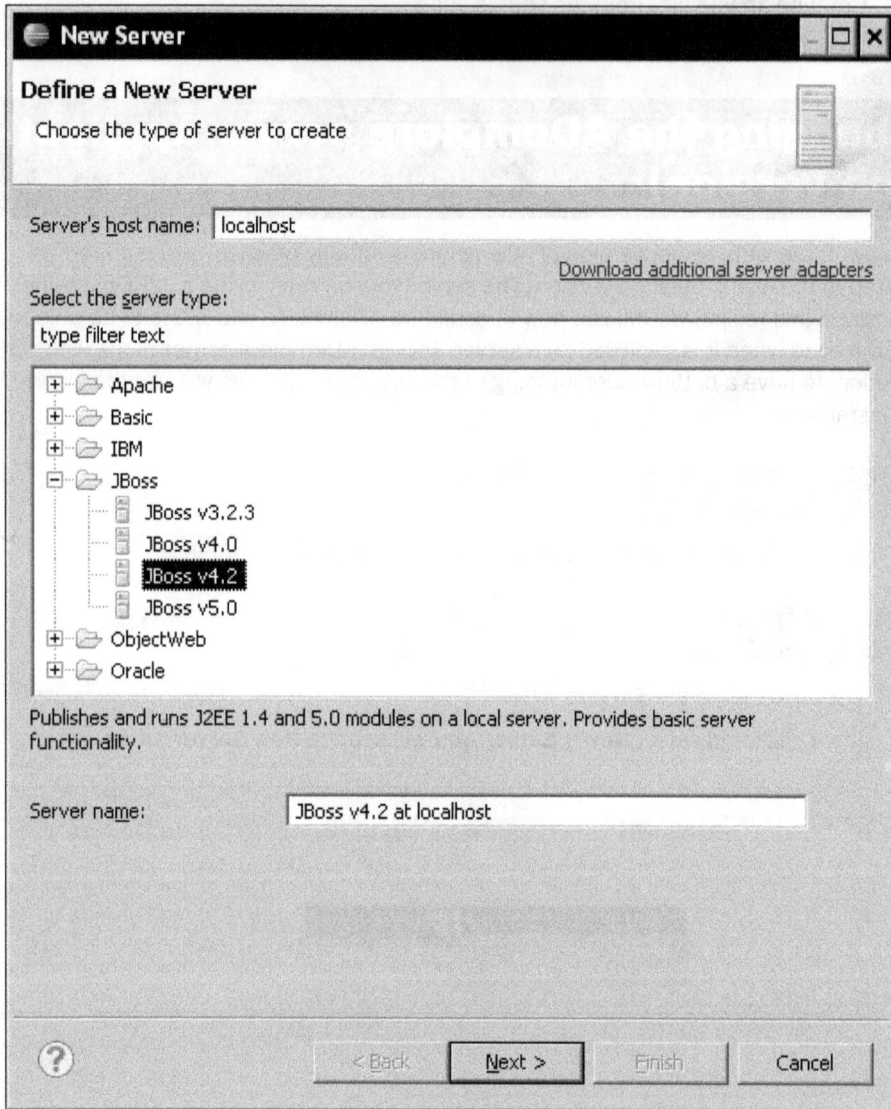

4. On the runtime window, enter the following values and click the **Next** button:

JRE: Choose JDK 1.6 or above

Application Server Directory: Set this to your JBoss installation folder (which is JBOSS_HOME)

This will take you to the following **New JBoss V4.2 Server** window:

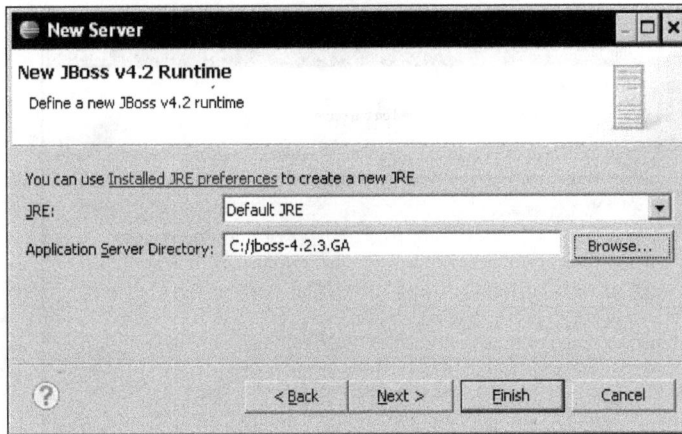

5. On the **New JBoss v4.2 Server** window, enter the following and click the **Next** button:

- ❏ **Address**: 127.0.0.1

- ❏ **Port**: 9080 (make sure that this port is not being used by any other application on your system)

- ❏ **JNDI Port**: 1099 (make sure that this port is not being used by any other application on your system)

- ❏ **Server Configuration**: default

Clicking on the **Next** button will take you to the **Add and Remove** window:

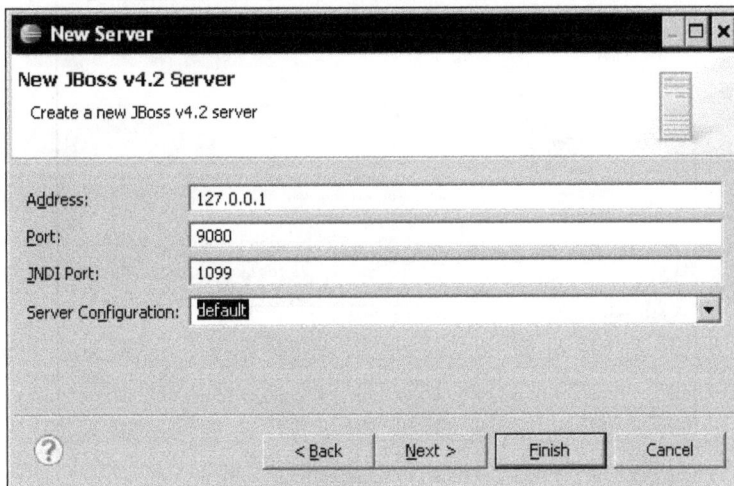

6. On the **Add and Remove** window, select `Adempiere_trunk` from the **Available** list, and add it to the **Configured** list.

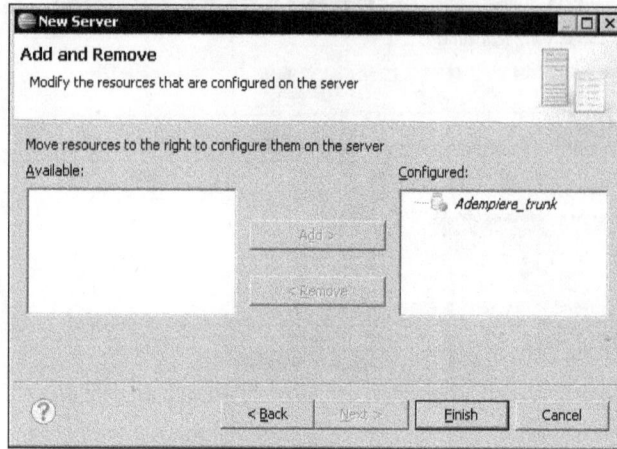

7. Click on the **Finish** button. This will add an entry in the **Servers** view.

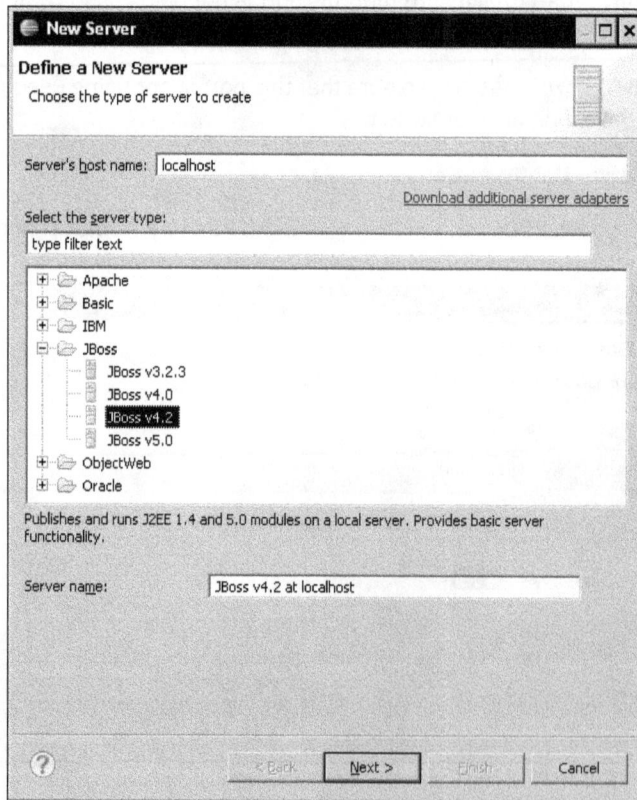

8. Open `org.adempiere.webui.AdempiereWebUI.java` and add a break-point inside the constructor.

9. Right-click on the server entry, which we just created, and select the **Open** menu option.

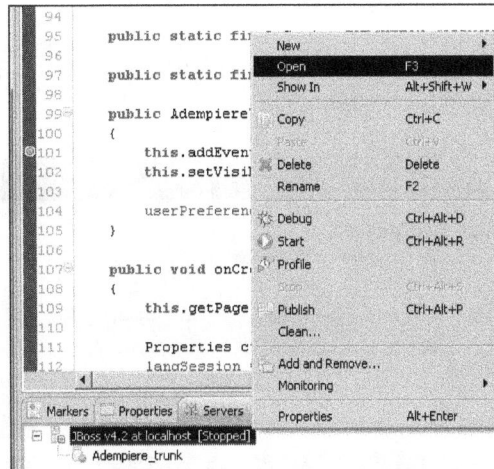

This will open the JBoss server Overview.

10. On the **Overview** screen, change the **Start** value under the **Timeouts** category to **500**.

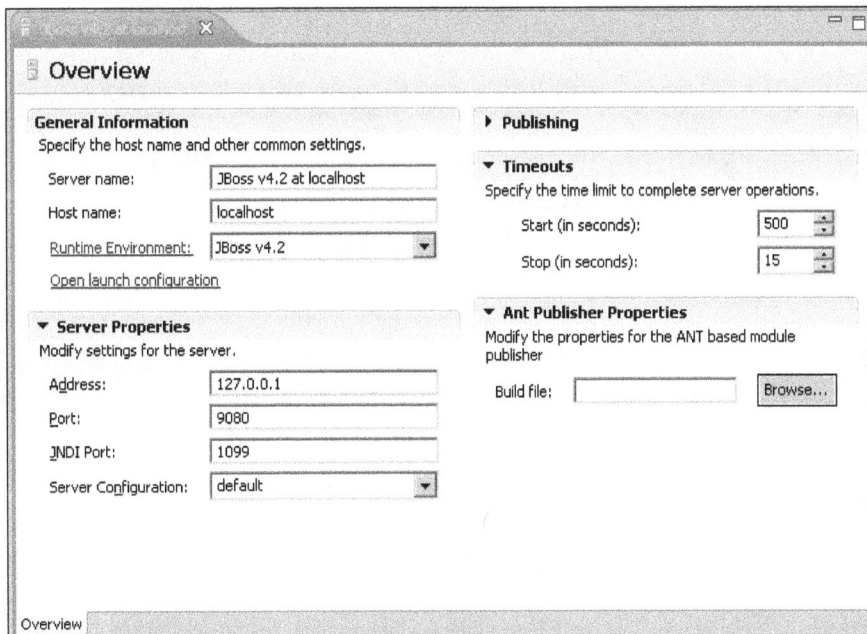

For the `default` **Server Configuration**, the port number is defaulted to `8080` unless you go and change the `config` files of JBoss, which we'll see in the subsequent recipe. For now, note that even though you enter `9080` as the port, the JBoss server will run on port `8080`. So, make sure that port `8080` is free on your system.

11. Click on the **Open launch** configuration. This will bring up the **Edit configuration** window to edit the JBoss configuration.

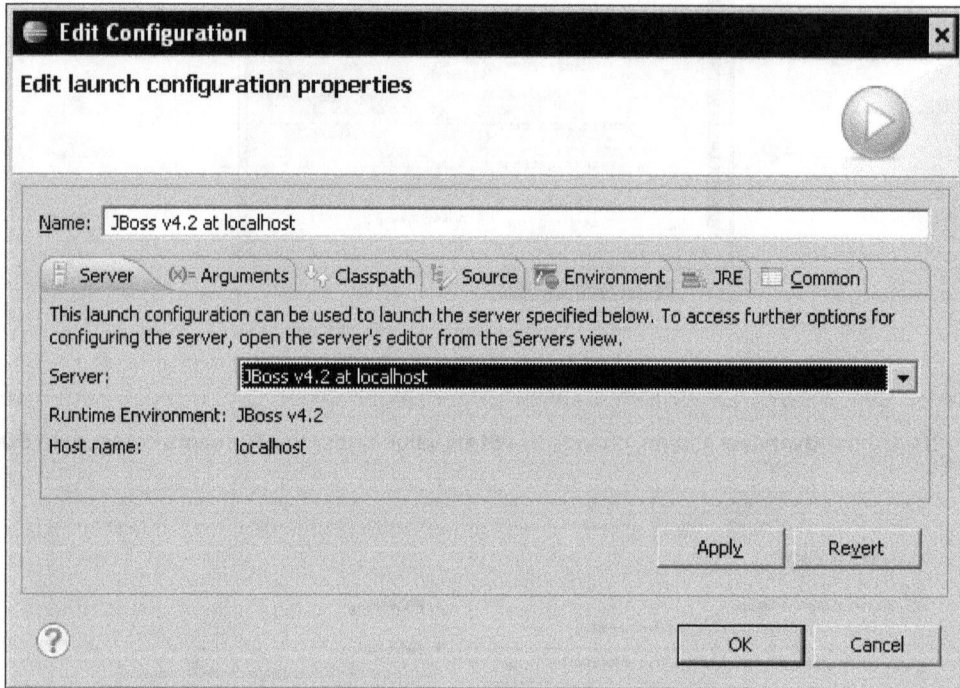

Edit Configuration

Edit launch configuration properties

Name: JBoss v4.2 at localhost

| Server | (x)= Arguments | Classpath | Source | Environment | JRE | Common |

This launch configuration can be used to launch the server specified below. To access further options for configuring the server, open the server's editor from the Servers view.

Server: JBoss v4.2 at localhost

Runtime Environment: JBoss v4.2

Host name: localhost

Apply   Revert

OK   Cancel

---

12. On the **Arguments** tab, add the following to the **VM arguments**:

```
-DPropertyFile="C:\adempiere_svn\tags\adempiere360lts\ADempiere.
properties" -
DADEMPIERE_HOME="C:\adempiere_svn\tags\adempiere360lts"
```

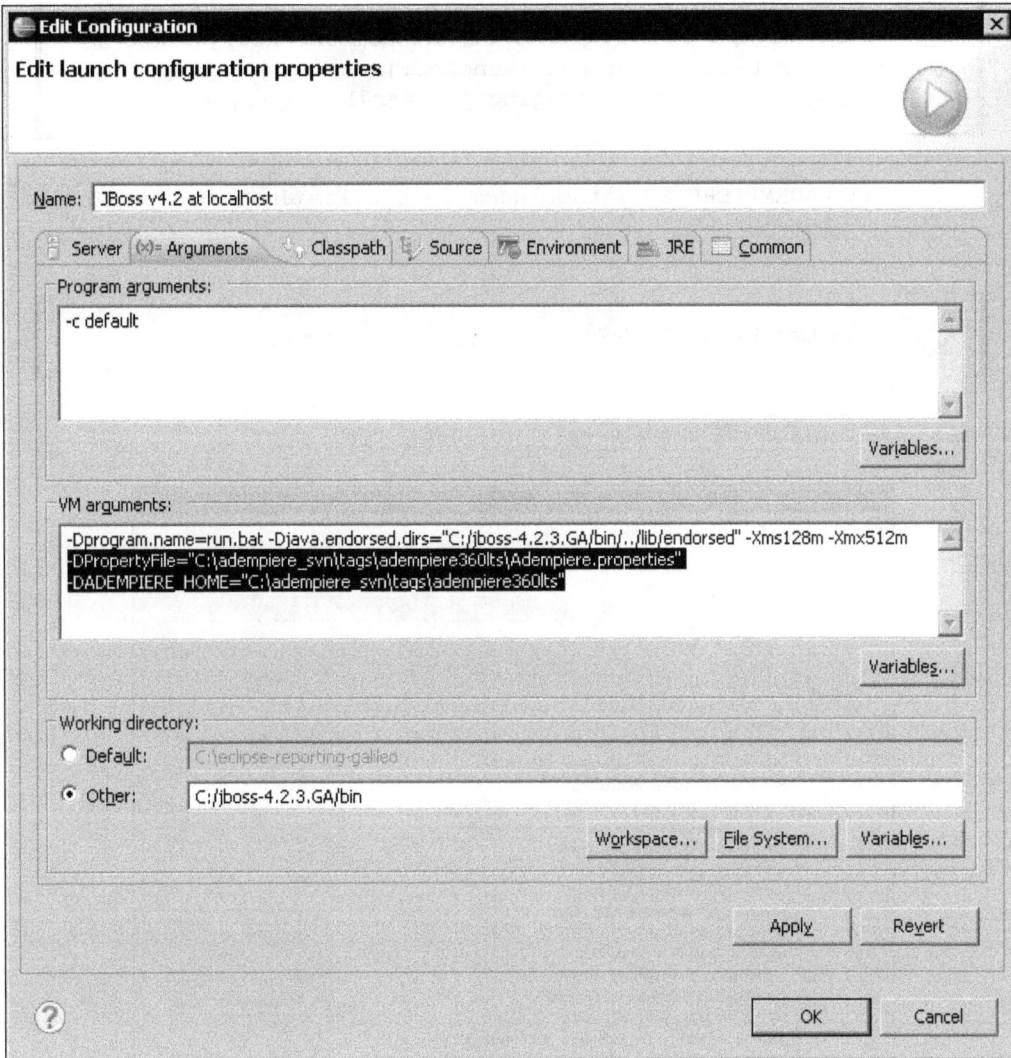

13. On the **Classpath** tab, click on the **Add External JARs** button to add the JARs from the following folders:

   ❑ `<ADEMPIERE_SVN>\tags\adempiere360lts\tools\lib`

> Exclude the following JARs: `ant.jar`, `ant-commons-net.jar`, `ant-contrib-1.0b1.jar`, `ant-launcher.jar`, `j2ee.jar`, `jnlp.jar`, `log4j.jar`, `commons-logging.jar`, `servlet-api.jar`

   ❑ `<ADEMPIERE_SVN>\tags\adempiere360lts\JasperReportsTools\lib`

> Exclude the following JARs: `jfreechart-1.0.13.jar`

   ❑ Add `<JAVA_HOME>\jre\lib\javaws.jar`

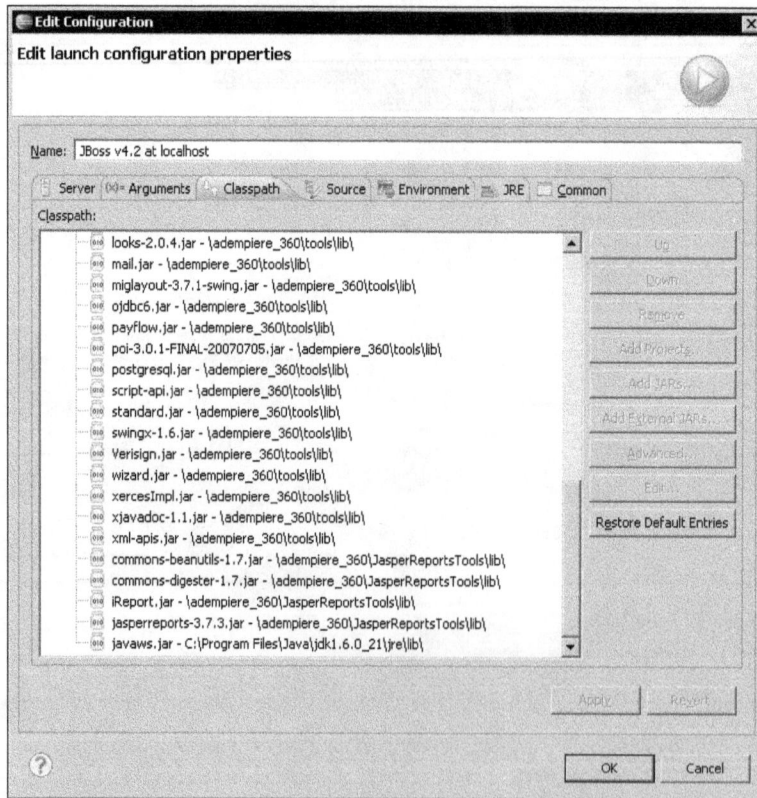

14. Click **Apply** followed by the **OK** button.

15. Refresh the project `adempiere_360`.

16. Right-click on the JBoss server entry on the **Servers** view and select the **Publish** menu option. This will start the process of build and deployment. The application is deployed with the context name `Adempiere_trunk`.

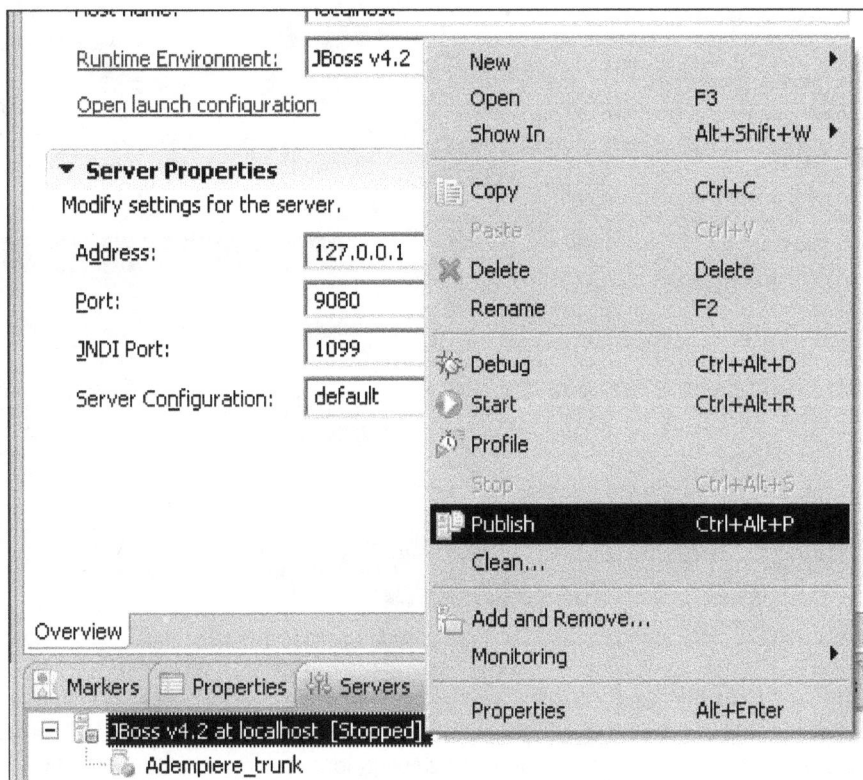

4. After publish is completed (you will see the **Synchronized** text next to the JBoss server entry in the **Servers** view), right-click on the server and select the **Debug** menu option.

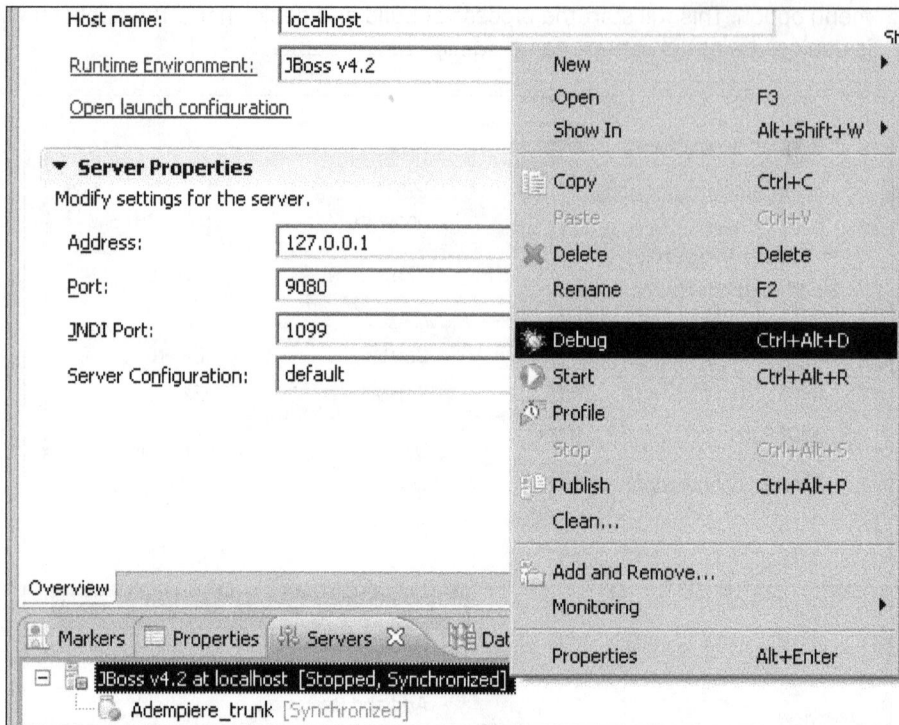

Host name:	localhost		
Runtime Environment:	JBoss v4.2	New	▶
Open launch configuration		Open	F3
		Show In	Alt+Shift+W ▶
▼ **Server Properties**		Copy	Ctrl+C
Modify settings for the server.		Paste	Ctrl+V
Address:	127.0.0.1	Delete	Delete
Port:	9080	Rename	F2
JNDI Port:	1099	Debug	Ctrl+Alt+D
Server Configuration:	default	Start	Ctrl+Alt+R
		Profile	
		Stop	Ctrl+Alt+S
		Publish	Ctrl+Alt+P
		Clean...	
Overview		Add and Remove...	
		Monitoring	▶
Markers Properties Servers ✕ Dat		Properties	Alt+Enter
⊟ JBoss v4.2 at localhost [Stopped, Synchronized]			
Adempiere_trunk [Synchronized]			

This will start the JBoss server in the debug mode and the debugger will stop at your break-point. Using the **Debug** toolbar, you will be able to debug ADempiere as a server application. If you resume the application, the server will run and you will see the following screen when you access the URL `http://localhost:8080/ Adempiere_trunk/` in your browser.

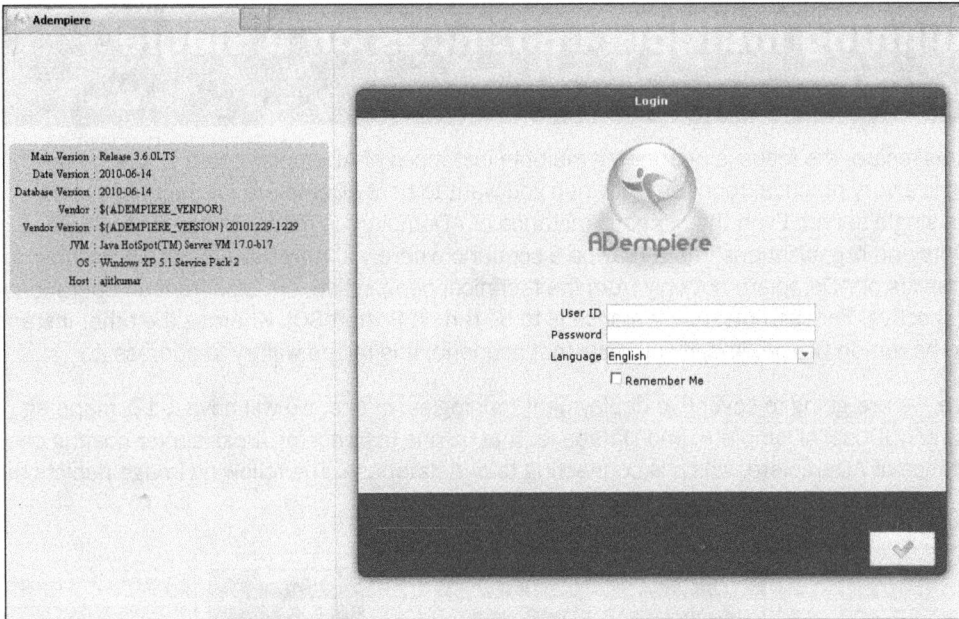

How it works...

Steps 1 through 7 take care of creating a JBoss server entry in Eclipse and adding the ADempiere project deployment resource to the JBoss server runtime. It is important to verify that the JBoss and JNDI port numbers (9080 and 1099) are free. Steps 9 through 14 are where the project related detail (for example, classpath) is configured in the JBoss server runtime. This is important for the deployment of the ADempiere server version in JBoss and running the same. The configuration adds the required JAR files and ADempiere classes to the JBoss configuration so that they are available to the runtime when we run the server.

See also

- ▶ Creating the installer from the source code
- ▶ Installing ADempiere

Running multiple instances on a single server

In this recipe, the focus is on running multiple instances of ADempiere on a single server. This is a very practical requirement when you want to host ADempiere for multiple clients on a single server. Even though each instance of ADempiere is meant to handle multiple clients and organizations, there may be a scenario where you may have to put up multiple instances of ADempiere not only from the technical perspective, but also from an operational perspective. For example, one instance is to be run on PostgreSQL whereas the other instance is to be run on Oracle. And, if you have that scenario, this recipe will try to address it.

Here, we are going to cover two deployment topologies. In one, we will have 1-1-1 mapping between JBoss, ADempiere, and Database, that is, one instance of JBoss server hosting one instance of ADempiere, which is connecting to one database. The following image depicts the 1-1-1 setup.

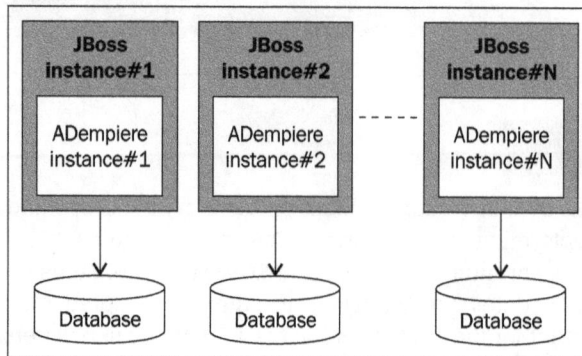

In the second instance, we will have 1-N-1 mapping where one instance of the JBoss server will host multiple instances of ADempiere instances and each one of them will connect to a single database. The following image depicts the 1-N-1 setup:

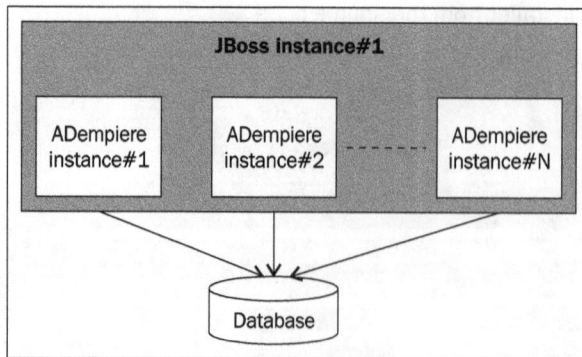

Getting ready

These steps are common to 1-1-1 as well as 1-N-1 setup.

- Copy the `<ADEMPIERE_SVN>\tags\adempiere360lts` to `<ADEMPIERE_SVN>\tags\adempiere360lts_2`.

- Change the project name to `adempiere_360_2` in the `<ADEMPIERE_SVN>\tags\adempiere360lts_2\.project` file.

- Import the `<ADEMPIERE_SVN>\tags\adempiere360lts_2` project into Eclipse.

- Create the `adempiere360_2` database in PostgreSQL and set up the schema and the initial data by following the steps mentioned in the *Installing ADempiere* recipe. Remember to use the already created user `adempiere`.

How to do it...

1. Running instance with 1-1-1 Setup.

    Here we will set up one more JBoss and ADempiere instance.

    - Go to the `<JBOSS_HOME>\server` folder

    - Copy the default folder to `adempiere360lts_2`. You may have any name for your server

    - Modify the port numbers in the following files so that they are not shared with the default server ports and they are available on your system:

    `< JBOSS_HOME>\server\ adempiere360lts_2\conf\jboss-service.xml`: Modify the following ports—8083, 1099, 1098, 4444, 4445

    `< JBOSS_HOME>\server\ adempiere360lts_2\deploy\ejb3.deployer\META-INF\jboss-service.xml`: Modify the following port—3873

    `< JBOSS_HOME>\server\ adempiere360lts_2\deploy\jms\uil2-service.xml`: Modify the following port—8093

    `< JBOSS_HOME>\server\ adempiere360lts_2\deploy\jboss-web.deployer\server.xml`: Modify the following ports—8080, 8443, 8009

    - Open the `<ADEMPIERE_SVN>\tags\adempiere360lts_2\.settings\org.eclipse.wst.common.component` file and change the deploy-name from `Adempiere_trunk` to `Adempiere_360_2` (you may have any name or your choice)

    - Go to Eclipse and refresh the `adempiere_360_2` project

- ❏ Follow the steps mentioned in *Debugging ADempiere server application* recipe to add a new JBoss server pointing to `<JBOSS_HOME>\server\ adempiere360lts_2` and deploy `Adempiere_360_2` to it. Make sure, your `PropertyFile` VM argument points to the `Adempiere.properties` created in `<ADEMPIERE_SVN>\tags\adempiere360lts_2` folder and `ADEMPIERE_HOME` VM argument points to `<ADEMPIERE_SVN>\tags\ adempiere360lts_2`

- ❏ Now, run the JBoss default server, where you had `Adempiere_trunk` deployed, and also run the second JBoss server where you have `Adempiere_360_2` deployed

2. Running an instance with 1-N-1 Setup.

   - ❏ Go to Eclipse

   - ❏ Right-click on the JBoss server entry in the **Servers** view, which we had created with the default configuration and to which `Adempiere_trunk` was deployed, and click **Add** and **Remove**. You will see `Adempiere_trunk` listed under the **Configured** items and `Adempiere_360_2` listed under the **Available** items

   - ❏ Add `Adempiere_360_2` to the **Configured** list and click on the **Finish** button

   - ❏ Right-click on the JBoss server entry and click **Publish** to deploy `Adempiere_360_2`. `Adempiere_360_2` will be the context for this ADempiere instance

   - ❏ Right-click on the JBoss server entry and click on Start the server with two instances of ADempiere deployed. You can now access the two instances by accessing the following URLs:

     `http://localhost:8080/Adempiere_trunk/`

     `http://localhost:8080/ Adempiere_360_2/`

Both ADempiere instances will be pointing to the same database as the database connection detail is mentioned in the `Adempiere.properties` file and a common property file is used in the VM arguments of the JBoss server.

How it works...

In order to have an instance with 1-1-1 setup, important point to make is making sure that we are able to run multiple instances of the JBoss server on a single machine. This requires us to make changes to the different port numbers, which one or another service in JBoss uses. If this is not done, some or some other service would not run and that would lead to an error while we try to deploy and run the application.

In the 1-N-1 setup, JBoss ports are not of concern as we will be running a single instance of it. However, the important point here is the deployment name for the multiple instances of the ADempiere application. Uniqueness must be maintained across ADempiere instances in terms of `deploy-name`, otherwise the deployment of one instance will overwrite the deployment of a second instance, as it uses the `deploy-name` as the WAR filename.

See also

- ▸ Creating an installer from the source code
- ▸ Installing ADempiere

Giving ADempiere your identity

If you are reading this book, you have, or may have, some customization or enhancement needs in your mind. Be it look and feel (UI color, CSS, icons and so on), name, or logo. Effectively, we would have a practical need to give ADempiere our own identity. Here we will discuss the various points where you may make the changes to have your own identity of the application.

Getting ready

Verify that you have completed the following recipes:

1. Creating the Installer from the source code.
2. Installing ADempiere.
3. Debugging the ADempiere server application.

How to do it...

- ▸ Change, say, NAME to your application name in `base/src/org/compiere/ADempiere.java`. Additionally, you may also change the `splash images, product images, product sub-title`, and so on
- ▸ Change, say, APP_NAME to your application name in `zkwebui/WEB-INF/src/org/adempiere/webui/ADempiereWebUI.java`
- ▸ CSS—For the web application, which is based on the ZK UI framework, you can modify the `<ADEMPIERE_SVN>\tags\adempiere360lts\zkwebui\css\default.css.dsp` file to modify the styles

▶ Images—There are lots of images. They include images used as ADempiere logos/icons of various kinds, button icons, toolbar icons, and other UI-related images. The simplest way to replace an existing image with yours is to:

> ❑ Search for the files with `.ico`, `.png`, `.jpg`, `.jpeg`, and `.gif` extensions in the `<ADEMPIERE_SVN>\tags\adempiere360lts` folder

> **Search by any or all of the criteria below.**
> All or part of the file name:
> `*.ico,*.png,*.jpg,*.jpeg,*.gif`
> A word or phrase in the file:
>
> Look in:
> 📁 adempiere360lts ▾
> **When was it modified?** ▶
> **What size is it?** ▶
> **More advanced options** ▶
>
> Back | Search

> ❑ Find the image of your interest and note down that image dimension and type (`jpg/png/gif/ico`/and so on)

> ❑ Create your image of the same dimension and type

> ❑ Replace the existing image with your image

> ❑ Launch the ADempiere application and notice the difference

Here is a custom identity that I have given by changing the application name and the logo:

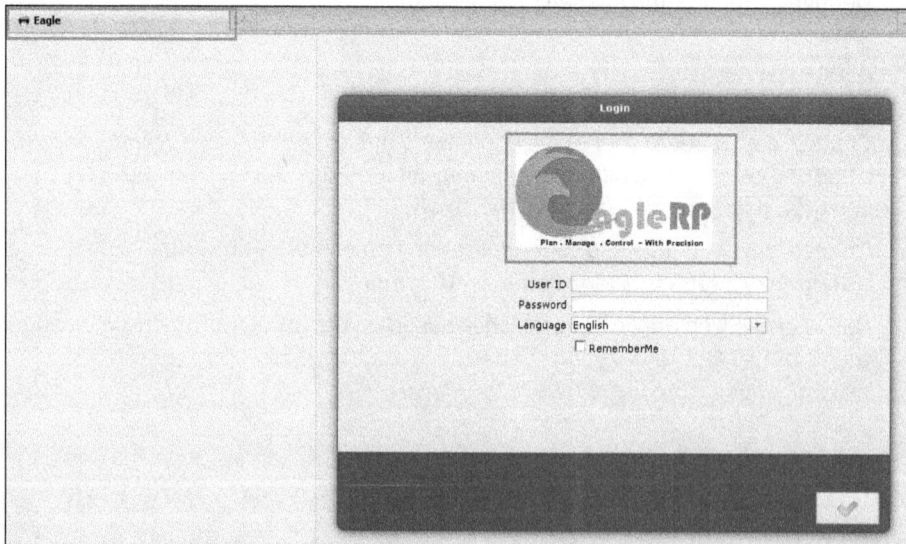

In the preceding diagram, we have changed the application name to Eagle and the logo with my **EagleRP** product logo. Similarly, you shall be able to make other changes you may need to give ADempiere your identity.

After you have done this, you may also want to commit the same in your project repository so that for all the subsequent builds and deployments, you will use this repository where all the CSS and new images will be part of the installer.

See also

- ▶ Creating the installer from the source code
- ▶ Installing ADempiere

2
ADempiere Customization – Part I

In this chapter, we will cover:

- ▶ Creating a new window
- ▶ Customizing an existing window
- ▶ Creating a window with multiple tabs
- ▶ Creating a search widget
- ▶ Populating a combo-box list
- ▶ Configuring a zoom window
- ▶ Creating a read-only window
- ▶ Creating a read-only tab
- ▶ Creating read-only fields
- ▶ Creating a new menu tree
- ▶ Role setup and assigning menu tree to a role
- ▶ Defaulting the data display to the single/multi row mode
- ▶ Showing the entity and line items on the same tab

Introduction

In this chapter, we are going to look at the overall customization capability of ADempiere. Many of them can be achieved by configuring ADempiere. However, many of them require a combination of customization and configuration. Here we will deal with words like Table, Column, Window, Tab, Field, Process, Model, Validation Rules, and so on and see how to create a new entity of each kind.

To make the topics relevant and have a logical flow, II will be taking a case study and implementing a small module called **Minutes Of Meeting** (**MOM**). This module is intended to allow the user to capture the minutes of a meeting and carry out various tasks related to it. As we progress through the recipes, we will cover the concept, its application to the business, how it maps to this MOM case study, and then we would look at what it takes to implement in ADempiere. Going forward, I will be using the following MOM template, as shown in the following screenshot, to map ADempiere capability.

Minutes of Meeting			
Location : Skype Conference		Date : 20th January 2010	
		Start Time : 9.30 IST	
Chairperson:	Ajit Kumar	End Time : 10:30 IST	
Participants			
Attendees: Suman Ravuri, Ajit Kumar – Walking Tree			
Sanjay Gupta – XYZ Corp			
Agenda :	• Purchase Order work-flow walkthrough • Request for Quotation workflow walkthrough • Price list walkthrough		
Item	Item Discussion	Actioned by	Status
1.			
2.			

Before we embark on the journey of customization, let us get our tools ready. Let us ensure that:

▶ We are able to compile the `adempiere_360` project

▶ We are able to run the desktop as well as the Web version of Adempiere using the `adempiere_360` project

▶ We are able to access the `adempiere360` database using `adempiere/adempiere`

You may refer to *Chapter 1, Preparing the Ground*, to learn how to complete the previously mentioned tasks.

Creating a new window

A window provides **create**, **read**, **update**, and **delete** (**CRUD**) access to the data to a user. These functionalities are provided by the standard tools and menus. A standard layout of a window has the following parts:

▶ **Title bar**

▶ **Menu bar**

▶ **Tool bar**

▶ **Tabs panel**

▶ **Status bar**

The following screenshot shows the different parts:

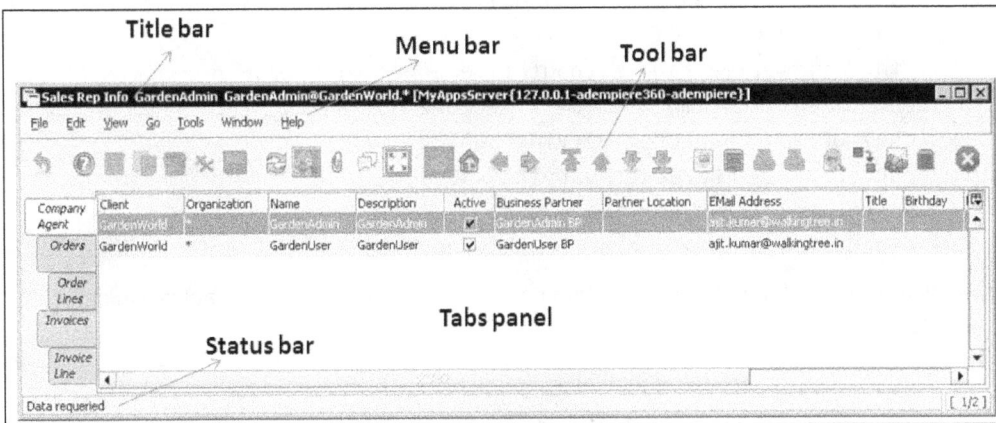

Given the ADempiere architecture, as an author of a new window, you do not have to worry about how and what gets displayed in the **Title**, **Menu bar**, **Tool bar**, and **Status bar**. All we need to focus on is the **Tabs panel**. And, in this recipe, we will go through the steps required to create a complete working new window in ADempiere, which will act as the foundation for building our MOM window.

Getting ready

Connect to the database `adempiere360` using `adempiere` as the user using your favorite PostgreSQL client (for example, `phpPgAdmin` or `pgAdmin III` or command based `psql`)

How to do it...

1. Create the following table in your `adempiere` schema:

```
CREATE TABLE adempiere.c_mom (
c_mom_id numeric(10,0) NOT NULL,
ad_client_id numeric(10,0) NOT NULL,
ad_org_id numeric(10,0) NOT NULL,
isactive character(1) DEFAULT 'Y'::bpchar NOT NULL,
created timestamp without time zone DEFAULT now() NOT NULL,
createdby numeric(10,0) NOT NULL,
updated timestamp without time zone DEFAULT now() NOT NULL,
updatedby numeric(10,0) NOT NULL,
value character varying(30) NOT NULL,
name character varying(255) NOT NULL,
start_date date NOT NULL,
start_time timestamp without time zone NOT NULL,
end_time timestamp without time zone NOT NULL,
chairperson character varying(80),
participants character varying(4000),
agenda character varying(4000),
discussion_detail character varying(8000));
```

ADempiere requires the following standard columns to be present on the tables, which ADempiere populates on its own:

`ad_client_id`: Client Identifier

`ad_org_id`: Organization Identifier

`isactive`: Flag to indicate whether the record is active

`created`: Time when the record was created

`createdby`: ID of the user who created the record

`updated`: Time when the record was last updated

`updatedby`: ID of the user who last updated the record

Additionally, every table must have a primary key, which must follow the naming convention of `<table name>_id`. `c_mom_id` which is the primary key of the `c_mom` table.

2. Run the desktop version of ADempiere and log in using **System/System**. Select the **System Administrator** as **Role**. After a successful login, You will see the **Menu** on the left-hand side of the window, and you will see the **Application Dictionary** related items:

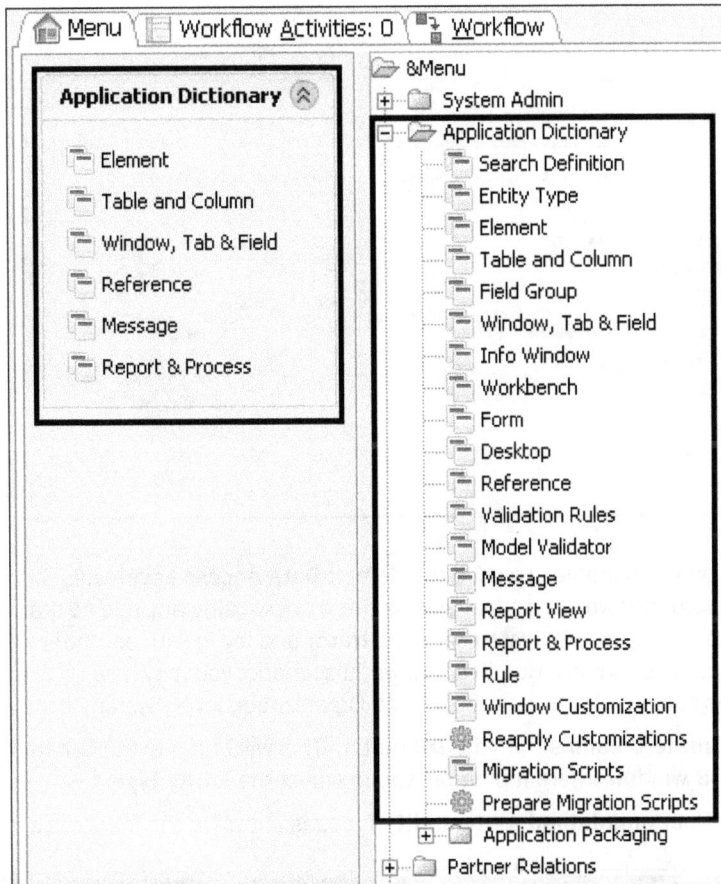

3. Click the **Table and Column**. It will pop up the **Lookup Record: Table** window where you click on the **New Record** button on the bottom-left corner.

4. Enter the following details on to the **Table** tab as shown in the following screenshot:

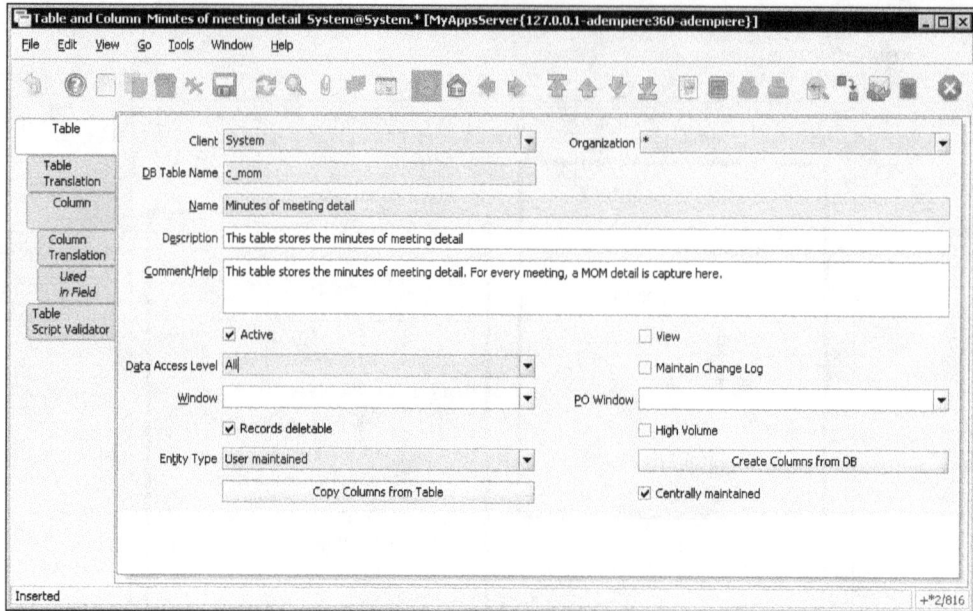

5. In the previous image, we used the default **Data Access Level—All**. This is only to make sure that we are able to access the window using any role so that we don't have to log out as the **System Administrator** and log in with another role to be able to access the window. But, in a real world scenario, you may have to use other options such as Client level, Client and Organization level, System level, and so on.

6. Click **Create Columns** from the **DB** button. This will bring up the **Create Columns from DB** window where it prompts you to select the **Entity Type**.

7. Select **User maintained** as the **Entity Type,** as shown in the following screenshot:

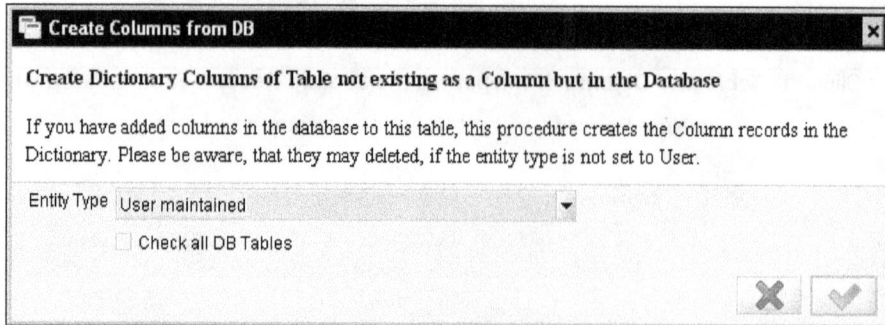

Selecting the **Entity Type** as **User maintained** will keep your table from being overwritten as part of future migrations. Tables with entity type **Dictionary** are subject to migration, whereas **User** maintained are not.

8. Click the tick button. It will pop-up a window showing all the columns generated from the table, as shown in the following screenshot:

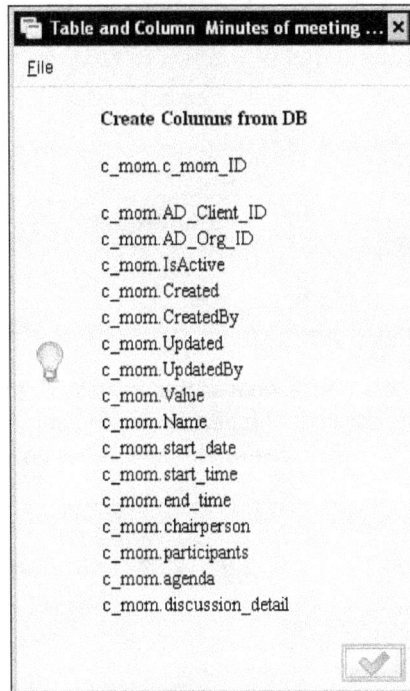

9. Click the tick button. This completes the creation of the columns, which you can verify by clicking on the **Column** tab.

Based on the data type of the columns in your database table, ADempiere guesses the data type of the columns, which you may want to use to store and retrieve data. For example, the **Date** on the column defaults to **Date+Time** in ADempiere, which may not be appropriate always as you may want to only store the date part of the timestamp. So, it is worth spending some time reviewing the **Reference** for the generated columns and making the required changes, if any.

10. Click on the **Window**, **Tab**, and **Field** menu option under **Application Dictionary**. This will pop-up the **Lookup Record: Window** window where you click on the **New Record** button in the bottom-left corner.

11. Enter the values on the **Window** tab, as shown in the following screenshot:

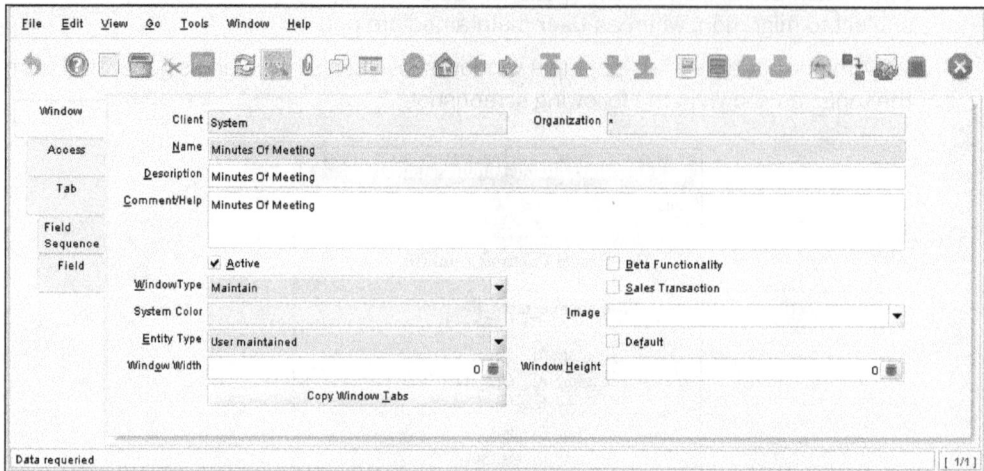

12. Verify the window access on the **Access** tab. By default, the access is given to all the roles in the system, as shown in the next screenshot. If you want, you can control the access using the **Active** field. However, for now, let us go ahead with the default.

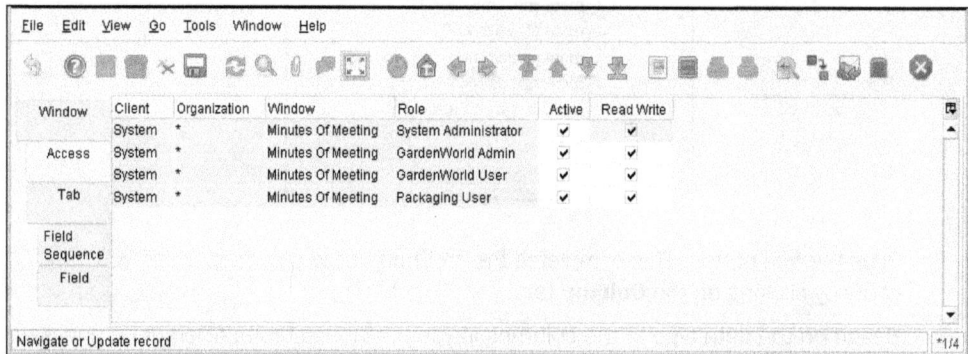

13. Now that we have created the window, we will move on to creating tabs within the window.

14. Click on the **Tab** tab and click on the **New Record** toolbar button. Fill in the details about the first tab of MOM where we would display the following basic details of a MOM:

- MOM name
- Date
- Start time
- End time

- ❏ Chairperson
- ❏ Agenda

An Important field is:

Table: Select the MOM table that we had created in the previous steps.

15. Click on the **Create Fields** button to create tab fields from the table columns. This will pop-up an information window showing additional details about this process, as shown in the next screenshot. Click on the tick button.

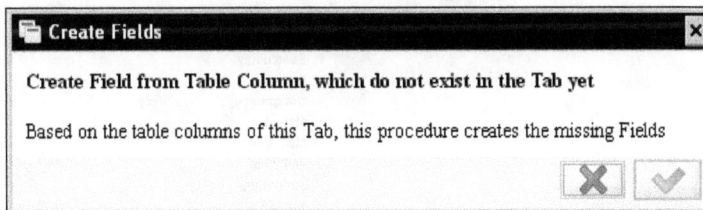

If everything goes well, you will be presented with a list of fields that will be generated, as shown in the following screenshot:

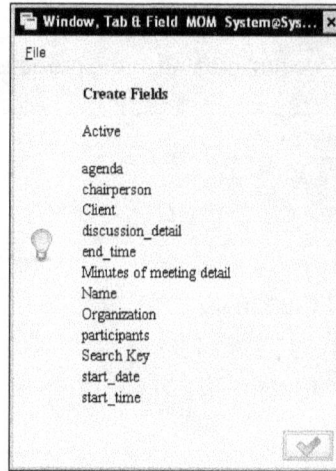

Click on the tick button. This will complete the process of creating fields from the table columns.

16. Go to the **Field Sequence** tab to see the default sequence in which the fields will appear on the tab. In case you want to change the sequence, you can do it in the **Sequence** area. Select the field, whose sequence you want to change, and use the up and down arrow keys on the right to change the position of that field. Alternatively, you can also use the drag-n-drop for quicker re-ordering. The following screenshot shows our fields after ordering:

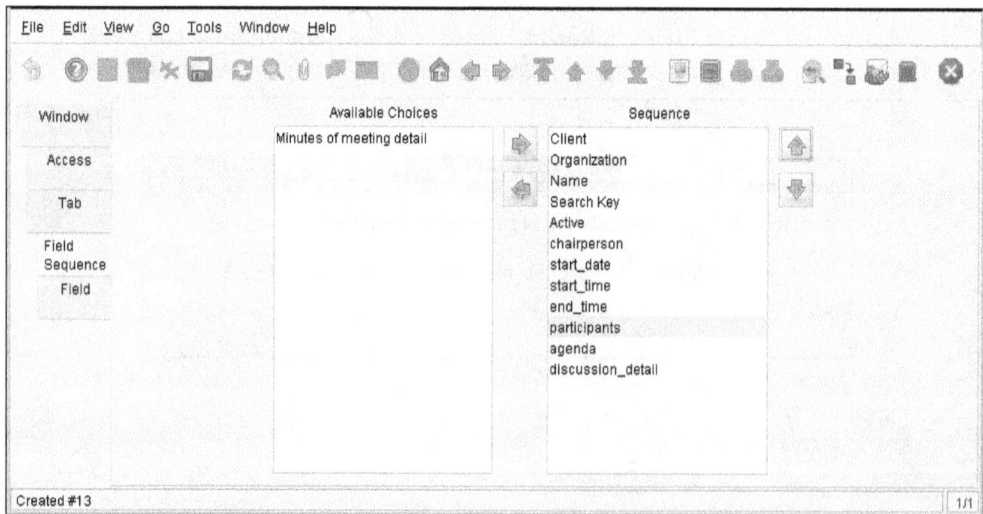

17. Another thing you must have noticed is the field names. They do not look readable and do not conform to the human language. For example, names with '_' (underscore) is not something that we would like to use in our field labels on the UI. To correct this, go to the **Field** tab and correct the **Name** field values. As a good practice, also add in the **Description** for the fields. ADempiere automatically generates descriptions for various standard fields like **Client**, **Organization**, and so on. So, effectively, you will have to enter the description for the fields that are specific to your need.

18. Alternatively, you can change the Name, Description, and Comment/Help of the fields on the Column tab of the Table and Column windows. This is the preferred way if you want the same name to appear on all the windows/tabs you create using the table. However, if you need to have different labels on the windows/tabs even though all the windows/tabs are generated from the same table, then you shall make the changes on the respective fields on the Window, Tab and Field. An important point to keep in perspective is that, when you regenerate the tab and fields, the Name, Description, and Comment/Help of the fields will be overwritten by the ones set on the fields.

19. The following screenshot shows the fields after we have corrected the **Name**, **Description**, and **Comment/Help**.

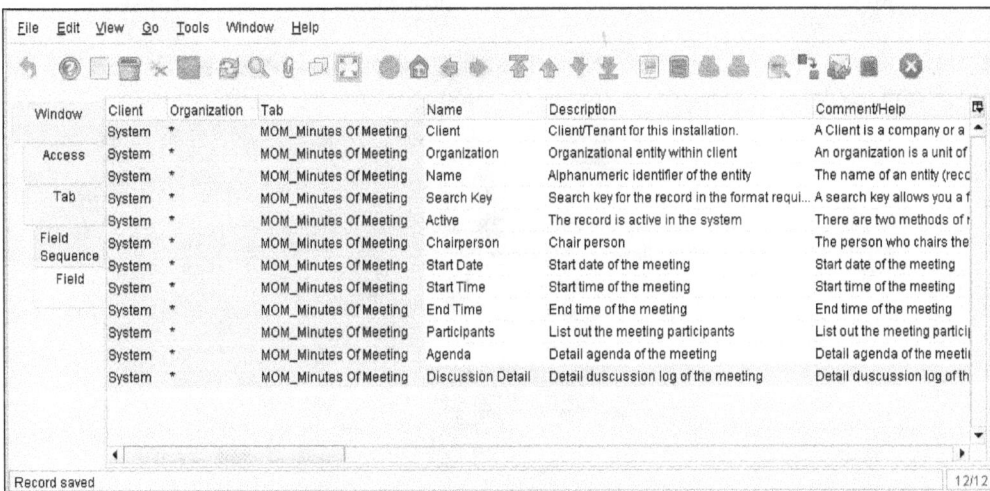

Window	Client	Organization	Tab	Name	Description	Comment/Help
	System	*	MOM_Minutes Of Meeting	Client	Client/Tenant for this installation.	A Client is a company or a
Access	System	*	MOM_Minutes Of Meeting	Organization	Organizational entity within client	An organization is a unit of
	System	*	MOM_Minutes Of Meeting	Name	Alphanumeric identifier of the entity	The name of an entity (reco
Tab	System	*	MOM_Minutes Of Meeting	Search Key	Search key for the record in the format requi...	A search key allows you a f
	System	*	MOM_Minutes Of Meeting	Active	The record is active in the system	There are two methods of r
Field	System	*	MOM_Minutes Of Meeting	Chairperson	Chair person	The person who chairs the
Sequence	System	*	MOM_Minutes Of Meeting	Start Date	Start date of the meeting	Start date of the meeting
Field	System	*	MOM_Minutes Of Meeting	Start Time	Start time of the meeting	Start time of the meeting
	System	*	MOM_Minutes Of Meeting	End Time	End time of the meeting	End time of the meeting
	System	*	MOM_Minutes Of Meeting	Participants	List out the meeting participants	List out the meeting partici
	System	*	MOM_Minutes Of Meeting	Agenda	Detail agenda of the meeting	Detail agenda of the meeti
	System	*	MOM_Minutes Of Meeting	Discussion Detail	Detail discussion log of the meeting	Detail duscussion log of th

Record saved

12/12

20. Click on **Menu** | **System Admin** | **General Rules** | **System Rules** | **Menu**. This pops up the **Lookup Record: Menu** window, as shown in the following screenshot:

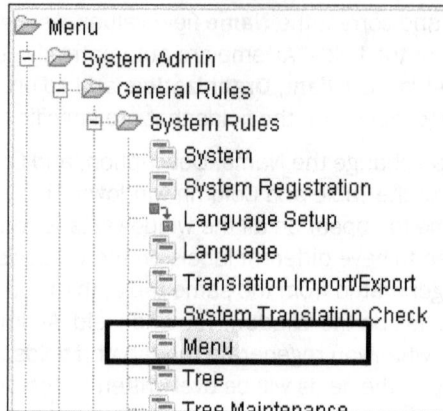

21. On **Lookup Record: Menu** window, click on the **New Record** button in the bottom-left corner. Fill in the details, as depicted in the following screenshot, and save it.

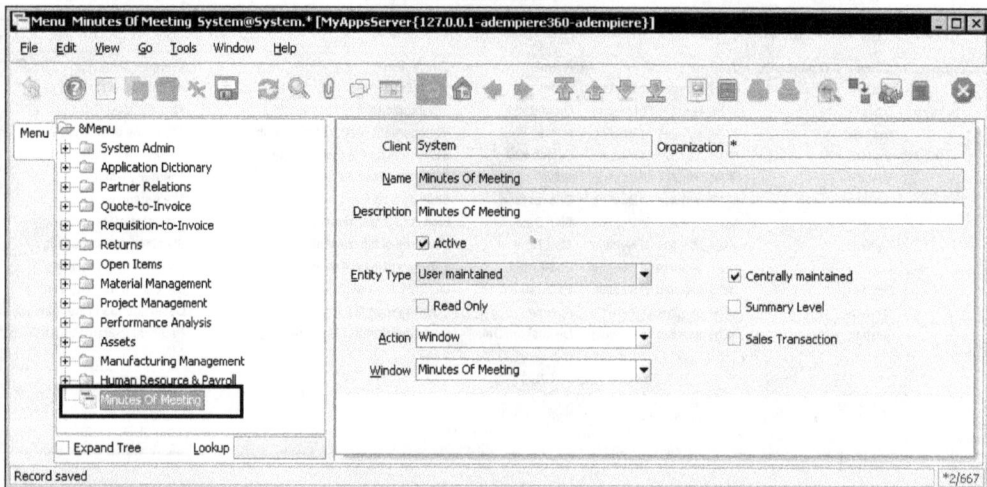

22. Log out and log in as **GardenAdmin/GardenAdmin**. You will see the following **Minutes Of Meeting menu** item:

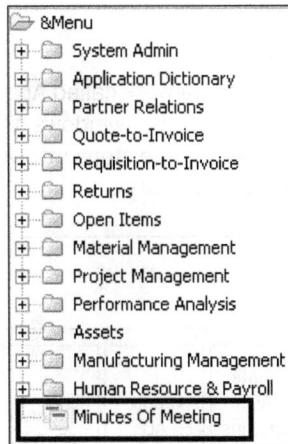

23. Click on the **Minutes Of Meeting** menu item. This will bring up the **Minutes Of Meeting** window with one tab, **MOM**. You will now be able to enter your MOM details and save it, as shown in the following screenshot:

At this stage, we have got our basic MOM window ready where we are able to save/update the information. As a standard practice in ADempiere, the **Search Key** shall appear before the Name field. We will do this in the later part of this chapter. However, you may work with the field sequence to accomplish this.

How it works...

ADempiere has a powerful, yet flexible, framework called Application Dictionary. It is called the core/kernel/heart of ADempiere. To generate the windows, tabs, and fields, ADempiere uses the dictionary. The following diagram depicts the steps involved in creating a new window in ADempiere (**AD** stands for **Application Dictionary**):

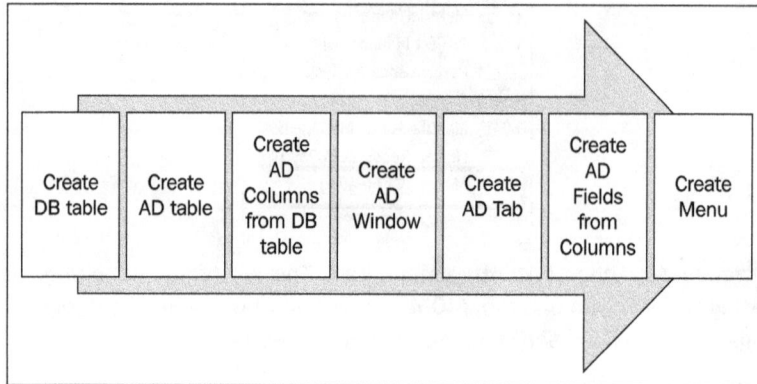

> ▸ The last step—**Create Menu**—allows us to access the window

In step 1, we created the database table, `c_mom`. step 2 through to 9 is where we created the AD table and columns using the `c_mom` table. In steps 10 through to 16, we created the AD window, tab, and fields using the AD table and columns created in the previous steps. After that we created a menu item and linked the window with it so that the same can be accessed by a click on the menu item.

There's more...

ADempiere's Application Dictionary is not just about Table, Columns, Window, Tabs, and Fields; it is much more than this. There are other entities like Process, Report, Workflow, Reference, and so on. ADempiere uses a set of application code and database tables. All the dictionary related tables have the prefix AD_ (for example, `AD_Window`, `AD_Table`, and so on). You may learn more about the Application Dictionary at `http://en.wikiversity.org/wiki/ADempiere_Application_Dictionary`.

Customizing an existing window

Practically, there will be a situation when we will have to make changes to the existing screens. For example, label change, data type change, logically grouping the fields, and so on. In this recipe, we will take our newly created MOM window and we will customize it further to understand the process involved in customizing an existing window.

In the previous recipe, our window had a **Start Date**, **Start Time**, and **End Time**. All of them display both the date and time. Now, say, we want to achieve the following:

- **Start Date** displays only the date
- **Start Time** and **End Time** displays only the time
- **Start Time** and **End Time** shall appear in the same line

Given this customization need, let us see how we can achieve it.

How to do it...

1. Log in as **System/System** with the **System Administrator** role.
2. Click on the **Menu | Application Dictionary | Table and Column** menu. This pops up the lookup window and prompts for table details. Enter the details to find the MOM related table.
3. Go to the **Column** tab for the MOM table and take a look at the fields that interest us, as shown in the following screenshot:

4. Select **end_time** in the **DB Column Name** and select **Time** in the **Reference** field.

5. Repeat step 5 for **start_time**.

6. For **start_date**, select the **Reference** field as **Date**. The following screenshot shows the fields with their updated **Reference**.

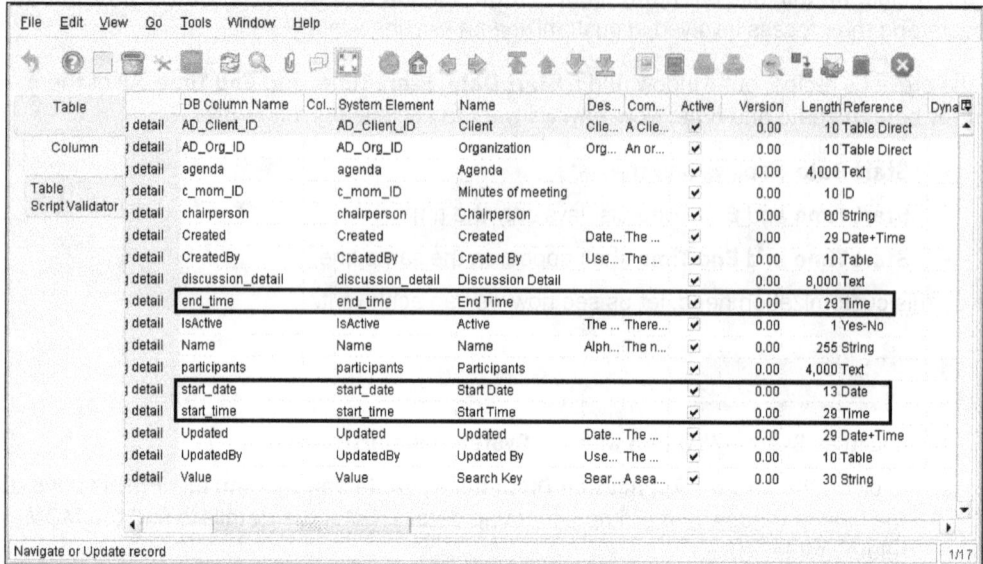

7. Go to the **Window**, **Tab**, and **Field** window for the **Minutes Of Meeting** and go to the **Field** tab.

8. Check the **Same Line** checkbox for the **end_time** field to show **Start Time** and **End Time** in the same line, as shown in the following screenshot:

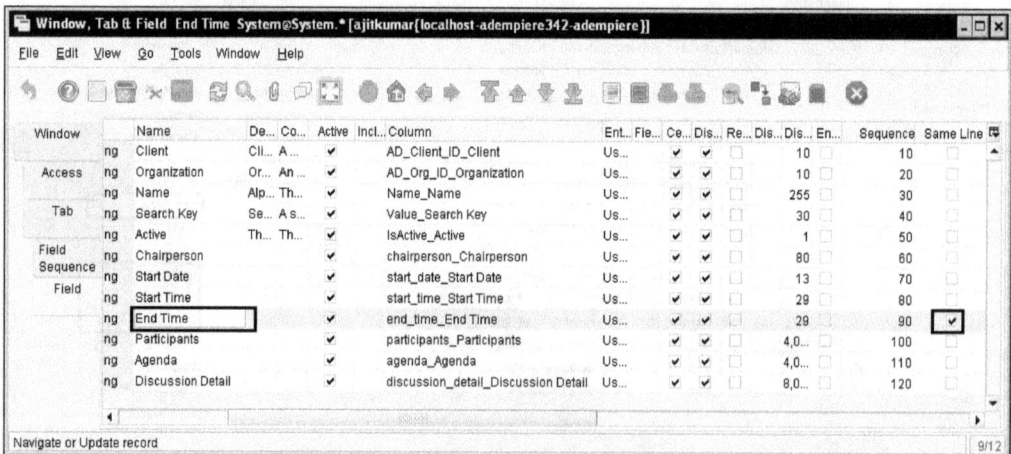

With this, we are done with our customization. The following screenshot shows how the window looks after the changes:

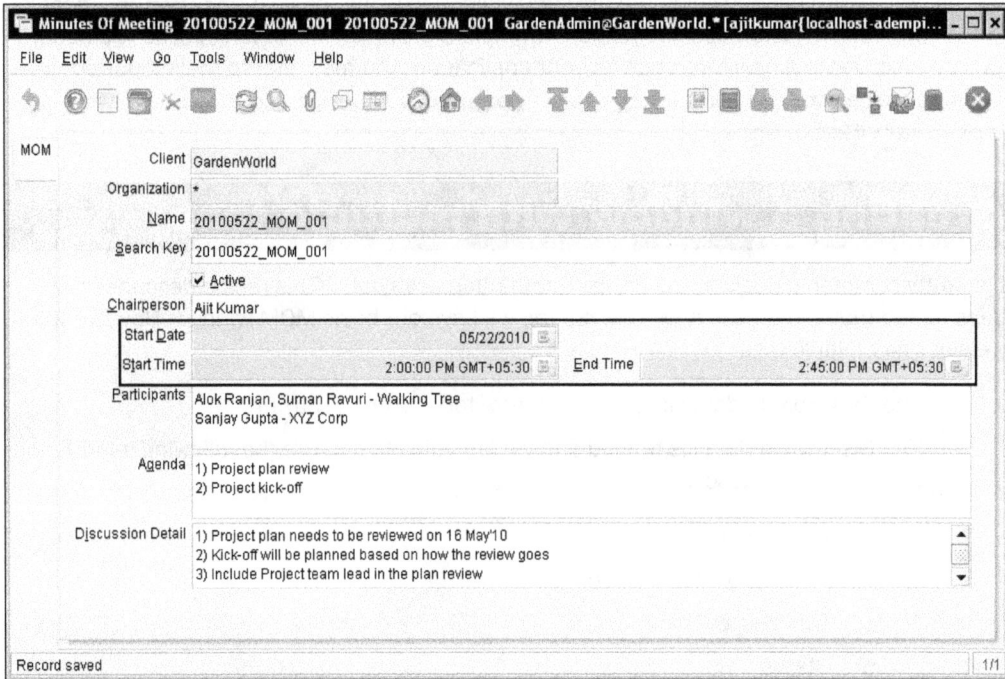

How it works...

In this recipe, we changed the data types of **Start Date**, **Start Time**, and **End Time** in steps 1 through to 6 and placed **Start Time** and **End Time** fields in the same line in the steps 7-8. The default **Reference Date+Time**, which ADempiere guesses for the timestamp columns, would show the date as well as the time. So, in order to change the type, the following is the field and **Reference** mapping:

Field	Reference
Start Date	Date
Start Time	Time
End Time	Time

When it comes to showing multiple fields on the same line, ADempiere uses the Same Line flag at the field level to determine whether the field needs to be rendered to the next line or to the same line. ADempiere uses a two column layout for the tab panel. Hence, at most, only two fields can be displayed in a single line.

There's more...

ADempiere determines the field data type and validation using the field `Reference`. There is a list of pre-defined Reference lists, which ADempiere provides. Moreover, in case you need, you can also create a new reference for your application. You may refer to the supported Reference list at `http://en.wikiversity.org/wiki/ADempiere_Application_Dictionary#Reference`.

Creating a window with multiple tabs

It is pretty common to logically relate the information using tabs. This recipe describes the steps to add multiple tabs in a window. So far, we have our basic MOM window. Now, we will break it into multiple tabs:

- The Participants detail is moved to a new tab—`Participants`
- The Discussion detail is refined and we are going to capture the following information as part of every discussion item:

  - Item number
  - Discussion description
  - Actioned by
  - Status

  This is also moved to a new tab—`Discussion Detail`

Getting ready

Connect to the database `adempiere360` using `adempiere` as a user using your favorite PostgreSQL client (for example, `phpPgAdmin` or `pgAdmin III` or command based `psql`).

How to do it...

1. Delete the records from the `c_mom` table.
2. Delete the menu—**Minutes Of Meeting**.
3. Related to MOM, delete the following from the **Window**, **Tab**, and **Field** windows, as per the order mentioned:

   - **Field**(s)
   - **Tab**
   - **Window**

4. Related to MOM, delete the following from the **Table** and **Column** windows, as per the order mentioned:

   ❑ **Columns**

   ❑ **Table**

5. Drop the `adempiere.c_mom` table by running the following SQL:

   ```
   DROP TABLE adempiere.c_mom;
   ```

6. Apply the following SQL to your `adempiere` schema:

   ```
   CREATE TABLE adempiere.c_mom (
   c_mom_id numeric(10,0) NOT NULL,
   ad_client_id numeric(10,0) NOT NULL,
   ad_org_id numeric(10,0) NOT NULL,
   isactive character(1) DEFAULT 'Y'::bpchar NOT NULL,
   created timestamp without time zone DEFAULT now() NOT NULL,
   createdby numeric(10,0) NOT NULL,
   updated timestamp without time zone DEFAULT now() NOT NULL,
   updatedby numeric(10,0) NOT NULL,
   value character varying(30) NOT NULL,
   name character varying(255) NOT NULL,
   start_date date NOT NULL,
   start_time timestamp without time zone NOT NULL,
   end_time timestamp without time zone NOT NULL,
   chairperson character varying(80),
   agenda character varying(4000),
   CONSTRAINT c_mom_pkey PRIMARY KEY (c_mom_id)
   );


   CREATE TABLE adempiere.c_mom_discussionline (
     c_mom_discussionline_id numeric(10,0) NOT NULL,
     c_mom_id numeric(10,0) NOT NULL,
     ad_client_id numeric(10,0) NOT NULL,
     ad_org_id numeric(10,0) NOT NULL,
     isactive character(1) DEFAULT 'Y'::bpchar NOT NULL,
     created timestamp without time zone DEFAULT now() NOT NULL,
     createdby numeric(10,0) NOT NULL,
     updated timestamp without time zone DEFAULT now() NOT NULL,
     updatedby numeric(10,0) NOT NULL,
     item_nbr numeric (10,0) NOT NULL,
     discussion_desc character varying(2000),
     actionedby character varying(80) NOT NULL,
   ```

```
      status character varying(80),
   CONSTRAINT cmom_cdiscussionline FOREIGN KEY (c_mom_id)
         REFERENCES adempiere.c_mom (c_mom_id) MATCH SIMPLE
         ON UPDATE NO ACTION ON DELETE NO ACTION DEFERRABLE INITIALLY
   DEFERRED
   );


   CREATE TABLE adempiere.c_mom_participantsline (
      c_mom_participantsline_id numeric(10,0) NOT NULL,
      c_mom_id numeric(10,0) NOT NULL,
      ad_client_id numeric(10,0) NOT NULL,
        ad_org_id numeric(10,0) NOT NULL,
      created timestamp without time zone DEFAULT now() NOT NULL,
      createdby numeric(10,0) NOT NULL,
      updated timestamp without time zone DEFAULT now() NOT NULL,
      updatedby numeric(10,0) NOT NULL,
      participant character varying(80),
      company character varying(80) NOT NULL,
   CONSTRAINT cmom_cparticipantsline FOREIGN KEY (c_mom_id)
         REFERENCES adempiere.c_mom (c_mom_id) MATCH SIMPLE
         ON UPDATE NO ACTION ON DELETE NO ACTION DEFERRABLE INITIALLY
   DEFERRED
   );
```

c_mom: Represents the basic MOM detail

c_mom_discussionline: Represents each MOM discussion detail

c_mom_participantsline: Represents each MOM participant detail

7. Follow the steps mentioned in the Create a new window recipe to create the tables and their columns. The following screenshot shows the list of tables after the completion of the steps:

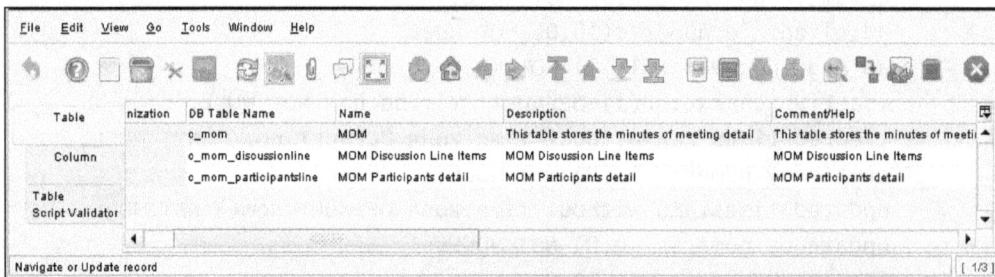

8. Also, create a **Minutes Of Meeting** window with the MOM tab, as per the steps mentioned in the Create a new window recipe. Similarly, add the **Participants** and **Discussion Detail** tabs using the `c_mom_participantsline` and `c_mom_discussionline` tables, respectively, as shown in the following screenshot:

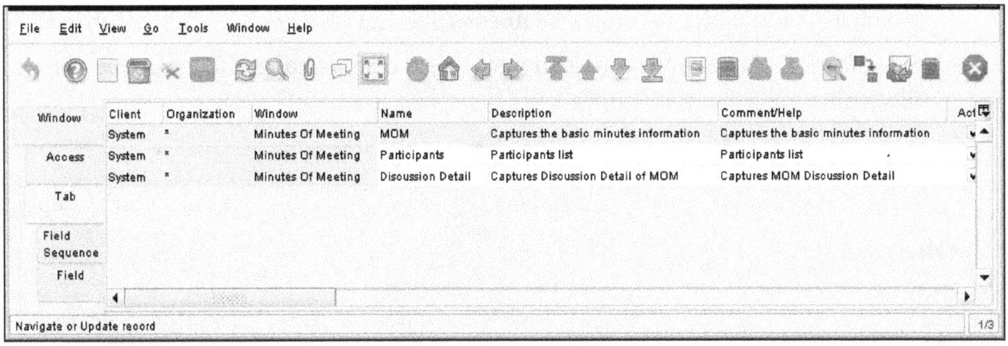

9. The **Sequence** field on the **Tab** screen determines the tab sequence. A tab with the least value of **Sequence** appears as the first tab and the one with the largest value appears as the last tab.

10. Select the **Participants** tab and switch to the single row view. The important fields are:

    ❑ **Table**: Select the participants table

    ❑ **Link Column**: Select the MOM ID on the `c_mom` table

    ❑ **Tab Level**: 1

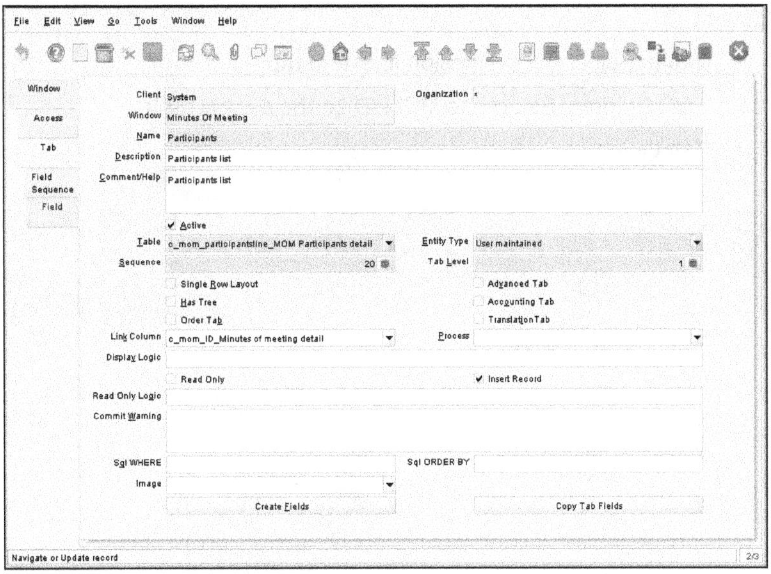

ADempiere uses **Tab Level** to indent the tab on a window and also, internally, uses it to create SQL joins to fetch the related records. The main tab has the tab level as 0, by default. Moreover, a tab with level 1' becomes the child of the main tab and is indented accordingly. For example, in the previous image, the tab **Access** has a tab level of the main tab—**Window**. Tabs with the same tab level are siblings or peers. For example, in the previous image, the **Access** and **Tab** tabs are at the same tab level.

11. Review the **Field Sequence** tab and make the required changes to the sequence, as shown in the following screenshot:

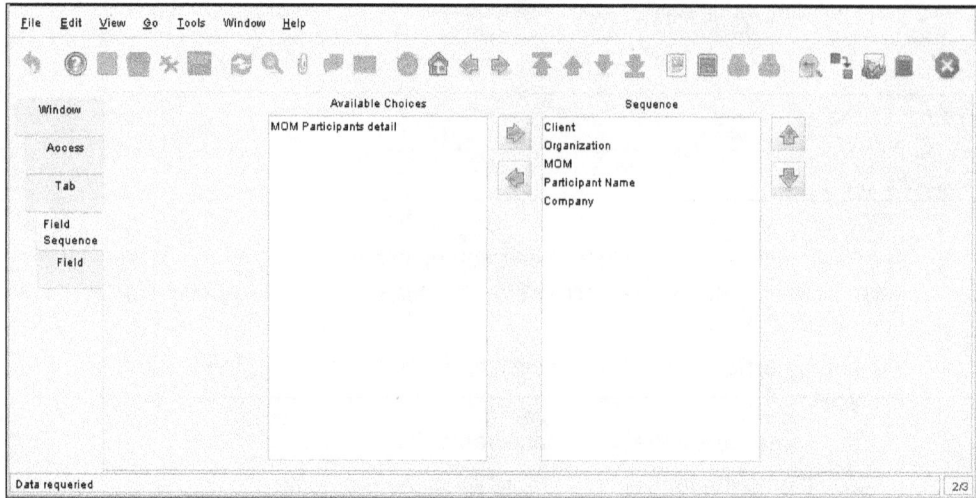

12. Select the **Discussion Detail** tab and switch to the single row view. The important fields are:

   □ **Table**: Select the discussion line item table

   □ **Link Column**: Select the MOM ID on the c_mom table

   □ **Tab Level**: 1

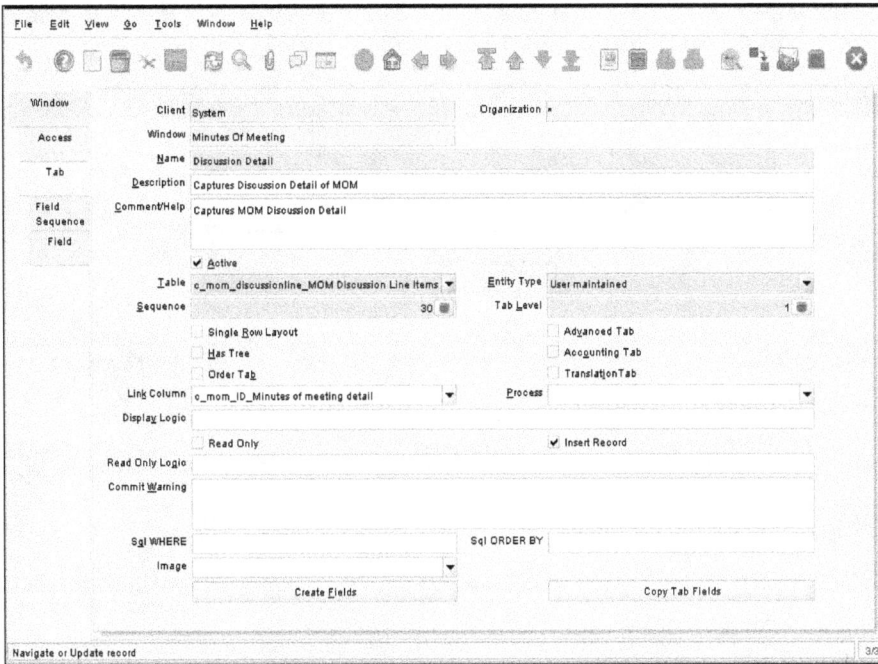

13. Review the **Field Sequence** tab and make the required changes to the sequence, as shown in the following screenshot:

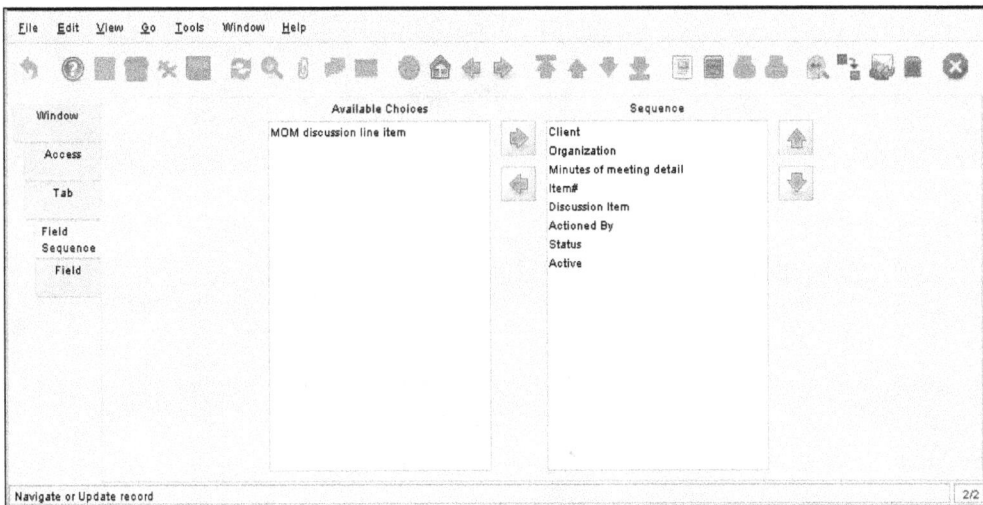

14. Follow the steps 18-19, mentioned in the Create a new window recipe, to create a menu, as shown in the following screenshot:

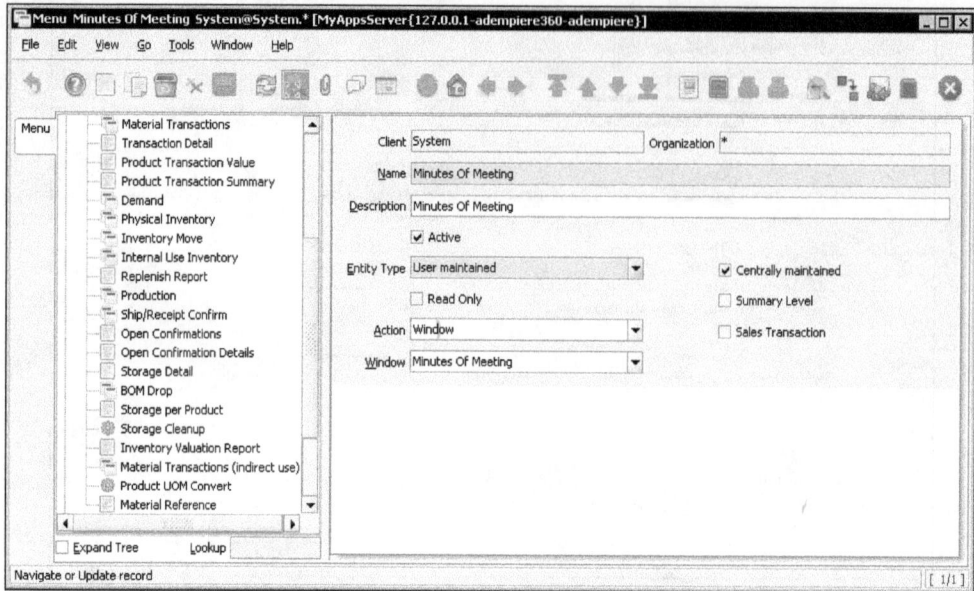

15. Log out and log in as **GardenAdmin**/**GardenAdmin**. You will see the **Minutes Of Meeting** menu item, as it appears in the following screenshot:

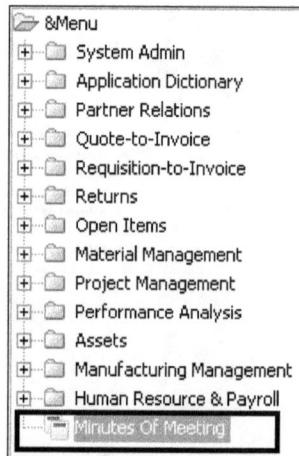

16. Click on the **Minutes Of Meeting** menu item. This will bring up the **Minutes Of Meeting** window with one tab, **MOM**. Our MOM window now has three tabs and looks more organized, as shown here in the following screenshot:

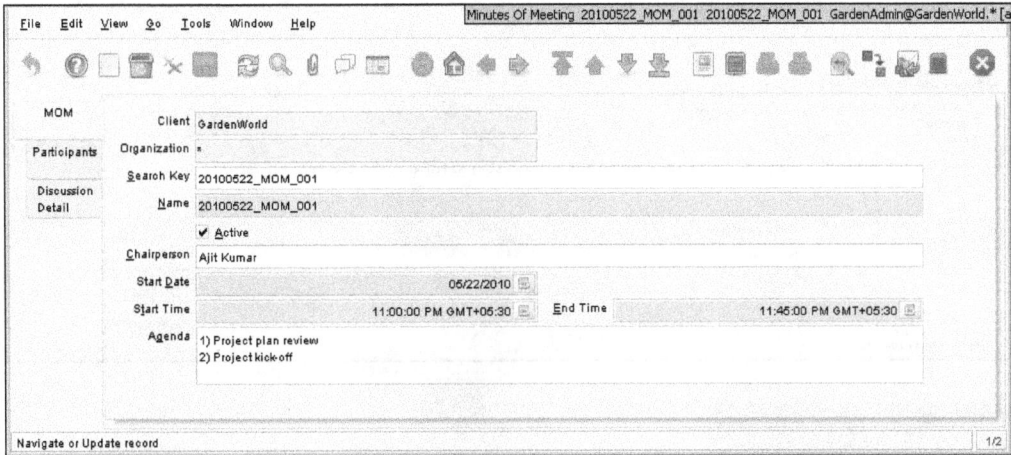

17. Add one or more participants for a MOM:

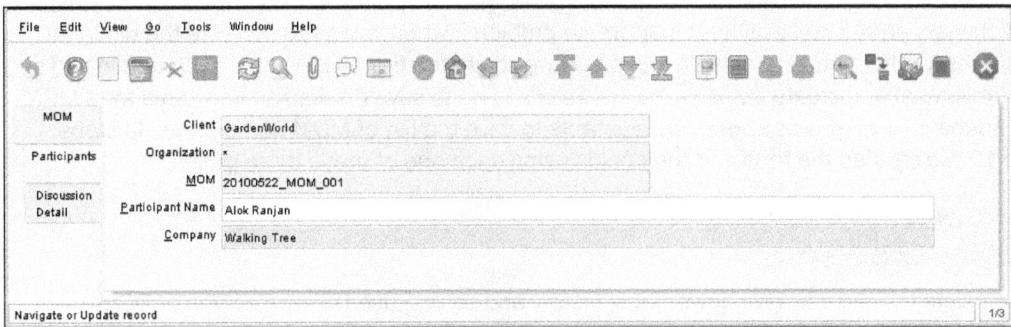

18. Add one or more discussion items for a MOM:

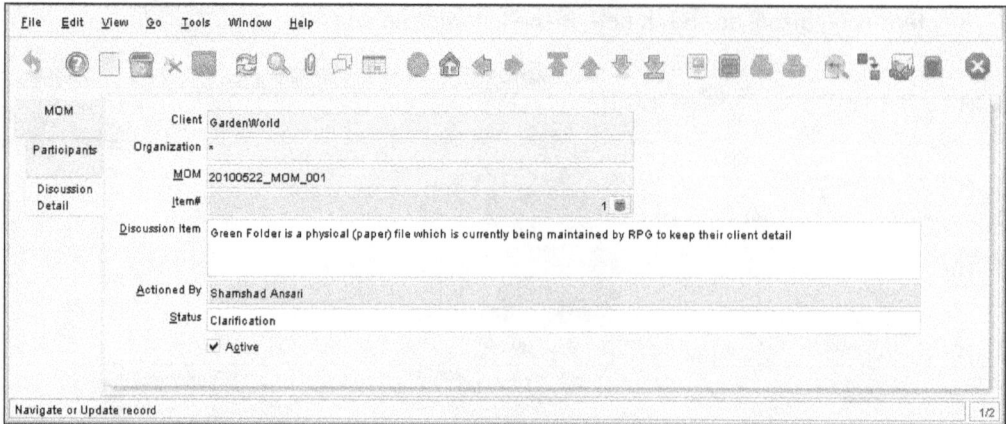

How it works...

In steps 1-5, we cleaned up the dictionary entries that were created so far, as we have changed the table structure of the c_mom table in this recipe and also introduced new tables, namely, c_mom_discussionline and c_mom_participantsline. If we don't do this, the dictionary entries will exist and may create problems when you try to recreate the dictionary entries for the modified table. In steps 6-7, we recreated the c_mom table (with a modified set of columns) and created c_mom_discussionline to save discussion line items for a MOM and the c_mom_participantsline table to save the list of MOM participants. In steps 9-12, we created the tabs and their fields using each one of these three tables.

There's more...

To delete the records, (Windows, Tabs, Fields, and so on.) use Delete Records or Delete Selected Items toolbar buttons ( ) instead of deleting the records directly from the database tables using SQL statements. This is important for the proper cleanup of the records from that database. For example, ADempiere has translation tables (table name ending with _trl) where the entries get created, internally, by ADempiere. If you directly try to delete using SQL statements, you may miss these records.

Creating a search widget

On the MOM tab, we have the Chairperson field where we are entering the username. Similarly, we have the participant's name on the Participants tab and the Actioned By person name on the Discussion Detail tab. ADempiere maintains User/Contact detail. To provide a better finishing of our MOM window, it would be good if we can connect these fields with ADempiere's User/Contact so that a user can find the right User/Contact and assign them to a MOM. This way, all these fields need to be made like a search widget where a Search button appears next to these fields. When a user clicks on the **Search** button, he/ she will be able to find the User/Contact, and upon selection, the selected User/Contact will appear in the field. As part of this recipe, we will follow through the steps required to convert each of these fields into a search widget.

Getting ready

Drop the adempiere.c_mom_participantsline table by executing the following SQL:

```
DROP TABLE adempiere.c_mom_participantsline;
```

Delete the Fields, Tabs, Window, Columns, and Table entries for the c_mom_participantsline table.

How to do it...

1. Create the adempiere.c_mom_participantsline table by executing the following SQL:

```
CREATE TABLE adempiere.c_mom_participantsline (
        c_mom_participantsline_id numeric(10,0) NOT NULL,
        c_mom_id numeric(10,0) NOT NULL,
        ad_client_id numeric(10,0) NOT NULL,
        ad_org_id numeric(10,0) NOT NULL,
    created timestamp without time zone DEFAULT now() NOT NULL,
    createdby numeric(10,0) NOT NULL,
    updated timestamp without time zone DEFAULT now() NOT NULL,
    updatedby numeric(10,0) NOT NULL,
        ad_user_id numeric(10),
        company character varying(80) NOT NULL,
CONSTRAINT cmom_cparticipantsline FOREIGN KEY (c_mom_id)
        REFERENCES adempiere.c_mom (c_mom_id) MATCH SIMPLE
        ON UPDATE NO ACTION ON DELETE NO ACTION DEFERRABLE INITIALLY
DEFERRED,
CONSTRAINT cmom_aduser FOREIGN KEY (ad_user_id)
        REFERENCES adempiere.ad_user (ad_user_id) MATCH SIMPLE
        ON UPDATE NO ACTION ON DELETE NO ACTION DEFERRABLE INITIALLY
DEFERRED
);
```

Here, I have removed the participant column and added the `ad_user_id` column, which has a foreign key relationship with the `adempiere.ad_user` table.

2. Log in as **System/System** with the **System Administrator** role.

3. Go to the **Window Tab & Field** window and look at the detail of the **Minutes Of Meeting** window.

4. Select the **Participants** tab on the **Tab** tab and go to the **Field** tab.

5. Remove the **Participant** field from the list.

6. Go to the **Table and Column** window and go to the `c_mom_participantsline` table entry, as shown in the following screenshot:

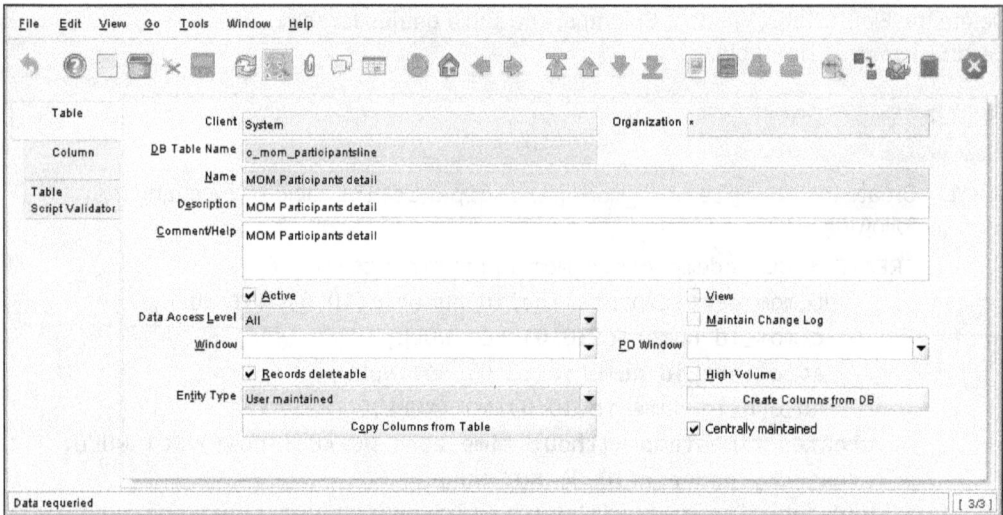

7. Click on the **Create Columns from DB** button. This will create the new column **AD_ User_ID**, as shown in the following screenshot:

Table	Client	Organization	Table	DB Column Name	Column SQL	System Element	
	System	*	c_mom_participantsline_MOM Participants detail	AD_Client_ID		AD_Client_ID	
Column	System	*	c_mom_participantsline_MOM Participants detail	AD_Org_ID		AD_Org_ID	
	System	*	c_mom_participantsline_MOM Participants detail	AD_User_ID		AD_User_ID	
Table	System	*	c_mom_participantsline_MOM Participants detail	c_mom_ID		c_mom_ID	
Script Validator	System	*	c_mom_participantsline_MOM Participants detail	c_mom_participantsline_ID		c_mom_participantsline_ID	
	System	*	c_mom_participantsline_MOM Participants detail	company		company	
	System	*	c_mom_participantsline_MOM Participants detail	Created		Created	
	System	*	c_mom_participantsline_MOM Participants detail	CreatedBy		CreatedBy	
	System	*	c_mom_participantsline_MOM Participants detail	participant		participant	
	System	*	c_mom_participantsline_MOM Participants detail	Updated		Updated	
	System	*	c_mom_participantsline_MOM Participants detail	UpdatedBy		UpdatedBy	

Navigate or Update record   1/11

8. Verify that there is no data in the c_mom_participantsline table and that the **Participant** column is not referenced elsewhere and also remove **Participant** from the **Column** list.

9. Select the **AD_User_ID** column and specify the following values for the two important fields, which are more relevant in this context (search widget):

   ❑ **Reference**: Select **Search**

   ❑ **Reference Key**: Select **AD_User**

10. Go to the **Window, Tab**, and **Field** window and look at the details of the **Minutes Of Meeting** window.

11. Select the **Participants** tab on the **Tab** tab and view its details in single row view. You will see the **Create Fields** button, as shown in the following screenshot:

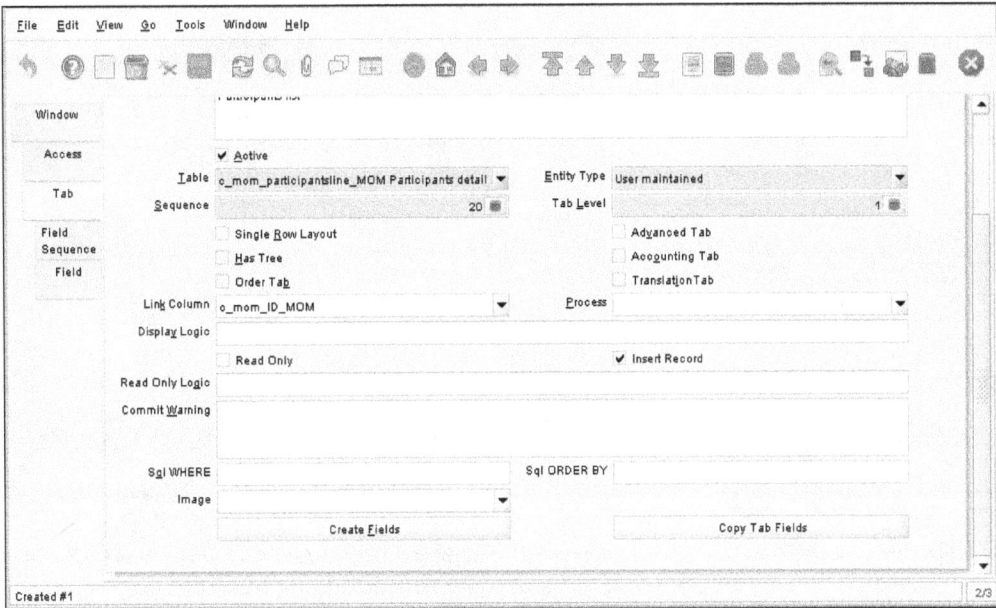

12. Click on **Create Fields** button so that the newly added **User/Contact** column is added as a field.

13. Change the sequence of the **User/Contact** field such that it comes before **Company**.

14. Log out and log in as **GardenAdmin/GardenAdmin** with the **GardenWorld Admin** role.

15. Go to the **Minutes Of Meeting** window and go to the **Participants** tab. You will notice that the **User/Contact** field is populated, by default, with the current logged in username and a search button appears next to the field, as shown in the following screenshot:

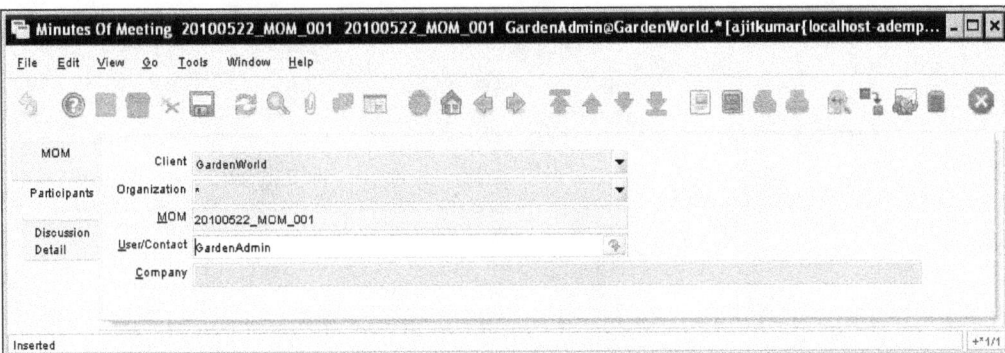

16. Click on the search button. This will pop-up the **Info User/Contact** window and will allow you to search and select the intended user, as shown in the following screenshot:

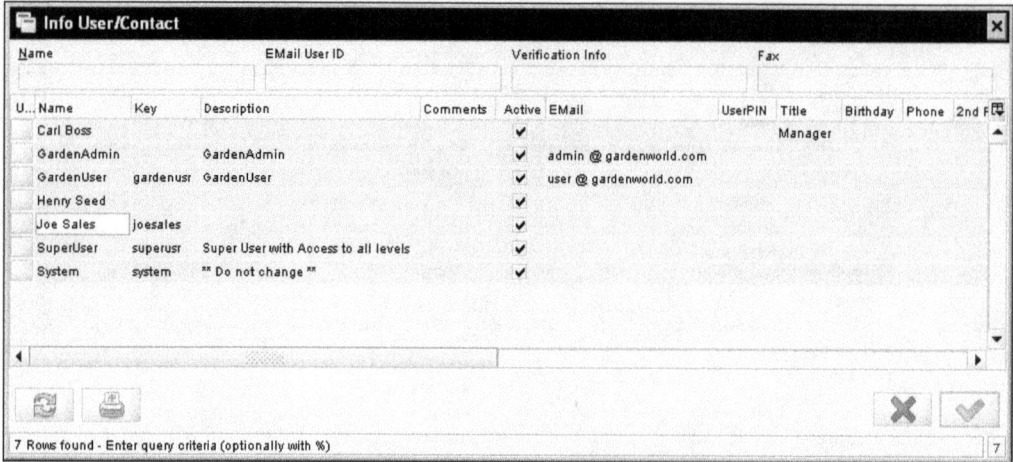

17. Click on the tick button. You will see the selected user appearing in the **User/Contact** field. So, the **Participants** tab will look more connected with ADempiere, as shown in the following screenshot:

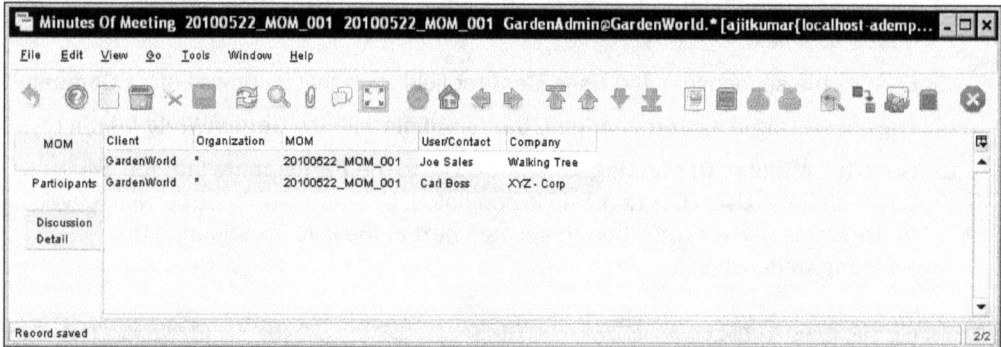

18. Make similar changes to the **Chairperson** field on the **MOM** tab, and the **Chairperson** field appears as a search field, as shown in the following screenshot:

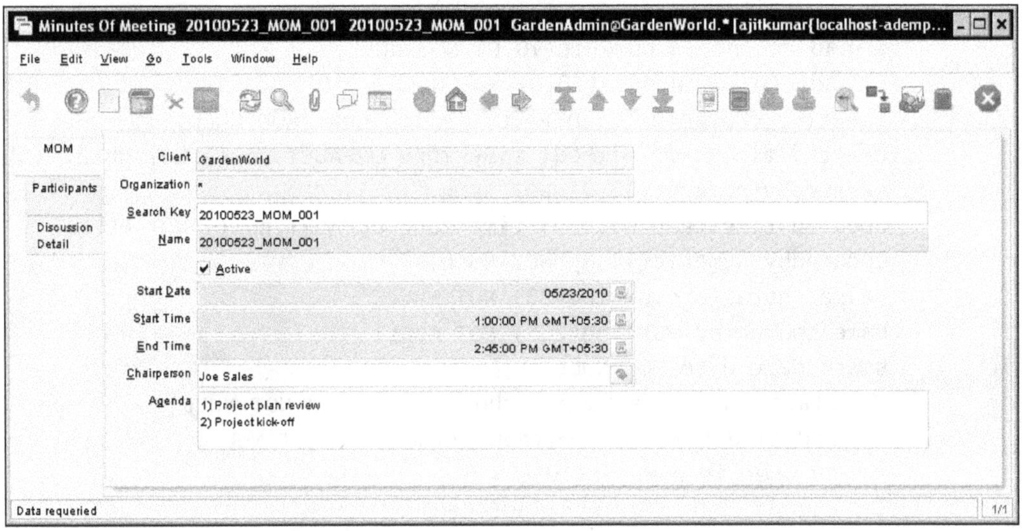

19. Similarly, make changes to the **Actioned By** field on the **Discussion Detail** tab, and the **Actioned By** field appears as a search field, as shown in the following screenshot:

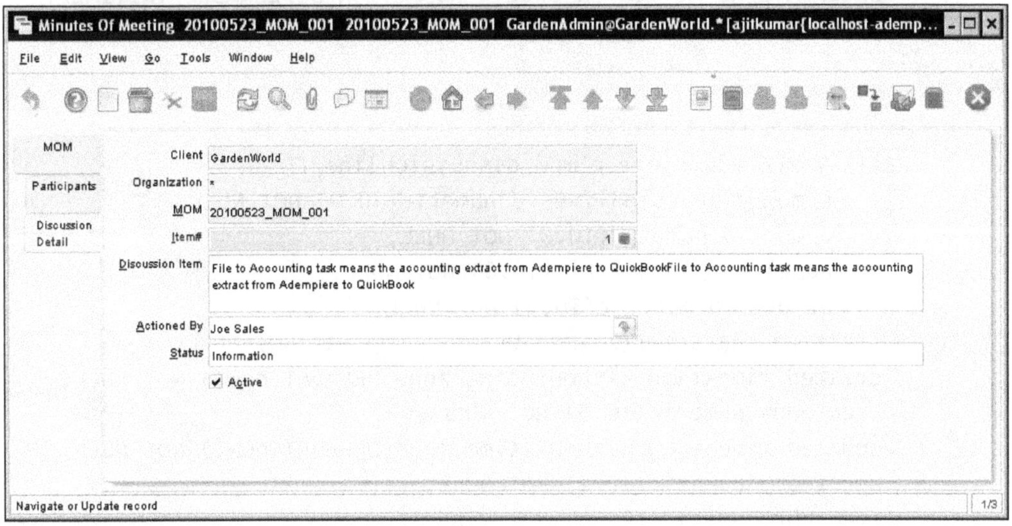

Here is the final schema:

```
CREATE TABLE adempiere.c_mom (
        c_mom_id numeric(10,0) NOT NULL,
        ad_client_id numeric(10,0) NOT NULL,
        ad_org_id numeric(10,0) NOT NULL,
    isactive character(1) DEFAULT 'Y'::bpchar NOT NULL,
    created timestamp without time zone DEFAULT now() NOT NULL,
    createdby numeric(10,0) NOT NULL,
    updated timestamp without time zone DEFAULT now() NOT NULL,
    updatedby numeric(10,0) NOT NULL,
    value character varying(30) NOT NULL,
    name character varying(255) NOT NULL,
    start_date date NOT NULL,
        start_time timestamp without time zone NOT NULL,
        end_time timestamp without time zone NOT NULL,
        ad_user_id numeric(10),
        agenda character varying(4000),
    CONSTRAINT c_mom_pkey PRIMARY KEY (c_mom_id),
    CONSTRAINT cmom_aduser FOREIGN KEY (ad_user_id)
      REFERENCES adempiere.ad_user (ad_user_id) MATCH SIMPLE
      ON UPDATE NO ACTION ON DELETE NO ACTION DEFERRABLE INITIALLY
DEFERRED
    );


CREATE TABLE adempiere.c_mom_discussionline (
        c_mom_discussionline_id numeric(10,0) NOT NULL,
        c_mom_id numeric(10,0) NOT NULL,
        ad_client_id numeric(10,0) NOT NULL,
        ad_org_id numeric(10,0) NOT NULL,
    isactive character(1) DEFAULT 'Y'::bpchar NOT NULL,
    created timestamp without time zone DEFAULT now() NOT NULL,
    createdby numeric(10,0) NOT NULL,
    updated timestamp without time zone DEFAULT now() NOT NULL,
    updatedby numeric(10,0) NOT NULL,
    item_nbr numeric (10,0) NOT NULL,
        discussion_desc character varying(2000),
        ad_user_id numeric(10),
        status character varying(80),
    CONSTRAINT cmom_cdiscussionline FOREIGN KEY (c_mom_id)
```

```
        REFERENCES adempiere.c_mom (c_mom_id) MATCH SIMPLE
        ON UPDATE NO ACTION ON DELETE NO ACTION DEFERRABLE INITIALLY
DEFERRED,
    CONSTRAINT cmomdl_aduser FOREIGN KEY (ad_user_id)
        REFERENCES adempiere.ad_user (ad_user_id) MATCH SIMPLE
        ON UPDATE NO ACTION ON DELETE NO ACTION DEFERRABLE INITIALLY
DEFERRED
    );


    CREATE TABLE adempiere.c_mom_participantsline (
        c_mom_participantsline_id numeric(10,0) NOT NULL,
        c_mom_id numeric(10,0) NOT NULL,
        ad_client_id numeric(10,0) NOT NULL,
        ad_org_id numeric(10,0) NOT NULL,
    created timestamp without time zone DEFAULT now() NOT NULL,
    createdby numeric(10,0) NOT NULL,
    updated timestamp without time zone DEFAULT now() NOT NULL,
    updatedby numeric(10,0) NOT NULL,
        ad_user_id numeric(10),
        company character varying(80) NOT NULL,
    CONSTRAINT cmom_cparticipantslinemom FOREIGN KEY (c_mom_id)
        REFERENCES adempiere.c_mom (c_mom_id) MATCH SIMPLE
        ON UPDATE NO ACTION ON DELETE NO ACTION DEFERRABLE INITIALLY
DEFERRED,
    CONSTRAINT cmom_aduser FOREIGN KEY (ad_user_id)
        REFERENCES adempiere.ad_user (ad_user_id) MATCH SIMPLE
        ON UPDATE NO ACTION ON DELETE NO ACTION DEFERRABLE INITIALLY
DEFERRED
    );
```

How it works...

In this recipe, we replaced the free text user columns in the c_mom_participantsline and c_mom_discussionline tables with ad_user_id, which is having a foreign key reference to the AD_User table. The AD_User table contains the ADempiere user detail. This is not a mandatory step. However, from a good database design perspective, it is advisable that we save the ID of an entity, which is referred to in a table and also has the constraint (foreign key) in place.

In step 9, we had to set the **Reference** to **Search** and **Reference Key** to **AD_User** for the **User/Contact** field on the **Participants** tab, **Actioned By** on the **Discussion Detail** tab, and **Chairperson** on the **MOM** tab. ADempiere interprets the **Reference—Search**—and displays a search button ([image]) next to the field. By clicking on it, ADempiere takes care of showing the Info **User/Contact** pop-up to allow the user to search for a user and select a user from the search result.

Populating the combo-box list

There is a **Status** field on the **Discussion Detail** tab. Currently, this field accepts free text. For various practical reasons, such as, to maintain the consistency in communication, to support project guidelines, to have clean data for further analysis and reporting, and so on, it makes sense to convert the **Status** field into a combo-box and the possible values are listed for the user selection. In this recipe, we will follow the steps to convert the **Status** field into a combo-box and configure it in such a way that it is populated with values.

Getting ready

Drop the status column by executing the following SQL:

```
ALTER TABLE c_mom_discussionline DROP COLUMN status;
```

How to do it...

1. Create a new table, c_momstatus, to capture the list of status values by executing the following SQL:

```
CREATE TABLE adempiere.c_momstatus
(
    c_momstatus_id numeric(10) NOT NULL,
    ad_client_id numeric(10) NOT NULL,
    ad_org_id numeric(10) NOT NULL,
    isactive character(1) NOT NULL DEFAULT 'Y'::bpchar,
    created timestamp without time zone NOT NULL DEFAULT now(),
    createdby numeric(10) NOT NULL,
    updated timestamp without time zone NOT NULL DEFAULT now(),
    updatedby numeric(10) NOT NULL,
    "name" character varying(60) NOT NULL,
    description character varying(255),
    isdefault character(1) NOT NULL DEFAULT 'N'::bpchar,
    "value" character varying(40) NOT NULL,
    CONSTRAINT c_momstatus_pkey PRIMARY KEY (c_momstatus_id),
    CONSTRAINT c_momstatus_isactive_check CHECK (isactive = ANY
(ARRAY['Y'::bpchar, 'N'::bpchar]))
);
```

2. Modify the `c_mom_discussionline` table to add a new column `c_momstatus_id`, which has a foreign key relationship with the `c_momstatus` table, by executing the following SQLs:

    ALTER TABLE adempiere.c_mom_discussionline ADD COLUMN c_momstatus_id numeric(10);

    ALTER TABLE adempiere.c_mom_discussionline ADD CONSTRAINT cmomdl_cmomstatus FOREIGN KEY (c_momstatus_id) REFERENCES adempiere.c_momstatus (c_momstatus_id) MATCH SIMPLE ON UPDATE NO ACTION ON DELETE NO ACTION DEFERRABLE INITIALLY DEFERRED

3. Log in as **System/System** with the **System Administrator** role.

4. Set up the table and column detail for the `c_momstatus` table using the **Table and Column** window.

5. Set up the window with a tab and the fields for the `c_momstatus` table using the **Window, Tab & Field** window.

6. Click on **Application Dictionary | Reference**. This will show the **Reference** window and will allow the user to create a new one. Fill in the detail on the **Reference** tab and click on the save icon to create a reference for our MOM status, as shown in the following screenshot:

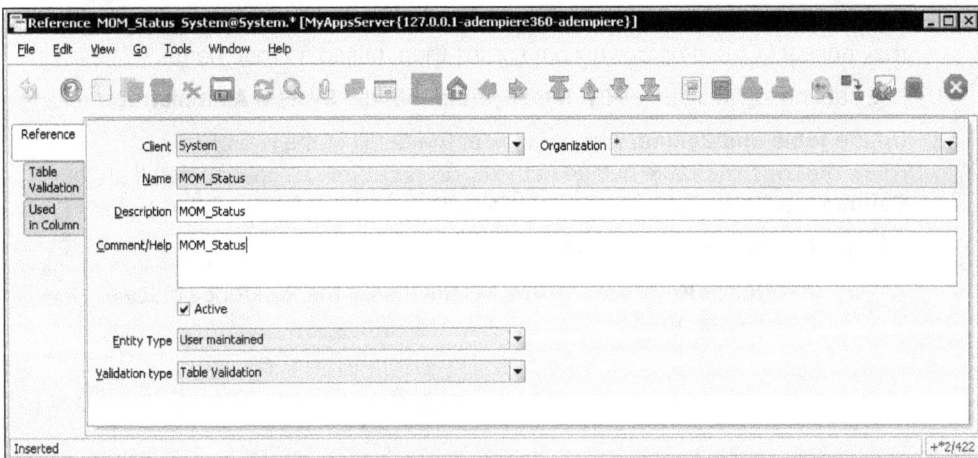

Since we had selected **Table Validation** as the **Validation Type**, the **Table Validation** tab is enabled (red colored cross disappears).

7. Enter the **Table, Key column**, and **Display column**, besides other details, on the **Table Validation** tab, as shown in the following screenshot:

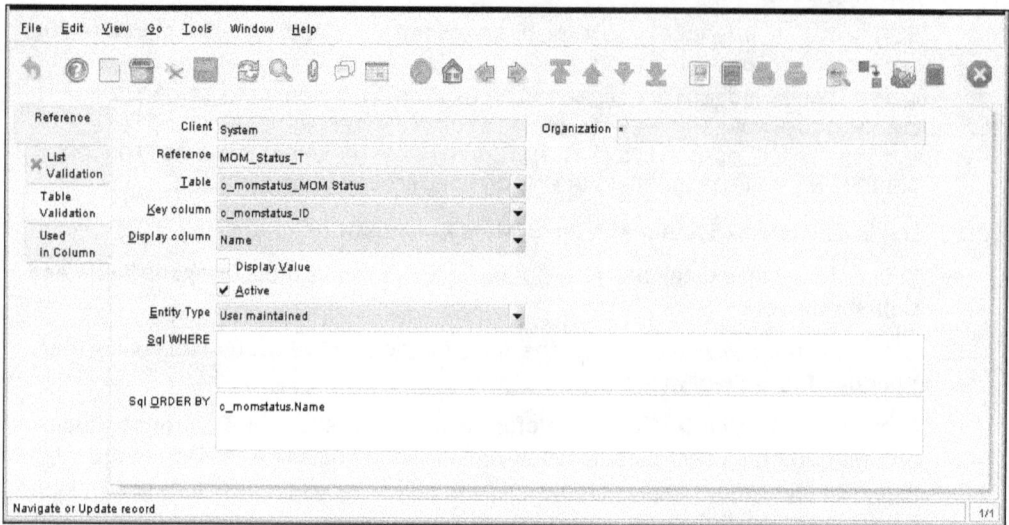

8. In the **Sql ORDER BY**, I have mentioned the ORDER BY clause to sort the values when they appear in the drop down. I am sorting them based on their name.

9. Log out and log in again as **System/System** with the **System Administrator** role.

10. On the **Table and Column** window, look at the detail of the c_mom_discussionline table and go to the c_momstatus_ID column detail on the **Column** tab. Enter the following field values:

   ❑ **Reference**: Select **Table**

   ❑ **Reference Key**: Select **MOM_Status** (this is the Reference that we have created)

The following screenshot shows the fields and values entered:

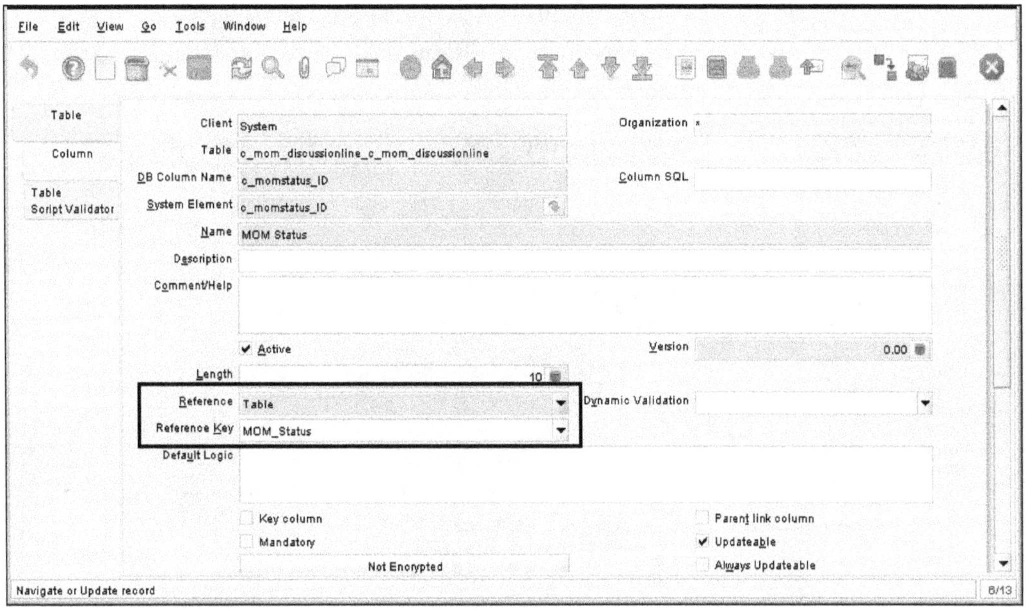

11. Create a **Menu** by name **MOM Status** as we created the one in the Create a new window recipe.

12. Log out and log in as **GardenAdmin/GardenAdmin** with the **GardenWorld Admin** role.

13. Go to the **MOM Status** window and create different statuses. For example, Let us say that **Open** is marked as the default status, as shown in the following screenshot:

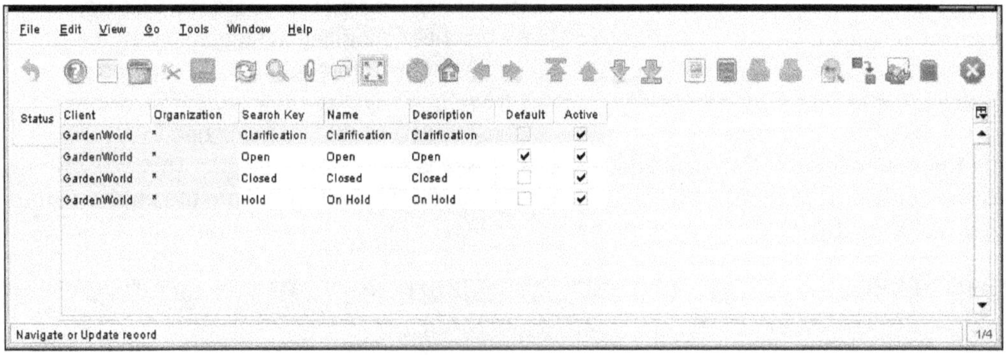

14. Go to the **Minutes Of Meeting** window and go to the **Discussion Detail** tab. The **Status** field is now a combo-box and all the statuses, which we created in the previous step, are available in the drop-down list. As **Open** is set as default, when we create a new discussion line item, the **Status** field will be populated with **Open**, by default, as shown in the following screenshot:

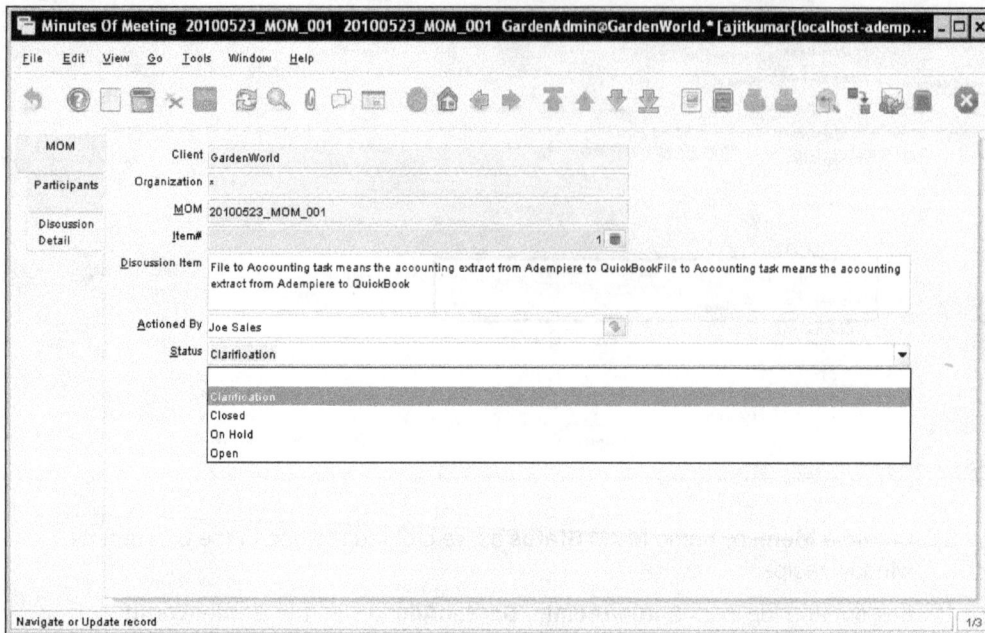

How it works...

In step 1, we created a new table c_momstatus where the MOM statuses will be saved. The status column in c_mom_dicussionline has been modified in step 2 so that the column is now linked with the c_momstatus. In the steps 3 through to 8, we created a Reference MOM_Status that gets the records from the c_momstatus table. This reference is then used on the **Status** column on the discussion detail table in the dictionary for which the **Reference** is set to **Table** and the **Reference Key** is set to MOM_Status. This way, the **Status** field is rendered as a combo-box and the values are populated from the entries in the c_momstatus table.

Configuring a zoom window

In the previous recipe, we created a c_momstatus table and created a column, c_momstatus_id, in the c_mom_discussionline, which has a foreign key relationship with the c_momstatus table. This is a useful detail in the context of the Zoom window, as ADempiere automatically generates a link (called hyperlink in the web version) and when we click on the link, the system takes us to the linked window, which is called zooming in ADempiere. This is useful when you are on a window and quickly jump on to another window, which is linked through one of the fields to look at more details. However, there are some other details that need to be configured before it starts working and this recipe will cover these details.

How to do it...

Say, we want to zoom to the **MOM Status** table when a user clicks on the **MOM Status** link on the **Discussion Detail** table. With this in perspective, the following are the steps:

1. Log in as **System/System** with the **System Administrator** role.

2. Go to the **Table and Column** window and open the details of the **MOM Status** table, as shown in the following screenshot:

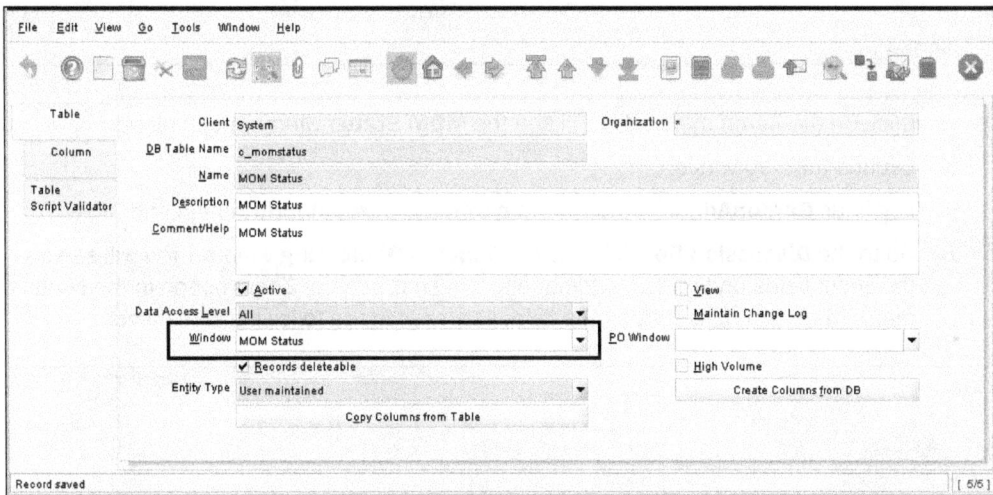

3. Set the **Window** field to **MOM Status**.

4. Log out and log in as **GardenAdmin/GardenAdmin** with the **GardenWorld Admin** role.

5. Go to the **Discussion Detail** tab of the **Minutes Of Meeting** window.

6. Right-click on the **MOM Status** field. You will get a menu with the **Zoom** option, as shown in the following screenshot.

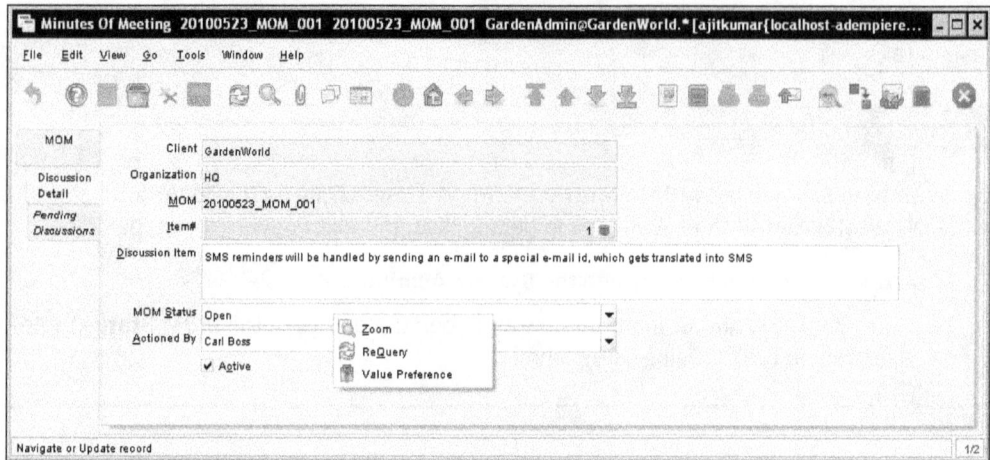

7. Click on the **Zoom** menu. You will see the **MOM Status** window popping up.

8. Launch the web version.

9. Log in as **GardenAdmin/GardenAdmin** with the **GardenWorld Admin** role.

10. Go to the **Discussion Detail** tab of the **Minutes Of Meeting** window. You will see all the zoom fields underlined. Additionally, you shall see the **Zoom** option in the context menu when you right-click on the field, as shown in the following screenshot:

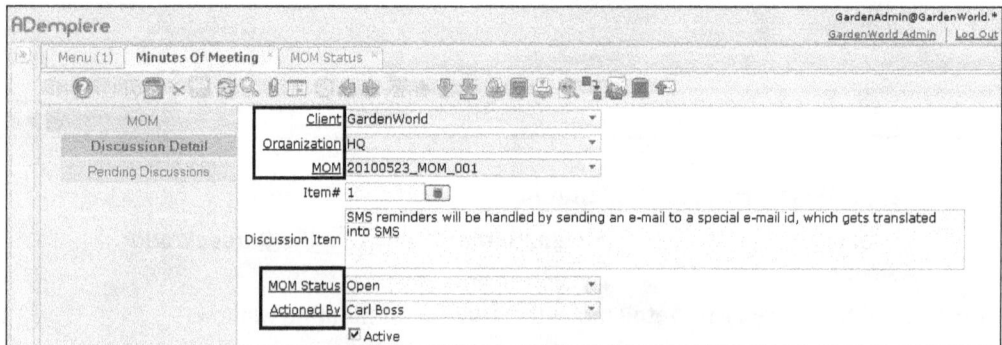

11. Click on the **MOM Status** hyperlink. The system will open the **MOM Status** window and make it the active one.

Creating a read-only window

In contrast, there will be situations where a user is required to only look at the details and not required to create the record. For example, a customer service representative only requires view permission on most of the data so that they can answer customer enquiries effectively. This recipe describes how we can create a read-only window.

How to do it...

To demonstrate, I have taken the **MOM Status** window. However, you may apply the same steps to your **Minutes Of Meeting** window.

1. Log in as **System/System** with the **System Administrator** role.

2. Go to the **Window, Tab**, and **Field** window and look for the **MOM Status** window.

3. Change the **Window Type** to **Query Only** and save it, as shown in the following screenshot:

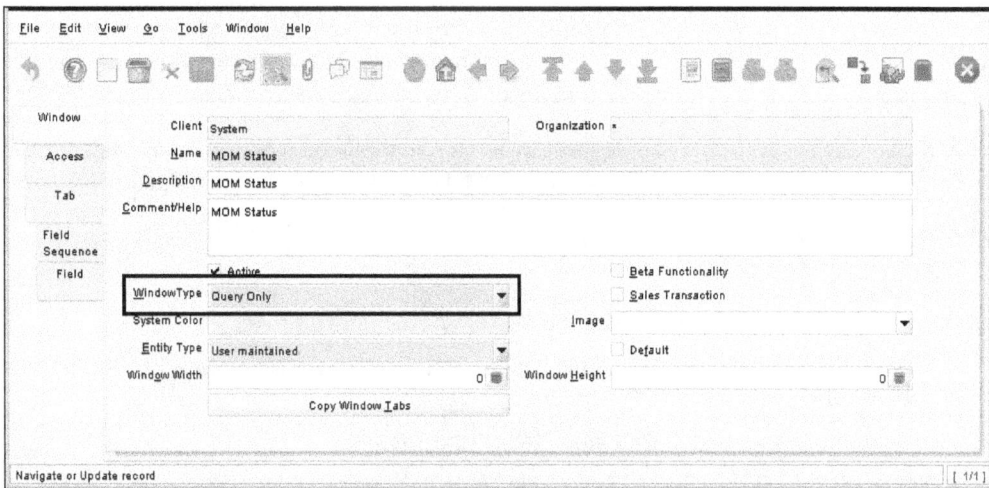

4. Log out and log in as **GardenAdmin/ GardenAdmin** with the **GardenWorld Admin** role.

5. Go to the **MOM Status** window. System will show you the list and the **New Record** button will be disabled, as shown in the following screenshot:

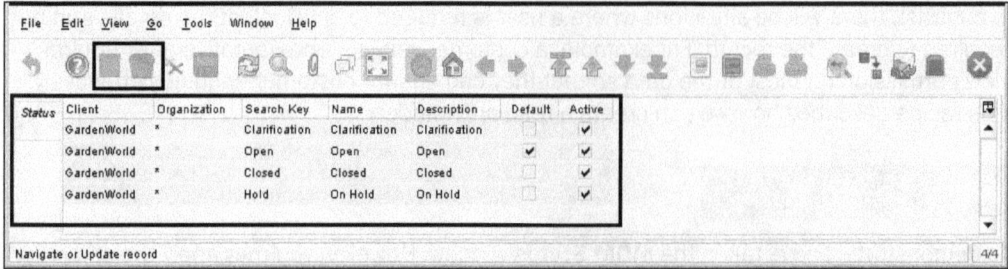

Creating a read-only tab

Sometimes there may be a need where not the complete window should be made read-only. Rather, a particular tab needs to be made read-only. For example, there is a user who, as per their role, shall capture the payments against an invoice. He/she should not be allowed to create an invoice in the system. To address this need, we can have a window where one tab is to capture the payment detail and another one showing the outstanding invoices, which we will make read-only. This way, on the single window, the user will be able to refer to the outstanding invoices and at the same time receive payments towards them.

In our MOM case study, Let us say we want to add a rule that states only an admin user shall be allowed to edit the discussion items of an MOM. Let us see how we can do this.

How to do it...

1. Log in as **System/System** with the **System Administrator** role.
2. Go to the **Window, Tab**, and **Field** window and look for the **Minutes Of Meeting** window.
3. Go to the **Discussion Detail** tab detail on the **Tab**.
4. Specify the following in the **Read Only Logic** field, as shown in the following screenshot:

    @#AD_Role_Name@='GardenWorld User'

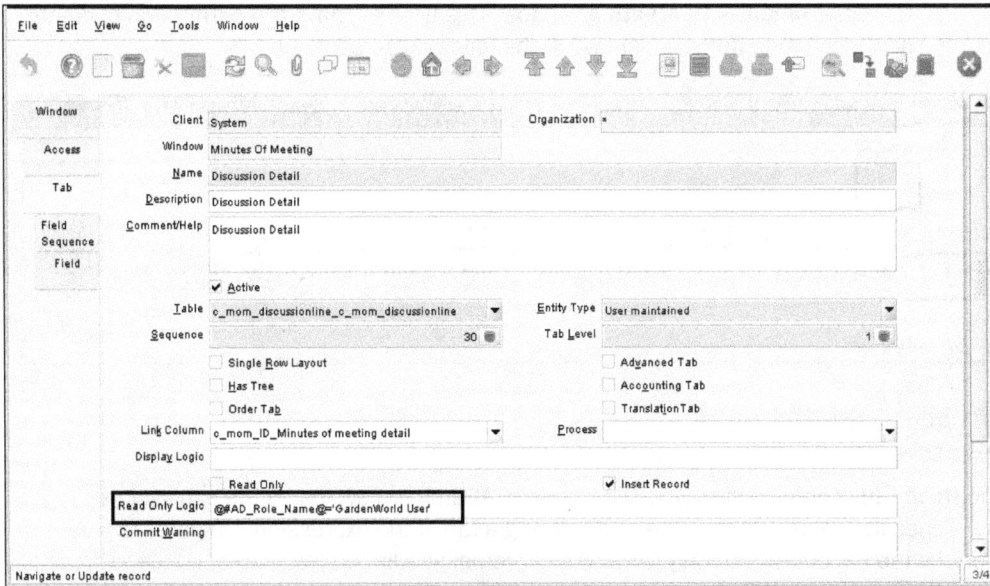

5. Log out and log in as **GardenUser/GardenUser** with the **GardenWorld User** role.

6. Go to the **Minutes Of Meeting** window. The system will show you the list and the **New Record** button will be disabled, because, for this role, we have set the read-only logic. Also notice that the read-only tab label is displayed in italic, as shown in the following screenshot:

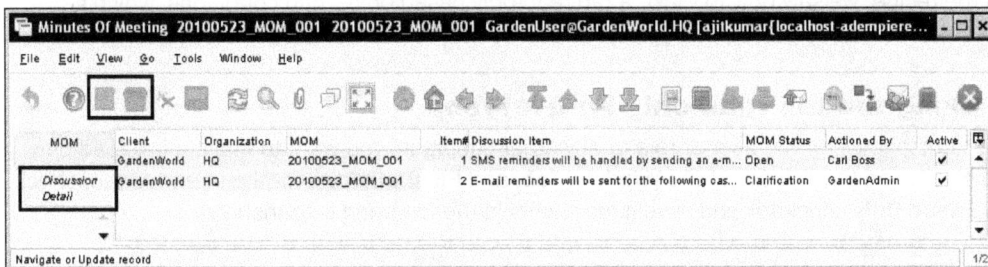

7. Log out and log in as **GardenAdmin/GardenAdmin** with the **GardenWorld Admin** role.

8. Go to the **Minutes Of Meeting** window. This user will have the permission to create new discussion items, as shown in the following screenshot:

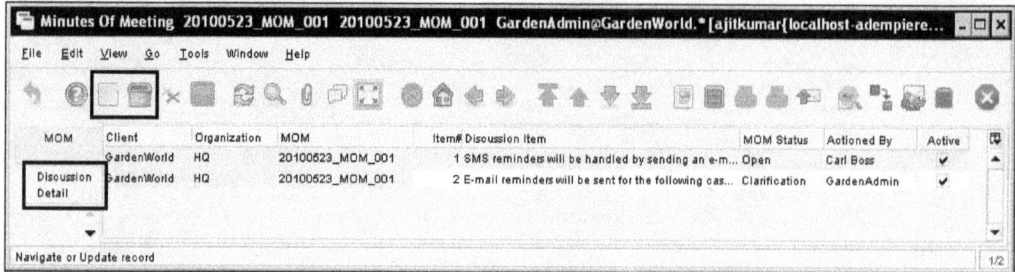

How it works...

The **Read Only Logic**, in step 3, is the key here. ADempiere evaluates the expression mentioned in this field at the time of displaying a tab. If the expression evaluates to true, then the tab becomes read-only. Otherwise, it remains editable. You can build the expressions using this context. In this recipe, we used the #AD_Role_Name context variable in the expression to check if the role name of the current logged in user is "GardenWorld user", and then made the tab read-only. To view the context information, click on **Tools | Preference** on any window and go to the **Context** tab.

There's more...

In the recipe, we saw how to make a tab read-only based on certain conditions, which get evaluated at runtime. There may be a case where a tab has to be read-only in all the cases.

Making the tab read-only for everyone

Say, irrespective of the user or role or any other condition, you want to make a tab read-only. To do this, on the **Tab** tab of the **Window, Tab**, and **Field** windows for the intended tab, check the **Read Only** checkbox and save it, as shown in the following screenshot:

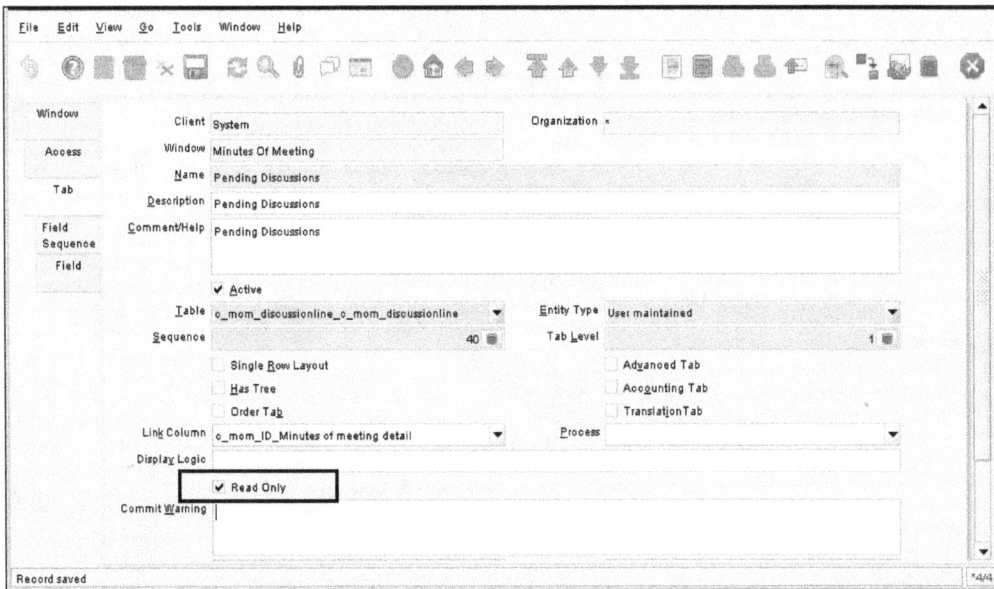

Creating read-only fields

Another situation is where neither a window is read-only nor is the tab. It is there that we want to make a few fields read-only on a tab. For example, on our MOM window, the **Client** and **Organisation** fields need to be read-only as they are populated, by default, based on the logged in user's details and does not require any modification. This recipe describes the steps to achieve this.

How to do it...

1. Log in as **System/System** with the **System Administrator** role.

2. Go to the **Window**, **Tab**, and **Field** window and look for the **Minutes Of Meeting** window.

3. Select the target tab on **Tab** and go to the **Field** tab.

4. Check the **Read Only** checkbox for the **Client** field, as shown in the
following screenshot:

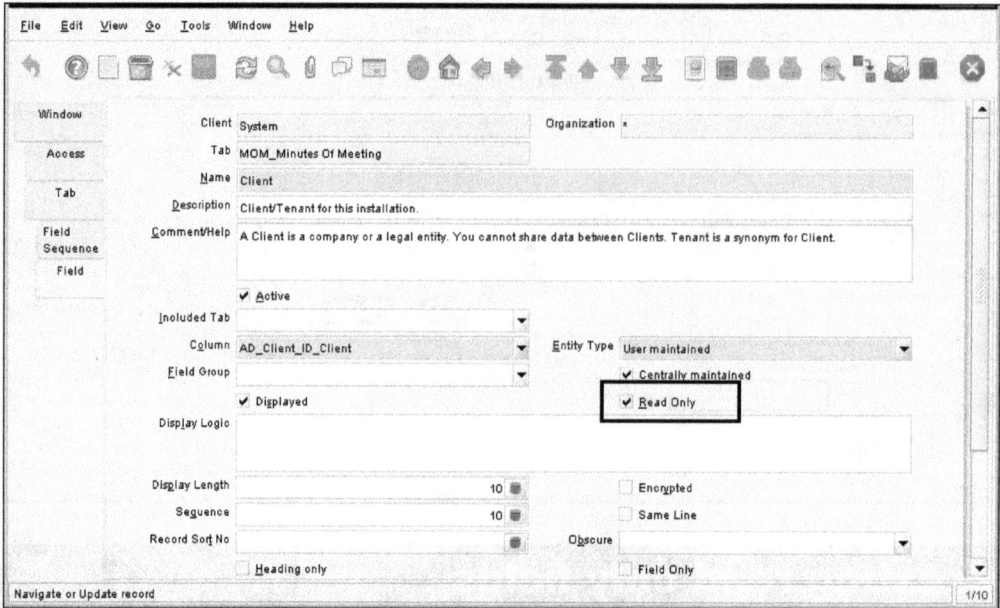

5. Repeat the same for **Organisation** and any other field that you want to be read-only.

6. Log out and log in as **GardenAdmin/ GardenAdmin** with the **GardenWorld Admin** role.

7. Go to the **Minutes Of Meeting** window. Editing will not be allowed for all the fields we
marked as read-only—**Client**, **Organization**—as shown in the following screenshot:

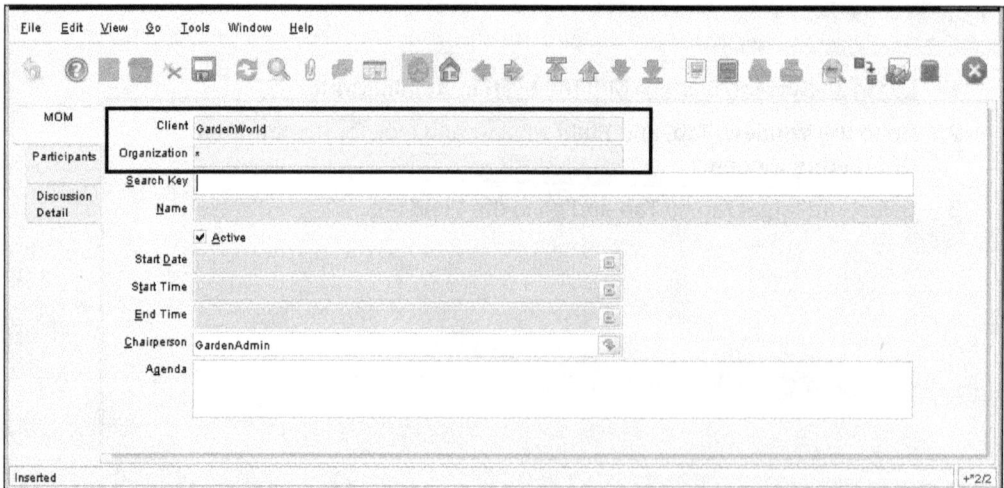

Creating a new menu tree

As part of the customization, we may build windows and may want to keep them logically grouped. For example, in ADempiere, we have Quote-to-Invoice where everything related to the sales is grouped. Let us say we want to group all our MOM-related windows under a node MOM in the Menu tree so that they are all in one place. Here we will look into the procedure to create such a menu structure.

How to do it...

1. Log in as **System/System** with the **System Administrator** role.
2. Go to **Menu | System Admin | General Rules | System Rules | Menu**.
3. Click on the **New Record** button to create a new menu and fill in the details, as shown in the following screenshot:

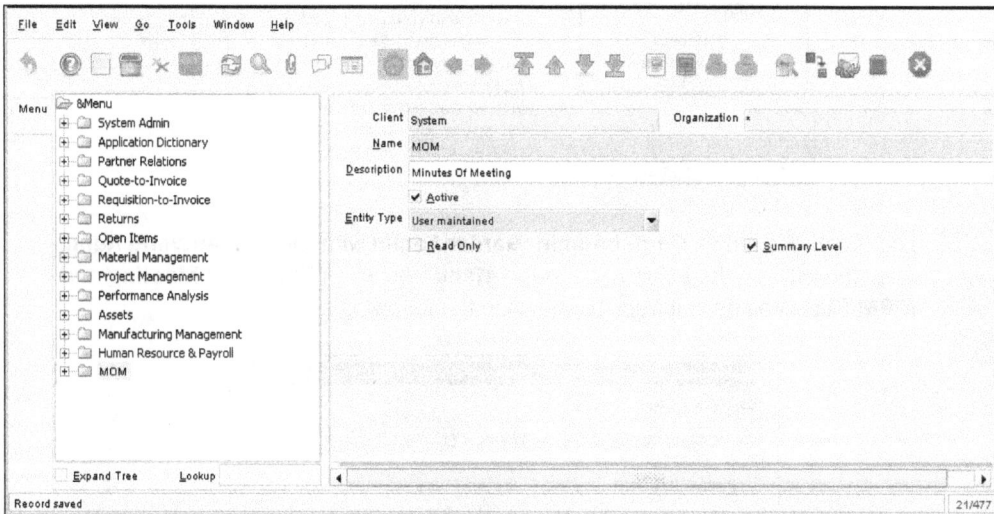

Check the **Summary Level** to create a folder entry in the **Menu** tree to which further menus can be added. If the **Summary Level** is not checked, the newly created menu will be added a leaf node to the **Menu** tree.

4. Go to **Menu | System Admin | General Rules | System Rules | Tree Maintenance** and select **Menu** from the **Tree** drop-down. You will see the newly created **MOM** node on the left-hand side. All the windows appear on the right-hand side.

5. Select the **MOM** node and add the **Minutes Of Meeting** and **MOM Status** windows to it by clicking on the **Add to Tree** button, as shown in the following screenshot:

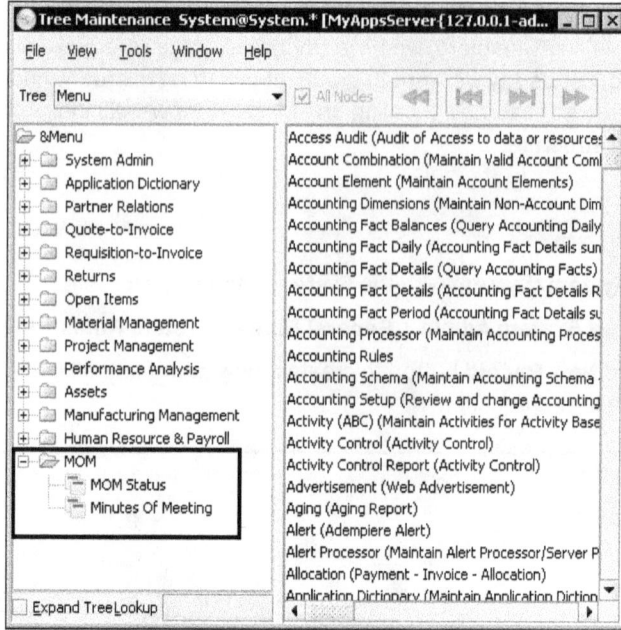

6. Log out and log in as **GardenAdmin/GardenAdmin** with the **GardenWorld Admin** role. You will see the **MOM** node in the **Menu** tree with **Minutes Of Meeting** and **MOM Status** as its children, as shown in the following screenshot:

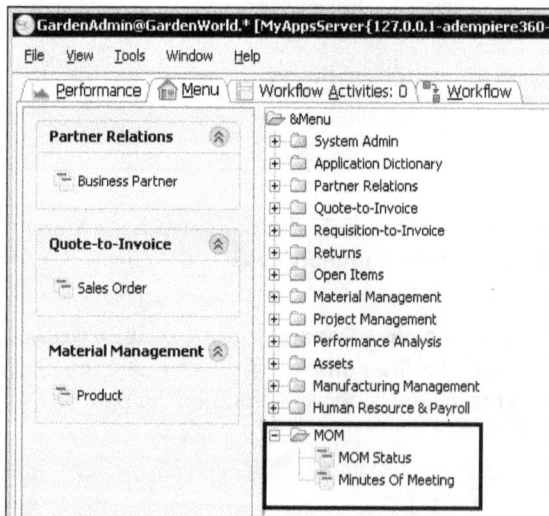

Role set up and assigning a menu tree to a role

By default, to every role in ADempiere, we see a **Menu** tree, which shows the items that the role has access to. It is imperative that, for a role, we may have to build an altogether different menu tree. For example, a sales representative in an organization requires access to Quote-to-Invoice. In that case, that role shall see only the **Quote-to-Invoice** node in its Menu tree.

Let us say, in our MOM example, there is a user role, which only needs to work with the MOM-related windows. To such a role, we would like to ensure that only the **MOM** node appears in their **Menu** tree. This recipe provides us with the required details to implement our requirement.

How to do it...

1. Log in as **System/System** with the **System Administrator** role.
2. Go to the **Menu | System Admin | General Rules | System Rules | Tree** window.
3. Click on **New Record** and fill in the required details. For **Type | Area**, select **Menu**, as shown in the following screenshot:

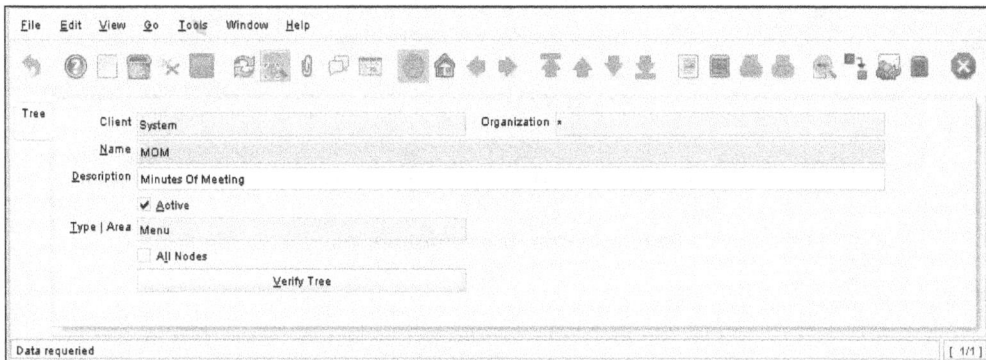

4. Click on the **Verify Tree** button.
5. Go to the **Menu | System Admin | General Rules | System Rules | Tree Maintenance** window.

6. Select the newly created tree, **MOM**, as **Tree** and add the **Minutes Of Meeting** and **MOM Status** windows to it, as shown in the following screenshot:

7. Log out and log in as **GardenAdmin/GardenAdmin** with the **GardenWorld Admin** role.

8. Go to the **Menu | System Admin | General Rules | Security | Role** window and create a new role by name, say, **GardenWorld TestUser**, for which select **MOM** as the **Menu Tree**, as shown in the following screenshot:

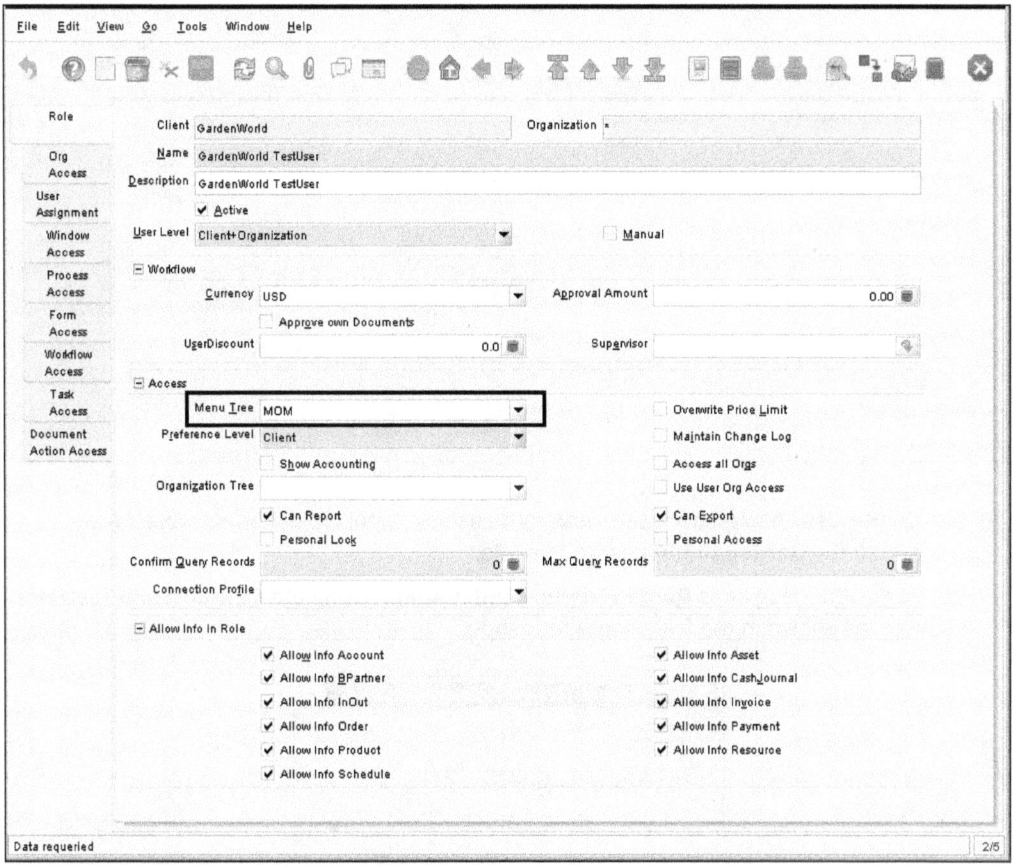

On the **Org Access** tab or the **Role** window, assign the organizations that this role will have access to, as shown here in the following screenshot:

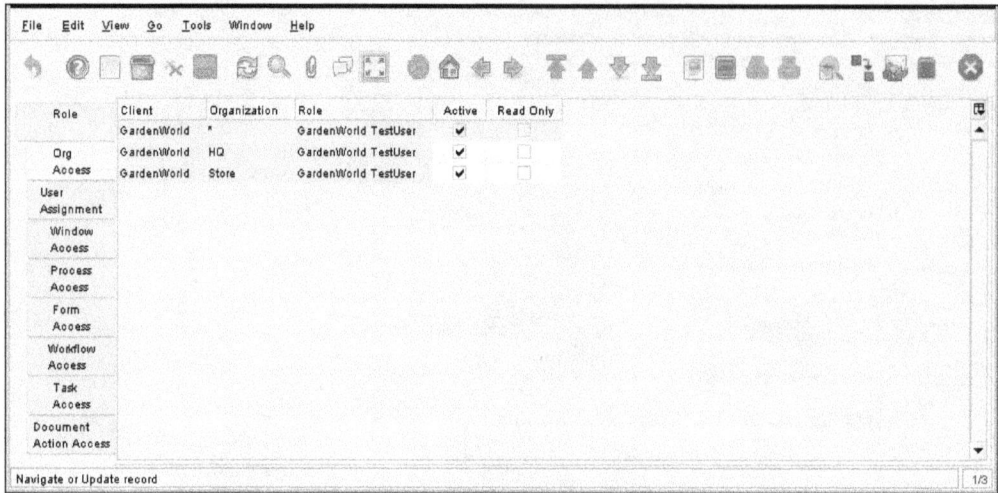

9. On the **User Assignment** tab, assign the user(s) to this role. For example, I have added the **GardenAdmin** user to this role.

10. Log out and log in as **GardenAdmin/GardenAdmin** using the **GardenWorld TestUser** role, as shown in the following screenshot:

In the **Menu** tree, you would see only the **MOM** node and its children, as shown in the following screenshot:

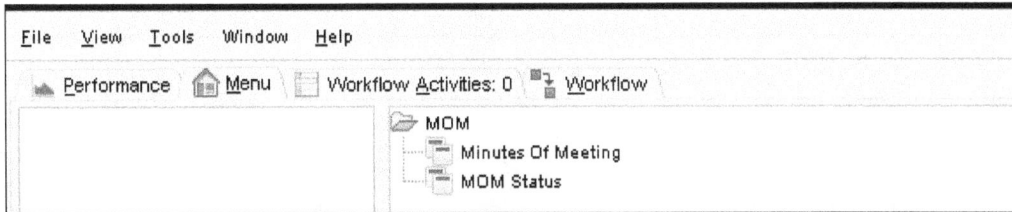

Defaulting the data display to single/multi-row mode

By default, ADempiere shows data in a window in multi-row mode, where it shows multiple records in a tabular format. It allows complete data entry in the tabular form, as well. However, in many instances, it is more logical and convenient to show the window as a form to allow easy understanding and filling of the data. Irrespective of the default mode, using the Grid Toggle toolbar button, a user can switch between these two modes. However, from a usability perspective, many a times, it makes sense to show the window as a form or as a table. For example, if the workflow says that a user has to always create the data in the system, it is more appropriate to provide the single-row mode (window is shown as a form) of the window to that user. Whereas, if the workflow requires the user to create the data (only if it does not exist in the system), it is more appropriate to show the window in the multi-row mode (tabular representation). This recipe covers this aspect of our customization need.

How to do it...

1. Log in as **System/System** with the **System Administrator** role.
2. Go to the **Window, Tab**, and **Field** window and select the target tab on **Tab**.

3. Check the **Single Row Layout** to default the record display on the tab to form representation. If unchecked, the record display on the tab defaults to the tabular representation, as shown in the following screenshot:

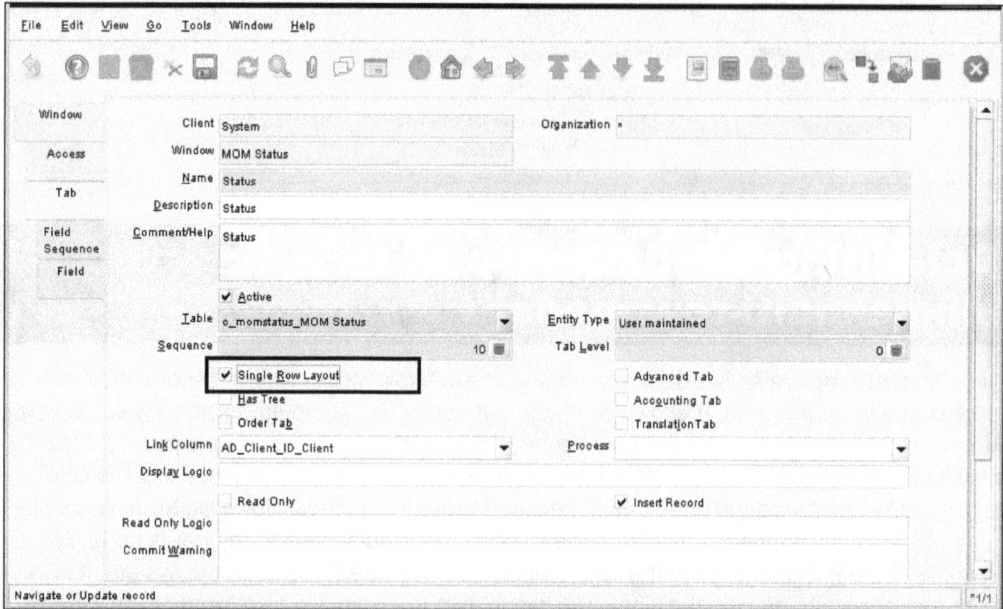

Showing the entity and line items on the same tab

On our MOM window, we have **MOM**, **Participants**, and **Discussion Detail** tabs. Let us say we think it would be better if Participants information is displayed on the first tab, MOM. This way, one can quickly find out who all attended the meeting, if that is the only interest they have in this window. Here we will go through the steps required to have a tab included inside another tab.

How to do it...

1. Add a new column to the `adempiere.c_mom` table by executing the following SQL:

   ```
   ALTER TABLE adempiere.c_mom ADD COLUMN tab_participants
   numeric(10);
   ```

2. Go to the **Table and Column** window and generate the new column from the database table, as shown in the following screenshot:

3. Go to the **Window**, **Tab**, and **Field** window and generate the new field.

4. Verify the field sequence. Usually, we would like to keep these kinds of things at the end, as shown in the following screenshot:

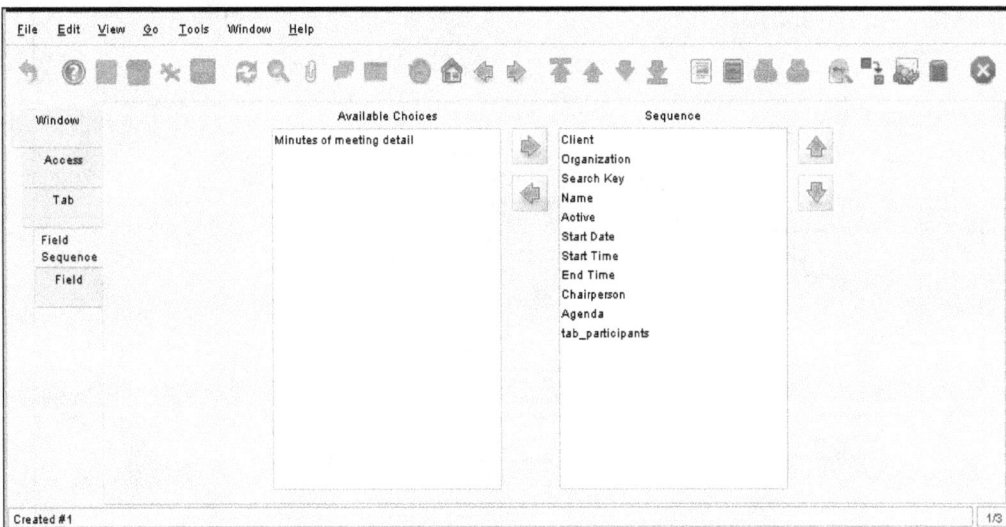

5. Go to the **Field** tab and select **Participants** from the **Included Tab** drop-down of the **tab_participants** field, as shown in the following screenshot:

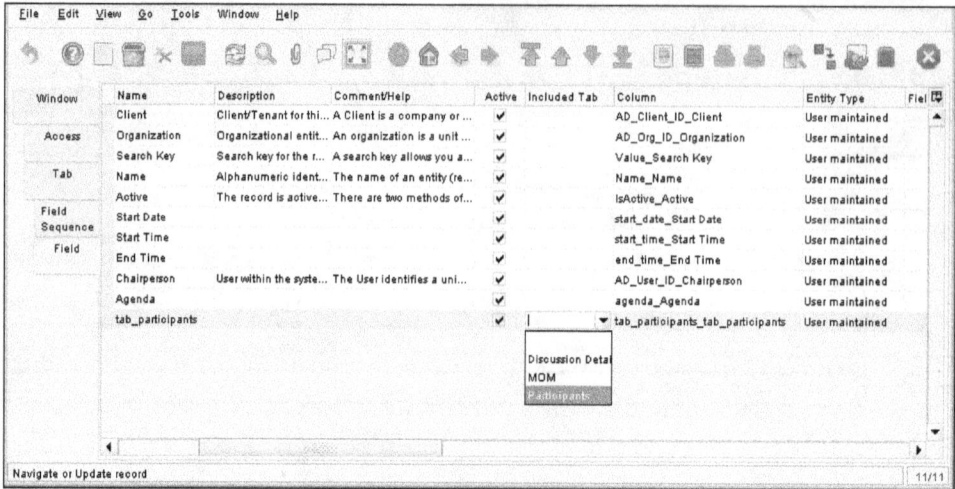

6. Log out and log in as **GardenAdmin/GardenAdmin** with the **GardenWorld Admin** role.

7. Go to the **Minutes Of Meeting** window. You will see the **Participants** tab details appearing as an included tab on the **MOM** tab, as shown in the following screenshot:

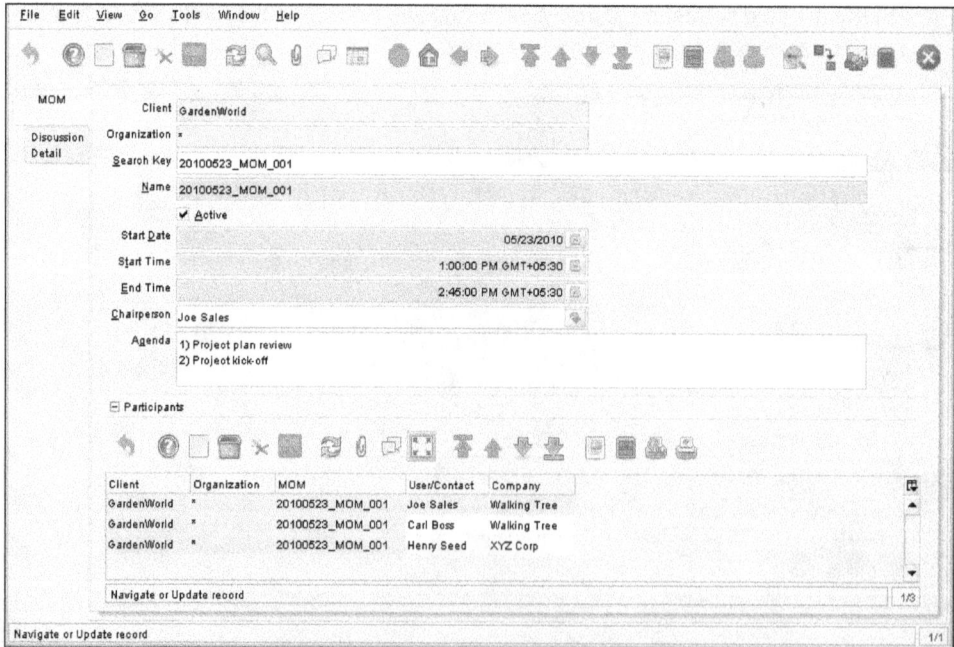

3
ADempiere Customization – Part II

In this chapter, we will cover:

- ► Copying another tab widget into this tab
- ► Filtering data at tab level
- ► Configuring display logic
- ► Configuring default logic
- ► Creating a new window from an existing window
- ► Configuring a lookup record
- ► Dynamic validations
- ► Customizing a default print format of a window
- ► Configuring a new print format for a window
- ► Generating a model
- ► Creating a new info window for the desktop version
- ► Creating a new info window for the web version
- ► Creating a callout
- ► Modifying hooks for a model
- ► Creating a process
- ► Extending the desktop version of the toolbar
- ► Extending the web version of the toolbar
- ► Grouping the fields in tab

Introduction

This chapter is a continuation of *Chapter 2, ADempiere Customization – Part I*. Here we will extend our discussion about ADempiere's customization capability and will look at other aspects of customization and extending ADempiere's capability.

I will continue using the MOM template, which I mentioned in *Chapter 2*, to map ADempiere's capability and demonstrate how we can extend its capability by making use of the constructs like model, process, callout, and toolbars.

Copy another tab widget into this tab

Say, in our MOM window, we want to provide an additional tab, **Pending Discussion**, which shows the pending items awaiting closure. For example, items which are in the *Open* or *On Hold* status shall appear on a different tab, so that one can quickly look at the pending items without going through the **Discussion Detail** tab. Here, **Pending Discussion** is an exact replica of the **Discussion Detail** tab. The only difference is that the **Pending Discussion** is a read-only tab and shows only the *Open* and *On Hold* items.

Now, to quickly create a replica of an existing tab, ADempiere provides a nice time-saving feature, which we will look at in this recipe. Here we will look at creating the replica rather than concentrating on the pending items.

How to do it...

1. Log in as **System/System** with the **System Administrator** role.

2. Go to the **Window, Tab** and **Field** window and open the **Minutes Of Meeting window** detail

3. Go to the **Tab** and click on the **New Record** toolbar button to create a new tab—**Pending Discussion**.

4. Fill in the **Table** and **Link Column**, and click on the **Copy Tab Fields** button. This pops up a window prompting you to select the **Tab**, as shown in the following screenshot:

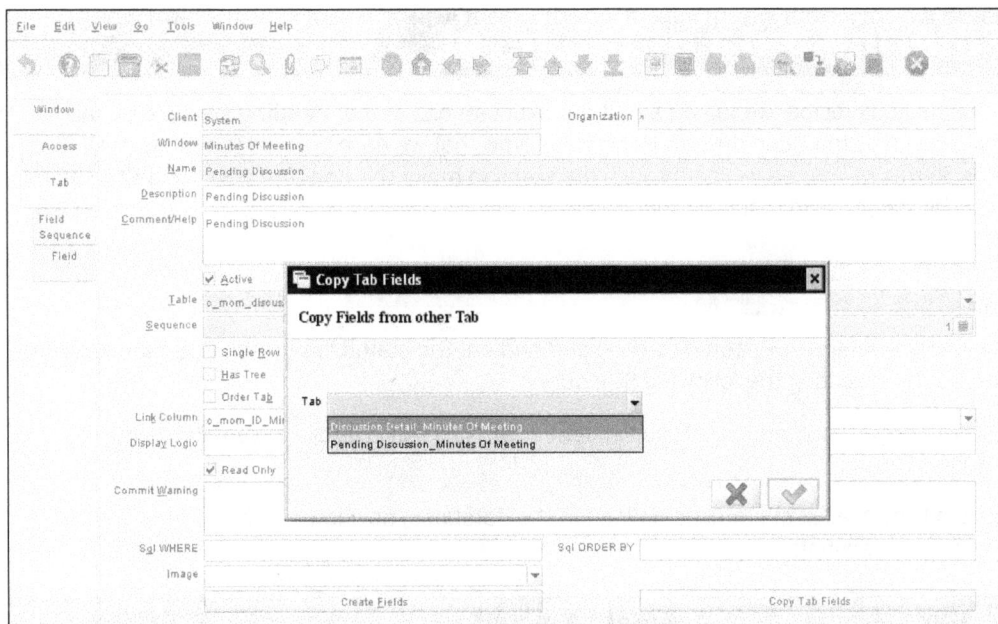

Note that the **Read Only** flag is checked for the **Pending Discussion** tab.

5. Select **Discussion Detail_Minutes Of Meeting** from the drop-down menu and click on the tick button. This will copy the fields from the **Discussion Tab** to the **Pending Discussion** tab. You may verify this on the **Field** tab.

6. Log out and log in as **GardenAdmin/GardenAdmin** with the **GardenWorld Admin** role.

7. Go to the **Minutes Of Meeting** window. You will see a read-only tab—**Pending Discussion**.

8. Go to the **Pending Discussion** tab. You will see the same fields and values appearing as they appear on the **Discussion Detail** tab, as shown in the following screenshot:

Filtering data at tab level

In the previous recipe, we talked about our expectations of the **Pending Discussion** tab—it shall show only the Open and On Hold items. Now that we have created the tab with all the fields, in this recipe, we will go through the steps to make the **Pending Discussion** tab more business friendly and meet the requirements.

Getting ready

Log in to the `adempiere360` database and find out the status IDs for the Open and On Hold statuses by executing the following SQL query:

```
select c_momstatus_id,name,description,isdefault,value from c_
momstatus;
```

You shall see the list of statuses defined in the database, as shown in the following screenshot:

```
 c_momstatus_id |     name      |  description   | isdefault |    value
----------------+---------------+----------------+-----------+--------------
        1000000 | Clarification | Clarification  | N         | Clarification
        1000001 | Open          | Open           | Y         | Open
        1000002 | Closed        | Closed         | N         | Closed
        1000003 | On Hold       | On Hold        | N         | Hold
(4 rows)
```

How to do it...

1. Log in as **System/System** with the **System Administrator** role.

2. Go to the **Window**, **Tab**, and the **Field** window and select the **Pending Discussion** tab on the **Tab**.

3. Enter the following in the **Sql WHERE** field:

   ```
   c_momstatus_ID IN (1000001, 1000003)
   ```

4. Enter `item_nbr` in the **Sql ORDER BY** field, so that the records are sorted by the item number, as shown in the following screenshot:

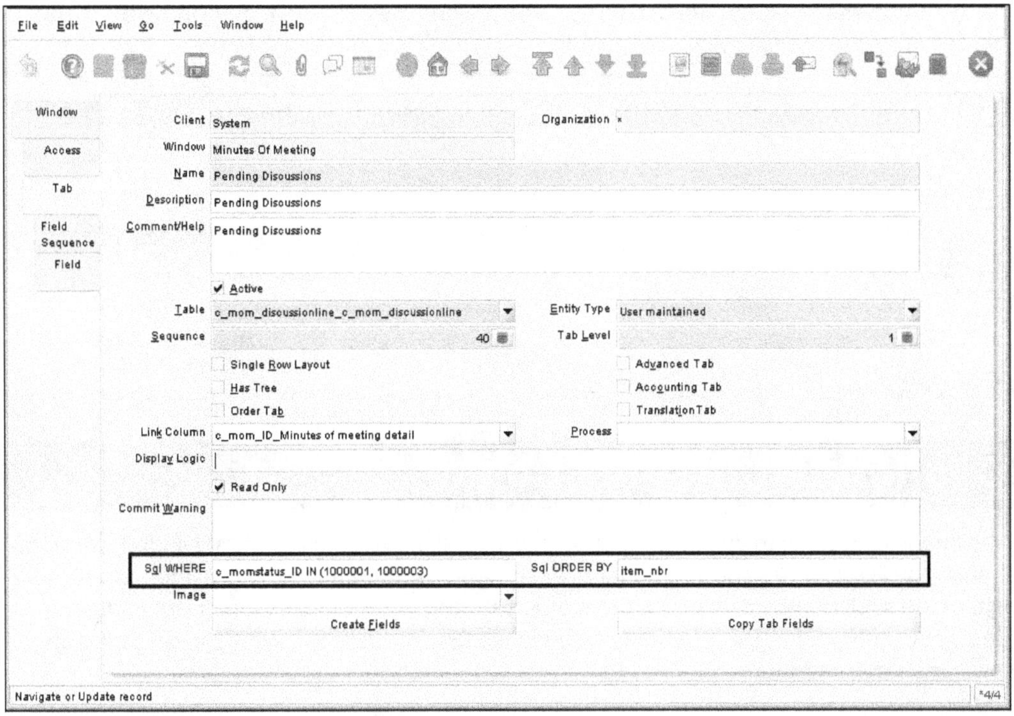

5. Log out and log in as **GardenAdmin/GardenAdmin** with the **GardenWorld Admin** role.

6. Go to the **Minutes Of Meeting** window. On the tab **Discussion Detail**, you will see all the discussion items, as shown in the following screenshot:

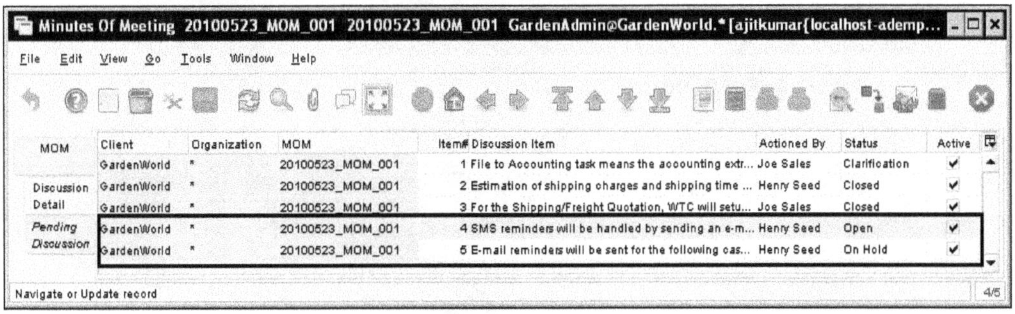

7. Go to the **Pending Discussion** tab. You will see only the Open and On Hold items, as shown in the following screenshot:

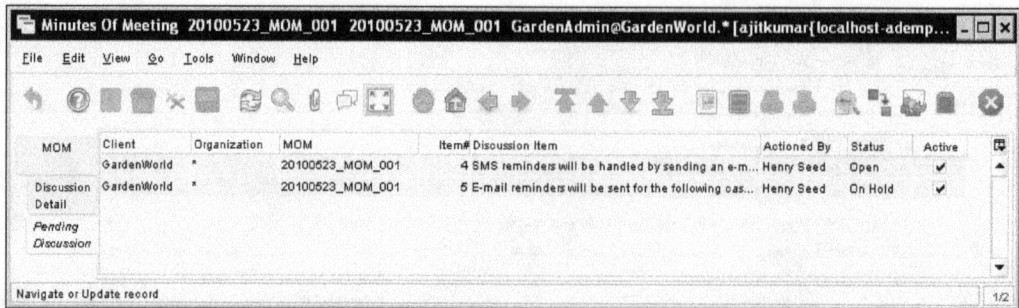

Configuring Display Logic

Display Logic helps us to dynamically show or hide a field. Say, on the MOM window, we want to show the **Pending Discussion** detail to a user who had created the MOM and we want to display the **Actioned By** field only if the status selected is not Clarification. If this is the need, then what shall we do? This is where ADempiere's Display Logic is useful and we would see how it is useful, shortly.

How to do it...

1. Log in as **System/System** with the **System Administrator** role.

2. Go to the **Window**, **Tab**, and the **Field** window and open the **Pending Discussion** tab detail on **Tab**.

3. Enter the following logic in the **Display Logic** field, as shown in the next screenshot, and save it:

```
@CreatedBy@=@#AD_User_ID@
```

4. The values for `CreatedBy` and `#AD_User_ID` comes from the context, which you can see by clicking on the **Tools | Preference** menu item and then selecting the **Context** tab. You may also read about the syntax of the **Display Logic** expression on `http://www.adempiere.com/index.php/ManPageW_WindowCustomization`

5. Select the **Discussion Detail** tab on the **Tab** and go to the **Field** tab.

6. Select the **Actioned By** field, as shown in the next screenshot, and enter the following in the **Display Logic**: `@c_momstatus_ID@!1000000`. (1000000 is the ID of the *Clarification* status.)

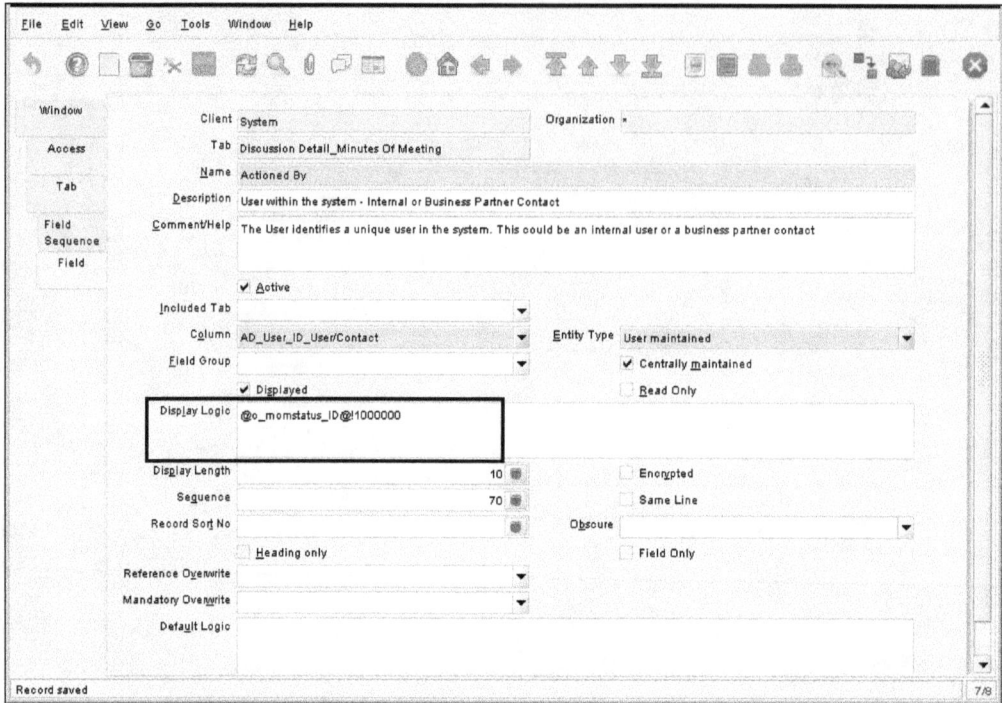

7. Log out and log in as **GardenAdmin/GardenAdmin** with the **GardenWorld Admin** role.

8. Go to the **Minutes Of Meeting** window. The **Pending Discussion** items are visible (otherwise a red colored cross appears on the tab) as there are *Open* or *On Hold* items, as shown in the next screenshot:

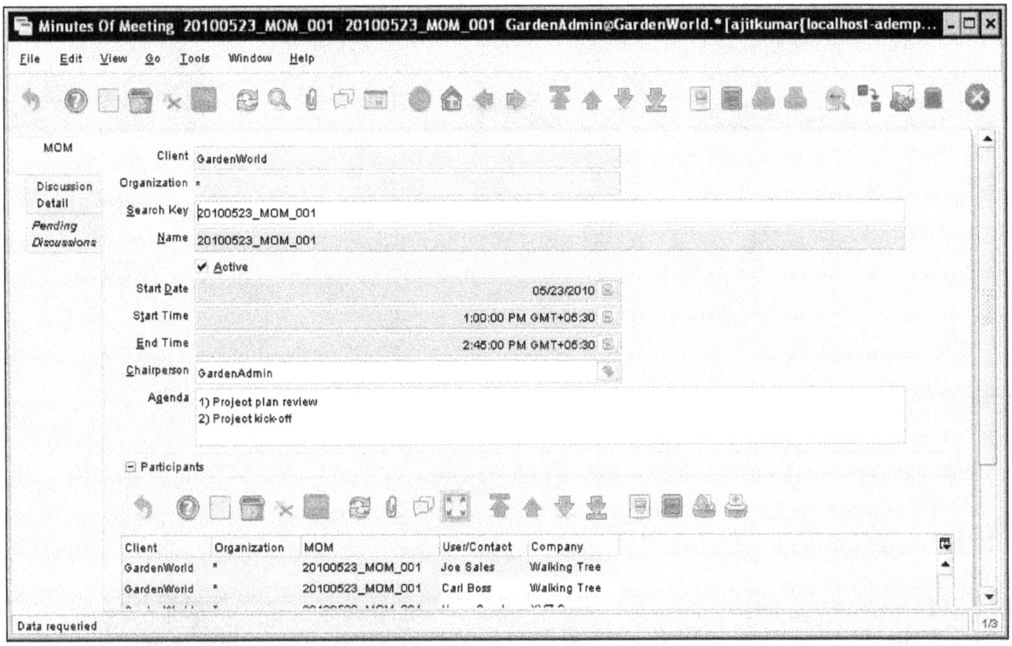

9. Go to the **Discussion Detail** tab and select **Clarification** as the status. The field **Actioned By** does not appear, as shown in the following screenshot:

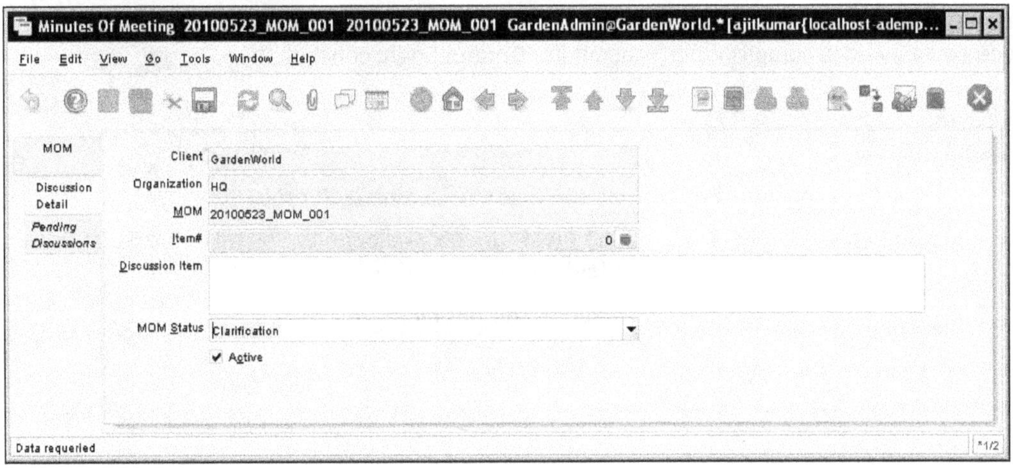

10. Select a status other than **Clarification**. The field **Actioned By** appears, as shown in the following screenshot:

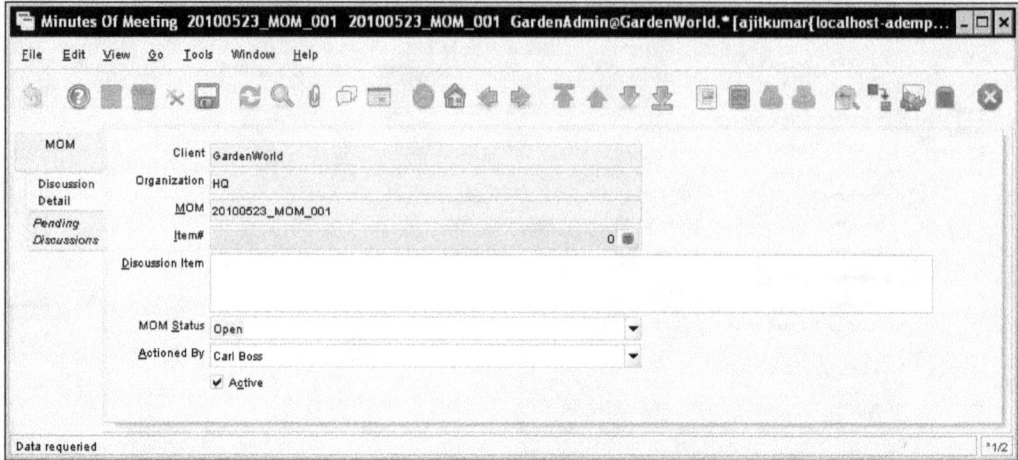

Configuring Default Logic

ADempiere's Default Logic concept is useful when we want to assign some default value to a field. The default value can be a static value or can be a derived value. In the MOM window, we have the **Start Date** field, which we would like to default to the current date so that when a user creates a MOM, it is pre-populated and the user is allowed to change it, if needed. Let us see how we can accomplish this by using the **Default Logic** concept.

How to do it...

1. Log in as **System/System** with the **System Administrator** role.
2. Go to the **Window**, **Tab**, and the **Field** window and open the detail of the **Start Date** field of the **MOM** tab on the **Field** tab.
3. Specify @Date@ as the field value of **Default Logic**.

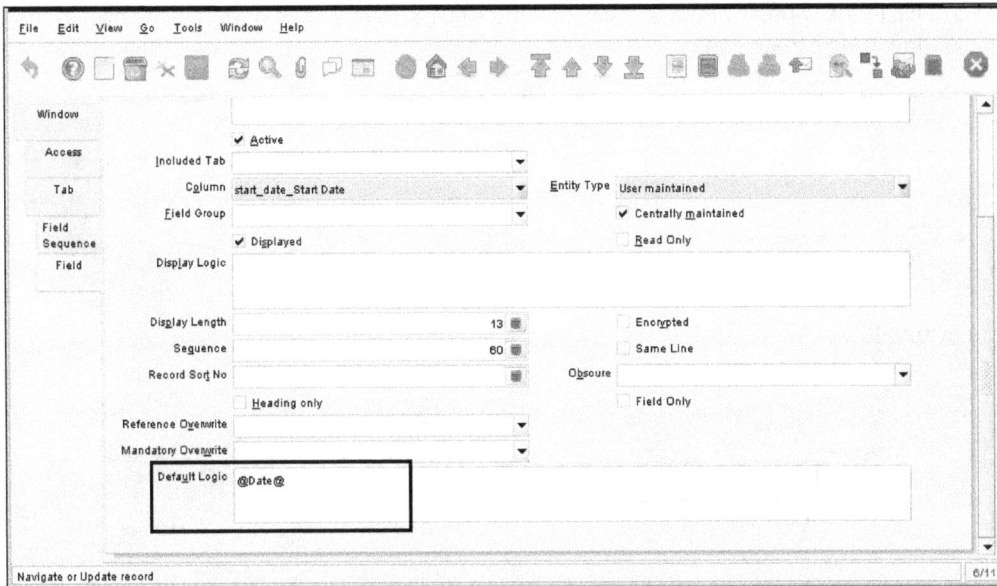

4. Log out and log in as **GardenAdmin/GardenAdmin** with the **GardenWorld Admin** role.

5. Go to the **Minutes Of Meeting** window.

6. Click on the **New Record** toolbar button. This will populate the **Start Date** with the current date, using the Default Logic.

Creating a new window from an existing window

Suppose there is a business need where a business wants two MOM windows to be available for two different purposes—one for a Query Only (search) window and another for a Transaction (create) window. Moreover, there is no change in the number of tabs and fields on these windows. If this is a need, ADempiere provides an efficient way to replicate a complete window (including its tabs and fields) from an existing window. In this recipe, we'll see what that way is.

How to do it...

1. Log in as **System/System** with the **System Administrator** role.

2. Go to the **Window, Tab**, and the **Field** window and click on the **New Record** toolbar button.

3. Fill in the window detail and click on the **Copy Window Tabs** button, as shown in the following screenshot:

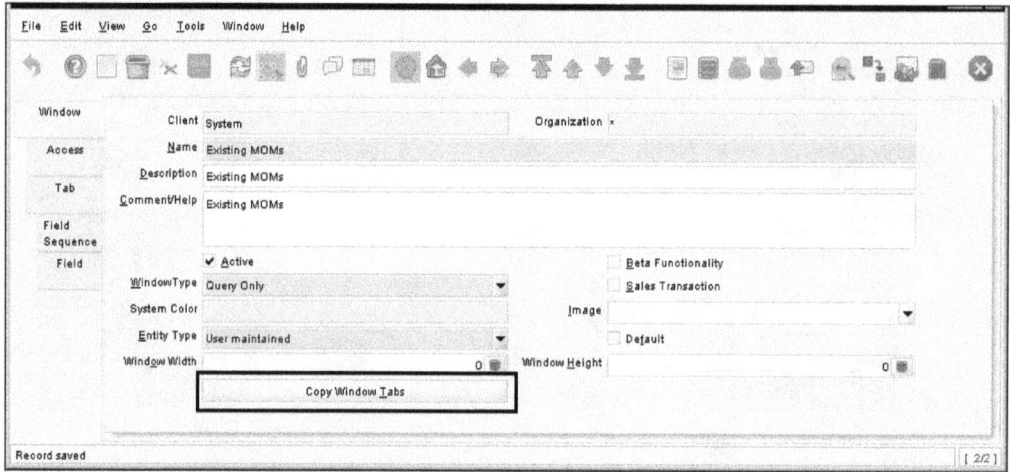

4. On the pop-up window, select the **Minutes Of Meeting** window and click on the tick button. This will copy all the tabs and their respective fields from the **Minutes Of Meeting** window to the **Existing MOM** window, as shown in the following screenshot:

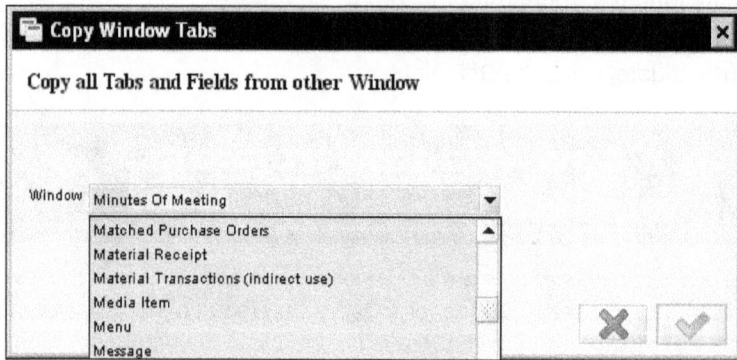

5. Verify the **Tab** to ensure that all the tabs are copied, as shown in the following screenshot:

6. Verify the **Field** tab to ensure that all the fields of different tabs are copied, as shown in the next screenshot:

Configuring a Lookup Record

ADempiere, for the tables where we have too many transactions happening and the volume of data is generally high, can automatically provide a Lookup Record window to filter the data and access the requested data efficiently. This window pops up when you click on the menu item. In this section, we will look at the steps involved in configuring a Lookup Record window.

How to do it...

1. Log in as **System/System** with the **System Administrator** role.

2. Go to the **Table and Column** window.

3. Look up the details of the c_mom table.

4. Check the **High Volume** checkbox, as shown in the following screenshot:

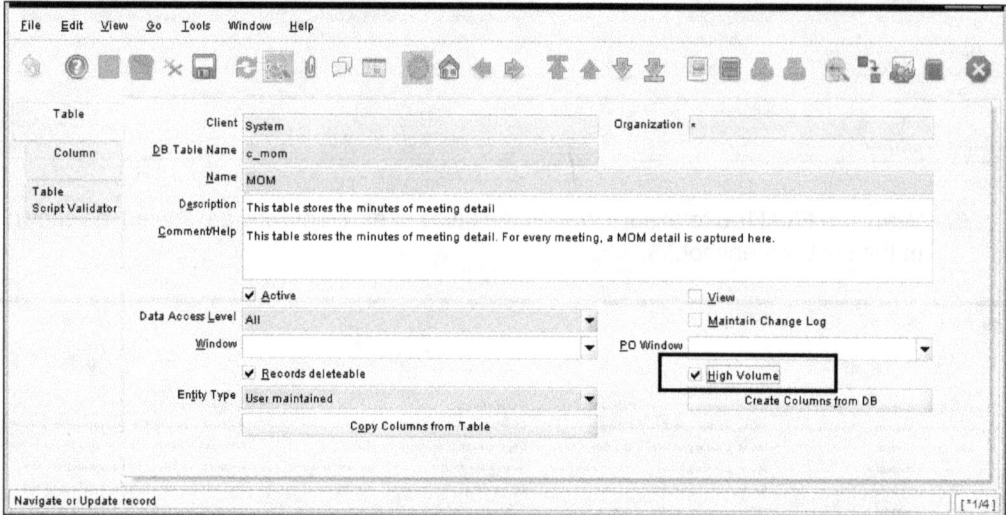

With this done, the **Lookup Record** window is configured. It will, by default, prompt the user for the **Key** and the **Name**. Further steps are required in case we want to add more fields to the **Lookup Record.**

5. Go to the **Column** tab.

6. Check the **Selection Column** checkbox from the columns, which you want to appear on the **Lookup Record** window. Say, I have checked the selection for **Start Date**, as shown in the next screenshot:

Table	...Col...	Syst...	Name	Des...	Co...	Acti...	Ver...	Len...	Ref...	Dyn...	Value Format	Process	Reference Key	Selection Column
	..	AD...	Client	Cli...	A C...	✔	0.00	10 Ta...						☐
Column	..	AD...	Organization	Org...	An ...	✔	0.00	10 Ta...						☐
	..	AD...	Chairperson	Use...	Th...	✔	0.00	10 Se...					AD_User	☐
Table	...	age...	Agenda			✔	0.00	4,000			Text			☐
Script Validator		c_...	Minutes of meeting detail				0.00	10 ID						☐
	..	Cre...	Created	Dat...	Th...	✔	0.00	29 Dat...						☐
	..	Cre...	Created By	Use...	Th...	✔	0.00	10 Ta...					AD_User	☐
	...	end...	End Time			✔	0.00	29 Time						☐
	..	IsA...	Active	Th...	Th...	✔	0.00	1 Yes...						☐
	..	Na...	Name	Alp...	Th...	✔	0.00	255 Stri...						✔
	..	star...	Start Date			✔	0.00	13 Date						✔
	..	star...	Start Time			✔	0.00	29 Time						☐
	..	tab...	tab_participants			✔	0.00	10 Inte...						☐
	..	Up...	Updated	Dat...	Th...	✔	0.00	29 Dat...						☐
	..	Up...	Updated By	Use...	Th...	✔	0.00	10 Ta...					AD_User	☐
	..	Val...	Search Key	Se...	A s...	✔	0.00	30 Stri...						☐

Navigate or Update record   1/16

7. Log out and log in as **GardenAdmin/GardenAdmin** with the **GardenWorld Admin** role.

8. Click on the **Menu | MOM | Minutes Of Meeting**. If there are not many records in the table, you would see the **Minutes Of Meeting** window, directly, without seeing the **Lookup Record** window.

> The **Lookup Record** window appears only if the number of records in the table is more than 10.

So how do we test to see if I have fewer records?'. Don't worry. There is another way to verify how your **Lookup Record** window will look and function. Click on the **Lookup Record** toolbar button on the **Minutes Of Meeting** window. Besides **Key** and **Name** columns, you will see the other columns for which you had checked the **Selection Column** on the **Table and Column** window.

Dynamic validations

Dynamic validation is used to filter the valid choices based on the value entered/selected in some other field on the screen. For example, on a screen, say, you want to load the business partners who belong to a selected business partner group.

In this recipe, we will apply this functionality of ADempiere to see how we can make use of it to achieve our specific goal.

Getting ready

On the **Discussion Detail** tab, we see duplicate values in the **MOM Status** drop-down list, as shown in the next screenshot:

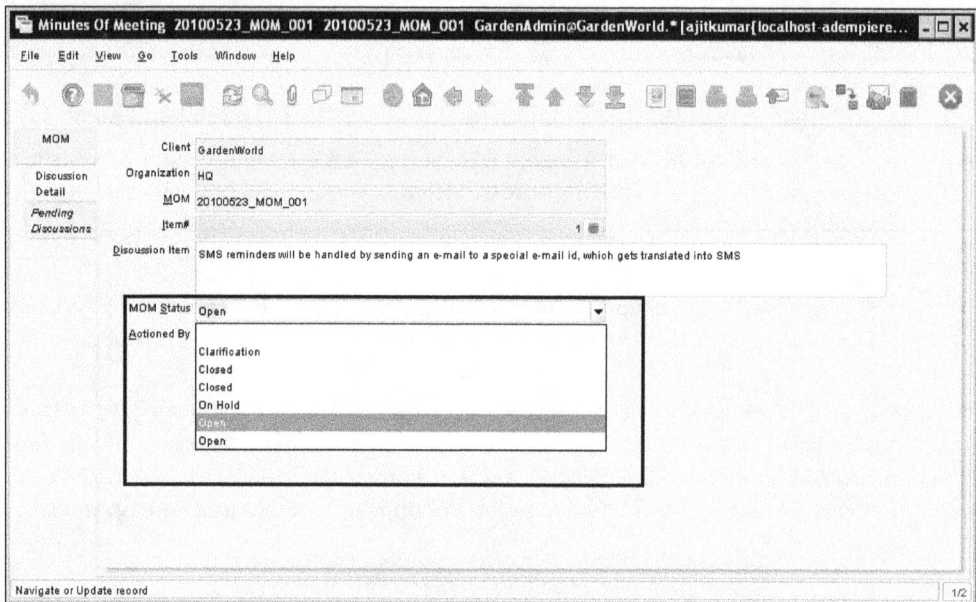

Find out the details about all the statuses, as shown in the next screenshot, by running the following SQL query:

```
SELECT ad_client_id,c_momstatus_id,name,isdefault,value FROM
c_momstatus;
```

ad_client_id	c_momstatus_id	name	isdefault	value
11	1000000	Clarification	N	Clarification
11	1000001	Open	Y	Open
11	1000002	Closed	N	Closed
11	1000003	On Hold	N	Hold
0	1000006	Open	N	Open
0	1000007	Closed	N	Closed

(6 rows)

Note down the `ad_client_id`, as 0 shows that it was created by the `System` user. We need to filter these out.

How to do it...

1. Log in as **System/System** with the **System Administrator** role.

2. Go to the **Menu | Application Dictionary | Validation Rules** window and create a new validation rule of the type **SQL**, as shown in the next screenshot, and specify the following as **Validation code**:

   ```
   ad_client_id<>0
   ```

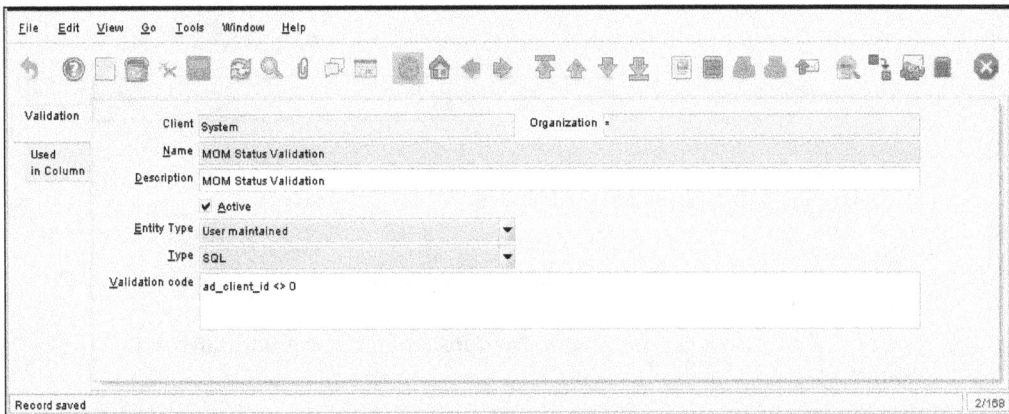

3. Log out and log in back as **System Administrator** so that the newly created validation rule gets loaded.

4. Go to the **Table and Column** window and open the details of the **MOM Status** column on the **Discussion Detail** table.

5. Select `MOM Status Validation` as the **Dynamic Validation**, as shown in the following screenshot:

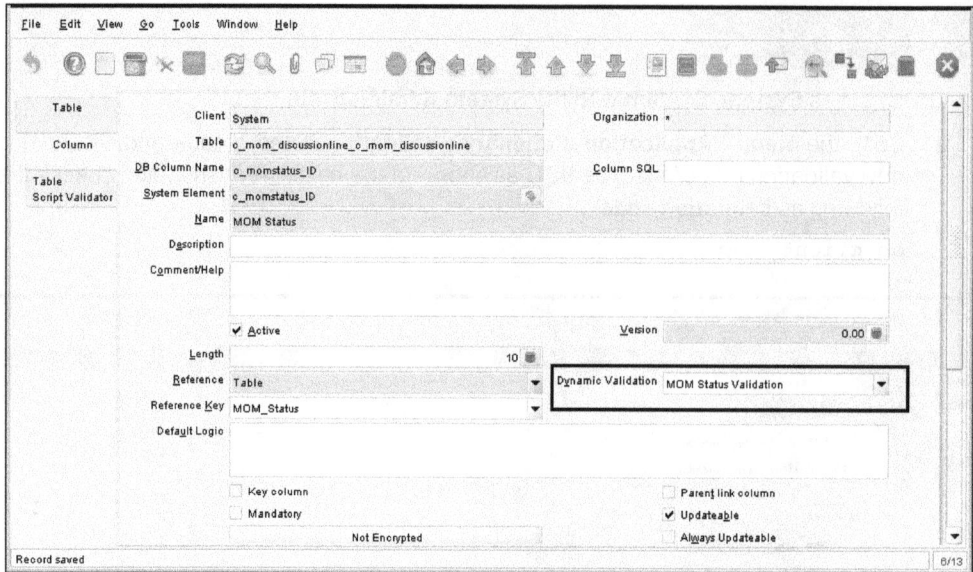

6. Log out and log in as **GardenAdmin/GardenAdmin** with the **GardenWorld Admin** role.

7. Go to the **Discussion Detail** tab of the **Minutes Of Meeting** window. Notice that the status values are filtered, as shown in the following screenshot:

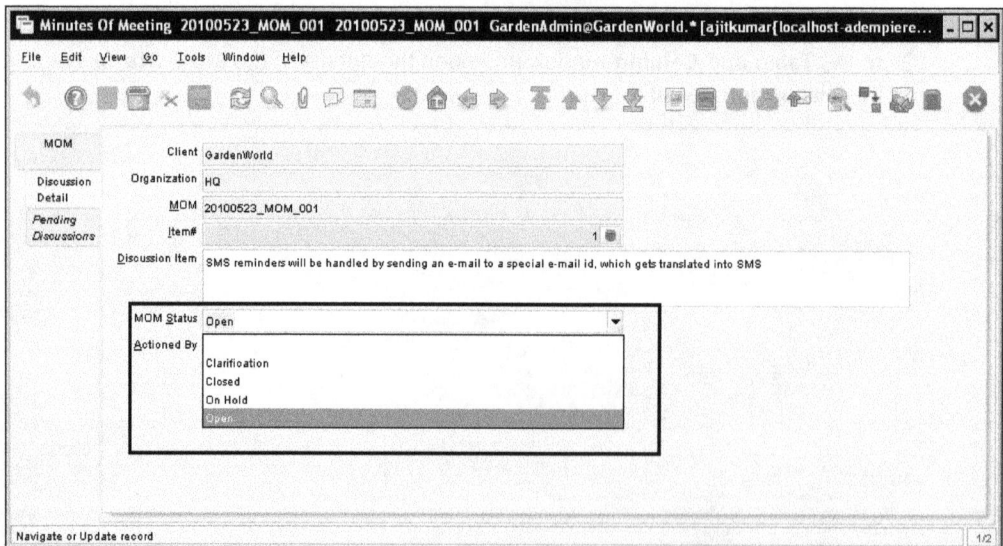

Customizing the default print format of a window

This recipe describes the steps to customize the default print format of a window, which displays the information of an active tab only.

How to do it...

1. Log in as **GardenAdmin/GardenAdmin** with the **GardenWorld Admin** role.

2. Go to the **Minutes Of Meeting** window.

3. Click on the **Report** toolbar button. This will show the report in the default format, as shown in the next screenshot:

4. Click on the **Customize** toolbar button. This will show the **Print Format** window, as shown in the following screenshot:

5. Go to **Display Order** tab and verify the sequence of the items, as shown in the following screenshot:

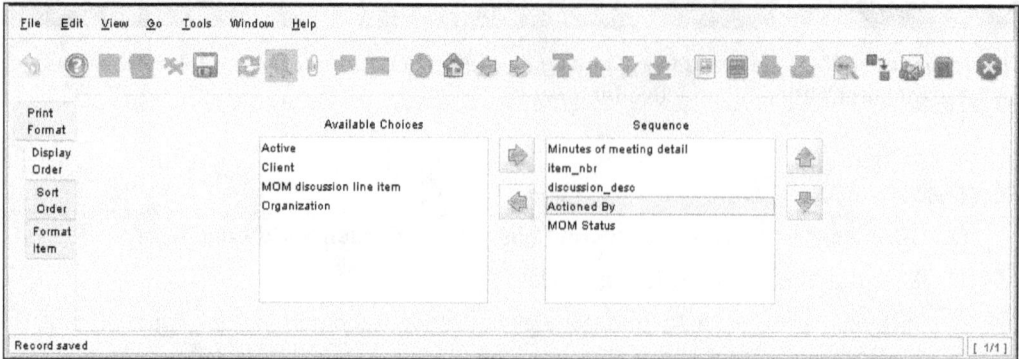

6. Go to the **Sort Order** tab and select the field that you want to use for record sorting, say, `item_nbr`, as shown in the following screenshot:

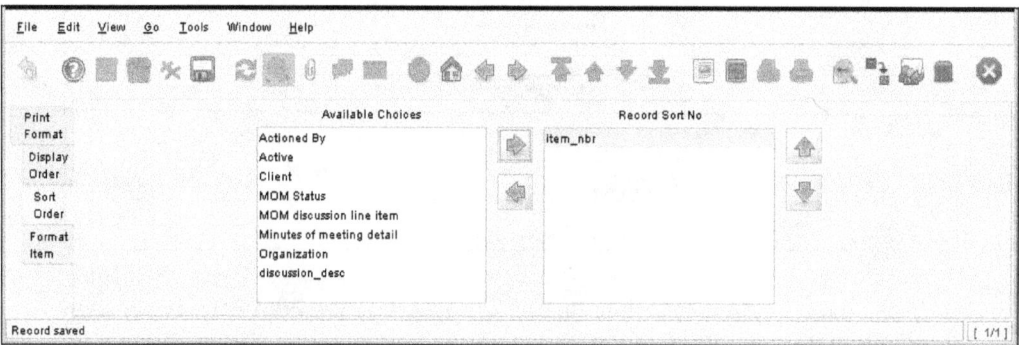

7. Go to the **Format Item** tab. Correct the **Print Text** of the items, if any. Values in the **Print Text** are displayed as a column header on the print format, as shown in the following screenshot:

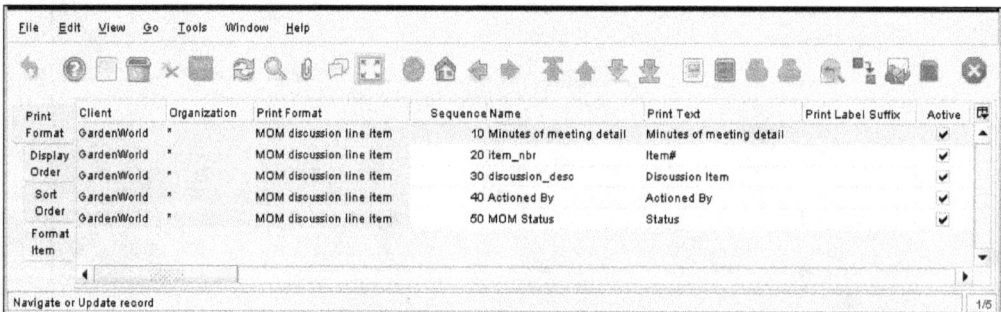

8. Save and close the **Print Format** window.

9. Click again on the **Report** toolbar button on the **Minutes Of Meeting** window, as shown in the following screenshot:

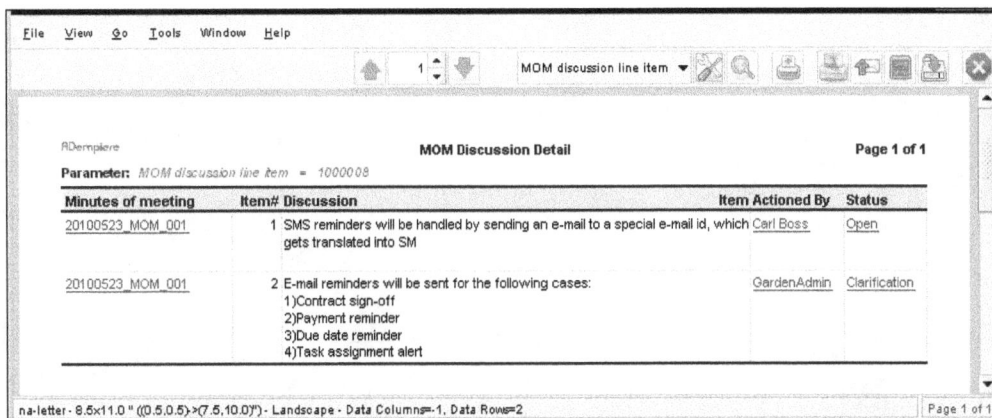

Configuring a new print format for a window

This recipe describes how we can configure a print format for a window where we can display information from different tabs on that window.

How to do it...

1. Create a view from the different tables, used in the window.

```
CREATE VIEW adempiere.c_mom_v AS
SELECT
    a.*,
    b.item_nbr,b.discussion_desc,b.ad_user_id AS actioned_by,b.c_
momstatus_id,
    c.ad_user_id AS participant,c.company,
    d.name AS status
FROM
    adempiere.c_mom a
    JOIN adempiere.c_mom_discussionline b ON a.c_mom_id=b.c_mom_id
    JOIN adempiere.c_mom_participantsline c ON c.c_mom_id=b.c_mom_
id
    JOIN adempiere.c_momstatus d ON b.c_momstatus_id=d.c_momstatus_
id;
```

2. Go to the **Table** and **Column** windows and create table and columns from the c_ mom_v view, as shown in the following screenshot:

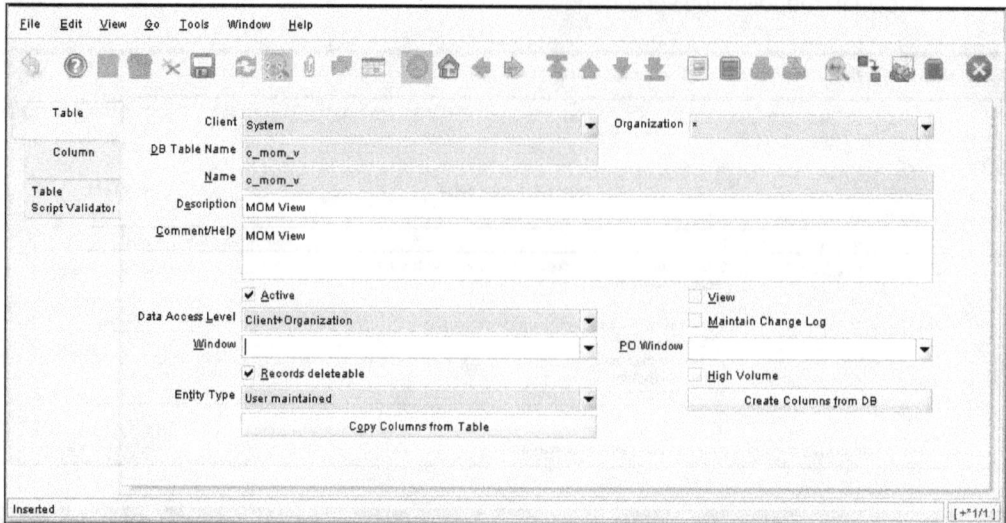

3. Go to the **Menu | System Admin | General Rules | Printing | Print Format** window and create a print format for, say, **MOM Print Format**, as shown in the following screenshot:

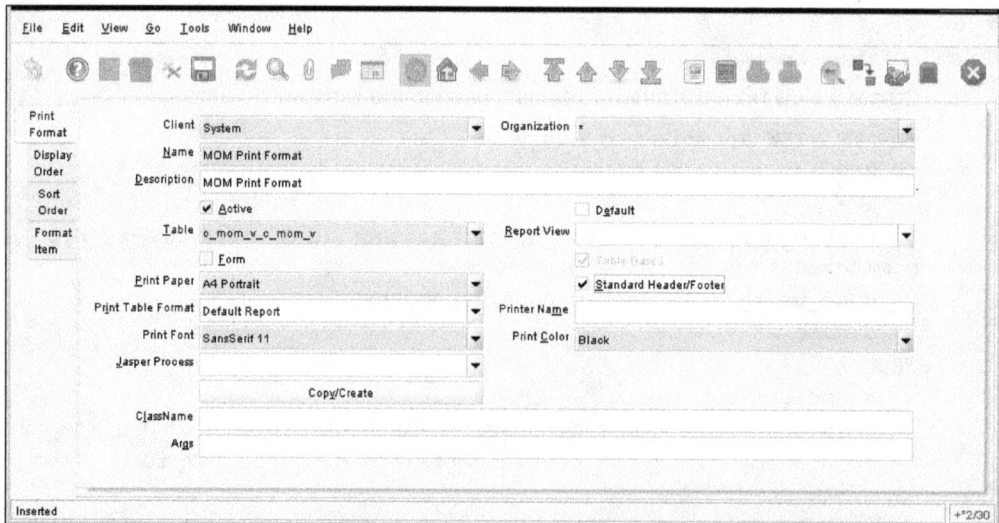

4. Click on the **Copy/Create** button. When prompted, select c_mom_v_c_mom_v as the **Table** and click on the tick button, as shown in the next screenshot:

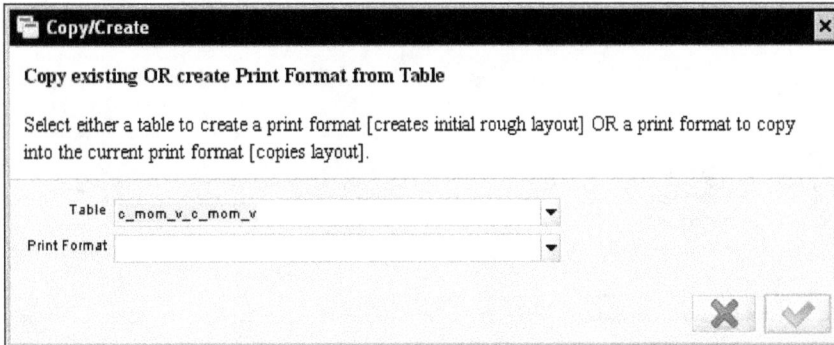

5. Go to the **Format Item** and correct the **Print Text** for the items, if any, as shown in the following screenshot:

6. Go to the **Menu | Application Dictionary | Report & Process** window and create a new report. Select the newly created format as the **Print Format**, as shown in the following screenshot:

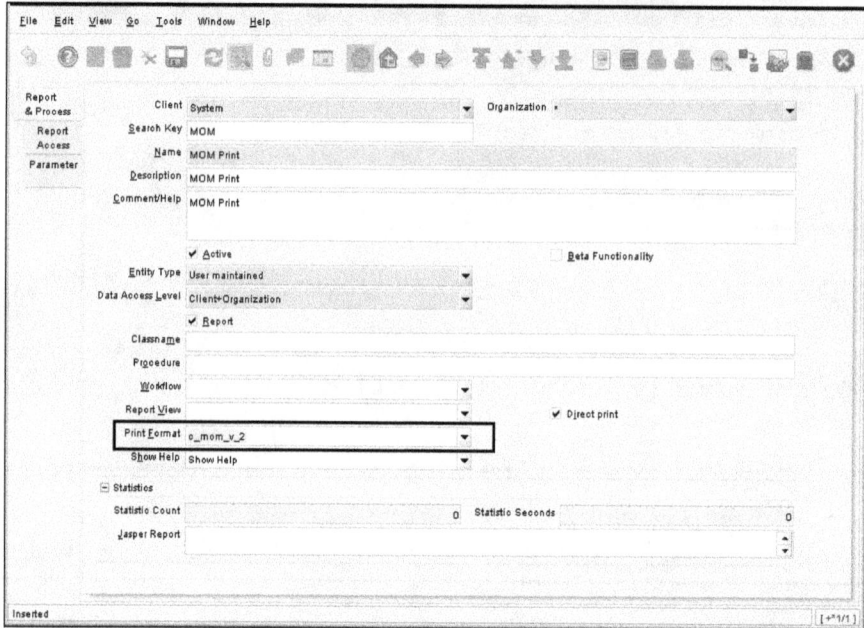

7. Go to the **Window, Tab,** and the **Field** windows and open the **Minutes Of Meeting** detail.

8. Go to the **Tab**, and for the **MOM** tab select the newly created report as **Process**, as shown in the following screenshot:

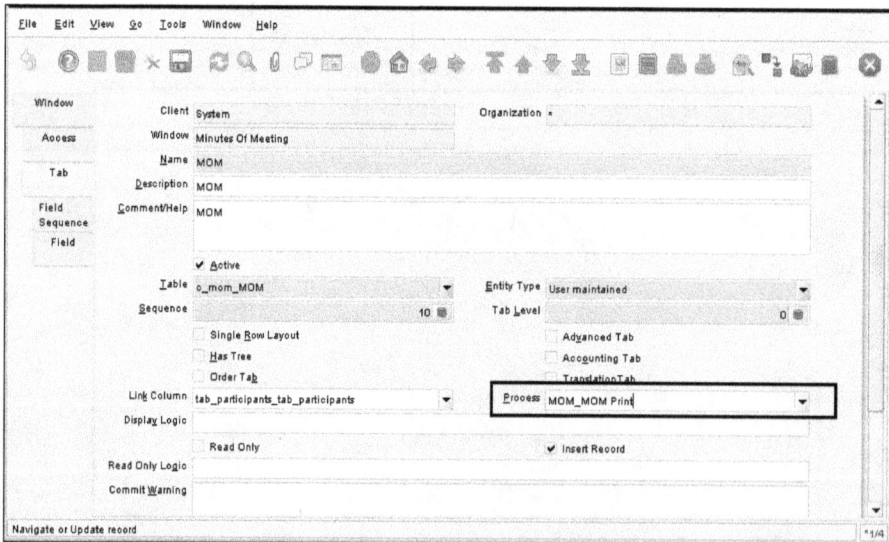

9. Log out and log in as **GardenAdmin/GardenAdmin** with the **GardenWorld Admin** role.

10. Go to the **Minutes Of Meeting** window and click on the **Report** toolbar button. This will show the report using the new print format, which we have configured, as shown in the following screenshot:

Generating a model

A model is the essential part of ADempiere as it allows us to implement business logic. A model represents a table in the database schema. Given a table, ADempiere provides the tools to generate the model which has the built-in persistence capability. A model is required if you want to write a process or validation logic, toolbar button actions, and so on. This recipe describes the steps to generate a model from a database table.

Getting ready

Launch **Eclipse** and open the `adempiere_360` project in it.

How to do it...

1. In **Eclipse**, click on the **Run | Run Configurations** menu. This will show the **Run Configuration** panel, as shown in the following screenshot.

2. Click on the **New Launch Configuration** toolbar button and fill in the following details on the **Main** tab:

   Project: `adempiere_360-`
   Main class: `org.adempiere.util.GenerateModel`

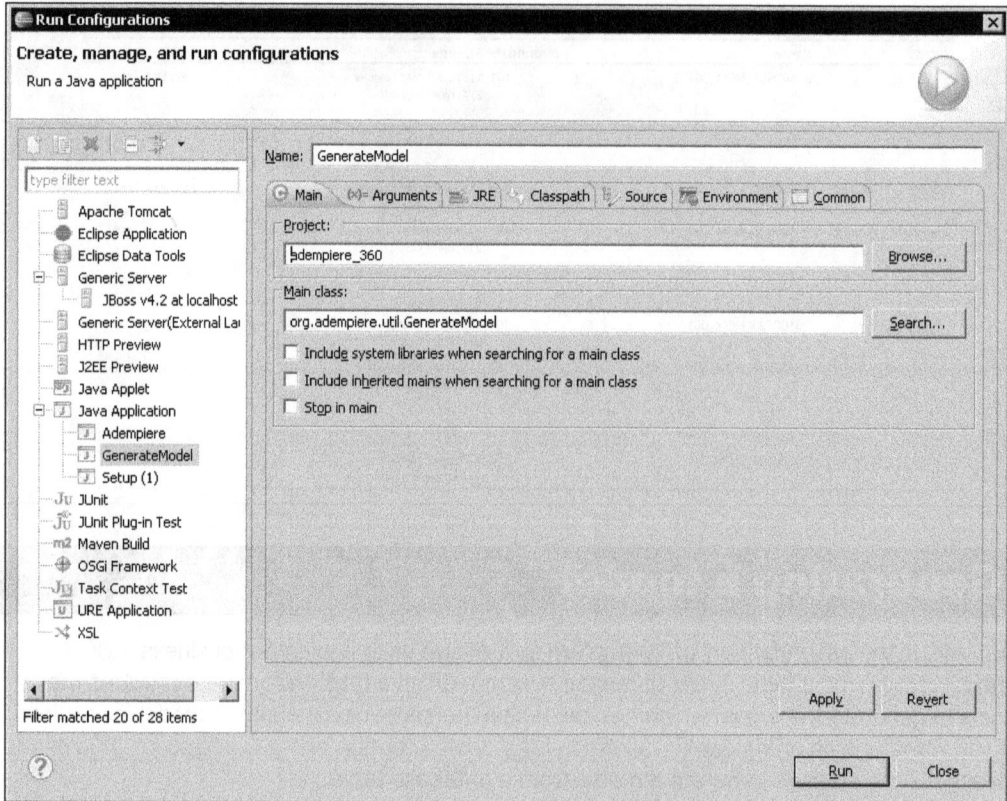

3. Go to the **Arguments** tab and fill in the following details, as shown in the following screenshot:

   Program arguments: `C:\\adempiere_svn\\tags\\adempiere360lts\\base\\src\\org\\compiere\\model org.compiere.model 'U' '%c_mom%'`
   VM arguments: `-DPropertyFile="C:\adempiere_svn\tags\adempiere360lts\Adempiere.properties" -DADEMPIERE_HOME="C:\adempiere_svn\tags\adempiere360lts"`

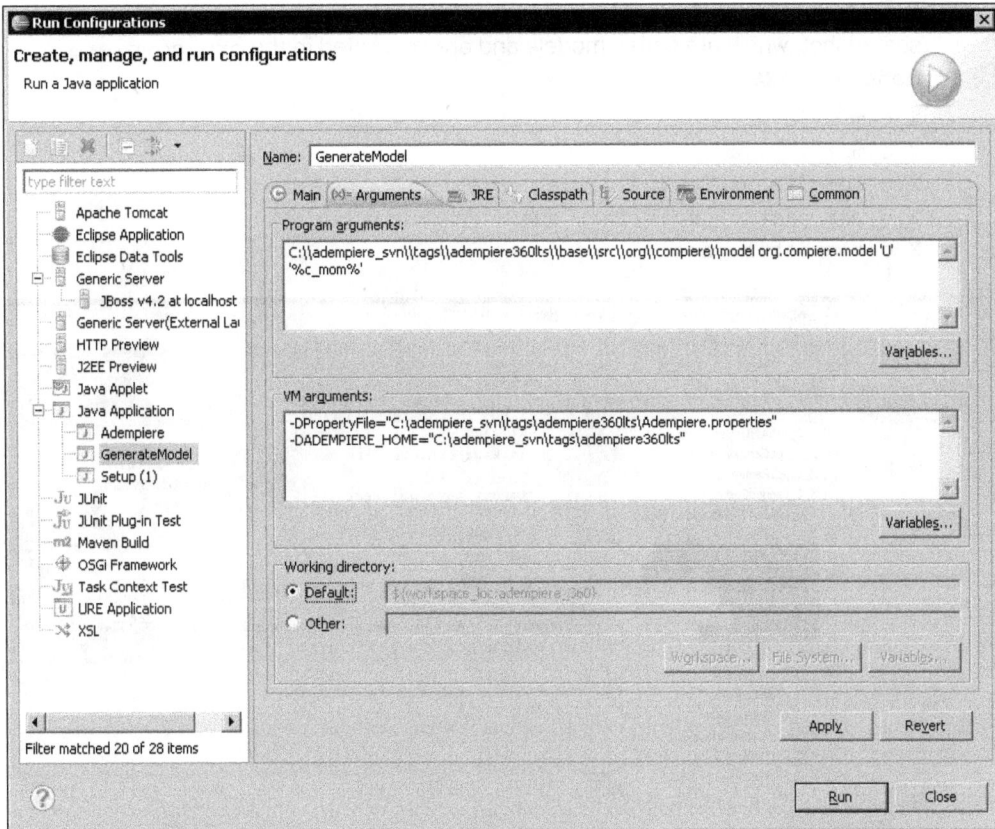

4. **Apply** and **Close** the **Run Configuration** panel.
5. Run the **GenerateModel** configuration, as shown in the following screenshot:

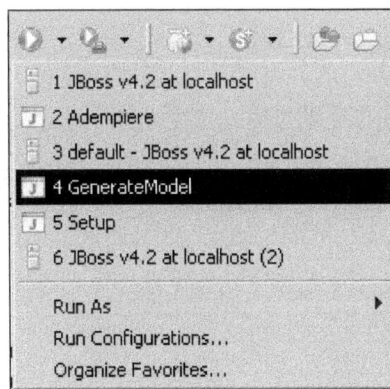

6. Refresh the project. You will see the following classes, as shown in the next screenshot, which are called models and are generated in the `org.compiere.model` package:

```
X_c_mom.java
X_c_mom_v.java
X_c_mom_discussionline.java
X_c_mom_participantsline.java
X_c_momstatus.java
```

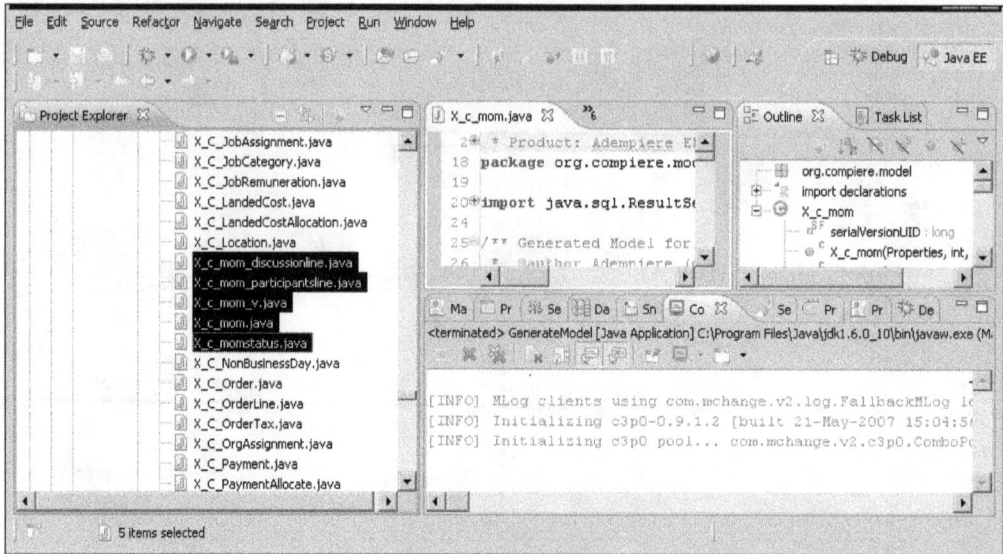

7. Create your own `Mmom` model, `Mmom`, by extending the generated `X_c_mom` model.

```
package org.compiere.model;

import java.util.Properties;

public class Mmom extends X_c_mom {

  public Mmom(Properties ctx, int c_mom_ID, String trxName) {
    super(ctx, c_mom_ID, trxName);
  }
}
```

Creating a new info window for the desktop version

There are various info windows in ADempiere, which provide the interface to a user to find an entity. Various search fields are added to allow data filtering. This window is very useful when a user has to find out the information about a particular entity. This recipe describes the steps involved in creating a new info window.

How to do it...

1. Go to the `client/src/org/compiere/apps/search` folder of your `adempiere_360` project and create an `InfoMOM` class which extends `Info` class and implements `ActionListener` interface. Make sure that the title is set to `InfoMOM`.

2. Add the following line in the `jbInit()` method in the `APanel.java` class:

    ```
    private AppsAction    aMOMInfo;
    ```

3. Add the following code in the `createMenu()` method in the `APanel.java` class:

    ```
    aMOMInfo =addAction("InfoMOM",  mView,   KeyStroke.
    getKeyStroke(KeyEvent.VK_I, Event.ALT_MASK),  false);
    ```

4. This will add an entry to the **View** menu.

5. Clean and build the `adempiere_360` project.

6. Launch the desktop version by running the `org.compiere.Adempiere.java` class.

7. Log in as **GardenAdmin/GardenAdmin** with the **GardenWorld Admin** role.

8. Launch the newly added **MOM Info** window from the **View | MOM Info** menu item.

There's more...

We saw how to create a new info window. After creation, it is equally important to ensure that the right role has the access to the right window. Let us see how we can set up the role-based access to the newly created window.

Role-based access to the info window

To grant access to the info window to a particular role, the following are the additional steps that we will have to execute:

1. Add a new column, `allow_info_mom`, to the `ad_role` table:

   ```
   ALTER TABLE adempiere.ad_role ADD COLUMN allow_info_mom
   character(1) DEFAULT 'Y'::bpchar;
   ```

2. Log in as **System/System** with the **System Administrator** role.

3. Go to the **Table and Column** window and create the additional column from the database for the **Role** table.

4. Go to **Window, Tab,** and the **Field** window and generate the new field for the **Role** tab of the **Role** window.

5. Log out and Log in as **GardenAdmin/GardenAdmin** with the **GardenWorld Admin** role.

6. Open the **Role** window for a role. You will see the **Allow Info MOM** checkbox. With this checkbox, you can now control which role shall have access to the **MOM Info** window.

7. Regenerate the `X_AD_Role` model from the `AD_User` table by following the steps mentioned in the *Generating a model* recipe. This will add an additional public method `isAllow_Info_Mom()` to the `X_AD_Role` model class.

8. In the `createMenu()` method of the `APanel.java` class, replace:

   ```
   aMOMInfo =addAction("InfoMOM",  mView,  KeyStroke.
   getKeyStroke(KeyEvent.VK_I, Event.ALT_MASK),  false);
   by
   if (MRole.getDefault().isAllow_Info_Mom())
   {
   aMOMInfo =addAction("InfoMOM",  mView,  KeyStroke.
   getKeyStroke(KeyEvent.VK_I, Event.ALT_MASK),  false);
   }
   ```

Creating a new info window for the web version

This recipe describes the steps applicable for the web version of ADempiere when it comes to creating a new info window.

How to do it...

1. Go to the `zkwebui/WEB-INF/src/org/adempiere/webui/panel` folder of your `adempiere_360` project and create an `InfoMOMPanel` class, which extends `InfoPanel` class and implements `EventListener` interface. Make sure that the title is set to `InfoMOM`.

2. Add the following code block in the `createViewPanel()` method in the `org.adempiere.webui.dashboard.DPViews.java` class:

```
if (MRole.getDefault().isAllow_Info_Mom())
{
ToolBarButton btnViewItem = new ToolBarButton("InfoMOM");
btnViewItem.setLabel(Msg.getMsg(Env.getCtx(), "InfoMOM"));
btnViewItem.addEventListener(Events.ON_CLICK, this);
vbox.appendChild(btnViewItem);
}
```

3. Add the new method in the `org.adempiere.webui.panel.InfoPanel.java` class:

```
public static void showMOM(int WindowNo)
{
   InfoPanel info = new InfoMOMPanel(WindowNo, "", false, "");
   AEnv.showWindow(info);
}
```

4. Add the following code block in the `onEvent` method in the `org.adempiere.webui.dashboard.DPViews.java` class:

```
else if (actionCommand.equals("InfoMOM") && AEnv.canAccessInfo("MOM"))
{
    InfoPanel.showMOM(WindowNo);
}
```

5. This will add an entry to the **Views** section of the dashboard.

6. Clean and build the `adempiere_360` project.

7. Launch the web version.

8. Log in as **GardenAdmin/GardenAdmin** with the **GardenWorld Admin** role.

9. Launch the newly added **MOM Info** window from **Views**.

Creating a callout

Callout is mainly used to perform some dynamic actions when a value in a particular field is changed. Each field in ADempiere maps to a column in a particular table, so callout is configured at column level. Callout is a Java method that gets invoked when there is a change in the field data in a tab.

Getting ready

Launch Eclipse and open the `adempiere_360` project in it.

How to do it...

1. Create a class, say, `CalloutMom`, in the `org.compiere.model` package.

    ```
    package org.compiere.model;

    import java.sql.PreparedStatement;
    import java.sql.ResultSet;
    import java.sql.SQLException;
    import java.util.Properties;
    import java.util.logging.Level;

    import org.compiere.util.DB;
    import org.compiere.util.Env;

    /**
     *
     * @author Ajit Kumar (ajit.kumar@walkingtree.in)
     *
     */
    public class CalloutMom extends CalloutEngine {

      /**
       *  Return the next item number available for a MOM
       *  @param ctx       Context
       *  @param WindowNo current Window No
       *  @param mTab      Model Tab
       *  @param mField    Model Field
       *  @param value     The new value
       *  @return Error message or ""
       */
      public String getNextItemNbr (Properties ctx, int WindowNo,
    GridTab mTab, GridField mField, Object value)
      {
    ```

```
Integer momId = (Integer)mTab.getValue("c_mom_ID");
String sql = "SELECT  MAX(item_nbr) "
    + "FROM C_Mom_DiscussionLine "
    + "WHERE C_Mom_ID=?";

PreparedStatement pstmt = null;
ResultSet rs = null;
try
{
  pstmt = DB.prepareStatement(sql, null);
  pstmt.setInt(1, momId);
  rs = pstmt.executeQuery();
  Integer maxItemNbr = 0;
  if (rs.next())
  {
    maxItemNbr = rs.getInt(1);
    Env.setContext(ctx, WindowNo, "item_nbr", maxItemNbr+1);
    mTab.setValue("item_nbr", maxItemNbr+1);
  }

  DB.close(rs, pstmt);
  rs = null;
  pstmt = null;
}
catch (SQLException e)
{
  log.log(Level.SEVERE, sql, e);
  return e.getLocalizedMessage();
}
finally
{
  DB.close(rs, pstmt);
  rs = null; pstmt = null;
}
return "";
  }

}
```

2. Compile the project.
3. Launch the desktop version of the project and log in as **System/System** with the **System Administrator** role.

4. Go to the **Table and Column** window and open the details of the c_mom_ID column in the c_mom_discussionline table and mention org.compiere.model. CalloutMom. getNextItemNbr as the **Callout**, as shown in the following screenshot:

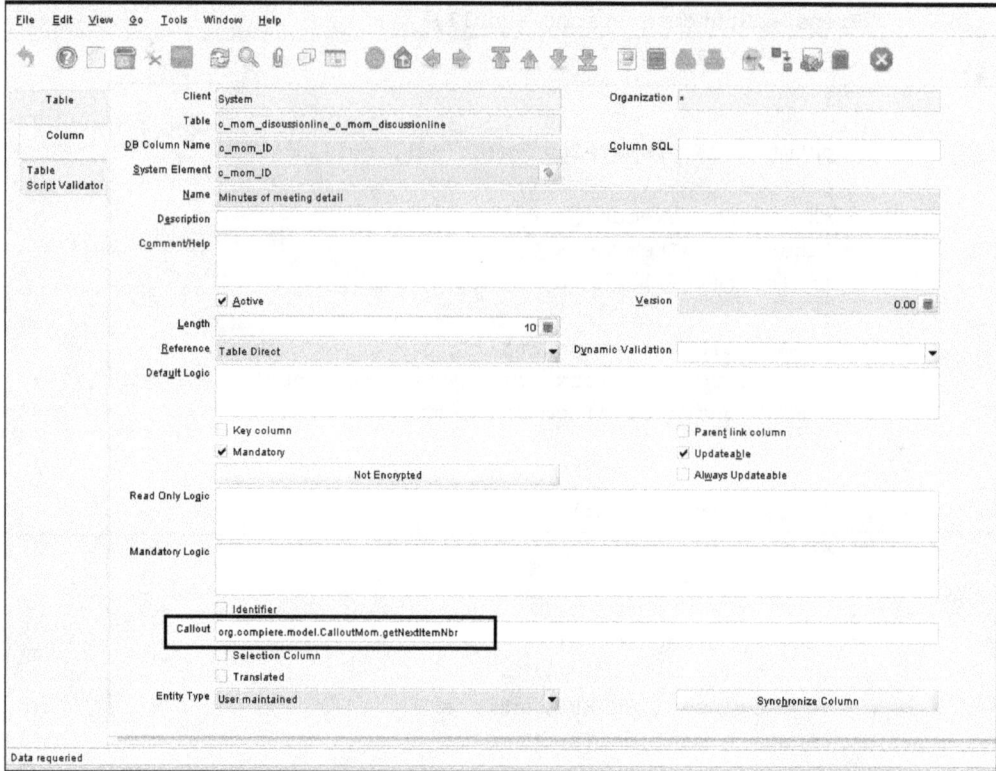

5. Log out and log in as **GardenAdmin/GardenAdmin** with the **GardenWorld Admin** role.

6. Go to the **Discussion Detail** tab of the **Minutes Of Meeting** window and click on the **New Record** toolbar button. The item number is automatically generated and the sequence is maintained, as shown in the next screenshot:

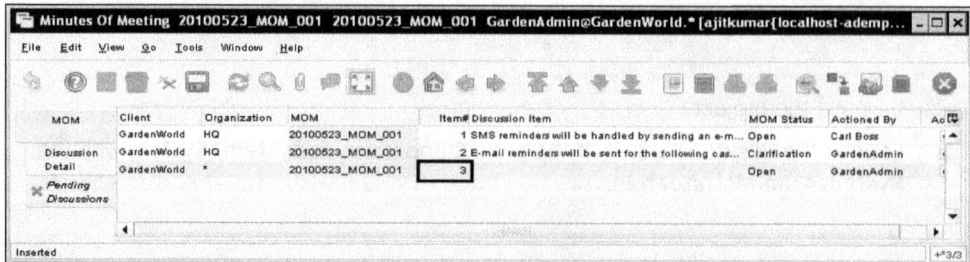

Modifying hooks for a model

Every model extends the PO class, which provides various hooks (methods) that one can override. They are `afterSave`, `beforeSave`, `afterDelete`, and `beforeDelete`. The syntax for these methods are:

```
protected boolean afterSave (boolean newRecord, boolean success)
protected boolean afterDelete (boolean success)
protected boolean beforeSave (boolean newRecord)
protected boolean beforeDelete ()
```

The main use of these methods is to perform additional tasks while a particular row of a table is being saved or deleted a particular row of a table. Let us say, we want to audit the activity, like create/update and delete, of the `C_Project` table. To accomplish this, we shall override the `beforeSave` and `beforeDelete` methods so that the audit information can be captured before the actual project information is updated or deleted.

In this recipe, we'll see how to override these hooks.

How to do it...

1. Implement the `afterSave` method in the Mmom model class to send the e-mail to the participants.

```
package org.compiere.model;

import java.sql.PreparedStatement;
import java.sql.ResultSet;
import java.sql.SQLException;
import java.util.Properties;
import java.util.logging.Level;

import org.compiere.util.DB;
import org.compiere.util.EMail;

//extend the generated x_c_mom model
public class Mmom extends X_c_mom {

    public Mmom(Properties ctx, int c_mom_ID, String trxName) {
        super(ctx, c_mom_ID, trxName);
    }

    protected boolean afterSave(boolean newRecord, boolean success)
    {
```

```
        String momId = String.valueOf(this.getc_mom_ID());
        int m_c_mom_ID = Integer.valueOf(momId);
        log.info("c_mom_ID=" + m_c_mom_ID);

    //  Client Info
    MClient m_client = MClient.get (getCtx());
    if (m_client.getAD_Client_ID() == 0)
      return false;
    if (m_client.getSMTPHost() == null || m_client.getSMTPHost().
length() == 0)
        return false;

    //send mail to the participants
    send2Participants(m_client, m_c_mom_ID);

    return success;
  }
  private void send2Participants(MClient m_client, int m_c_mom_ID)
  {
    log.info("C_Mom_ID=" + m_c_mom_ID);

    String sql = "SELECT a.ad_user_id "
        + "FROM adempiere.c_mom_participantsline a "
        + "WHERE a.c_mom_id=?";
    PreparedStatement pstmt = null;
    try
    {
      //get the participants
      pstmt = DB.prepareStatement(sql, get_TrxName());
      pstmt.setInt(1, m_c_mom_ID);
      ResultSet rs = pstmt.executeQuery();
      while (rs.next())  //for each participant
      {
        //send mail to the particiapant
        Boolean ok = sendIndividualMail (m_client, m_c_mom_ID,
rs.getInt(1));
        if (ok == null)
          ;
      }
      rs.close();
      pstmt.close();
      pstmt = null;
    }
    catch (SQLException ex)
```

```
    {
      log.log(Level.SEVERE, sql, ex);
    }
    try
    {
      if (pstmt != null)
        pstmt.close();
    }
    catch (SQLException ex1)
    {
    }
    pstmt = null;
  }


  //Method to send mail to a user
  private Boolean sendIndividualMail (MClient m_client, int m_c_
mom_ID, int AD_User_ID)
  {
    MUser to = new MUser (getCtx(), AD_User_ID, null);
    Mmom m_mom = new Mmom(getCtx(), m_c_mom_ID, get_TrxName());
    MUser m_from = new MUser (getCtx(), m_mom.getAD_User_ID(),
get_TrxName());

    String message = "Hi " + to.getFirstName() +
            "\n" + m_mom.getName() +
            " has been updated in the system! Following is the
agenda mentioned:\n" + m_mom.getagenda() +
            "\nThanks\nAfter Save!!";
    String subject = "AfterSave : " + m_mom.getName();
    //call createMail method available in MClient object
    EMail email = m_client.createEMail(m_from, to, subject,
message);
    email.setSubject (subject);
    email.setMessageText (message);

    if (!email.isValid() && !email.isValid(true))
    {
      log.warning("NOT VALID - " + email);
      to.setIsActive(false);
      to.addDescription("Invalid EMail");
      to.save();
      return Boolean.FALSE;
    }
    //send mail
    boolean OK = EMail.SENT_OK.equals(email.send());
```

```
    if (OK)
      log.fine(to.getEMail());
    else
      log.warning("FAILURE - " + to.getEMail());
    return new Boolean(OK);
  }
}
```

2. Launch the desktop version of ADempiere from your project and log in as **GardenAdmin/GardenAdmin** with the **GardenWorld Admin** role. The same works for the web version as well.

3. Go to the **Minutes Of Meeting** window, as shown in the following screenshot:

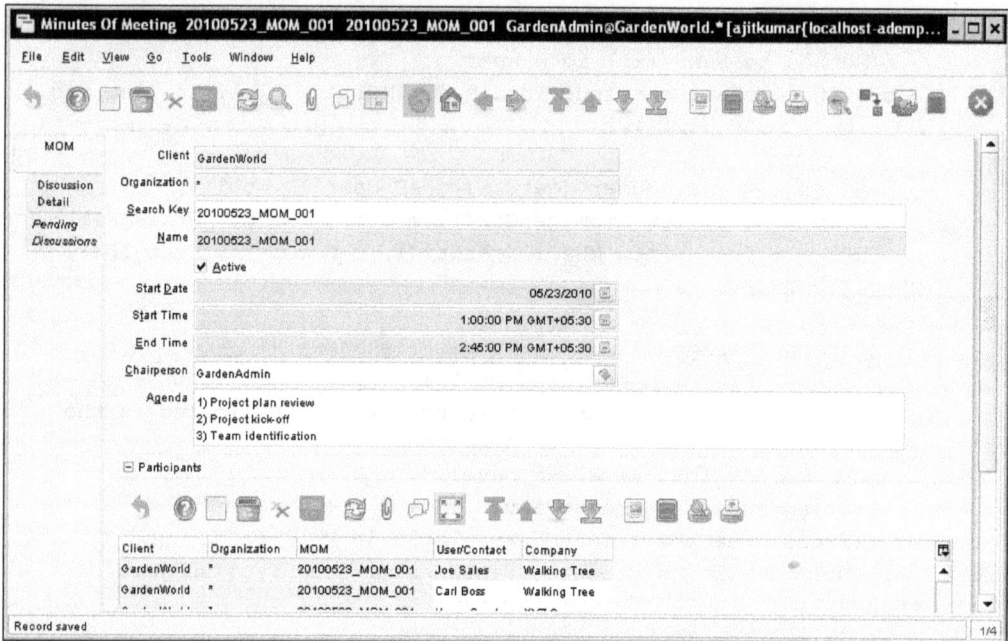

4. Make some changes and save it. You will receive a mail if your e-mail ID belongs to one of the participants of the MOM with the MOM and agenda detail in the body, as shown in the following screenshot:

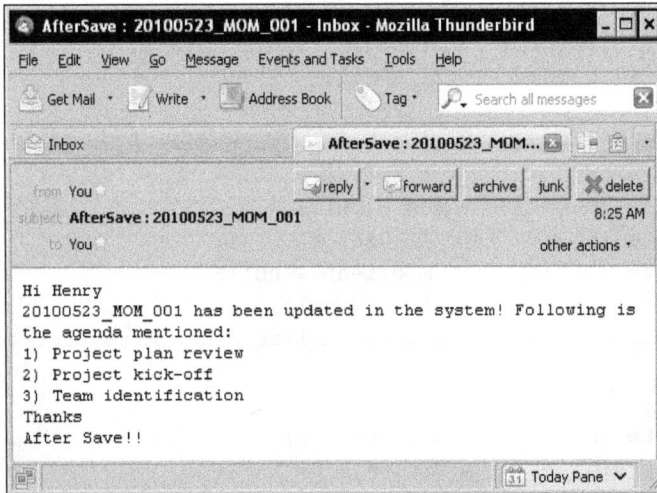

Creating a process

A process is another way to execute business logic. Usage of a process is not limited to a window, tab, or field. It is not related to any table or column. You can write a process and link it with a button on a window/tab for further processing (for example, the Complete button on the Sales Order window). Moreover, we can write any business logic inside it and invoke it directly. All the items that appear with an icon 🌸 in the Menu tree represent a process. This recipe will walk us through the steps to create a new process and invoke it. Here we are going to create a process, which prompts the user to select a MOM from the existing MOMs, and sends MOM-related mail to the participants of the selected MOM.

How to do it...

1. Add a new class, say, `SendMOMMail` to the `org.compiere.process` package. This class must extend `SvrProcess` in order to call itself an ADempiere **Process**.

    ```
    package org.compiere.process;

    import java.sql.PreparedStatement;
    import java.sql.ResultSet;
    import java.sql.SQLException;
    import java.util.ArrayList;
    import java.util.logging.Level;

    import org.compiere.model.MClient;
    import org.compiere.model.MUser;
    ```

```java
import org.compiere.model.Mmom;
import org.compiere.util.DB;
import org.compiere.util.EMail;

public class SendMOMMail extends SvrProcess {
  private int          m_c_mom_ID = -1;
  private Mmom        m_mom = null;
  private int          m_AD_User_ID = -1;
  private MClient       m_client = null;
  private MUser        m_from = null;
  private ArrayList<Integer>   m_list = new ArrayList<Integer>();


  private int          m_counter = 0;
  private int          m_errors = 0;

  @Override
  protected void prepare() {
    ProcessInfoParameter[] para = getParameter();
    for (int i = 0; i < para.length; i++)
    {
      String name = para[i].getParameterName();
      if (para[i].getParameter() == null)
        ;
      else if (name.equals("c_mom_ID"))
        m_c_mom_ID = para[i].getParameterAsInt();
      else
        log.log(Level.SEVERE, "Unknown Parameter: " + name);
    }
  }

  @Override
  protected String doIt() throws Exception {
    log.info("c_mom_ID=" + m_c_mom_ID);

    m_mom = new Mmom(getCtx(), m_c_mom_ID, get_TrxName());
    m_AD_User_ID = m_mom.getAD_User_ID();

    // Client Info
    m_client = MClient.get (getCtx());
    if (m_client.getAD_Client_ID() == 0)
      throw new Exception ("Not found @AD_Client_ID@");
    if (m_client.getSMTPHost() == null || m_client.getSMTPHost().
length() == 0)
```

```
        throw new Exception ("No SMTP Host found");

    if (m_AD_User_ID > 0)
    {
      m_from = new MUser (getCtx(), m_AD_User_ID, get_TrxName());
      if (m_from.getAD_User_ID() == 0)
        throw new Exception ("No found @AD_User_ID@=" + m_AD_User_
ID);
    }
    log.fine("From " + m_from);
    long start = System.currentTimeMillis();

    send2Participants();

    return "@Created@=" + m_counter + ", @Errors@=" + m_errors +
" - "
      + (System.currentTimeMillis()-start) + "ms";
  }

  private void send2Participants()
  {
    log.info("C_Mom_ID=" + m_c_mom_ID);

    String sql = "SELECT a.ad_user_id "
        + "FROM adempiere.c_mom_participantsline a "
        + "WHERE a.c_mom_id=?";
    PreparedStatement pstmt = null;
    try
    {
      pstmt = DB.prepareStatement(sql, get_TrxName());
      pstmt.setInt(1, m_c_mom_ID);
      ResultSet rs = pstmt.executeQuery();
      while (rs.next())
      {
        Boolean ok = sendIndividualMail (rs.getInt(1));
        if (ok == null)
          ;
        else if (ok.booleanValue())
          m_counter++;
        else
          m_errors++;
      }
      rs.close();
      pstmt.close();
```

```
        pstmt = null;
      }
    catch (SQLException ex)
    {
      log.log(Level.SEVERE, sql, ex);
    }
    try
    {
      if (pstmt != null)
        pstmt.close();
    }
    catch (SQLException ex1)
    {
    }
    pstmt = null;
  }


  /**
   *   Send Individual Mail
   *   @param AD_User_ID user
   *   @return true if mail has been sent
   */
  private Boolean sendIndividualMail (int AD_User_ID)
  {
    Integer ii = new Integer (AD_User_ID);
    if (m_list.contains(ii))
      return null;
    m_list.add(ii);

    MUser to = new MUser (getCtx(), AD_User_ID, null);

    String message = "Hi " + to.getFirstName() + "\n " + m_mom.
getName() + " has been updated in the system!\nThanks";
    String subject = "MOM : " + m_mom.getName();
    EMail email = m_client.createEMail(m_from, to, subject,
message);
    email.setSubject (subject);
    email.setMessageText (message);

    if (!email.isValid() && !email.isValid(true))
    {
      log.warning("NOT VALID - " + email);
      to.setIsActive(false);
      to.addDescription("Invalid EMail");
```

```
        to.save();
        return Boolean.FALSE;
    }
    boolean OK = EMail.SENT_OK.equals(email.send());
    if (OK)
        log.fine(to.getEMail());
    else
        log.warning("FAILURE - " + to.getEMail());
    addLog(0, null, null, (OK ? "@OK@" : "@ERROR@") + " - " +
to.getEMail());
        return new Boolean(OK);
    }


}
```

2. Compile the project and launch the desktop version of ADempiere from the project.

3. Log in as **System/System** with the **System Administrator** role.

4. Go to the **Menu | Application Dictionary | Reference** window and create a new reference, MOM, as shown in the following screenshot:

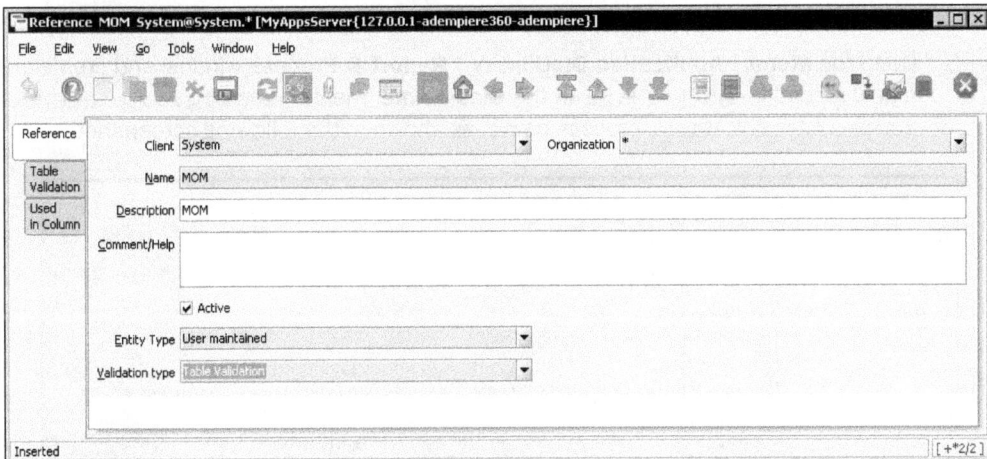

5. Go to the **Table Validation** tab and create a new record for the c_mom table and the c_mom_ID column, as shown in the following screenshot:

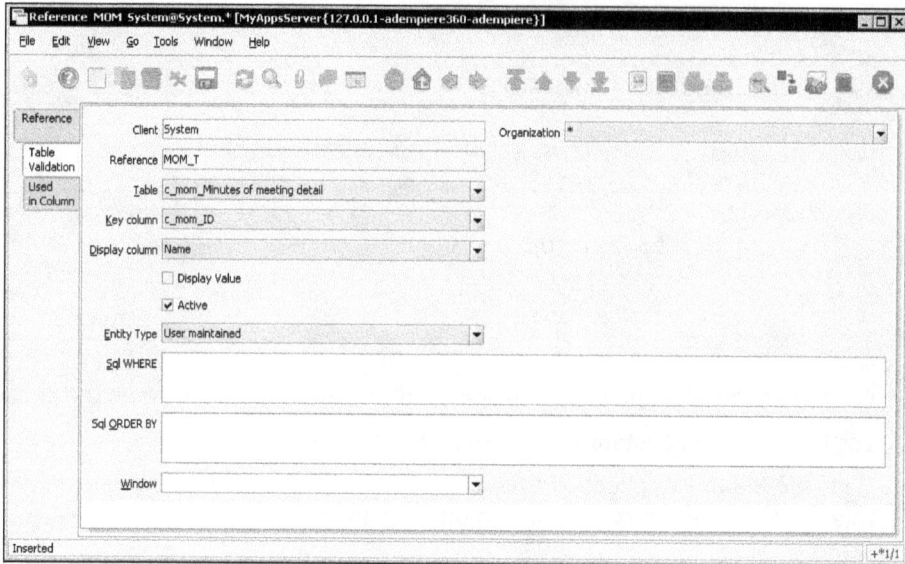

6. Go to the **Menu | Application Dictionary | Report & Process** window and create a new record—Send MOM Mail. In the **Classname**, mention the org.compiere. process SendMOMMail process name, as shown in the following screenshot:

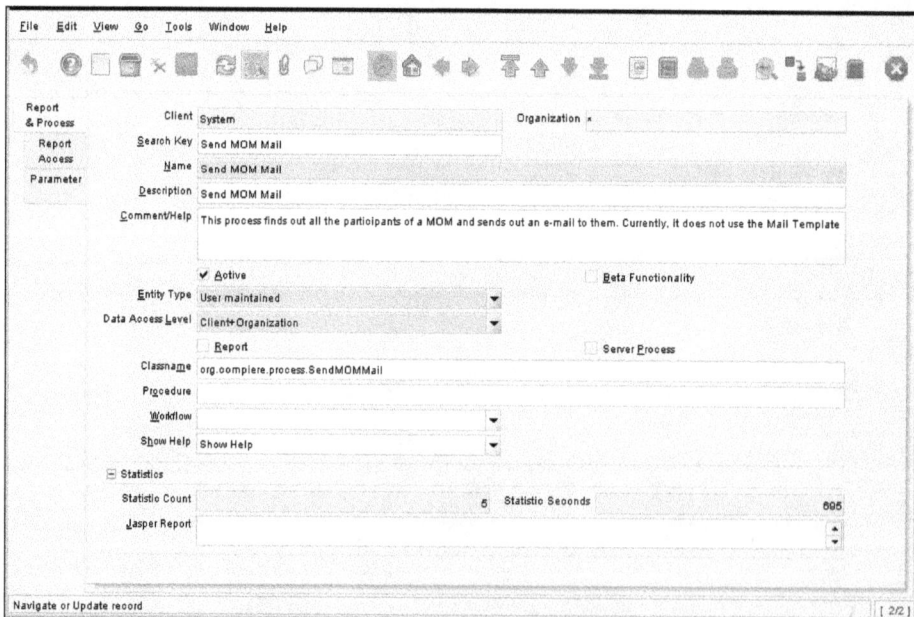

7. Go to the **Parameter** tab to create a process parameter where we can select the MOM for which e-mail needs to be sent to their participants.

8. Create a new parameter, as shown in the following screenshot, with the following important details:

   DB Column Name: c_mom_ID

   System Element: c_mom_ID

   Reference: Table

   Reference Key: MOM (this is the reference that we created in the previous steps)

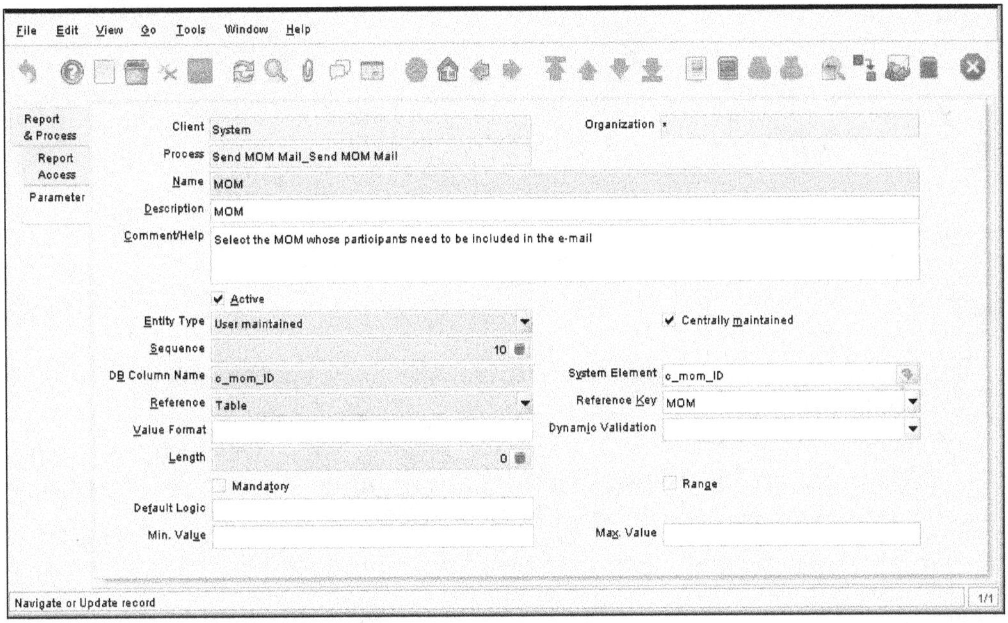

9. Save the record.

10. Go to the **Menu | System Admin | General Rules | System Rules | Menu** window and create a new menu item—Send MOM Mail. Add this menu item to the **MOM** node, as shown in the following screenshot:

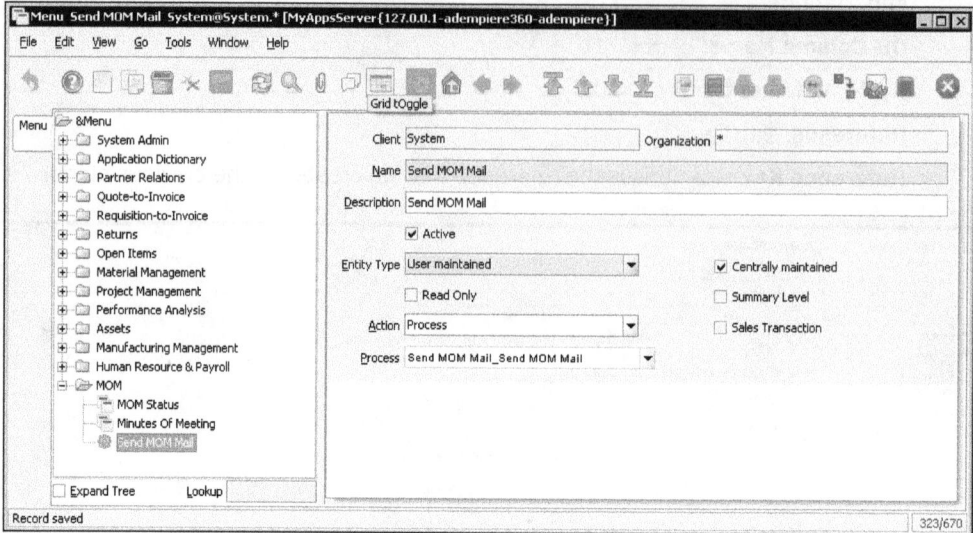

11. Log out and log in as **GardenAdmin/GardenAdmin** with the **GardenWorld Admin** role.

12. Go to the **Client** window and verify the mail server setting on the **Client** tab. To verify the settings, click on the **Test EMail** button. If everything is correct, you will see a success message, as shown in the following screenshot:

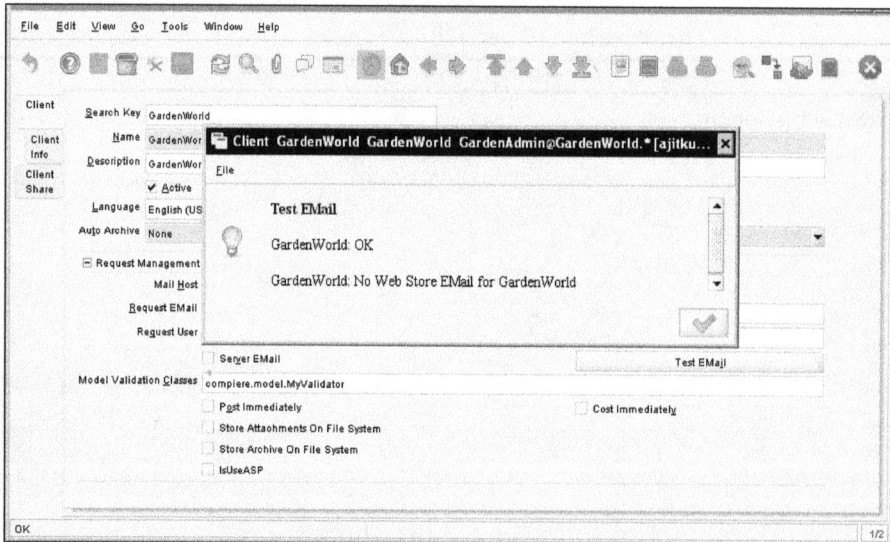

13. Click on the **Send MOM Mail** process. It will prompt you to select a **MOM**, as shown in the following screenshot:

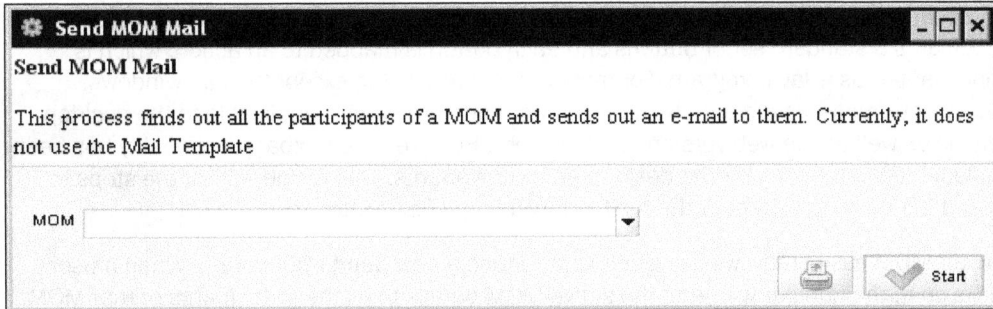

14. Select an MOM from the drop-down list and click on the **Start** button. This will send the e-mail and present the status, finally, as shown in the following screenshot:

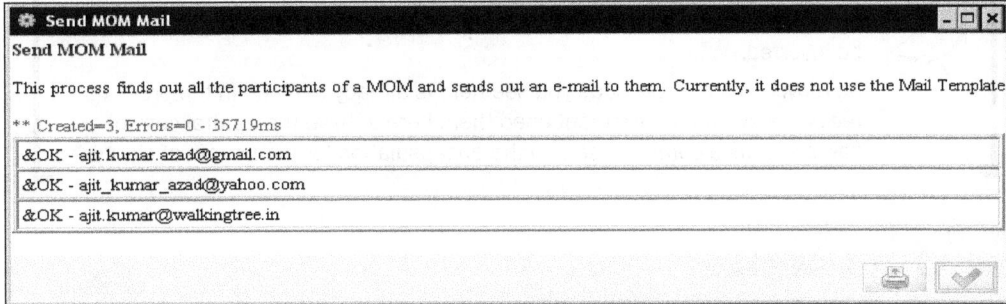

15. Check your mailbox to see if you have received e-mail with the MOM details, as shown in the next screenshot:

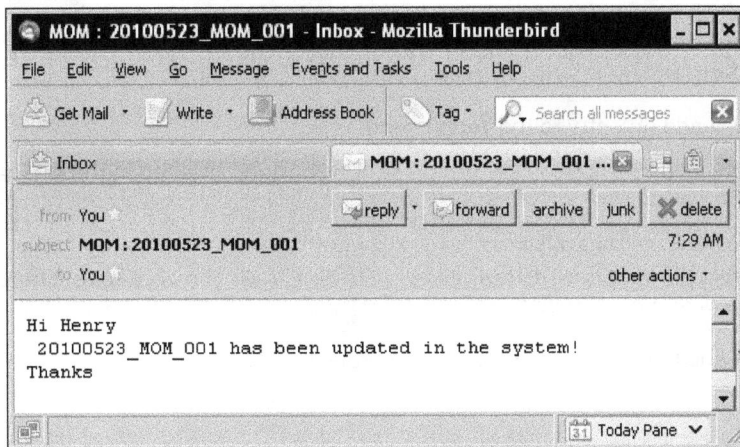

Extending the desktop version of the toolbar

The toolbar is another great way to extend the capability of ADempiere. In ADempiere, a toolbar is a standard set of buttons and each button is mapped to an action, which is implemented as a Java program. For most of the parts so far, except the info windows, the configurations we did and the changes we made are equally applicable to the desktop version as well as the web version of ADempiere. However, the toolbar functionality has been implemented differently for the desktop and web variants. This recipe will list the steps to extend the desktop variant of the toolbar by adding a new button to it.

For our MOM case study, we are going to introduce a new **Send Mail** button. When a user clicks on it, the handler will send the active MOM details to all the participants of that MOM.

> Wherever applicable, I have mentioned the line number, next to the code, where the mentioned code shall be inserted in the existing Java file. While I don't guarantee the correctness of the line number, I have mentioned them so that they indicate the logical location of where the mentioned code may be inserted.
>
> Moreover, some of the code you see here is already outlined in the previous recipes. However, I have mentioned them here to have the natural control flow and hence compromised on the encapsulation for the benefit of clarity.

How to do it...

1. Add the following line in the `jbInit()` method in the `APanel.java` class:

   ```
   private AppsAction aSendMail;
   ```

2. Add the following code in the `createMenu()` method in the `APanel.java` class:

   ```
   aSendMail = addAction("SendMail", mTools,    KeyStroke.
   getKeyStroke(KeyEvent.VK_M, 0),   false);
   toolBar.add(aSendMail.getButton()); //Line# 414.
   ```

3. This will add an entry to the **Tools** menu.

4. Add the following code in the `dataStatusChanged` method in the `APanel.java` class:

   ```
   aSendMail.setEnabled(true); //Line# 968
   aSendMail.setEnabled(false); //Line# 1234 to disable the button if
   there are no records.
   ```

5. Clean and build the `adempiere_360` project.

6. Add the following code in the `actionPerformed` method in the `APanel.java` class:

```
else if (cmd.equals(aSendMail.getName())) //Line# 1536 to handle
the action
        cmd_sendMail();
```

7. Add the following method definitions to the `APanel.java` class:

```
private void cmd_sendMail() {
  m_errorDisplayed = false;

  String momId = m_ctx.getProperty(m_curWindowNo + "|c_mom_ID");
  if (momId == null || momId.equals(""))
    return;
  int m_c_mom_ID = Integer.valueOf(momId);
  log.info("c_mom_ID=" + m_c_mom_ID);

  //  Client Info
  MClient m_client = MClient.get (getCtx());
  if (m_client.getAD_Client_ID() == 0)
    return;
  if (m_client.getSMTPHost() == null || m_client.getSMTPHost().
length() == 0)
      return;

  send2Participants(m_client, m_c_mom_ID);
  return;
}

private void send2Participants(MClient m_client, int m_c_mom_ID)
{
  log.info("C_Mom_ID=" + m_c_mom_ID);

  String sql = "SELECT a.ad_user_id "
        + "FROM adempiere.c_mom_participantsline a "
        + "WHERE a.c_mom_id=?";
  PreparedStatement pstmt = null;
  try
  {
    String trx = Trx.createTrxName();
    pstmt = DB.prepareStatement(sql, trx);
    pstmt.setInt(1, m_c_mom_ID);
    ResultSet rs = pstmt.executeQuery();
    while (rs.next())
    {
```

```
            Boolean ok = sendIndividualMail (m_client, m_c_mom_ID,
       rs.getInt(1));
           if (ok == null)
              ;
       }
     rs.close();
     pstmt.close();
     pstmt = null;
   }
   catch (SQLException ex)
   {
     log.log(Level.SEVERE, sql, ex);
   }
   try
   {
     if (pstmt != null)
       pstmt.close();
   }
   catch (SQLException ex1)
   {
   }
   pstmt = null;
 }


 /**
  *   Send Individual Mail
  *  @param AD_User_ID user
  *  @return true if mail has been sent
  */
 private Boolean sendIndividualMail (MClient m_client, int m_c_
 mom_ID, int AD_User_ID)
   {
     MUser to = new MUser (getCtx(), AD_User_ID, null);
     Mmom m_mom = new Mmom(getCtx(), m_c_mom_ID, m_client.get_
 TrxName());
     MUser m_from = new MUser (getCtx(), m_mom.getAD_User_ID(), m_
 client.get_TrxName());

     String message = "Hi " + to.getFirstName() +
             "\n" + m_mom.getName() +
             " has been updated in the system! Following is the
 agenda mentioned:\n" + m_mom.getagenda() +
             "\nThanks\n!!";
     String subject = "MOM : " + m_mom.getName();
     EMail email = m_client.createEMail(m_from, to, subject,
```

```
message);
    email.setSubject (subject);
    email.setMessageText (message);

    if (!email.isValid() && !email.isValid(true))
    {
      log.warning("NOT VALID - " + email);
      to.setIsActive(false);
      to.addDescription("Invalid EMail");
      to.save();
      return Boolean.FALSE;
    }
    boolean OK = EMail.SENT_OK.equals(email.send());
    if (OK)
      log.fine(to.getEMail());
    else
      log.warning("FAILURE - " + to.getEMail());
    return new Boolean(OK);
}
```

8. Compile the code and launch the desktop version of ADempiere from your project.

9. Log in as **GardenAdmin/GardenAdmin** with the **GardenWorld Admin** role.

10. Go to the **Minutes Of Meeting** window. You will see the **Send Mail** item in the **Tools** menu and an icon on the toolbar.

11. Click on the **Send Mail** toolbar button. This will send e-mails to the participants. The same can be achieved by clicking the **Send Mail** item in the **Tools** menu, as shown in the following screenshot:

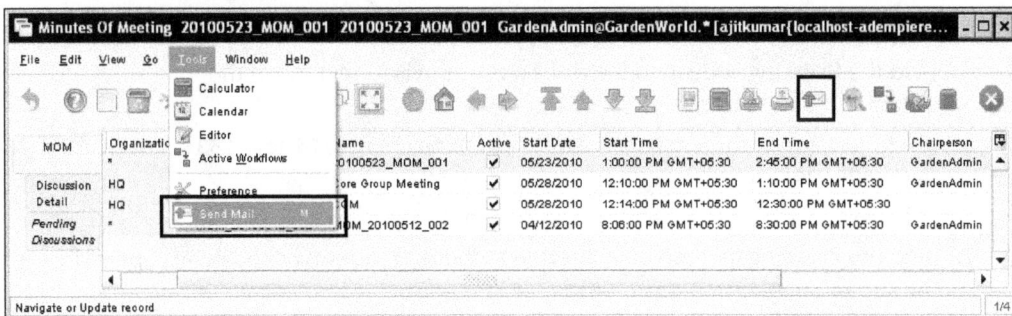

Extending the web version of the toolbar

This recipe presents the steps to accomplish exactly what we had done in the previous recipe, but for the web version of ADempiere.

How to do it...

1. Add a `btnMail` as a member of the `org.adempiere.webui.component.CWindowToolbar` class by adding the following line:

   ```
   private ToolBarButton btnMail;
   ```

2. Add the following code in to the `init` method in the `CWindowToolbar.java` class:

   ```
   btnMail = createButton("SendMail", "SendMail","SendMail"); //Line#
   156
   btnMail.setVisible(true);
   btnMail.setDisabled(false); //Line#168 after all the toolbar
   buttons are initialized
   ```

3. Add the following code in to the `configureKeyMap` method in the `CWindowToolbar.java` class:

   ```
   ctrlKeyMap.put(VK_M, btnMail);//Line# 277
   ```

4. Add the following method in to the `org.adempiere.webui.event.ToolbarListener` class:

   ```
   /**
    * Send Mail
    */
   public void onSendMail();
   ```

5. Clean and build the `adempiere_360` project.

6. Add the following code in to the `actionPerformed` method in the `APanel.java` class:

   ```
   else if (cmd.equals(aSendMail.getName())) //Line# 1536 to handle
   the action
           cmd_sendMail();
   ```

7. Add the following method definitions in to the `org.adempiere.webui.panel.AbstractADWindowPanel` class:

   ```
   public void onSendMail()
   {
   String momId = Env.getContext(ctx, "2|c_mom_ID");
   int m_c_mom_ID = Integer.valueOf(momId);

   //  Client Info
   MClient m_client = MClient.get (ctx);
   ```

```
    if (m_client.getAD_Client_ID() == 0)
        return;
    if (m_client.getSMTPHost() == null || m_client.getSMTPHost().
length() == 0)
        return;

    send2Participants(m_client, m_c_mom_ID);
    }


  private void send2Participants(MClient m_client, int m_c_mom_ID)
  {
    String sql = "SELECT a.ad_user_id "
          + "FROM adempiere.c_mom_participantsline a "
          + "WHERE a.c_mom_id=?";
    PreparedStatement pstmt = null;
    try
    {
      String trx = Trx.createTrxName();
      pstmt = DB.prepareStatement(sql, trx);
      pstmt.setInt(1, m_c_mom_ID);
      ResultSet rs = pstmt.executeQuery();
      while (rs.next())
      {
        Boolean ok = sendIndividualMail (trx, m_client, m_c_mom_
ID, rs.getInt(1));
        if (ok == null)
          ;
      }
      rs.close();
      pstmt.close();
      pstmt = null;
    }
    catch (SQLException ex)
    {
    }
    try
    {
      if (pstmt != null)
        pstmt.close();
    }
    catch (SQLException ex1)
    {
    }
    pstmt = null;
```

```
        }

    /**
     *    Send Individual Mail
     *    @param AD_User_ID user
     *    @return true if mail has been sent
     */
    private Boolean sendIndividualMail (String trx, MClient m_
client, int m_c_mom_ID, int AD_User_ID)
    {
      MUser to = new MUser (ctx, AD_User_ID, null);
      Mmom m_mom = new Mmom(ctx, m_c_mom_ID, trx);
      MUser m_from = new MUser (ctx, m_mom.getAD_User_ID(), trx);

      String message = "Hi " + to.getFirstName() +
              "\n" + m_mom.getName() +
              " has been updated in the system! Following is the
agenda mentioned:\n" + m_mom.getagenda() +
              "\nThanks\nAfter Save!!";
      String subject = "AfterSave : " + m_mom.getName();
      EMail email = m_client.createEMail(m_from, to, subject,
message);
      email.setSubject (subject);
      email.setMessageText (message);

      if (!email.isValid() && !email.isValid(true))
      {
        to.setIsActive(false);
        to.addDescription("Invalid EMail");
        to.save();
        return Boolean.FALSE;
      }
      boolean OK = EMail.SENT_OK.equals(email.send());
      return new Boolean(OK);
    }
```

8. Compile the code and launch the web version of ADempiere from your project.

9. Log in as **GardenAdmin/GardenAdmin** with the **GardenWorld Admin** role.

10. Go to the **Minutes Of Meeting** window. You will see the **Send Mail** icon on the toolbar.

11. Click on the **Send Mail** toolbar button. This will send e-mails to the participants, as shown in the following screenshot:

Grouping the fields in a tab

If there are too many fields on a tab, it may sound appropriate to group them logically, so that the user can see the connection between them. As part of this recipe, we are going to do this and see how we can do it.

We are going to group the basic MOM fields on the MOM tab under a collapsible panel with the title 'MOM Basic Detail'.

How to do it...

1. Log in as **System/System** with the **System Administrator** role.

2. Go to the **Menu | Application Dictionary | Field Group** window and create a new **Field Group** by the name of **MOM Basic Detail**, as shown in the following screenshot:

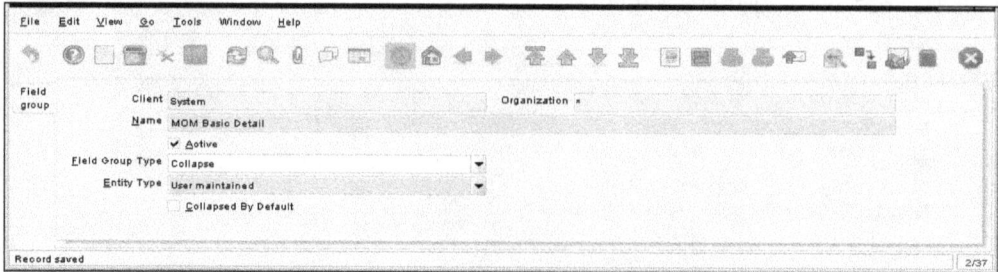

3. Go to the **Window, Tab**, and the **Field** window, and open the details of **Minutes Of Meeting** window.

4. Go to the **Tab** window and select the **MOM** tab.

5. Go to the **Field** tab and set the **Field Group** to **MOM Basic Detail**, as shown in the next screenshot

> The Field Group appears with the first item and all the items below it are considered to be in that group, until a new field group is specified.

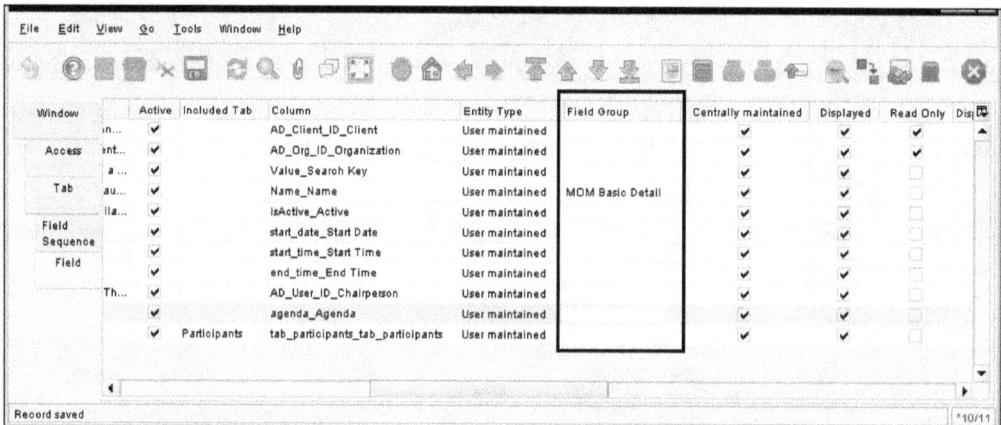

6. Log out and log in as **GardenAdmin/GardenAdmin** with the **GardenWorld Admin** role.

7. Go to the **Minutes Of Meeting** window. You will see the fields grouped under a collapsible group, **MOM Basic Detail**, as shown in the following screenshot:

4
Web services

In this chapter, we will cover:

- ▶ Building Web services support
- ▶ Configuring Web services
- ▶ Configuring a Web service to create a record
- ▶ Configuring a Web service to read a record
- ▶ Configuring a Web service to read a list of records
- ▶ Configuring a Web service to update a record
- ▶ Configuring a Web service to remove a record
- ▶ Configuring a Web service to run a process

Introduction

ADempiere has various modules and processes to provide the ERP, SCM, and CRM capability to the user. However, as ADempiere is still evolving, so are our business processes in the constant quest for efficiency and effectiveness. With this in perspective, there may be instances where an enterprise would have multiple applications, including ADempiere, sitting side-by-side and providing some specialized services to the user or complementing ADempiere's functionality. This, in most of the instances, calls for an integration of different systems. Moreover, if the enterprise uses ADempiere as its centralized system, then all other applications may have to integrate themselves with ADempiere so that they can read the common data and make their data available in it. For example, a shopping cart application needs product information. To achieve this, ADempiere provides the Web services interface. There are four types of Web service interfaces provided:

- ▶ **UI oriented Web services**: Provides APIs based on ADempiere's Window, Tab, and Field constructs

- **Model oriented Web services**: This provides APIs based on ADempiere's data model
- **eCommerce Integration Web services**: Provides integration of external eCommerce packages, such as Online Store or POS
- **Openbravo POS integration Web services**: Custom APIs provided for integration with Openbravo

Out of the previously listed types, model-oriented Web services will be the focus of this chapter. UI Web services are special services and unless you understand the ADempiere's Application Framework, it would be very difficult for any third party integrator to understand them and use them. Besides, the security layer has not been implemented yet in it, so it is not recommended for production use. Openbravo services are still at the alpha stage.

Model oriented services are built on top of ADempiere's data model and provides the following generic APIs to execute any ADempiere Web service:

- `createData`: For creating one record on a table
- `readData`: To return values from one record on a table
- `queryData`: To query records on a table
- `getList`: To get data from a list (reference list or reference table)
- `updateData`: To modify one record on a table
- `deleteData`: To delete one record from a table
- `runProcess`: To run a process or raise a process that starts a document workflow
- `setDocAction`: To trigger a change in document action, that is, complete a material receipt

In this chapter, we will look into the model oriented Web services and understand what it takes to consume them. Since these are generic APIs, it requires us to configure the security and our specific Web services detail in ADempiere, which will be the first thing/process we will cover to ensure our installation is built and configured for Web services.

> For all the Web services execution, we will be using the **soapUI** (`http://www.eviware.com`) client. So, kindly install it on your system and keep it ready before we start. **soapUI** is a Web services testing tool.

Also, the APIs require various details to be specified (for example, login details, warehouse, language, and so on). With reference to the WSDL of the model-oriented Web services, keep the following detail handy, as it will be useful during the execution of the Web services.

Tag	Description	Value	SQLs to find the value
User	Web services security will be configured for this user	GardenUser	
Pass	User Password	GardenUser	
Lang	Language ID for the user, GardenUser	192	`SELECT ad_language_id FROM ad_language WHERE ad_language='en_US'`
ClientID	Client ID has access to the Web services to which the user belongs to	11	`SELECT ad_client_id FROM ad_client WHERE name='GardenWorld'`
RoleID	Role of the GardenUser user, has access to the Web services	103	`SELECT ad_role_id FROM ad_role WHERE name='GardenWorld User'`
OrgID	Organisation ID Here, say, we want to give access to the Web services at the HQ (Head Quarters) level	11	`SELECT ad_org_id FROM ad_org WHERE name='HQ'`
WarehouseID	Warehouse ID HQ Warehouse	103	`SELECT m_warehouse_id FROM m_warehouse WHERE ad_client_id=11 AND ad_org_id=11`
Stage	Login stage This is related to the two stages we have when we login. In the first stage, we enter the username and password, and in the second stage, we select the role, organisation, client, and warehouse details	0	This is not used in the Web services. So, set the value to 0

Building Web services support

Support for Web services is not in-built into ADempiere and is also not part of the trunk (main branch) in the SVN repository. The Web services support was sponsored and the seed code was provided by 3E and the complete code resides, at the time of writing this book, in the `branches\3E_WebServices` folder of the ADempiere SVN repository. This recipe takes us through the steps required to build and deploy the Web services so that they can be used in conjunction with our ADempiere application.

Getting ready

To execute the steps mentioned in this recipe, we need to ensure that we have got the working and deployable version of the `adempiere_360` project in Eclipse. You may refer to *Chapter 1, Preparing the Ground* to do so, if you have not already done it.

How to do it...

1. Check out the `https://adempiere.svn.sourceforge.net/svnroot/adempiere/branches/3E_WebServices` SVN URL in `<ADEMPIERE_SVN>\branches`.

2. Launch Eclipse.

3. Import the newly checked out `3E_WebServices` project in Eclipse.

4. Right-click on the project and go to **Properties**. This will pop-up the **Properties** window.

5. Click on **Java Build Path**. You will see the build-related details on the right-hand side.

6. Click on the **Projects** tab and remove all the existing entries from the **Required projects on the build path** list.

7. Add the `adempiere_360` project to the **Required projects on the build path** and click on the **OK** button.

8. Edit the `build.xml` file and make the following changes:

   ❑ Set the `Adempiere.dir` property value to `${basedir}/../../tags/adempiere360lts/lib` to point it to our `adempiere_360` project folder

   ❑ Add the following to the `war target` before the WAR file is being created (`war` element):

```
<copy todir="${WEBINF.dir}/lib">
    <fileset dir="${Adempiere.dir}">
        <include name="*.jar"/>
    </fileset>
</copy>
<copy todir="${WEBINF.dir}/classes">
        <fileset dir="${Adempiere.dir}/../bin">
                <include name="**"/>
        </fileset>
</copy>
```

9. Right-click on **build.xml | Run As | Ant Build** to build and create the WAR file. On a successful build, it will create the `ADInterface-1.0.war` file in the `3E_WebServices\dist` folder. You will have to refresh your project to see this in Eclipse.

10. Copy the `ADInterface-1.0.war` file to the `<JBOSS_HOME>\server\adempiere360lts\deploy` folder (refer to *Chapter 1* to understand creating the `adempiere360lts` server instance).

11. Go to Eclipse and go to **Server** view.

12. Start the JBoss server instance where we had deployed the `adempiere_360` project.

13. Access the `http://127.0.0.1:9080/ADInterface-1.0/services/ADService?wsdl` URL in the browser. This will download the UI Web services WSDL file and display it, which means the Web services have been deployed successfully.

14. Access the `http://127.0.0.1:9080/ADInterface-1.0/services/ModelADService?wsdl` URL in the browser. This will download the Model Web services WSDL file and display it, which means the Web services have been deployed.

15. Open the URLs mentioned in step 13 and 14 in the **soapUI** client.

16. Run the `getVersion` Web service from the UI Web services list. Upon success, you shall get the version number returned from the service, for example, `0.7.0`. With this, we have verified that the installation is working fine.

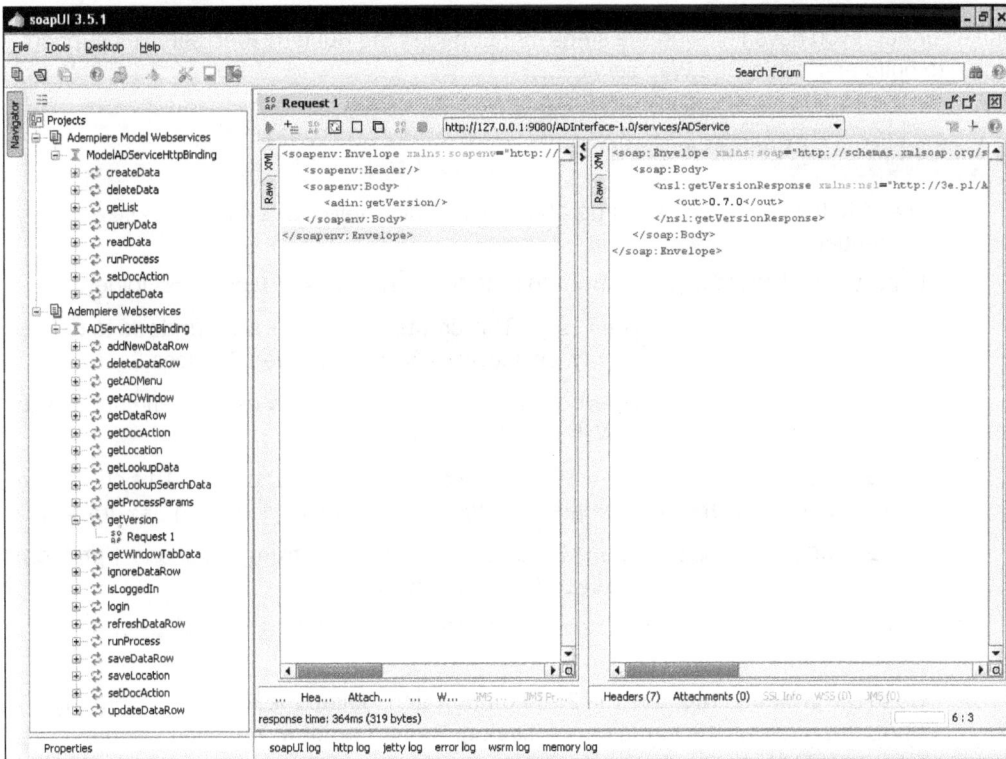

See also

▸ Creating the Installer from the source code

▸ Installing ADempiere

▸ Debugging the ADempiere client application (Desktop version)

▸ Debugging the ADempiere server application (Web version)

Configuring Web services

Now that we can build, deploy, and test the sample login service to verify the deployment, we can configure our ADempiere instance so that we can start configuring our new Web services and run them. Here we will see what we must do in order to configure our ADempiere instance for Web services support.

Getting ready

Make sure that you have followed the steps mentioned in the Building Web services support recipe to build and deploy the Web services.

How to do it...

1. Log in to the `adempiere360` database using the `adempiere/adempiere` credential.

2. Import the following SQL files from the `3E_WebServices\migration` folder:

   ❑ `WS001_WebServices.sql`: This creates the tables and windows to define the Web service security, as shown in ADempiere Web Services Security

   ❑ `WS002_WebServicesDefinition.sql`: This creates the definition of the currently supported Web services and methods

   ❑ `WS003_WebServicesConfigGardenWorldSample.sql`: This creates the role, user, and two sample tests for testing Web services with `GardenWorld`

   ❑ `WS004_WebServicesFixDict.sql`: This is for fixing a dictionary problem from the `WS001_WebServices.sql` script

3. Launch ADempiere from the `adempiere_360` project and log in as `SuperUser/System` with the `System Administrator` role.

4. Go to the **Window**, **Tab**, and the **Field** window and lookup the records by entering `%Web Service` as the name on the **Lookup Record** window. You shall see the following entries:

   ❑ Web Service Definition

   ❑ Web Service Security

5. Verify the **Access** of both the windows. Note that GardenUser has access to the Web services. We'll use it for all our Web services-related activities.

6. Go to the **Table and Column** window and lookup the records by entering %Web service as the **Name** on the **Lookup Record** window. You shall see the Web services-related tables. Verify that the **Data Access Level** is set to Client+Organization for all the table entries. Based on this setting, the data access security will be applied.

7. Log out and log in as `GardenUser/GardenUser` with the `GardenWorld User` role.

8. Lookup for Web service and make sure you have the following menus existing in your **Menu** tree:

    ❑ Web Service Security

    ❑ Web Services

> In case you are not seeing these menu items, follow the *Creating a new menu tree* recipe mentioned in *Chapter 2, ADempiere Customization – Part I*.

With this, we have verified the Web services configuration needed to configure and consume new Web services, which we will see in the subsequent recipes.

Configuring a Web service to create a record

This recipe describes the steps required to configure a Web service to create a new record in a table. It will be using the generic API, `createData`. We have taken an example where we would like to create a business partner in the system using the Web service.

Getting ready

Make sure that you have completed the steps mentioned in recipes 1 and 2 of this chapter.

How to do it...

1. Log in to ADempiere using `GardenUser/GardenUser` with the `GardenWorld User` role.

2. Go to the **Web Service Security** window.

3. Click on the **New Record** and enter the following on the **Web Service Type** tab, as shown in the next screenshot:

    ❑ **Search Key**: `CreateBPartner` (choose your text)

    ❑ **Name**: `Create BPartner` (choose your text)

    ❑ **Web Service**: `Model Oriented Web Services`

    ❑ **Web Service Method**: `Create Data_Model Oriented Web Services`

    ❑ **Table**: `C_BPartner_Business Partner`

    ❑ **Description**: `<your description of service>`

    ❑ **Comment/Help**: `<your text>`

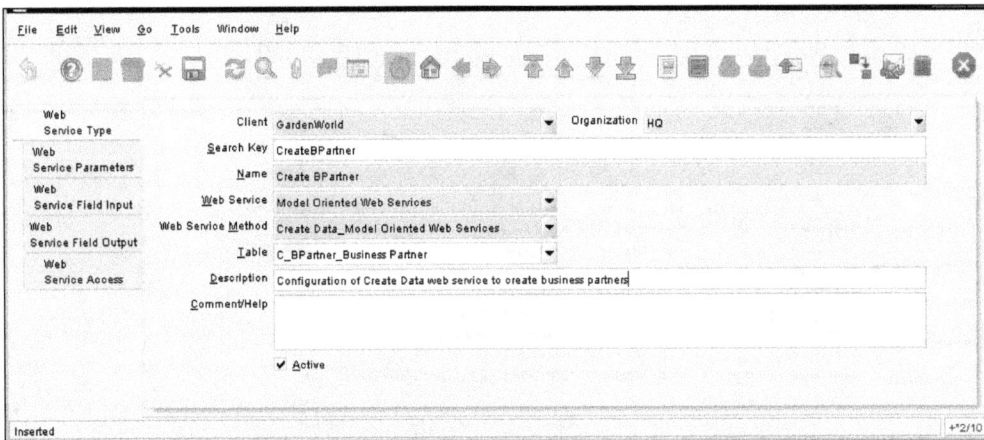

4. Go to **Web Service Parameter** and create the following parameters, as shown in the next screenshot:

  ❑ TableName: Set this to C_BPartner

  ❑ RecordID: The value for this will be passed from the Web service request

  ❑ Action: Set this to Create

5. Go to the **Web Service Field Input** tab and enter the following **Columns**, as shown in the next screenshot:

  ❑ Value_Search Key

  ❑ Name_Name

  ❑ TaxID_Tax ID

  ❑ IsVendor_Vendor

  ❑ IsCustomer_Customer

  ❑ IsTaxExempt_Tax exempt

- Name2_Name 2

- C_BP_Group_ID_Business Partner Group

6. Go to the **soapUI** client and run the following SOAP request:

```xml
<soapenv:Envelope xmlns:soapenv="http://schemas.xmlsoap.org/soap/
envelope/" xmlns:adin="http://3e.pl/ADInterface">
   <soapenv:Header/>
   <soapenv:Body>
      <adin:createData>
         <adin:ModelCRUDRequest>
            <adin:ModelCRUD>
               <adin:serviceType>CreateBPartner</adin:serviceType>
               <adin:TableName>C_BPartner</adin:TableName>
               <adin:RecordID>0</adin:RecordID>
               <adin:Action>Create</adin:Action>
               <!--Optional:-->
               <adin:DataRow>
                  <!--Zero or more repetitions:-->
                  <adin:field column="Value">
                     <adin:val>Ajit</adin:val>
                  </adin:field>
                  <adin:field column="Name">
                     <adin:val>Ajit Kumar</adin:val>
                  </adin:field>
                  <adin:field column="TaxID">
                     <adin:val></adin:val>
                  </adin:field>
                  <adin:field column="IsVendor">
                     <adin:val>N</adin:val>
                  </adin:field>
                  <adin:field column="IsCustomer">
                     <adin:val>N</adin:val>
```

```
            </adin:field>
            <adin:field column="IsTaxExempt">
                <adin:val>N</adin:val>
            </adin:field>
            <adin:field column="Name2">
                <adin:val>Walking Tree</adin:val>
            </adin:field>
            <adin:field column="C_BP_Group_ID">
                <adin:val>105</adin:val>
            </adin:field>
        </adin:DataRow>
    </adin:ModelCRUD>
    <adin:ADLoginRequest>
        <adin:user>GardenUser</adin:user>
        <adin:pass>GardenUser</adin:pass>
        <adin:lang>192</adin:lang>
        <adin:ClientID>11</adin:ClientID>
        <adin:RoleID>103</adin:RoleID>
        <adin:OrgID>11</adin:OrgID>
        <adin:WarehouseID>103</adin:WarehouseID>
        <adin:stage>0</adin:stage>
    </adin:ADLoginRequest>
  </adin:ModelCRUDRequest>
 </adin:createData>
</soapenv:Body>
</soapenv:Envelope>
```

The following is the response you shall receive indicating that the business partner has been created in the system:

```
<soap:Envelope xmlns:soap="http://schemas.xmlsoap.org/soap/
envelope/" xmlns:xsd="http://www.w3.org/2001/XMLSchema"
xmlns:xsi="http://www.w3.org/2001/XMLSchema-instance">
    <soap:Body>
        <ns1:createDataResponse xmlns:ns1="http://3e.pl/
ADInterface">
            <StandardResponse RecordID="1000002" xmlns="http://3e.pl/
ADInterface"/>
        </ns1:createDataResponse>
    </soap:Body>
</soap:Envelope>
```

7. Go to the **Business Partner** window in **ADempiere** and verify that the details of the newly created business partner appear in it.

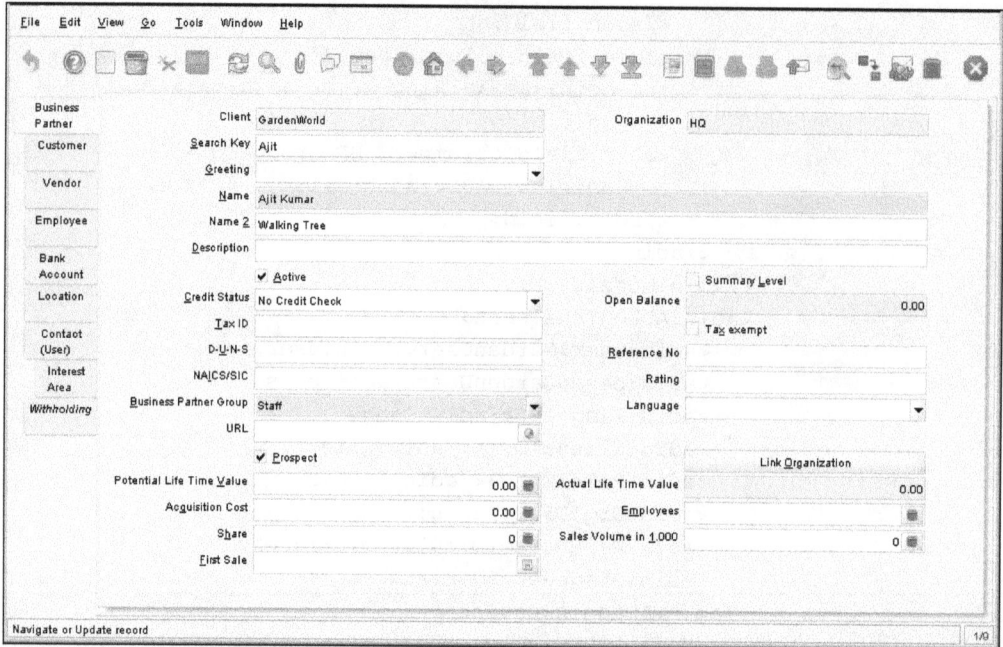

Configuring a Web service to read a record

Now let us look at how to configure a Web service to read the newly created business partner using the generic API—readData.

How to do it...

1. Log in to **ADempiere** using GardenUser/GardenUser with the GardenWorld User role.

2. Go to the **Web Service Security** window.

3. Click on the **New Record** and enter the following, as shown in the next screenshot:

   ❑ **Search Key**: ReadBPartner (choose your text)

   ❑ **Name**: Read BPartner (choose your text)

   ❑ **Web Service**: Model Oriented Web Services

   ❑ **Web Service Method**: Read Data_Model Oriented Web Services

   ❑ **Table**: C_BPartner_Business Partner

❏ **Description**: <your description of service>

❏ **Comment/Help**: <your text>

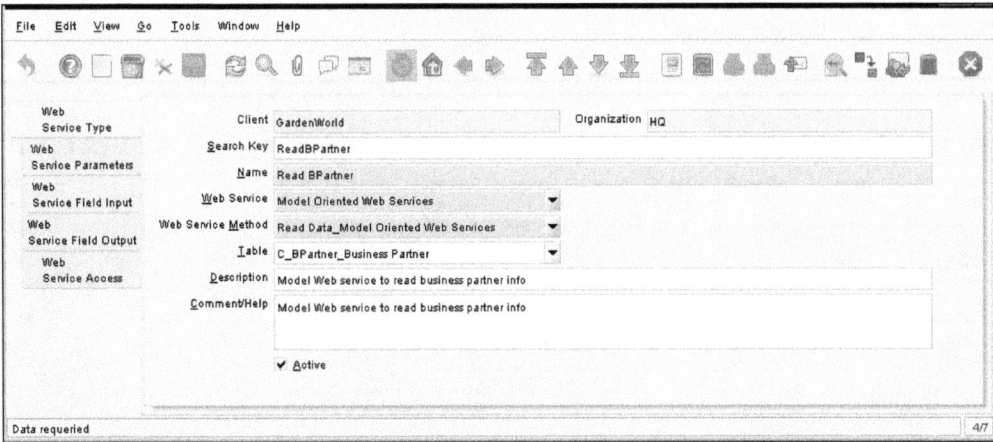

4. Go to the **Web Service Parameter** tab and create the following parameters, as shown in the next screenshot:

❏ TableName: Set this to C_BPartner

❏ RecordID: The value for this will be passed from the Web service request. You may get the RecordID from the response of the CreateData service response, as shown in the previous recipe

❏ Action: Set this to Read

5. Go to the **Web Service Field Output** tab and create the following parameters as shown in the following screenshot:

   ❑ Name_Name

   ❑ Name2_Name 2

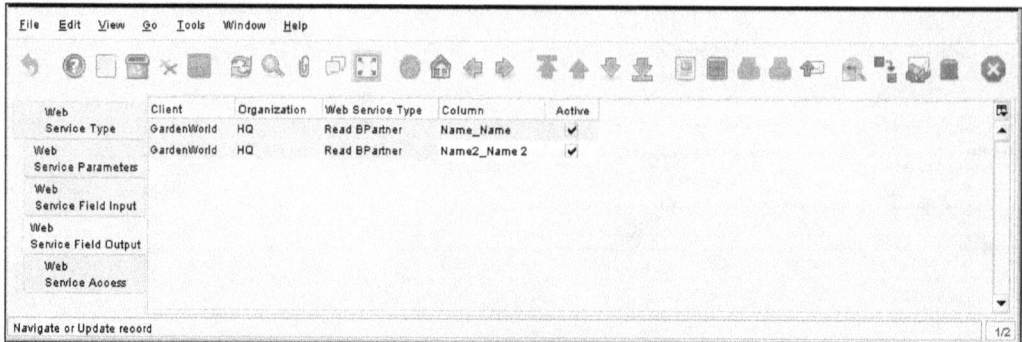

6. Go to the **soapUI** client and run the following SOAP request:

```
<soapenv:Envelope xmlns:soapenv="http://schemas.xmlsoap.org/soap/
envelope/" xmlns:adin="http://3e.pl/ADInterface">

   <soapenv:Header/>

   <soapenv:Body>

      <adin:readData>

         <adin:ModelCRUDRequest>

            <adin:ModelCRUD>

               <adin:serviceType>ReadBPartner</adin:serviceType>
               <adin:TableName>C_BPartner</adin:TableName>
               <adin:RecordID>1000002</adin:RecordID>
               <adin:Action>Read</adin:Action>
            </adin:ModelCRUD>
            <adin:ADLoginRequest>
               <adin:user>GardenUser</adin:user>
               <adin:pass>GardenUser</adin:pass>
               <adin:lang>192</adin:lang>
               <adin:ClientID>11</adin:ClientID>
               <adin:RoleID>103</adin:RoleID>
               <adin:OrgID>11</adin:OrgID>
               <adin:WarehouseID>103</adin:WarehouseID>
               <adin:stage>0</adin:stage>
            </adin:ADLoginRequest>
```

```
        </adin:ModelCRUDRequest>
      </adin:readData>
    </soapenv:Body>
  </soapenv:Envelope>
```

In the preceding request, `1000002` is the `RecordID` returned as part of the `CreateBPartner` service calls.

The following shall be the response showing the record detail:

```
<soap:Envelope xmlns:soap="http://schemas.xmlsoap.org/soap/
envelope/" xmlns:xsd="http://www.w3.org/2001/XMLSchema"
xmlns:xsi="http://www.w3.org/2001/XMLSchema-instance">
  <soap:Body>
    <ns1:readDataResponse xmlns:ns1="http://3e.pl/ADInterface">
      <WindowTabData NumRows="1" TotalRows="1" StartRow="1"
xmlns="http://3e.pl/ADInterface">
        <DataSet>
          <DataRow>
            <field column="Name">
              <val>Ajit Kumar</val>
            </field>
            <field column="Name2">
              <val>Walking Tree</val>
            </field>
          </DataRow>
        </DataSet>
        <RowCount>1</RowCount>
        <Success>true</Success>
      </WindowTabData>
    </ns1:readDataResponse>
  </soap:Body>
</soap:Envelope>
```

Configuring a Web service to read a list of records

There may be instances where you may have to provide an API to return a list of records, for example, list of purchase orders, list of products, list of business partners, and so on. In this recipe, we will see how we can configure a Web service to return a list of records, say business partners, using the generic API, `queryData`.

How to do it...

1. Log in to **ADempiere** using GardenUser/GardenUser with the GardenWorld User role.

2. Go to the **Web Service Security** window.

3. Click on the **New Record** and enter the following, as shown in the next screenshot:

   - **Search Key**: QueryBPartner (choose your text)
   - **Name**: Query BPartner (choose your text)
   - **Web Service**: Model Oriented Web Services
   - **Web Service Method**: Query Data_Model Oriented Web Services
   - **Table**: C_BPartner_Business Partner
   - **Description**: <your description of service>
   - **Comment/Help**: <your text>

4. Go to the **Web Service Parameter** tab and create the following parameters, as shown in the following screenshot:

   - TableName: Set this to C_BPartner
   - RecordID: The value for this will be passed from the Web service request
   - Action: Set this to Read

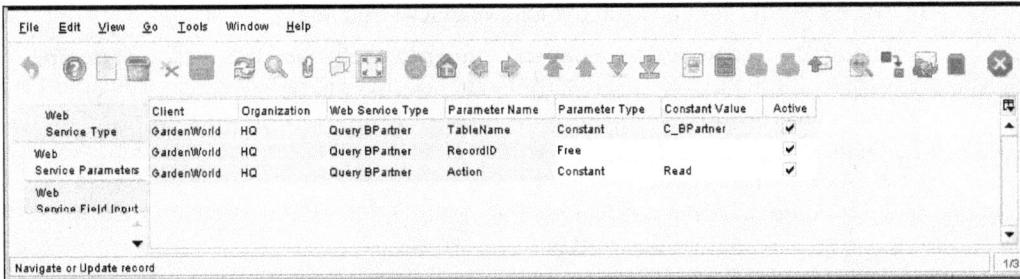

5. Go to the **Web Service Field Input** tab and enter the following **Columns**, as shown in the following screenshot:

   ❑   Name_Name

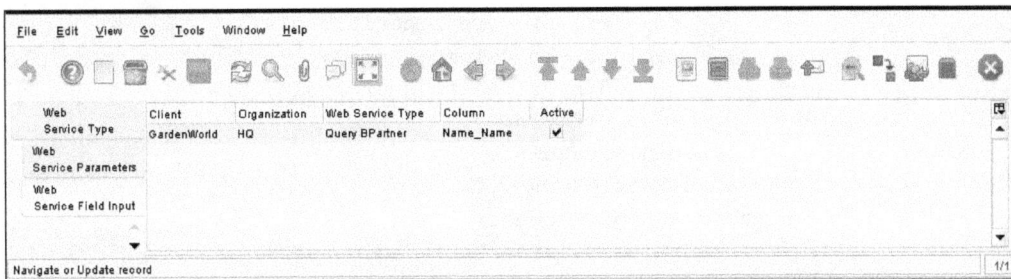

6. Go to the **Web Service Field Output** tab and create the following parameters, as shown in the following screenshot:

   ❑   Name_Name

   ❑   Name2_Name 2

   ❑   C_BP_Group_ID_Business Partner Group

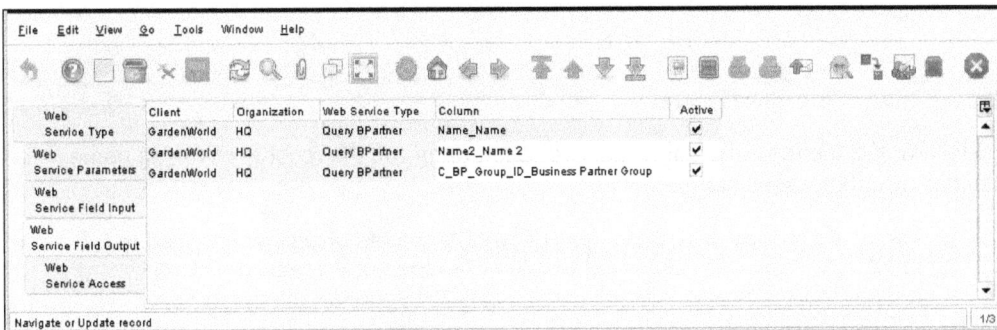

7. Go to the **soapUI** client and run the following SOAP request:

```
<soapenv:Envelope xmlns:soapenv="http://schemas.xmlsoap.org/soap/
envelope/" xmlns:adin="http://3e.pl/ADInterface">
   <soapenv:Header/>
   <soapenv:Body>
      <adin:queryData>
         <adin:ModelCRUDRequest>
            <adin:ModelCRUD>
               <adin:serviceType>QueryBPartner</adin:serviceType>
               <adin:TableName>C_BPartner</adin:TableName>
               <adin:RecordID>0</adin:RecordID>
               <adin:Action>Read</adin:Action>
               <!--Optional:-->
               <adin:DataRow>
                  <!--Zero or more repetitions:-->
                  <adin:field column="Name">
                     <adin:val>Ajit Kumar</adin:val>
                  </adin:field>
               </adin:DataRow>
            </adin:ModelCRUD>
            <adin:ADLoginRequest>
               <adin:user>GardenUser</adin:user>
               <adin:pass>GardenUser</adin:pass>
               <adin:lang>192</adin:lang>
               <adin:ClientID>11</adin:ClientID>
               <adin:RoleID>103</adin:RoleID>
               <adin:OrgID>11</adin:OrgID>
               <adin:WarehouseID>103</adin:WarehouseID>
               <adin:stage>0</adin:stage>
            </adin:ADLoginRequest>
         </adin:ModelCRUDRequest>
      </adin:queryData>
   </soapenv:Body>
</soapenv:Envelope>
```

The following is the response you shall receive, showing you the records of whose name matches with the passed name:

```
<soap:Envelope xmlns:soap="http://schemas.xmlsoap.org/soap/
envelope/" xmlns:xsd="http://www.w3.org/2001/XMLSchema"
xmlns:xsi="http://www.w3.org/2001/XMLSchema-instance">
   <soap:Body>
      <ns1:queryDataResponse xmlns:ns1="http://3e.pl/ADInterface">
         <WindowTabData NumRows="2" TotalRows="2" StartRow="1"
xmlns="http://3e.pl/ADInterface">
```

```
        <DataSet>
          <DataRow>
            <field column="C_BP_Group_ID">
              <val>105</val>
            </field>
            <field column="Name">
              <val>Ajit Kumar</val>
            </field>
            <field column="Name2">
              <val>Walking Tree</val>
                      </DataRow>
        </DataSet>
        <DataSet>
          <DataRow>
            <field column="C_BP_Group_ID">
              <val>105</val>
            </field>
            <field column="Name">
              <val>Ajit Kumar</val>
            </field>
            <field column="Name2">
              <val>SBI Bank</val>
            </field>
          </DataRow>
        </DataSet>
        <RowCount>2</RowCount>
        <Success>true</Success>
      </WindowTabData>
    </ns1:queryDataResponse>
  </soap:Body>
</soap:Envelope>
```

There's more...

There is another generic API, getList, which can be used to read a list of records using the table reference.

Reading a list of records using getList

The getList API requires a table reference, which can be found from the ad_reference table. For example, for the business partner table, the reference ID is 138. Now, configure a Web service by following these steps:

1. Log in as GardeUser/GardenUser with the GardenWorld User role.

2. Open the **Web Service Security** window and click on **New Record**.

3. Enter the following on the **Web Service Type** tab:

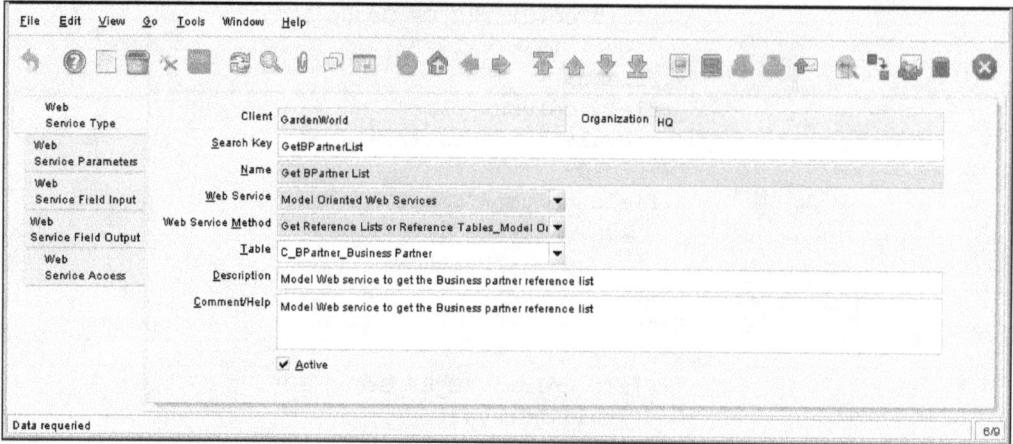

4. Enter the following on the **Web Service Parameters** tab:

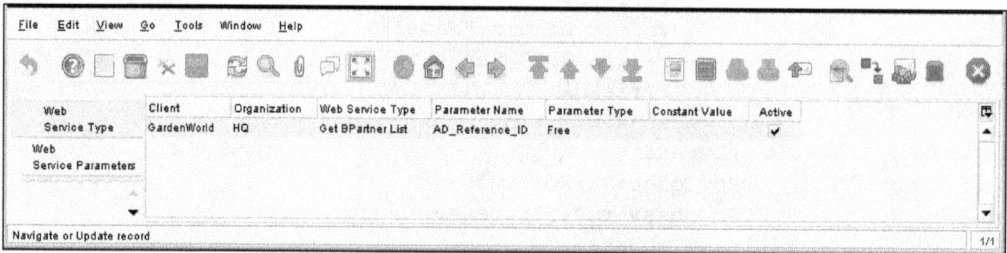

5. Enter the following on the **Web Service Field Output** tab:

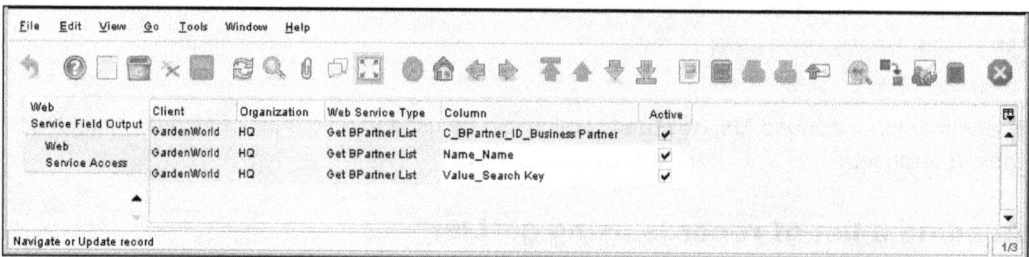

6. Run the following SOAP request in **soapUI**:

```
<soapenv:Envelope xmlns:soapenv="http://schemas.xmlsoap.org/soap/
envelope/" xmlns:adin="http://3e.pl/ADInterface">
    <soapenv:Header/>
    <soapenv:Body>
```

```
        <adin:getList>
            <adin:ModelGetListRequest>
                <adin:ModelGetList>
                    <adin:serviceType>GetBPartnerList</
    adin:serviceType>
                    <adin:AD_Reference_ID>138</adin:AD_Reference_ID>
                </adin:ModelGetList>
                <adin:ADLoginRequest>
                    <adin:user>GardenUser</adin:user>
                    <adin:pass>GardenUser</adin:pass>
                    <adin:lang>192</adin:lang>
                    <adin:ClientID>11</adin:ClientID>
                    <adin:RoleID>103</adin:RoleID>
                    <adin:OrgID>11</adin:OrgID>
                    <adin:WarehouseID>103</adin:WarehouseID>
                    <adin:stage>0</adin:stage>
                </adin:ADLoginRequest>
            </adin:ModelGetListRequest>
        </adin:getList>
    </soapenv:Body>
</soapenv:Envelope>
```

7. Verify that the response shows the records list.

Configuring a Web service to update a record

This recipe describes the steps required to configure a Web service to update a record in a table using the generic API, `updateData`.

How to do it...

1. Log in to **ADempiere** using `GardenUser/GardenUser` with the `GardenWorld User` role.

2. Go to the **Web Service Security** window.

3. Click on the **New Record** and enter the following, as shown in the next screenshot:

    ❑ **Search Key**: `UpdateBPartner` (choose your text)

    ❑ **Name**: `Update BPartner` (choose your text)

    ❑ **Web Service**: `Model Oriented Web Services`

    ❑ **Web Service Method**: `Update Data_Model Oriented Web Services`

    ❑ **Table**: `C_BPartner_Business Partner`

□ **Description**: <your description of service>

□ **Comment/Help**: <your text>

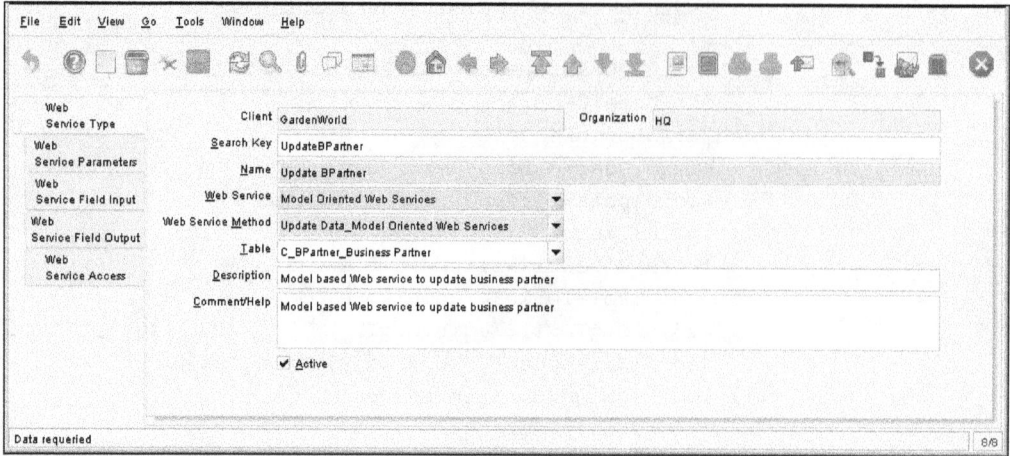

4. Go to the **Web Service Parameter** tab and create the following parameters, as shown in the next screenshot:

□ `TableName`: Set this to `C_BPartner`

□ `RecordID`: The value for this will be passed from the Web service request

□ `Action`: Set this to `Update`

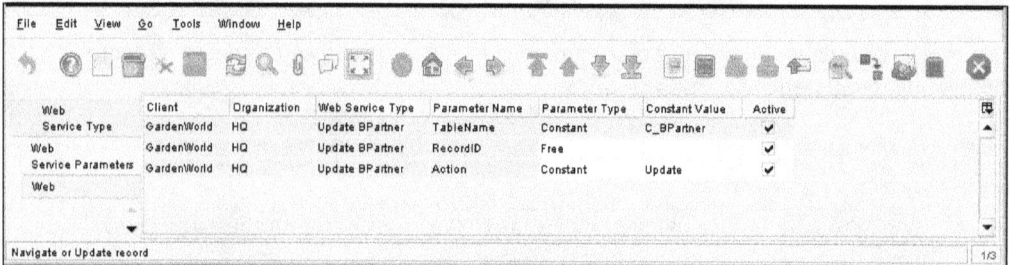

5. Go to the **Web Service Field Input** tab and enter the following **Columns**, as shown in the next screenshot:

▶ `Name2_Name 2`

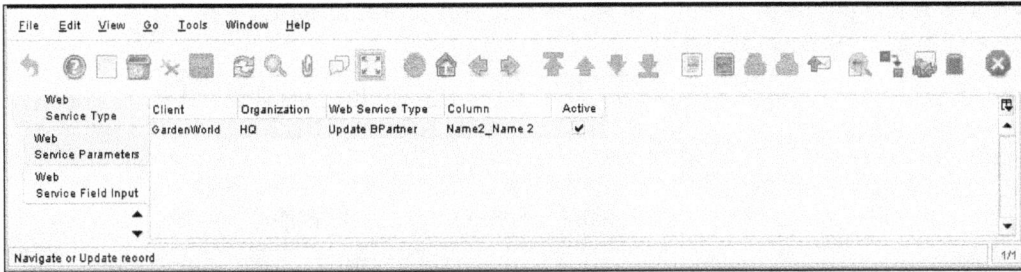

6. Go to the **soapUI** client and run the following SOAP request:

```
<soapenv:Envelope xmlns:soapenv="http://schemas.xmlsoap.org/soap/
envelope/" xmlns:adin="http://3e.pl/ADInterface">
    <soapenv:Header/>
    <soapenv:Body>
        <adin:updateData>
            <adin:ModelCRUDRequest>
                <adin:ModelCRUD>
                    <adin:serviceType>UpdateBPartner</adin:serviceType>
                    <adin:TableName>C_BPartner</adin:TableName>
                    <adin:RecordID>1000003</adin:RecordID>
                    <adin:Action>Update</adin:Action>
                    <!--Optional:-->
                    <adin:DataRow>
                        <!--Zero or more repetitions:-->
                        <adin:field column="Name2">
                            <adin:val>UIT Bank</adin:val>
                            <!--Optional:-->
                        </adin:field>
                    </adin:DataRow>
                </adin:ModelCRUD>
                <adin:ADLoginRequest>
                    <adin:user>GardenUser</adin:user>
                    <adin:pass>GardenUser</adin:pass>
                    <adin:lang>192</adin:lang>
                    <adin:ClientID>11</adin:ClientID>
                    <adin:RoleID>103</adin:RoleID>
                    <adin:OrgID>11</adin:OrgID>
                    <adin:WarehouseID>103</adin:WarehouseID>
                    <adin:stage>0</adin:stage>
                </adin:ADLoginRequest>
            </adin:ModelCRUDRequest>
        </adin:updateData>
    </soapenv:Body>
</soapenv:Envelope>
```

In the preceding request, `1000003` is the `RecordID` returned as part of the `CreateBPartner` service calls.

The following is the response you will receive, indicating that the business partner has been updated in the system:

```
<soap:Envelope xmlns:soap="http://schemas.xmlsoap.org/soap/
envelope/" xmlns:xsd="http://www.w3.org/2001/XMLSchema"
xmlns:xsi="http://www.w3.org/2001/XMLSchema-instance">
    <soap:Body>
        <ns1:updateDataResponse xmlns:ns1="http://3e.pl/
ADInterface">
            <StandardResponse RecordID="1000003" xmlns="http://3e.pl/
ADInterface"/>
        </ns1:updateDataResponse>
    </soap:Body>
</soap:Envelope>
```

7. Go to the **Business Partner** window and verify that the **Name 2** field is updated.

Configuring a Web service to remove a record

Here we will see how to configure a Web service to remove a record from a table using the generic API, `deleteData`.

How to do it...

1. Log in to **ADempiere** using `GardenUser/GardenUser` with the `GardenWorld User` role.
2. Go to the **Web Service Security** window.
3. Click on the **New Record** and enter the following, as shown in the next screenshot:
   - ❑ **Search Key**: `DeleteBPartner` (choose your text)
   - ❑ **Name**: `Delete BPartner` (choose your text)
   - ❑ **Web Service**: `Model Oriented Web Services`
   - ❑ **Web Service Method**: `Delete Data_Model Oriented Web Services`
   - ❑ **Table**: `C_BPartner_Business Partner`
   - ❑ **Description**: `<your description of service>`
   - ❑ **Comment/Help**: `<your text>`

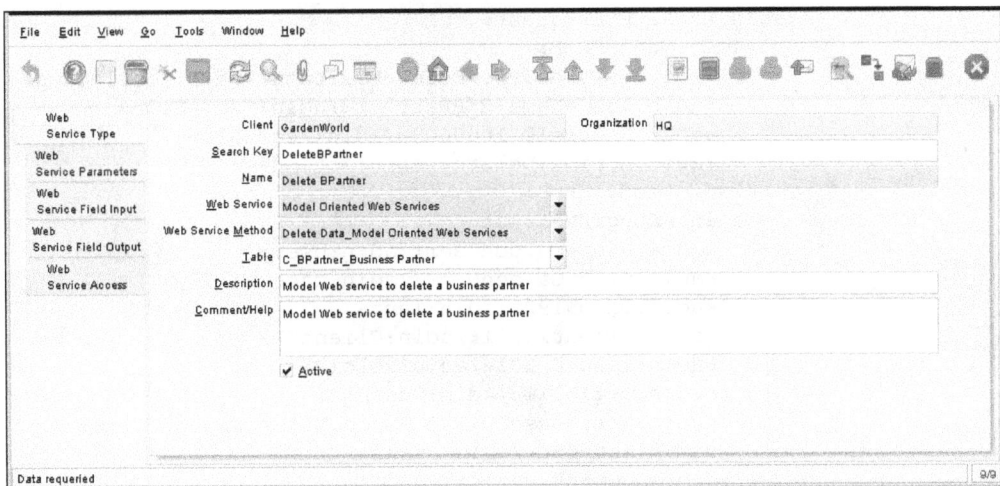

4. Go to the **Web Service Parameter** tab and create the following parameters, as shown in the following screenshot:

   - ❑ `TableName`: Set this to `C_BPartner`
   - ❑ `RecordID`: The value for this will be passed from the Web service request
   - ❑ `Action`: Set this to `Delete`

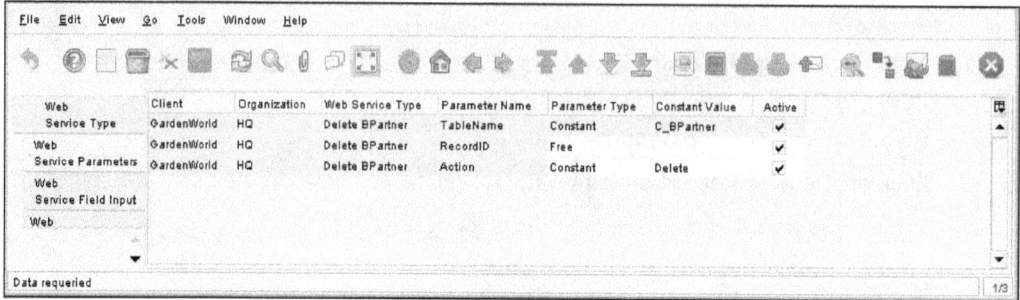

	Client	Organization	Web Service Type	Parameter Name	Parameter Type	Constant Value	Active
Web Service Type	GardenWorld	HQ	Delete BPartner	TableName	Constant	C_BPartner	✔
Web Service Parameters	GardenWorld	HQ	Delete BPartner	RecordID	Free		✔
	GardenWorld	HQ	Delete BPartner	Action	Constant	Delete	✔

Web Service Field Input
Web

Data requeried   1/3

5. Go to the **soapUI** client and run the following SOAP request:

```
<soapenv:Envelope xmlns:soapenv="http://schemas.xmlsoap.org/soap/
envelope/" xmlns:adin="http://3e.pl/ADInterface">
   <soapenv:Header/>
   <soapenv:Body>
      <adin:deleteData>
         <adin:ModelCRUDRequest>
            <adin:ModelCRUD>
               <adin:serviceType>DeleteBPartner</adin:serviceType>
               <adin:TableName>C_BPartner</adin:TableName>
               <adin:RecordID>1000003</adin:RecordID>
               <adin:Action>Delete</adin:Action>
            </adin:ModelCRUD>
            <adin:ADLoginRequest>
               <adin:user>GardenUser</adin:user>
               <adin:pass>GardenUser</adin:pass>
               <adin:lang>192</adin:lang>
               <adin:ClientID>11</adin:ClientID>
               <adin:RoleID>103</adin:RoleID>
               <adin:OrgID>11</adin:OrgID>
               <adin:WarehouseID>103</adin:WarehouseID>
               <adin:stage>0</adin:stage>
            </adin:ADLoginRequest>
         </adin:ModelCRUDRequest>
      </adin:deleteData>
   </soapenv:Body>
</soapenv:Envelope>
```

The following is the response you will receive indicating that the business partner has been deleted from the system:

```
<soap:Envelope xmlns:soap="http://schemas.xmlsoap.org/soap/
envelope/" xmlns:xsd="http://www.w3.org/2001/XMLSchema"
xmlns:xsi="http://www.w3.org/2001/XMLSchema-instance">
    <soap:Body>
        <ns1:deleteDataResponse xmlns:ns1="http://3e.pl/
ADInterface">
            <StandardResponse RecordID="1000003" xmlns="http://3e.pl/
ADInterface"/>
        </ns1:deleteDataResponse>
    </soap:Body>
</soap:Envelope>
```

Configuring a Web service to run a process

In this recipe, we would configure a Web service to run an ADempiere process using the generic API, `runProcess`. I have taken the `SendMOMMail` process as an example for demonstration purposes. You may refer to the *Creating a process* recipe in *Chapter 3, ADempiere Customization – Part II* to understand the `SendMOMMail` process.

Getting ready

The `SendMOMMail` process must be created and configured.

How to do it...

1. Log in to **ADempiere** using `GardenUser`/`GardenUser` with the `GardenWorld User` role.
2. Go to the **Web Service Security** window.
3. Click on the **New Record** and enter the following, as shown in the next screenshot:
   - **Search Key**: `SendMOMMail` (choose your text)
   - **Name**: `Send MOM Mail` (choose your text)
   - **Web Service**: `Model Oriented Web Services`
   - **Web Service Method**: `Run Process_Model Oriented Web Services`
   - **Table**: `C_mom_participantsline_MOM Participants`

- ❏ **Description**: <your description of service>
- ❏ **Comment/Help**: <your text>

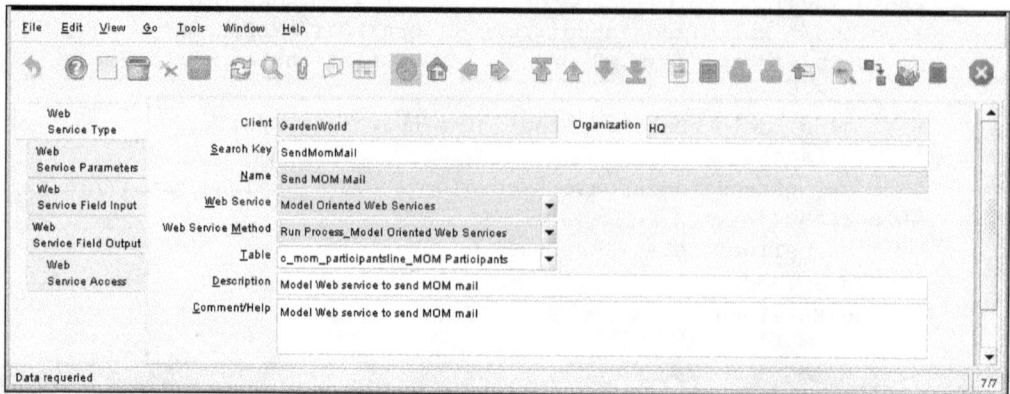

4. Go to **Web Service Parameter** tab and create the following parameters, as shown in the next screenshot:

- ❏ AD_Menu_ID: Set this to the menu ID of the **Send MOM Mail** menu item, as mentioned in the ad_menu table
- ❏ AD_Process_ID: Set this to the process ID of the SendMOMMail process, as mentioned in the ad_process table
- ❏ AD_Record_ID: The value for this will be passed from the Web service request

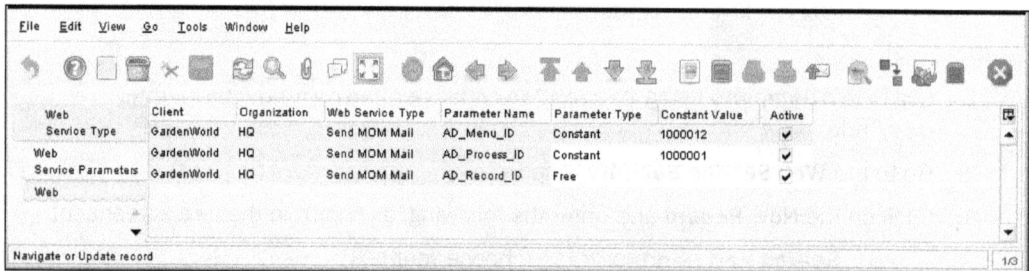

5. Go to the **Web Service Field Input** tab and create the following parameters, as shown in the following screenshot:

- ❏ C_mom_ID_Minutes of meeting detail

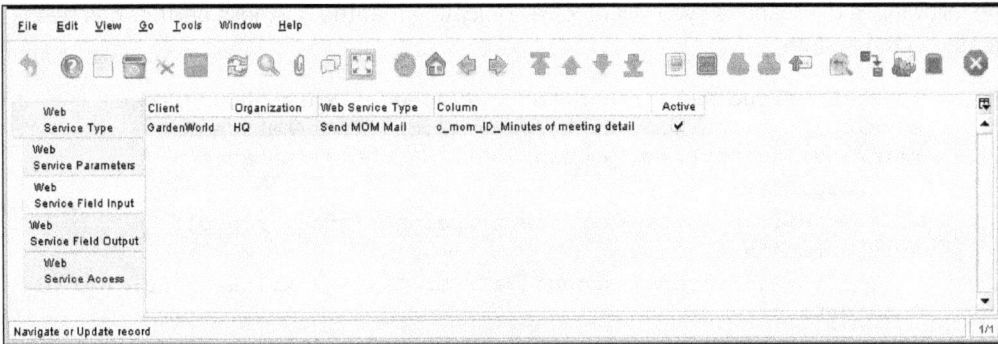

6. Go to the **soapUI** client and run the following SOAP request:

```
<soapenv:Envelope xmlns:soapenv="http://schemas.xmlsoap.org/soap/
envelope/" xmlns:adin="http://3e.pl/ADInterface">
    <soapenv:Header/>
    <soapenv:Body>
        <adin:runProcess>
            <adin:ModelRunProcessRequest>
                <adin:ModelRunProcess>
                    <adin:serviceType>SendMomMail</adin:serviceType>
                    <adin:ParamValues>
                        <!--Zero or more repetitions:-->
                        <adin:field column="c_mom_ID">
                            <adin:val>1000008</adin:val>
                        </adin:field>
                    </adin:ParamValues>
                </adin:ModelRunProcess>
                <adin:ADLoginRequest>
                    <adin:user>GardenUser</adin:user>
                    <adin:pass>GardenUser</adin:pass>
                    <adin:lang>192</adin:lang>
                    <adin:ClientID>11</adin:ClientID>
                    <adin:RoleID>103</adin:RoleID>
                    <adin:OrgID>11</adin:OrgID>
                    <adin:WarehouseID>103</adin:WarehouseID>
                    <adin:stage>0</adin:stage>
                </adin:ADLoginRequest>
            </adin:ModelRunProcessRequest>
        </adin:runProcess>
    </soapenv:Body>
</soapenv:Envelope>
```

The following is the response you will receive, indicating that the business partner has been created in the system:

```
<soap:Envelope xmlns:soap="http://schemas.xmlsoap.org/soap/
envelope/" xmlns:xsd="http://www.w3.org/2001/XMLSchema"
xmlns:xsi="http://www.w3.org/2001/XMLSchema-instance">
    <soap:Body>
        <ns1:runProcessResponse xmlns:ns1="http://3e.pl/
ADInterface">
            <RunProcessResponse IsError="false" xmlns="http://3e.pl/
ADInterface">
                <Summary>Created=3, Errors=0 - 21843ms</Summary>
                <LogInfo/>
            </RunProcessResponse>
        </ns1:runProcessResponse>
    </soap:Body>
</soap:Envelope>
```

There's more...

Another generic API, `setDocAction`, which is very specific to the document processes of ADempiere, can be used to manage the document actions on any kind of ADempiere-maintained document, for example, material receipt, purchase order, vendor invoice, and so on. A document action can initiate a workflow, send an e-mail, post accounting facts to the books, trigger material movement, and so on. In the service request (SOAP message), you will have to specify the `recordID` and the `docAction` (for example, `prepareIt`, `completeIt`, `voidIt`, and so on). The rest of the request is straightforward.

For brevity, the detailed discussion of the workflow and document actions is out of this book's scope. However, you may refer to the following URLs to read more about them:

 ▶ `http://www.adempiere.com/index.php/Workflow`
 ▶ `http://www.adempiere.com/index.php/HOWTO_Process_Documents`

> There is an important note about the `setDocAction` service on the ADempiere site (`http://www.adempiere.com/index.php/Adempiere_Web_Services`) that is worth mentioning so that we are better informed:
>
> This Web service completes documents not via workflow, so it jumps over any approval step considered in a document workflow. To complete documents using workflow, it's better to use the runProcess Web service.

5

VirtueMart Integration

In this chapter, we will cover:

- ▶ Setting up the environment
- ▶ Bridging with Apache ActiveMQ
- ▶ Building ActiveMQ adapters for ADempiere and VirtueMart
- ▶ Publishing products and prices to the VirtueMart
- ▶ Linking VirtueMart checkout with ADempiere

Introduction

In the previous chapter, we learnt about providing the Web Services interface to an application where ADempiere is a downstream application for it. In an enterprise environment, there is another possibility, as well. There, ADempiere will be an upstream application interfacing with other downstream applications. In this chapter, I have taken a popular shopping cart application—Joomla! VirtueMart—as the downstream application. Even though ADempiere has its own web store, for different practical reasons, an enterprise may opt for other shopping cart applications, such as VirtueMart, Magento, osCommerce, and so on and would like to have ADempiere use them as their web store rather than the built-in one.

Coming to the integration mechanism, there are various options available. One of the major points that we'll have to keep in perspective while choosing an integration technology/ framework is that VirtueMart is implemented in PHP whereas ADempiere is in Java. We are running our ADempiere instance on PostgreSQL whereas VirtueMart uses MySQL. Keeping this in perspective, we have options like message queues, Web Services, Service Bus, and so on. The mechanism you select would be based on the criteria on which we base our overall architecture. For demonstration purposes, in this chapter, we will be using JMS for integration and we will be using Apache's ActiveMQ implementation of it. It addresses our main design constraint—PHP and Java-based application integration—by providing the support for Stomp protocol and Stomp-JMS mapping.

In order to follow this chapter, we would have to first set up the development environment. For this purpose, we would need the following additional software to be downloaded and installed on the system:

▸ Apache ActiveMQ 5.3.2

▸ XAMPP: 1.7 or above

▸ Joomla!: 1.5

▸ VirtueMart 1.1.4

▸ Zend Eclipse: latest

Let us see how to set up each one of them and make use of them to provide the required integration between ADempiere and VirtueMart.

Setting up the environment

In this recipe, we will go through the steps required to set up the complete environment to get started with the integration between ADempiere and VirtueMart. It includes setting up the following:

▸ Apache ActiveMQ

▸ Joomla!

▸ VirtueMart

I have excluded the installation of Joomla!, as you may find documents on the Joomla! website or Google it. You may find one such document, which I had written sometime ago for one of the technology magazines, on http://wtcindia.wordpress.com/2009/11/27/build-your-professional-website-using-joomla-part-1/. Say, we refer to the Joomla! installation folder by <JOOMLA_HOME>.

Also excluded is the installation and Zend Eclipse setup.

How to do it...

1. Install and verify Apache ActiveMQ. First of all, we are going to install and verify Apache ActiveMQ. The following are the steps to download, install, and verify the installation:

    ❏ Download Windows Distribution of ActiveMQ from `http://activemq.apache.org/activemq-532-release.html`

    ❏ Follow the installation instructions outlined in the following URL http://activemq.apache.org/getting-started.html. Say, we have installed the ActiveMQ in `C:\Program Files\Apache Software Foundation\apache-activemq-5.3.2`. We'll refer to this path as `ACTIVEMQ_PATH` throughout the chapter

    ❏ Go to the `<ACTIVEMQ_PATH>\bin` folder and run `activemq.bat`. If everything goes well, you shall see the following output, indicating your ActiveMQ installation is ready for use

```
C:\WINDOWS\system32\cmd.exe
ACTIVEMQ_BASE: C:\Program Files\Apache Software Foundation\apache-activemq-5.3.2
\bin\..
Loading message broker from: xbean:activemq.xml
 INFO | Using Persistence Adapter: org.apache.activemq.store.kahadb.KahaDBPersis
tenceAdapter@c2b2f6
 INFO | Replayed 1 operations from the journal in 0.015 seconds.
 INFO | ActiveMQ 5.3.2 JMS Message Broker (localhost) is starting
 INFO | For help or more information please see: http://activemq.apache.org/
 INFO | Listening for connections at: tcp://ajitkumar:61616
 INFO | Connector openwire Started
 INFO | ActiveMQ JMS Message Broker (localhost, ID:ajitkumar-1531-1278835355187-
0:0) started
 INFO | Logging to org.slf4j.impl.JCLLoggerAdapter(org.mortbay.log) via org.mort
bay.log.Slf4jLog
 INFO | jetty-6.1.9
 INFO | ActiveMQ WebConsole initialized.
 INFO | Initializing Spring FrameworkServlet 'dispatcher'
 INFO | ActiveMQ Console at http://0.0.0.0:8161/admin
 INFO | Initializing Spring root WebApplicationContext
 INFO | Successfully connected to tcp://localhost:61616
 INFO | Camel Console at http://0.0.0.0:8161/camel
 INFO | ActiveMQ Web Demos at http://0.0.0.0:8161/demo
 INFO | RESTful file access application at http://0.0.0.0:8161/fileserver
 INFO | Started SelectChannelConnector@0.0.0.0:8161
```

2. Install and verify VirtueMart

    ❏ Download Joomla! from `http://www.joomla.org/download.html` and install it. You may grab a copy of the Quick Start Guide (`http://help.joomla.org/ghop/feb2008/task048/joomla_15_quickstart.pdf`) to understand the installation steps and how to get started with Joomla!. For simplicity, I will assume that you are using XAMPP to install and run Joomla!

- ❑ Download VirtueMart from `http://virtuemart.net/downloads` and install it inside Joomla!

- ❑ Enable the VirtueMart components and modules of your choice in Joomla!

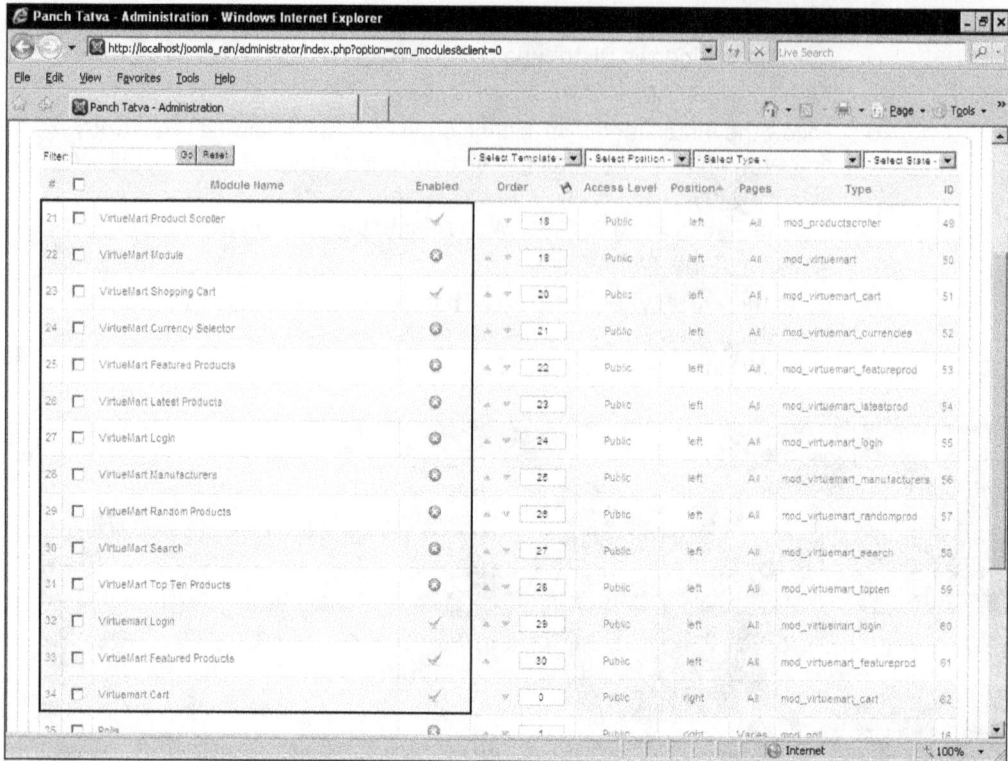

The following screenshot shows how the website will look with the **VirtueMart** modules enabled:

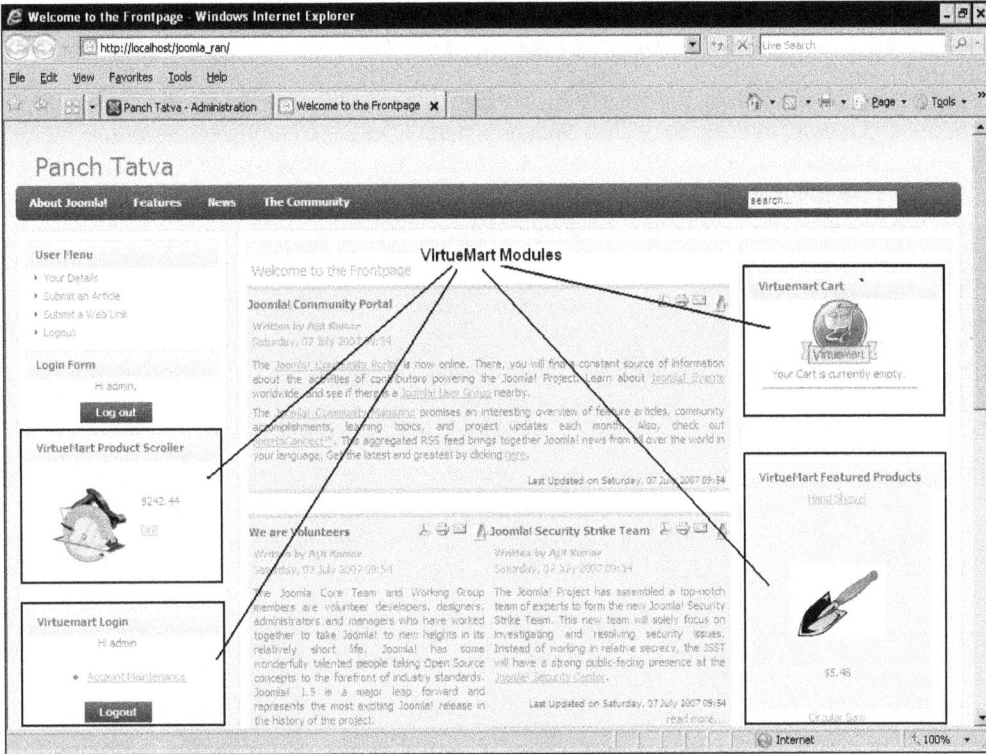

How it works...

XAMPP comes bundled with Web Server, PHP, MySQL, and phpMyAdmin, that are required for running Joomla! and VirtueMart, which runs as a Joomla! component. Once Joomla! is installed and set up on the system, using Joomla's administrator panel, we can install the VirtueMart component so that it becomes accessible through the Joomla! website.

ActiveMQ provides the communication channel between ADempiere (which is in Java) and Joomla! VirtueMart (which is in PHP). After it is installed, in the subsequent recipe, we will see how to configure it and have messages flowing between the two applications.

Bridging with Apache ActiveMQ

This recipe will talk about configuring Apache ActiveMQ to enable the integration between ADempiere and VirtueMart. We will also see how we can test and verify the setup to make sure that it works.

As discussed earlier, in order to allow a Java-based application to communicate with a PHP-based application, ActiveMQ provides Stomp. Stomp support is not configured in ActiveMQ, by default. In this recipe, we will look at the steps involved in configuring the support in ActiveMQ and verifying the configuration.

Getting ready

Make sure that you have got ActiveMQ and VirtueMart installed.

How to do it...

1. **Stomp setup**: Since ADempiere is implemented in Java and VirtueMart is in PHP, we will have to add the Stomp support in our ActiveMQ instance. To do this:

   - Stop ActiveMQ
   - Add the following lines in `<ACTIVEMQ_PATH>\conf\activemq.xml` as a child of the `transportConnectors` node

   `<transportConnector name="stomp" uri="stomp://0.0.0.0:61613"/>`

   - Make sure that the port `61613` is free on your system where you are running ActiveMQ. Also, add this in after the `openwire` transport connector node detail in the `activemq.xml` file
   - Run ActiveMQ. You shall see the following lines appearing on the console, indicating Stomp has been set up correctly and ready for use

   INFO | Listening for connections at: stomp://localhost:61613

   INFO | Connector stomp Started

   You may read more about Stomp on `http://activemq.apache.org/stomp.html`.

2. **Verify our environment**: Now we are going to write a small program in Java and another one in PHP to see if our environment is ready for further development.

   ❑ Start Eclipse and create a new Java project

   ❑ Create a class, `SimpleStompProducer.java`, and add the following code to it:

   ```
   import org.apache.activemq.transport.stomp.
   StompConnection;

   public class SimpleStompProducer {

     public static void main(String args[]) throws Exception
   {

       StompConnection connection = new StompConnection();
       connection.open("localhost", 61613);

       connection.connect("", "");
       connection.send("/queue/test", "Hello World!! from "
   + SimpleStompProducer.class.getName());
       connection.disconnect();
     }

   }
   ```

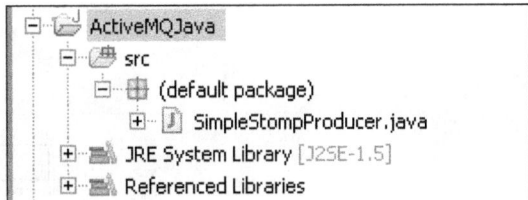

```
ActiveMQJava
  src
    (default package)
      SimpleStompProducer.java
  JRE System Library [J2SE-1.5]
  Referenced Libraries
```

❑ Add `<ACTIVEMQ_PATH>\activemq-all-5.3.2.jar` to the project libraries

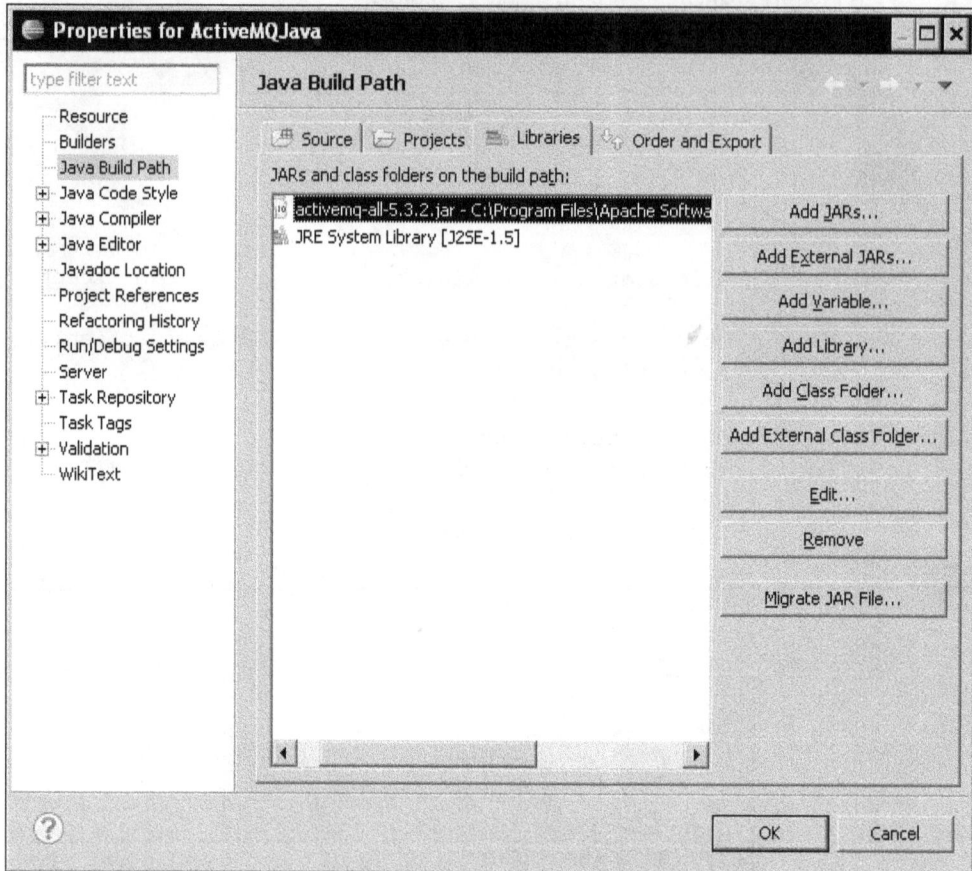

❑ Create a new PHP project and add a new PHP file, `SimpleStomConsumer.php`, and add the following code to it:

```php
<?php
require_once("Stomp.php");
$con = new Stomp("tcp://localhost:61613");
$con->connect();
$con->subscribe("/queue/test");
$msg = $con->readFrame();// do what you want with the
message
if ( $msg != null) {
  echo "Received message with body '$msg->body'\n";
  $con->ack($msg);
} else {
```

```
    echo "Failed to receive a message\n";
}
$con->disconnect();
?>
```

❏ Download the PHP Stomp client library from `http://stomp.fusesource.org/download.html`

❏ Extract the selected files to your PHP project folder

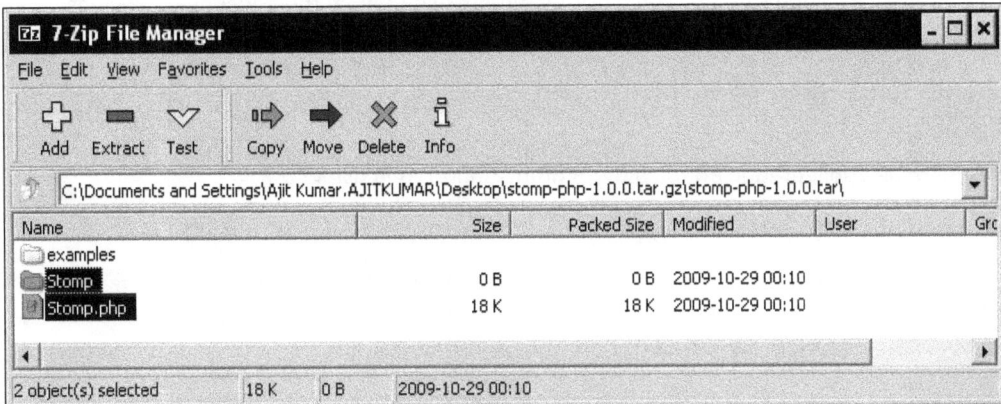

❏ Refresh your PHP project. You shall see the extracted files in the project

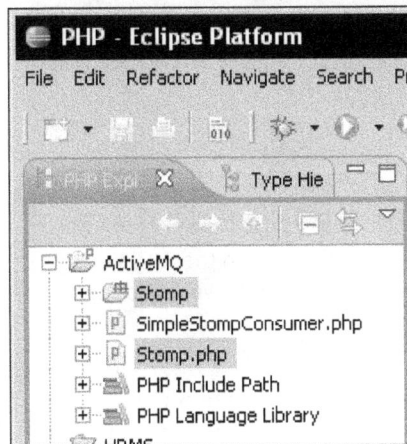

❏ Right-click on `SimpleStompProducer.java` and click on **Run As | Java Application**. The producer code will put a message on the queue and exit

        ❑   Now, right-click on `SimpleStompConsumer.php` and click on **Run As | PHP Script**. The consumer will read the message from the queue and display it. You shall see the following message in the **Eclipse Debug Output** view:

X-Powered-By: PHP/5.2.8

Set-Cookie: ZendDebuggerCookie=127.0.0.1%3A10000%3A0||004|7774 2D65|1003; path=/_

Received message with body 'Hello World!! from SimpleStompProducer'

With this, we are done with our configuration and verification. In the subsequent recipes, we will make use of this setup to integrate VirtueMart with ADempiere.

How it works...

The following configuration enables the Stomp support in ActiveMQ:

```
<transportConnector name="stomp" uri="stomp://localhost:61613"/>
```

It uses the port 61613 (which is different from the JMS port) for Stomp-based communications. In order to send and receive messages using the Stomp protocol, the Java application must use the Stomp APIs provided by ActiveMQ.

Building ActiveMQ adapters for ADempiere and VirtueMart

The recipe describes how to build the adapters for ADempiere and VirtueMart, which are the foundations for the integration.

How to do it...

1.   Add `<ACTIVEMQ_PATH>\activemq-all-5.3.2.jar` to the project libraries.

2.   Create a `MQClient.java` file, say, in the `<ADEMPIERE_SVN>\base\src\compiere\util` folder, with the following code:

```
package org.compiere.util;

import org.apache.activemq.transport.stomp.Stomp;
import org.apache.activemq.transport.stomp.StompConnection;
import org.apache.activemq.transport.stomp.StompFrame;
import org.apache.activemq.transport.stomp.Stomp.Headers.
Subscribe;

public class MQClient {
```

```
    public static void sendMessage(String messageText) {
      try {
        StompConnection connection = new StompConnection();
        connection.open("localhost", 61613);
        connection.connect("", "");
        connection.send("/queue/test", messageText);
        connection.disconnect();
      } catch (Exception e) {
        e.printStackTrace();
      }
    }
    public static String receiveMessage() {
      try {
        StompConnection connection = new StompConnection();
        connection.open("localhost", 61613);

        connection.connect("", "");
        connection.subscribe("/queue/test", Subscribe.AckModeValues.
CLIENT);
        StompFrame connect = connection.receive();
        if (!connect.getAction().equals(Stomp.Responses.CONNECTED))
{
            throw new Exception ("Not connected");
        }

        StompFrame message = connection.receive();
        connection.disconnect();

        return message.getBody();
      } catch (Exception e) {
        e.printStackTrace();
        return null;
      }
    }
  }
```

3. Add the following method to the PO.java class of ADempiere:

```
public String getXmlRepresentation() {
  try {
    if (null != this) {
      StringWriter res = new StringWriter();

      XMLStreamWriter writer = XMLOutputFactory.newInstance()
            .createXMLStreamWriter(res);
```

```
                      writer.writeStartDocument();
                      writer.writeStartElement("entityDetail");

                      writer.writeStartElement("type");
                          writer.writeCharacters(this.get_TableName().
        substring(this.get_TableName().indexOf('_') + 1).toUpperCase());
                      writer.writeEndElement();

                      writer.writeStartElement("detail");

                      Field[] fields = this.getClass().getFields();
                      for (int i = 0; i < fields.length; i++) {
                        Field tmp = fields[i];
                        if (tmp.getName().contains("COLUMNNAME")) {
                            writer.writeStartElement(tmp.getName().substring(11));
                            writer.writeCharacters(this.get_DisplayValue(tmp.
        getName().substring(11), true));
                          writer.writeEndElement();
                        }
                      }

                      writer.writeEndElement(); // detail
                      writer.writeEndElement(); // entityDetail
                      writer.writeEndDocument();
                      return res.toString();
                    } else {
                      return null;
                    }
                } catch (Exception ex) {
                    ex.printStackTrace();
                    return null;
                }
            }
```

4. Add the Stomp library to the `<JOOMLA_HOME>\administrator\components\com_virtuemart\classes` folder.

5. Create a `MQClient.php` file, say, in `<JOOMLA_HOME>\administrator\components\com_virtuemart\classes` folder, with the following code:

```php
<?php
require_once("Stomp.php");
function receiveMessage(){
  $con = new Stomp("tcp://localhost:61613");
  $con->connect();
  $con->subscribe("/queue/test");
```

```php
$msg = $con->readFrame();// do what you want with the message
if ( $msg != null) {
  echo "Received message with body '$msg->body'\n";
  $con->ack($msg);
} else {
  echo "Failed to receive a message\n";
}
$con->disconnect();
return $msg != null ? $msg->body : null;
}

function sendMessage($msg) {
  $con = new Stomp("tcp://localhost:61613");
  $con->connect();
  $con->send("/queue/test", $msg);
  echo "Sent message with body 'test'\n";
  $con->disconnect();
}
?>
```

6. Add the following function to a utility class or say `MQClient.php`, which will return the XML formatted string when a name-value map is passed. This function expects an entry in the map by name type:

```php
function getXmlRepresentation($fields){
  $dom = new DOMDocument;
    $dom->formatOutput = true;

    $entityDetail = $dom->createElement( "entityDetail" );
    $root = $dom->appendChild($entityDetail);

    $sxe = simplexml_import_dom( $dom );

    $sxe->addChild("type", $fields['type']);
    $detail = $sxe->addChild("detail");
    foreach($fields as $key => $value) {
      if ($key != 'type'){
        $detail->addChild($key, $value);
      }
    }

    return $sxe->asXML();
}
```

How it works...

In the beginning of this chapter, we discussed that there are numerous ways to integrate ADempiere and VirtueMart. Based on the problem's context, we choose the best, if not better, approach to solve it. The following are the important points that drove our overall integration:

- ▸ ADempiere will produce the messages in its data model format
- ▸ ADempiere will consume the messages from VirtueMart in its data model format
- ▸ VirtueMart will consume the messages from ADempiere and convert it into its data model
- ▸ VirtueMart will convert its data model to ADempiere and produce the messages for ADempiere
- ▸ All the messages will be represented in an XML format

In order to have the integration working, we are producing/consuming the data in the following XML format:

```
<?xml version="1.0" ?>
<entityDetail>
<type>entity name</type>
<detail>
    .....
    entity specific detail
    .....
</detail>
</entityDetail>
```

Following is an example XML for product:

```
<?xml version="1.0" ?>
<entityDetail>
<type>PRODUCT</type>
<detail>
<C_TaxCategory_ID>Standard</C_TaxCategory_ID>
<C_UOM_ID>Each</C_UOM_ID>
<Description>Alarm Clock</Description>
<DescriptionURL>./.</DescriptionURL>
<Discontinued>false</Discontinued>
<DiscontinuedBy>./.</DiscontinuedBy>
....................
....................
....................
<Volume>0</Volume>
```

```
<Weight>0</Weight>
</detail>
</entityDetail>
```

The following diagram depicts the typical components involved in the two-way integration of ADempiere with VirtueMart:

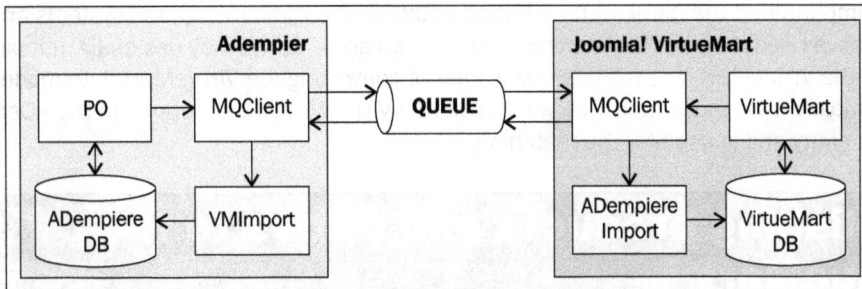

- ► **PO**: This is the Persistence Object class of ADempiere, which it uses to store/load a Java object into the relational database. This class will be modified to produce the XML from ADempiere models in a generic way. This will be useful when information needs to be published from ADempiere to VirtueMart. For example, supplier details, product, prices, and so on.

- ► **MQClient**: This is a utility class implementing the send/receive methods using the ActiveMQ APIs. It will be a Java class for ADempiere and PHP class for Joomla!.

- ► **VMImport**: VMImport's job is to import data in the ADempiere database from incoming VirtueMart messages. This job is useful in importing the information published by VirtueMart. For example, purchase order after the completion of the checkout process.

- ► **AdempiereImport**: ADempiereImport's job is to import data in the VirtueMart database from incoming ADempiere messages. This job is useful for importing the information published by ADempiere. For example, supplier details, products, prices, and so on. This can be a scheduled job.

- ► **VirtueMart**: This is the VirtueMart application, which will produce the XML data and send it as part of a message. This will be useful when information needs to be published from VirtueMart to ADempiere. For example, the purchase order.

There's more...

Another interesting integration challenge is the flow of different IDs (identifiers) helping us to map an entity in one system to the entity in another system. For example, an order ID will help us link an order detail in VirtueMart with an order detail in ADempiere. Again, there are different approaches to address this. In this recipe, I have demonstrated the integration with the assumption that the name of the entities would be the same in both the systems and hence I have used them for the matching rather than any IDs. You may use an ID mapping table on the VirtueMart side (as it is taking care of converting the VirtueMart data model into the ADempiere data model and vice versa) where a VirtueMart ID is mapped to the ADempiere ID for an entity and is used for the matching.

Publishing products and prices to the VirtueMart

This recipe talks about the real integration between ADempiere and VirtueMart, where data created in ADempiere is being published to the VirtueMart, and we are going to see what steps are involved in making sure that when a new product is created in ADempiere (and indicated that it shall be available in web store) it is also immediately available in the VirtueMart web store.

Before, we get started with the steps, it is worth looking at the VirtueMart entities and how they may affect the overall integration design. The following are the VirtueMart entities applicable in the context of integration:

- ▶ Store
- ▶ Products
- ▶ Shopper
- ▶ Orders
- ▶ Vendor
- ▶ Tax
- ▶ Shipping
- ▶ Manufacturer

The following is a typical process involved in setting up the entities in VirtueMart:

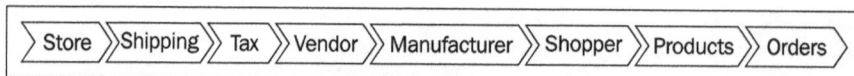

> Store ⟩⟩ Shipping ⟩⟩ Tax ⟩⟩ Vendor ⟩⟩ Manufacturer ⟩⟩ Shopper ⟩⟩ Products ⟩⟩ Orders ⟩

So, even before we think of setting up a product and its prices, we need to make sure that the other entities are set up correctly and they are in-sync with the corresponding entities in ADempiere. Some of the entities are optional and we'll ignore them for the brevity of this recipe. I am going to drop the Shipping, Tax, Vendor, and Shopper. After you complete this recipe and gain the basic understanding of the entities and their integration across the two systems, then you may include these optional items, as well, in your overall integration scope. So, our scope includes the following entities:

- Store
- Products
- Orders
- Manufacturer

Now, let us look at the mappings of the previous VirtueMart entities with that of ADempiere.

VirtueMart entity	Corresponding ADempiere entity
Store	Client + Organization
Products	Products
Order	Sales Order
Manufacturer	Business Partner

Here, I would like to make an assumption about the Store and Manufacturer entity setup. I would assume that these entities have been set up in ADempiere as well as VirtueMart manually, to focus really on the publishing of the products and their prices from ADempiere to VirtueMart. In the following recipe, we'll see how the purchase order, created in VirtueMart, flows into ADempiere.

How to do it...

1. Add the following line of code in the `afterSave` method of the `MProduct.java` class of ADempiere, before the `return` statement:

```
if (this.isSelfService()) {
    String productXML = this.getXmlRepresentation();
    MQClient.sendMessage(productXML);
}
```

The preceding code will send the product details in an XML format if the product has been marked for service (shall be available on the web store). The following XML will be produced:

```
<?xml version="1.0" ?>
<entityDetail>
<type>PRODUCT</type>
<detail>
<Classification>./.</Classification>
<C_RevenueRecognition_ID>./.</C_RevenueRecognition_ID>
```

```
<C_SubscriptionType_ID>./.</C_SubscriptionType_ID>
<C_TaxCategory_ID>Standard</C_TaxCategory_ID>
<C_UOM_ID>Each</C_UOM_ID>
<Description>Alarm Clock</Description>
<DescriptionURL>./.</DescriptionURL>
<Discontinued>false</Discontinued>
<DiscontinuedBy>./.</DiscontinuedBy>
<DocumentNote>./.</DocumentNote>
<Group1>./.</Group1>
<Group2>./.</Group2>
<GuaranteeDays>0</GuaranteeDays>
<GuaranteeDaysMin>0</GuaranteeDaysMin>
<Help>Alarm Clock</Help>
<ImageURL>./.</ImageURL>
<IsBOM>false</IsBOM>
<IsDropShip>false</IsDropShip>
<IsExcludeAutoDelivery>false</IsExcludeAutoDelivery>
<IsInvoicePrintDetails>false</IsInvoicePrintDetails>
<IsPickListPrintDetails>false</IsPickListPrintDetails>
<IsPurchased>true</IsPurchased>
<IsSelfService>true</IsSelfService>
<IsSold>true</IsSold>
<IsStocked>true</IsStocked>
<IsSummary>false</IsSummary>
<IsVerified>false</IsVerified>
<IsWebStoreFeatured>true</IsWebStoreFeatured>
<M_AttributeSet_ID>./.</M_AttributeSet_ID>
<M_AttributeSetInstance_ID>0</M_AttributeSetInstance_ID>
<M_FreightCategory_ID>./.</M_FreightCategory_ID>
<M_Locator_ID>101</M_Locator_ID>
<M_Product_Category_ID>Standard</M_Product_Category_ID>
<M_Product_ID>1000021</M_Product_ID>
<Name>AlarmClock</Name>
<Processing>false</Processing>
<ProductType>Item</ProductType>
<R_MailText_ID>./.</R_MailText_ID>
<SalesRep_ID>GardenUser</SalesRep_ID>
<S_ExpenseType_ID>./.</S_ExpenseType_ID>
<ShelfDepth>0</ShelfDepth>
<ShelfHeight>0</ShelfHeight>
<ShelfWidth>0</ShelfWidth>
<SKU>./.</SKU>
<S_Resource_ID>./.</S_Resource_ID>
<UnitsPerPallet>0</UnitsPerPallet>
```

```
<UPC>./.</UPC>
<Value>AlarmClock</Value>
<VersionNo>2.0</VersionNo>
<Volume>0</Volume>
<Weight>0</Weight>
</detail>
</entityDetail>
```

2. Add the following `afterSave` method in the `MBPartnerProduct.java` class of ADempiere:

```java
protected boolean afterSave(boolean newRecord, boolean success) {
  if (!success)
    return success;

  if (newRecord) {

    try {
      String xmlData = this.getXmlRepresentation();
      MQClient.sendMessage(xmlData);
    } catch (Exception e) {
      e.printStackTrace();
    }
  }
  return success;
}
```

3. Add the following `afterSave` method in the `MProductPrice.java` class of ADempiere:

```java
protected boolean afterSave(boolean newRecord, boolean success) {
  if (!success)
    return success;

  if (newRecord) {

    try {
      String xmlData = this.getXmlRepresentation();
      MQClient.sendMessage(xmlData);
    } catch (Exception e) {
      e.printStackTrace();
    }
  }
  return success;
}
```

4. Create the `AdempiereImport.php` file and code the following steps:

- Receive a message from the queue and get the XML message body

```
$msg = receiveMessage();
$entityDetail = new SimpleXMLElement($msg);
```

▸ If the `type` on the incoming message is `PRODUCT`:

- Create an `INSERT` SQL statement by fetching the relevant field values from the XML

```
if ($entityDetail->type == "PRODUCT") {
    $detail = $entityDetail->detail;
    $q = "INSERT INTO " . $dbprefix . "vm_product
(product_sku, product_s_desc, product_desc, product_
name....) VALUES ('". $detail->SKU . "','" . $detail-
>Description . "','" . $detail->Help . "','" . $detail-
>Name.....);
```

- Insert the record in the `jos_vm_product` table of VirtueMart (based on your Joomla installation you may have a different prefix than `jos`)

▸ If the `type` is `MBPARTNER_PRODUCT`:

- Update the `vendor_id` column of the product entry (created in the previous step) in the `jos_vm_product` table by reading the business partner ID from the incoming XML data

▸ If the `type` is `PRODUCTPRICE`:

- Create an `INSERT` SQL statement by fetching the relevant field values from the XML

- Insert the record in the `jos_vm_product_price` table of VirtueMart

After successful completion of the preceding steps, we shall be able to see the products listed in VirtueMart's products list, as shown in the following screenshot:

Linking VirtueMart checkout with ADempiere

In this recipe, we will understand what it takes to enable the flow of information from VirtueMart to ADempiere when a user checks out one or more products on the VirtueMart web store.

How to do it...

1. In the `ps_checkout.php` file, the `add()` function creates all the records related to the order after the order confirmation. Modify the `add()` function to include the following steps after all the records have been created in different tables:

   - Create a `$fields` array with all the relevant fields related to order, order history, order payment, and order items. Make sure that `type` is explicitly set on the array to, say, PURCHASEORDER

   - Create XML data from the `$fields` array by using the `getXmlRepresentation()` function of the `MQClient.php` file

- Send the XML data on the queue by calling the `sendMessage()` function of the `MQClient.php` file

2. Create the `VMImport.java` file and code the following steps:

- Receive a message from the queue and get the XML message body

- If the `type` on the incoming message is PURCHASEORDER:

- Create an `INSERT` SQL statement by fetching the relevant field values from the XML and insert the record in the `c_order` table of ADempiere that contains the purchase order details

- Create an `INSERT` SQL statement by fetching the relevant field values from the XML and insert the record in the `c_orderline` table that contains the line items (product and their quantities assigned) of a purchase order

The `c_order` and `c_orderline` tables contain a good amount of columns that require elaboration to be able to map the incoming VirtueMart data. You may refer to `http://www.adempiere.com/index.php/ManPageW_PurchaseOrder` for all the details related to the ADempiere purchase order and the two tables.

Alternatively, you may also use the Web Services to import data into ADempiere

- Update the inventory counts for the products that are part of the order

With this, the order placed in the VirtueMart is now available in ADempiere as well.

How it works...

When the order is confirmed in Stage 4 of VirtueMart's checkout process (Step 2, if shipping and payment is disabled), after the order is completely saved in VirtueMart and before informing the user of the successful creation of the order, it created a message with the type—PURCHASEORDER, and placed it on the queue. `VMImport.java` picks up the message, and based on the type and the entity details, creates a PO in ADempiere.

6
JasperReports with ADempiere

In this chapter, we will cover:

- ▶ Setting up the environment
- ▶ Developing a new report using view
- ▶ Developing a report without view
- ▶ Using the context in a report
- ▶ Developing a report with sub-report
- ▶ Using a custom report for printing

Reports are an integral and critical enterprise need. It is instrumental in providing the information for the strategy formulation and decision making. It would probably be a disaster for any enterprise application to be considered complete without the support provided for reports. Additionally, even if a system provides reports, architecturally and also from a CIO perspective, what is important is not how many off-the-shelf reports are provided by the product/solution, rather to what extent the product/solution is equipped with the necessary support to create new reports quickly to address the changing business need. From this perspective, while ADempiere provides numerous ready-made reports, it provides strong support to customize an existing report and build new reports quickly. While for the report layout design, it uses JasperReports capability, its `ReportEngine` provides a solid foundation for the extensibility and customization.

In order to follow this chapter, we will have to first set up the development environment. For this purpose, we will need the following additional software to be downloaded and installed on the system:

▸ **iReport**: This chapter is based on version 3.7.6
▸ PostgreSQL 8.x JDBC driver

Let us see how to set up each one of them and make use of them to provide the required integration between ADempiere and JasperReports.

Setting up the environment

This recipe is all about setting up the ground for us so that we can design and develop the new JasperReports and use them inside ADempiere.

Getting ready

Make a note of the following points, which we defined and set up in *Chapter 1, Preparing the Ground*, as we will be referring to them throughout this chapter:

▸ ADEMPIERE_HOME
▸ ADEMPIERE_SVN
▸ ADempiere database connection detail

How to do it...

1. Download the PostgreSQL JDBC driver from http://jdbc.postgresql.org/download.html.
2. Install iReport.
3. Run iReport and go to the **Tools | Options** menu, as shown in the following screenshot:

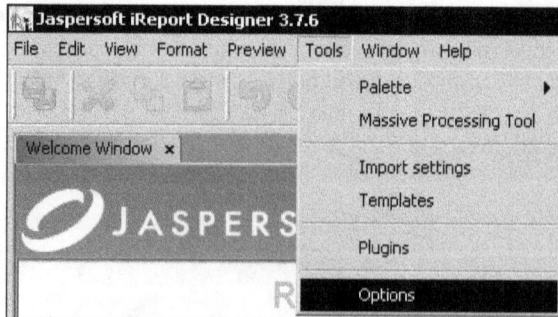

4. Go to the **iReport | Classpath** tab.

5. Click on the **Add JAR** button and browse through the filesystem and select the PostrgeSQL JDBC driver, as shown in the following screenshot:

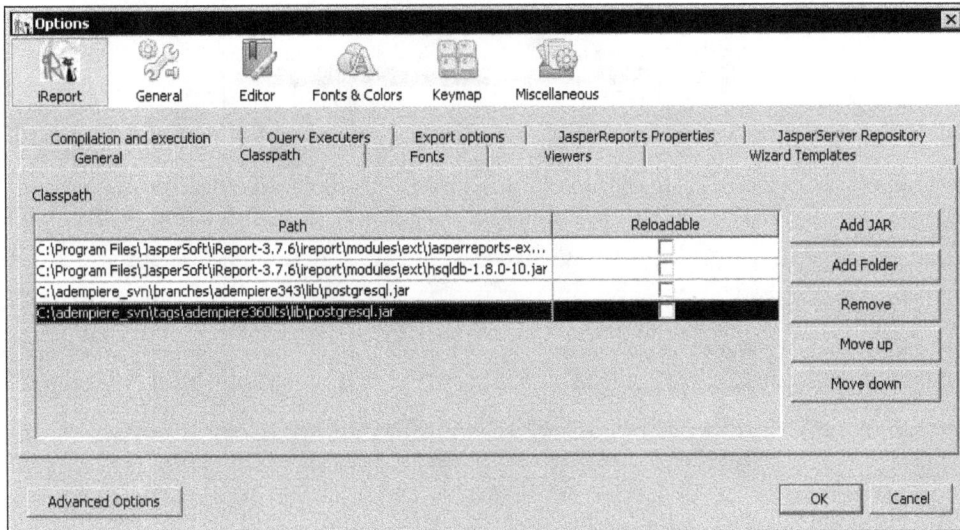

6. Click on the **OK** button to add the JAR into the iReport classpath.

7. Click on the [icon] icon on the toolbar or click on **Step 1** in **Quick Start**, as shown in the next screenshot. With this, we will set up the data source for the reports.

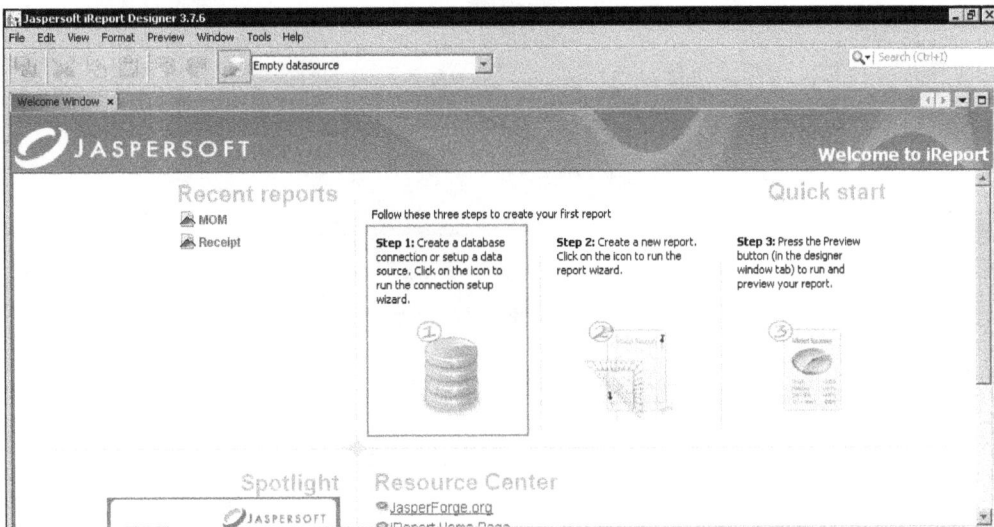

8. Select **Database JDBC Connection** and click on the **Next** button.

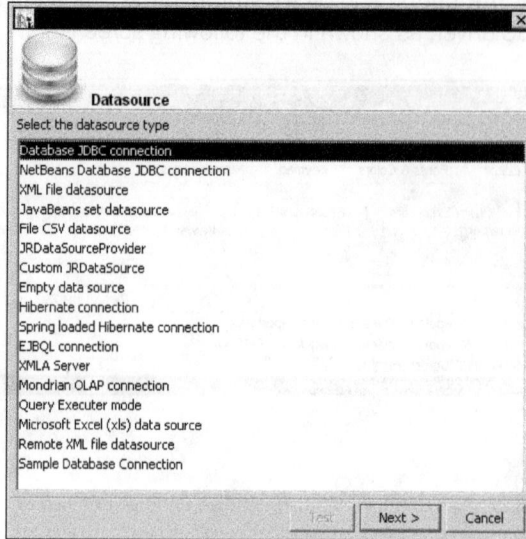

9. Enter the following database details:

▶ **Name**: `Adempiere360`

▶ **JDBC Driver**: `org.postgresql.Driver`

▶ **JDBC URL**: `jdbc:postgresql://localhost:5432/adempiere360`

▶ **User Name**: `adempiere`

▶ **Password**: `adempiere`

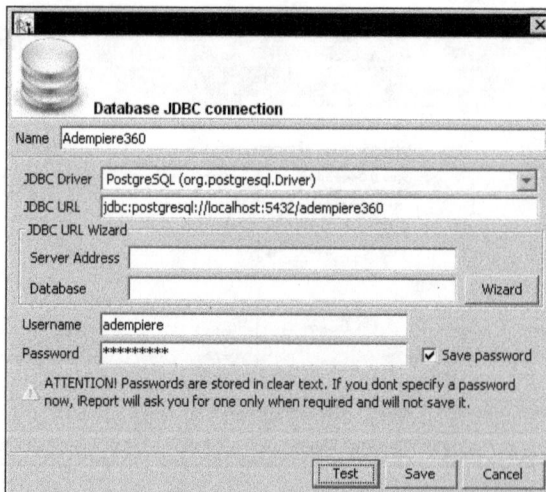

10. Click on the **Test** button to verify if the settings are correct.

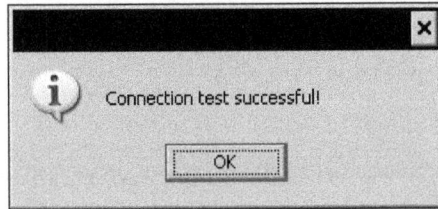

Connection test successful!

OK

11. Check the **Default** checkbox for the `Adempiere360` entry, as we'll be using it for all our reports design in this chapter.

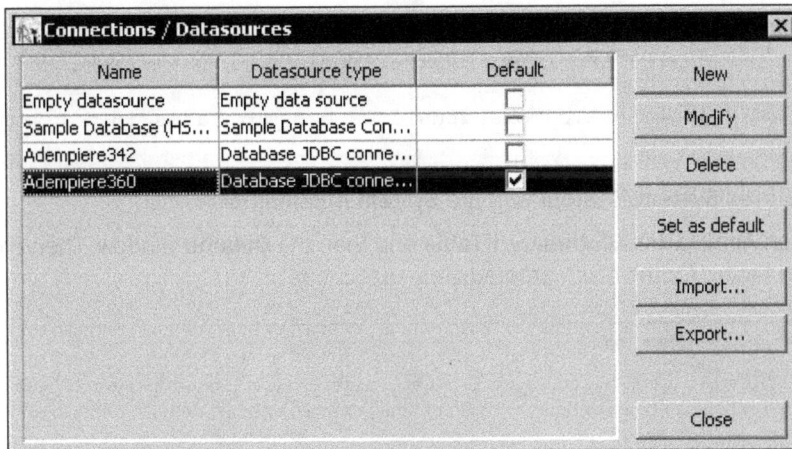

Name	Datasource type	Default
Empty datasource	Empty data source	☐
Sample Database (HS...	Sample Database Con...	☐
Adempiere342	Database JDBC conne...	☐
Adempiere360	Database JDBC conne...	☑

New
Modify
Delete
Set as default
Import...
Export...
Close

12. Click on the **Close** button to complete the data source setup.

Developing a new report using view

This recipe describes the steps involved in creating a database view and using it to generate reports.

Getting ready

Complete *Chapter 2, ADempiere Customization – Part I* and *Chapter 3, ADempiere Customization – Part II* and keep the final MOM-related schema handy, as we will be using it in this recipe.

How to do it...

1. Create the following database view:

```
CREATE VIEW adempiere.c_mom_v AS
SELECT
    a.*,
    b.item_nbr,b.discussion_desc,b.ad_user_id AS actioned_by,b.c_
momstatus_id,
    c.ad_user_id AS participant,c.company,
    d.name AS status
FROM
    adempiere.c_mom a
    JOIN adempiere.c_mom_discussionline b ON a.c_mom_id=b.c_mom_id
    JOIN adempiere.c_mom_participantsline c ON c.c_mom_id=b.c_mom_
id
    JOIN adempiere.c_momstatus d ON b.c_momstatus_id=d.c_momstatus_
id;
```

2. Log in as **System/System** with the **System Administrator** role.

3. Open **Application Dictionary | Table** and then the **Column** window. Then create a new record for the newly created view—c_mom_v.

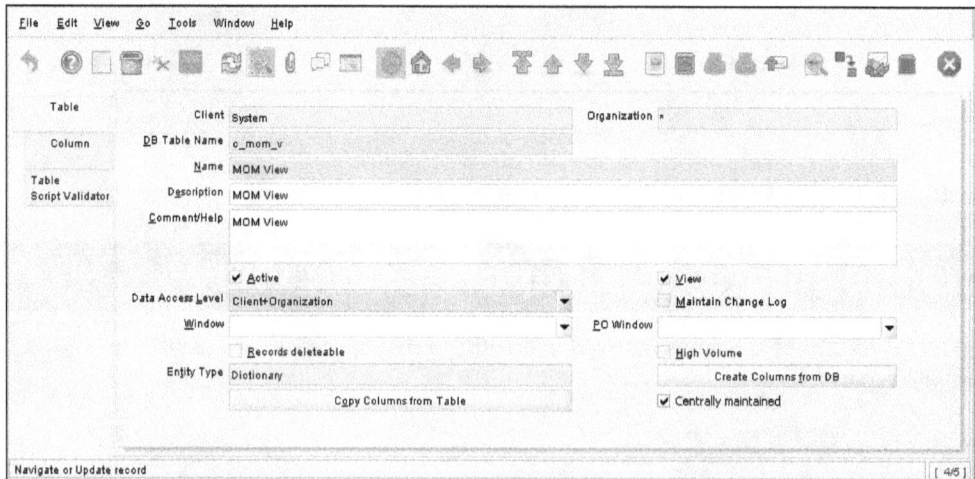

4. Click on the **Create Columns from DB** button and verify that all the columns are created on the **Column** tab.

5. Open the **Application Dictionary | Report View** window and create a new record using the newly created table in the dictionary—MOM View.

6. Open the **Application Dictionary** | **Report & Process** window, create a report entry, and select MOM View, which was created in the previous step, as the **Report View**.

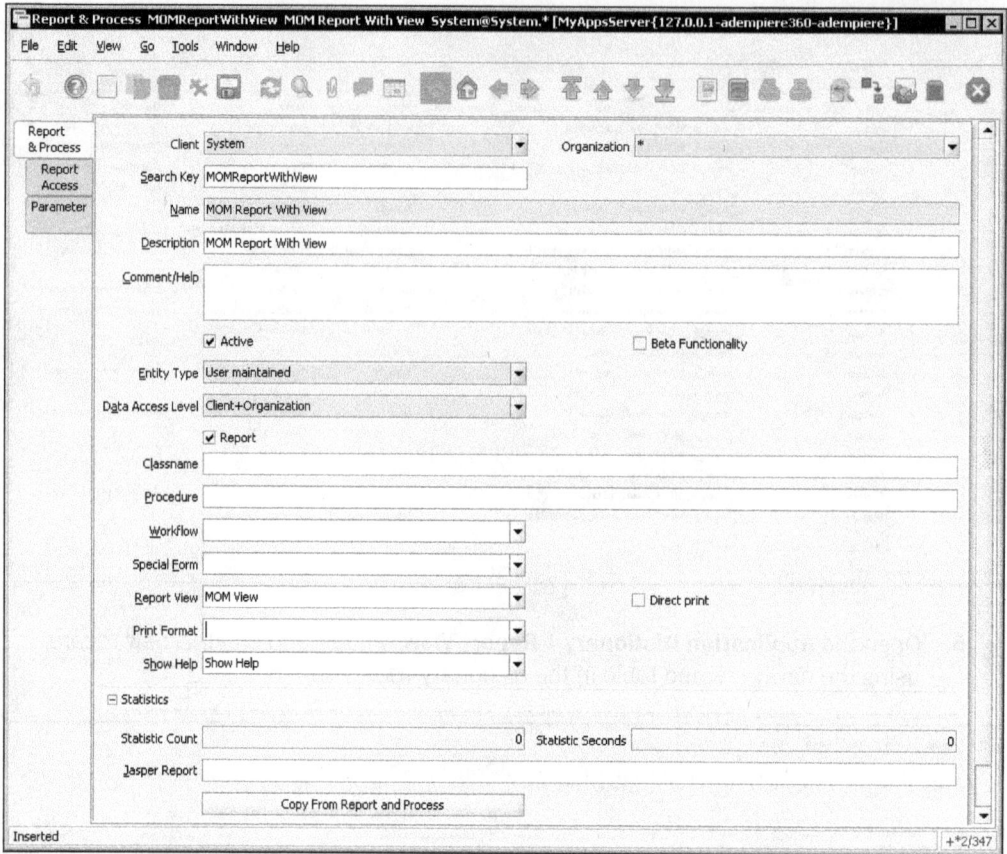

7. Verify the access to the report on the **Report Access** tab. By default, all the roles are given access. You may review the list and grant access to the roles according to your need.

8. Now, go to the **Menu** | **System Admin** | **General Rules** | **System Rules** | **Menu** window and create a new menu node for the report under the MOM menu.

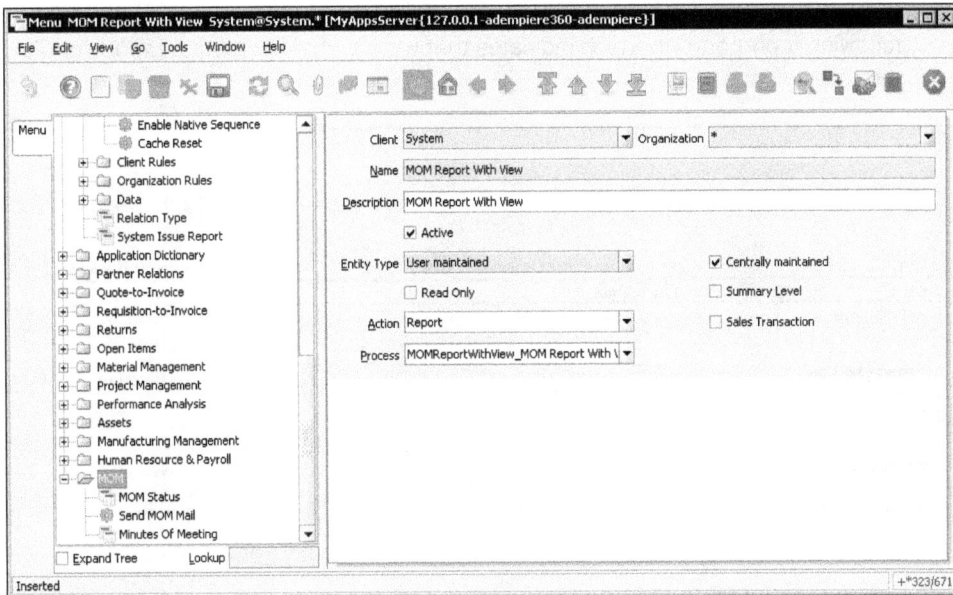

9. Log out and log in as **GardenAdmin/GardenAdmin** with the **GardenWorld Admin** role. You shall see the newly added menu item under the MOM menu.

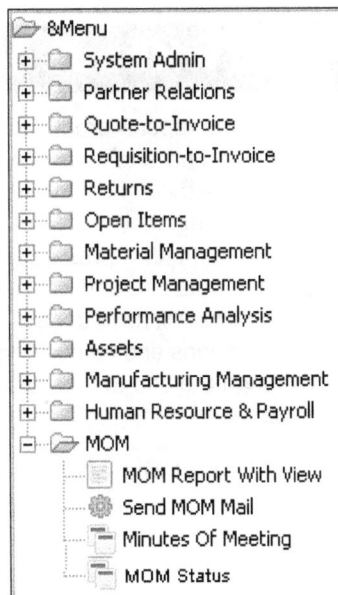

10. Click on the `MOM Report With View` menu and run the report. You shall get the following report output, which indicates that we are able to create a report from a database view.

Developing a report without a view

In the previous recipe, we saw how to get the reports produced from a database view. It is a great way to get reports out quickly as all you have to do is provide a view that can feed data to ADempiere's report engine. It can also use the in-built layout to present the data in a well formatted form. However, when we start talking about having a customized report layout, reading data from multiple data sets (for example, views, joined tables, and so on), applying conversions and calculations on top of the data set, and so on, the view-based approach starts to look very limiting. In these cases, we will have to have our own custom layouts dealing with data sets and applying conversions and calculation. Moreover, this is going to be the focus of this recipe. We'll go through the end-to-end steps required to design a custom report and use it in ADempiere to present our data.

For simplicity, I have taken a very basic data set where I will create a report that presents the basic MOM details in a very raw form.

Getting ready

Complete *Chapter 2* and *Chapter 3* and keep the final MOM-related schema handy, as we will be using it in this recipe.

How to do it...

1. Start iReport and create a New Document by name, say, MOM.

2. Click on the [icon] toolbar button on the Designer view of the report. It will bring up the **Report Query** window where we can add the SQL query for our new report.

3. On the **Report Query** tab, select SQL as the **Query Language** and enter your SQL query, which will fetch the data for your report. For example, I have entered the query that will return the MOM-related data from the c_mom table.

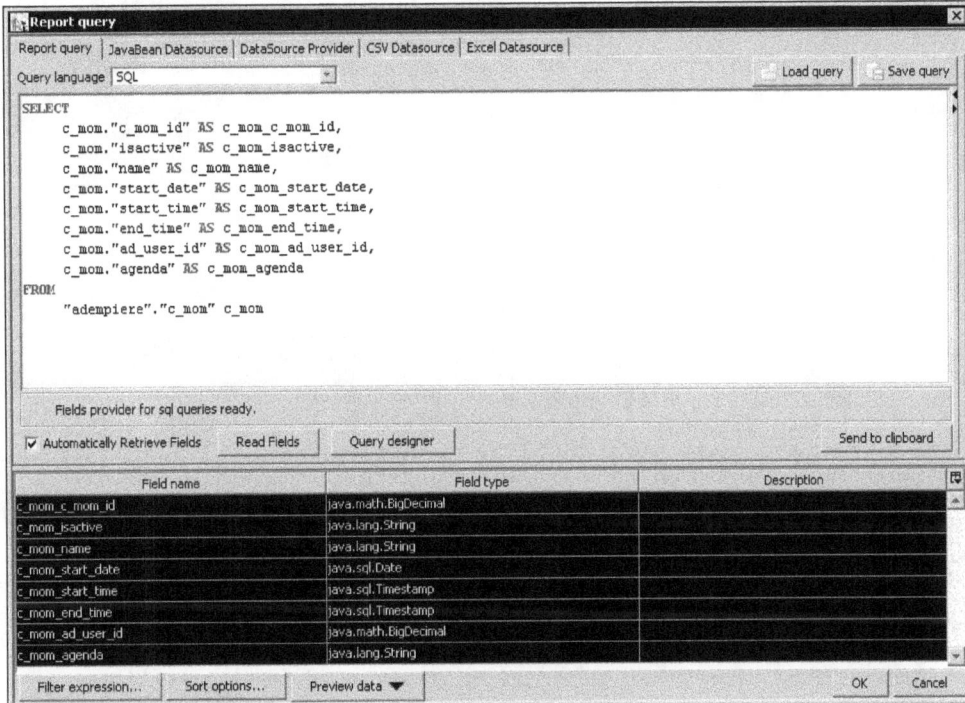

4. You may, optionally, use the **Query Designer** (clicking on the **Query Designer** button launches the designer) to construct your query graphically.

5. Click on the **Read Fields** button to get the fields generated based on the entered SQL query.

6. Click on the **OK** button, after the fields are generated.

7. Now, add the fields to the report and use the fields that we generated in the previous step, as shown in the following screenshot:

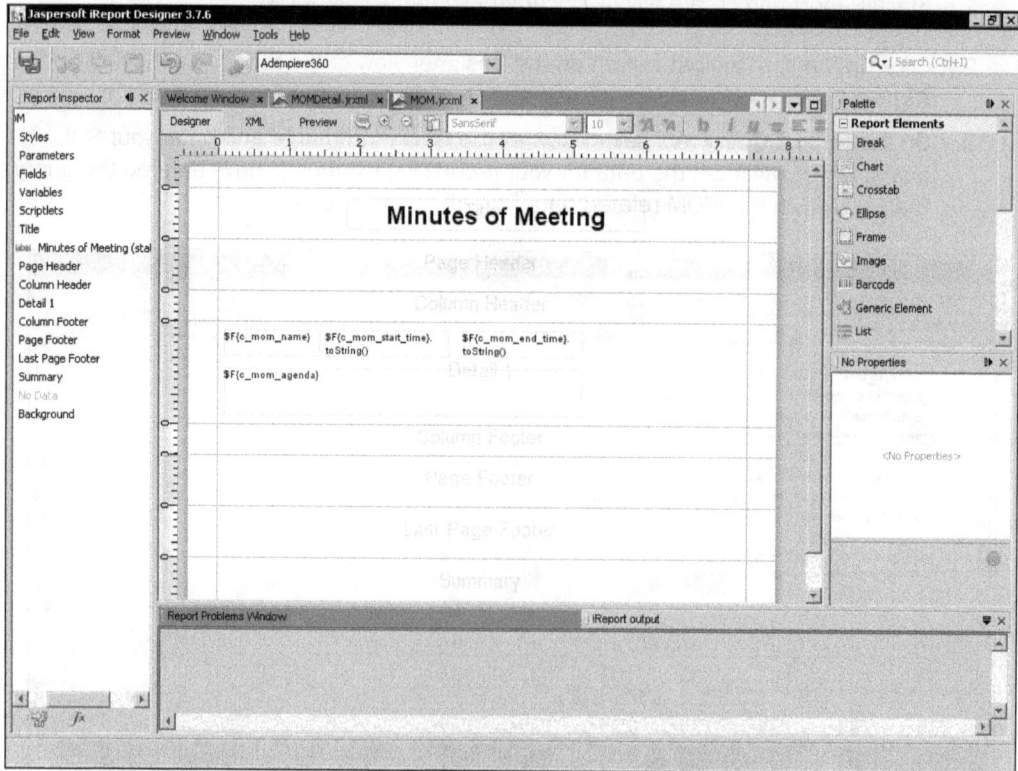

8. Save the report and copy the MOM.jrxml file to the <ADEMPIERE_HOME>\reports folder. ADEMPIERE_HOME should have been set to <ADEMPIERE_SVN>\tags\ adempiere360lts.

9. Open the **Application Dictionary | Report & Process** window, create a new report entry, and specify `MOM.jrxml` in the **Jasper Report** field. Also, mention `org.compiere.report.ResportStarter` as the **Classname**. This class takes care of running all the reports.

10. Add a new menu under MOM.

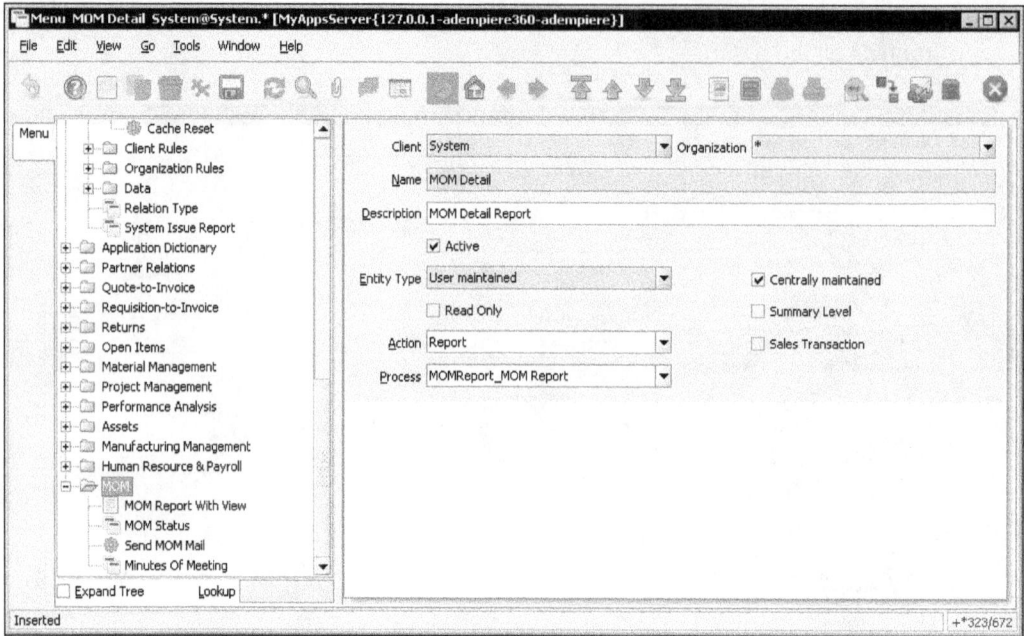

11. Log out and log back in as **GardenAdmin/GardenAdmin** with the **GardenWorld Admin** role.

12. Click on the MOM Report node under the MOM menu to run the report.

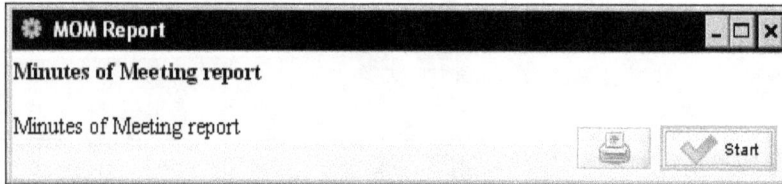

13. Click on the **Start** button to run the report. After a successful run, you shall see the report displayed in the viewer.

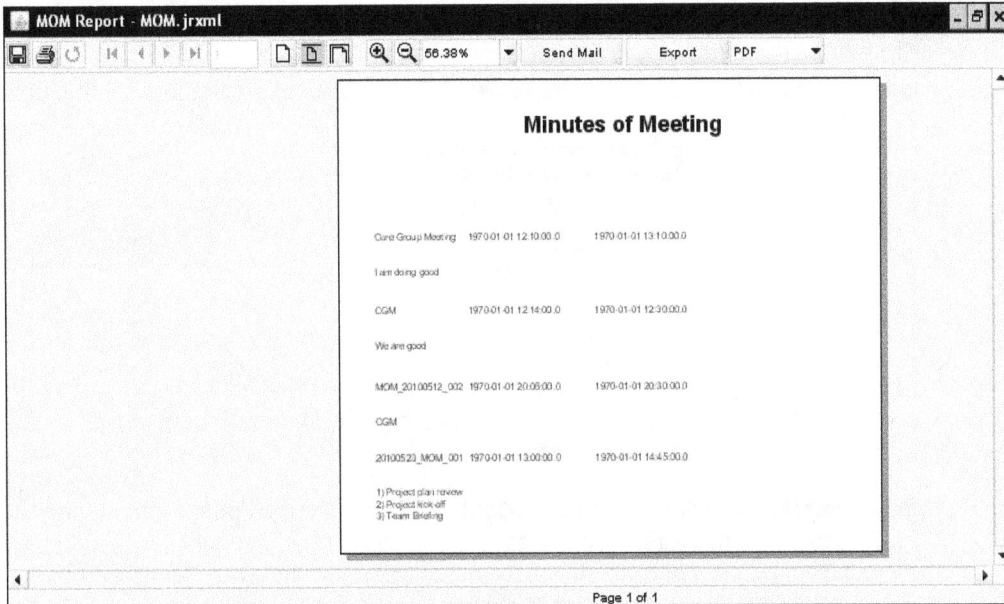

Using the context in a report

JasperReports allows us to add parameters to a report and their values can be passed by the caller. For example, we can create a parameter, `momId`, in the report and allow the user of the report to pass the value for it at runtime. Moreover, inside the report, different decisions (for example, filtering data) can be taken at runtime based on the parameter value. When we use a Jasper report inside ADempiere, it passes the following to every report:

- Current context
- Parameters specified in the report
- `RECORD_ID`: The primary key of the current record. This is passed as `Integer`
- `AP_INSTANCE_ID`: The ID of the current process. This is passed as `Integer`
- `CURRENT_LANG`: The current language. This is passed as `String`

While others are more straightforward, in this recipe, we will understand the steps it takes to use the ADempiere's current context in a Jasper report.

How to do it...

1. Launch ADempiere and click on the **Tools | Preferences** option on the top menu bar.

2. On the **Preferences** window, go to the **Context** tab to view the context information. It contains name-value pairs. Take a note of the context variable names that you intend to use in your report. For example, I have noted down #AD_Client_Name and #AD_Org_Name, which I will be using on the report.

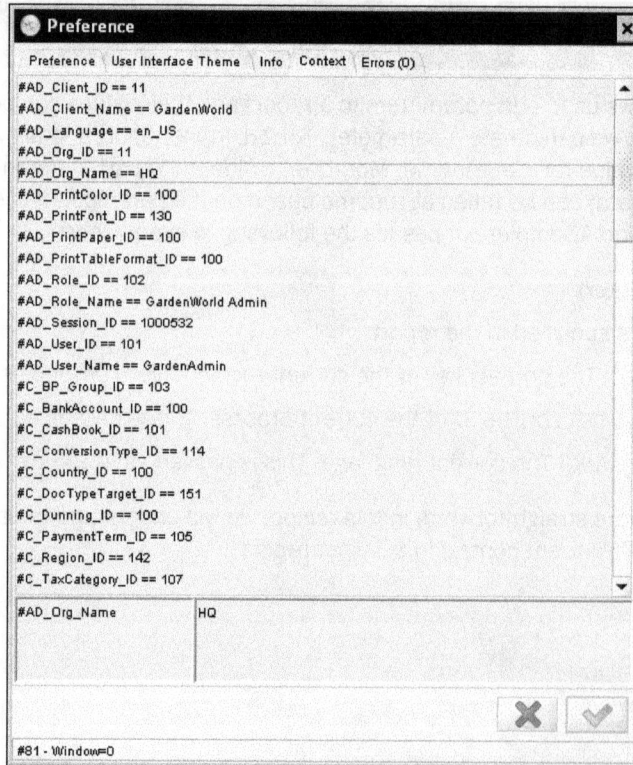

3. Go to iReport and open the `MOM.jrxml` file in it.

4. Right-click on the **Parameters** under **Report Inspector** and click on **Add Parameter** to add #AD_Org_Name as a report parameter.

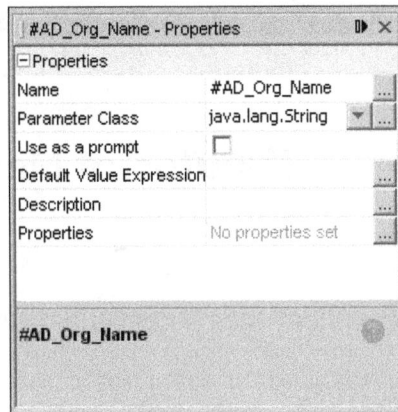

Similarly, add #AD_Client_Name as another parameter.

5. Add two fields on to the report and use the newly created parameters.

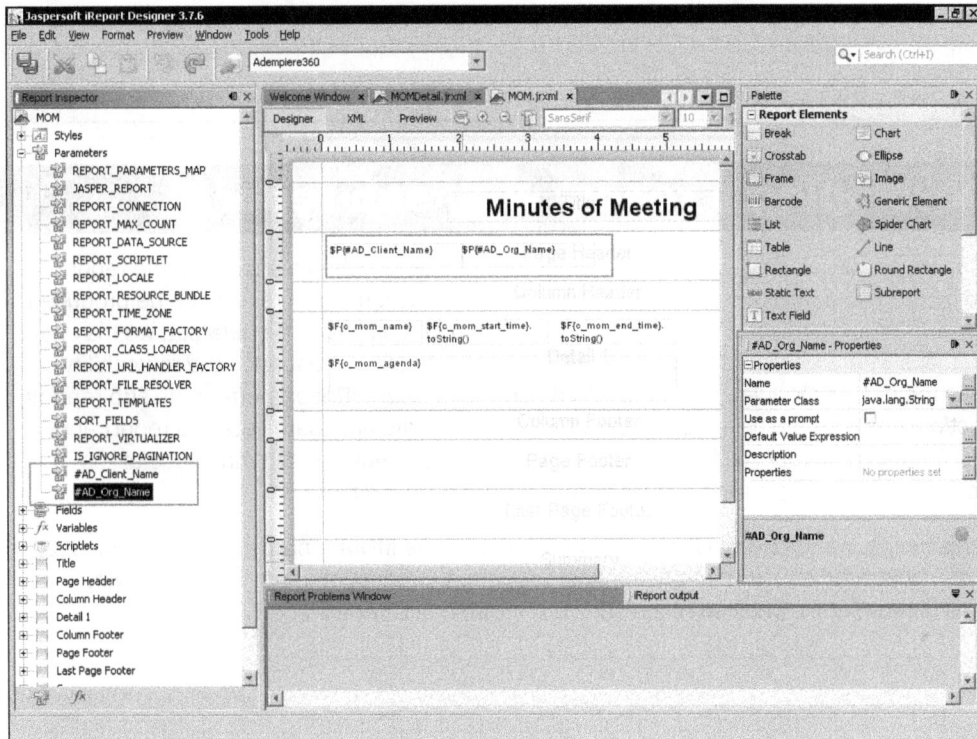

6. Save the report and place it in the `<ADEMPIERE_HOME>\reports` folder.

7. Click on the `MOM Report` node under the `MOM` menu and run the report. You will see the **Client** name and **Organization** name appearing on the report.

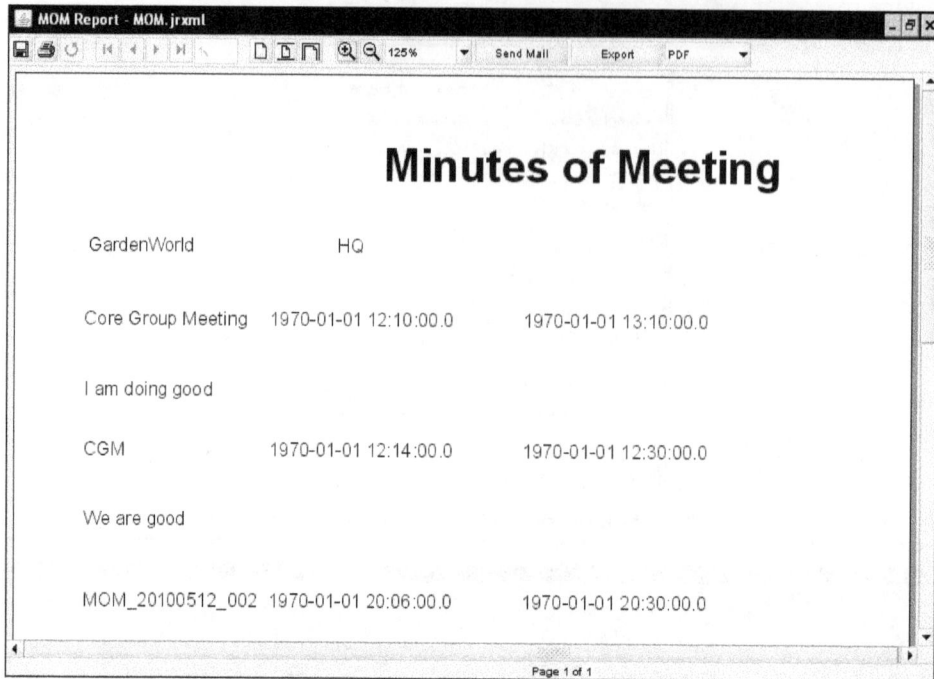

Developing a report with sub-report

When we are developing a report, there will be an instance when a section of the report can be produced with one data set whereas another section of the report can be produced with a different data set. Even if we combined them and still had one data set, we may have situations where we would have to keep them separate (say, to enhance the re-usability or make the design modular, and so on). In those cases, JasperReports offers the sub-reports functionality. With the use of sub-reports, one can use multiple data sets in a report and develop re-usable reports. In this section, we will discuss how we can make use of the sub-reports in our report and get them working inside ADempiere.

In this recipe, we will design the complete version of the MOM report so that the concept can be demonstrated and we can get our final formatted, production-ready report showing a MOM detail in the format, which we expressed our interest in *Chapter 2*.

How to do it...

1. Launch iReport.

2. Create a report, `MOMParticipants`, to display the participants list for a given MOM ID.

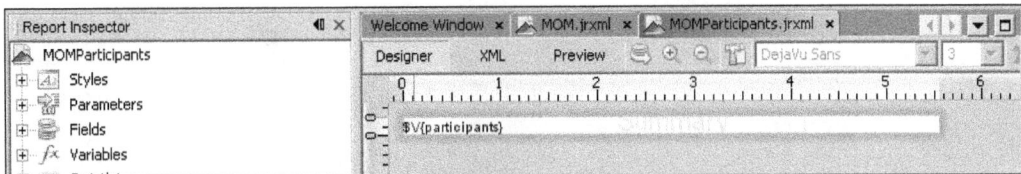

3. Create a report, `MOMDiscussionDetail`, to display the discussion line items for a given MOM ID.

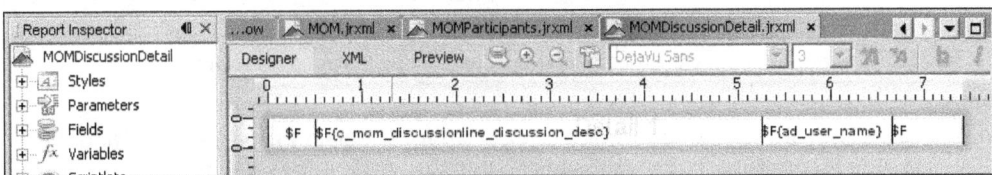

4. Create a report, say `MOMDetail`, to display the complete MOM detail, including the participants and discussion line items for a given MOM ID.

5. Add the `MOMParticipants` and the `MOMDiscussionDetail` reports as sub-reports on the `MOMDetail`.

6. Add the `momId` parameter to the main report, `MOMDetail`.

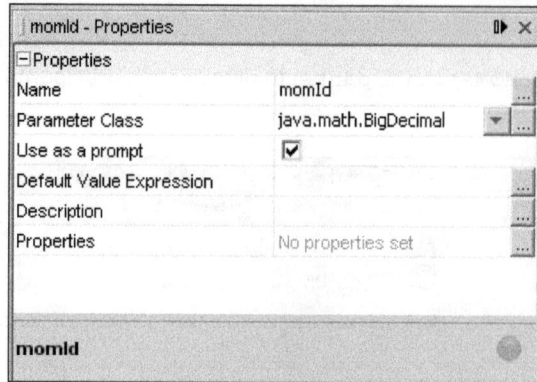

7. Add the `#AD_Client_Name` and the `#AD_Org_Name` as `String` type parameters to the main report.

8. Add the `momId` as a parameter to the `MOMParticipants` as well as to the `MOMDiscussionDetail` reports.

9. Right-click on the sub-report, `MOMParticipants`, select **Properties**, and add the `momId` as the sub-report parameter on the `Subreport(Other)` tab.

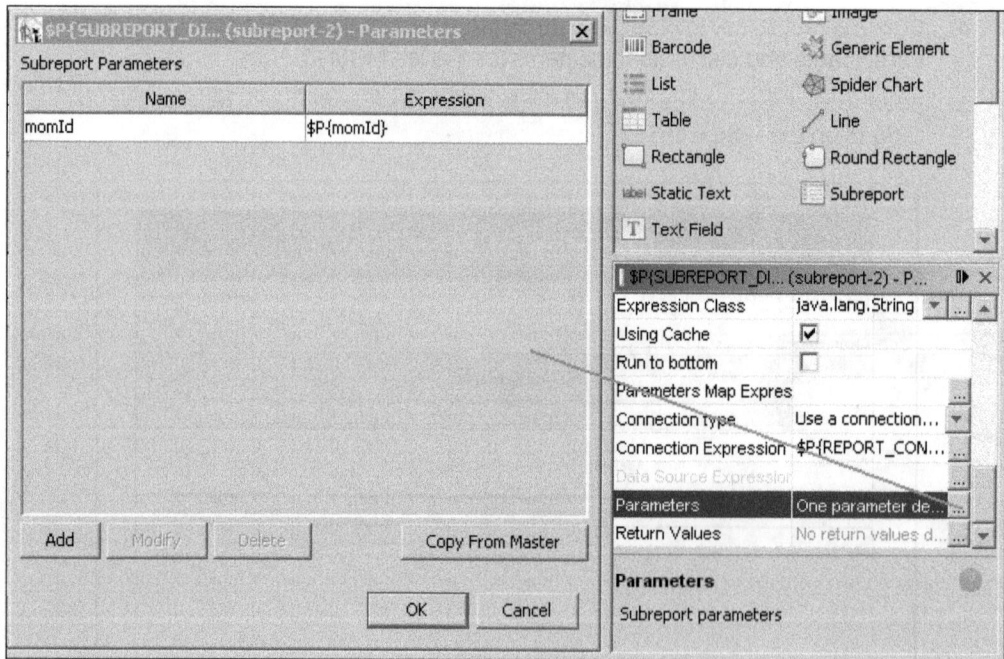

10. Similarly, add the `momId` as a sub-report parameter for the `MOMDiscussionDetail` as well.

11. Copy the `.jrxml` files of the main report and the two sub-reports to the `<ADEMPIERE_HOME>\reports`.

12. Create a new report on the **Application Dictionary | Report & Process** window and specify `MOMDetail.jrxml` as the **Jasper Report**.

13. Click on the **Parameter** tab to add a report parameter, momId, so that a MOM ID can be passed from the system to the reports.

14. Add a new menu node under the MOM menu by name, say, MoM Detail.

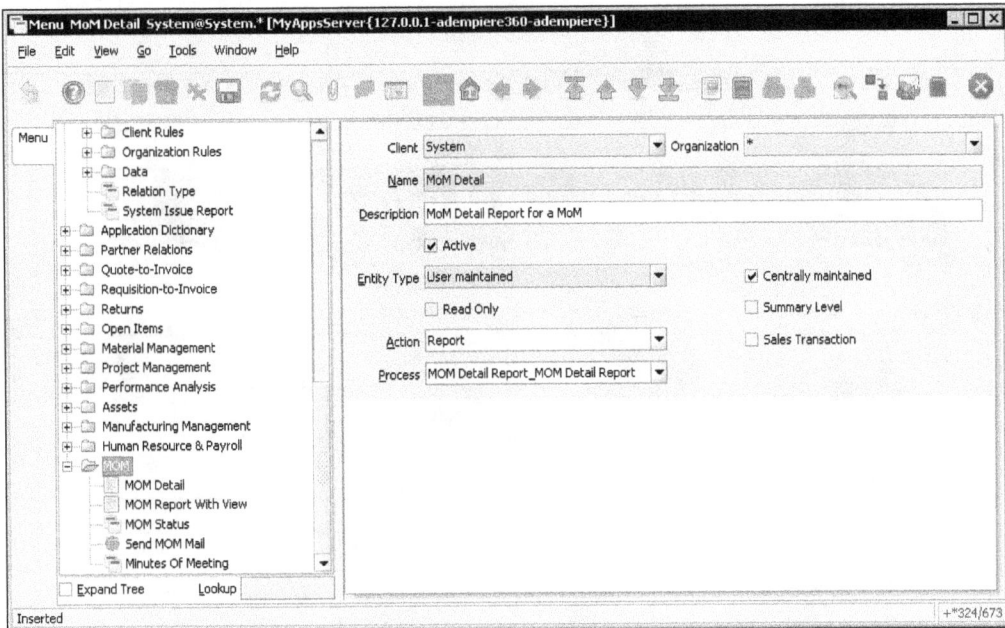

15. Log out and log in as **GardenAdmin/GardenAdmin** with the **GardenWorld Admin** role.

16. Click on the MoM Detail node under the MOM menu. This will prompt you to select the MOM of your choice.

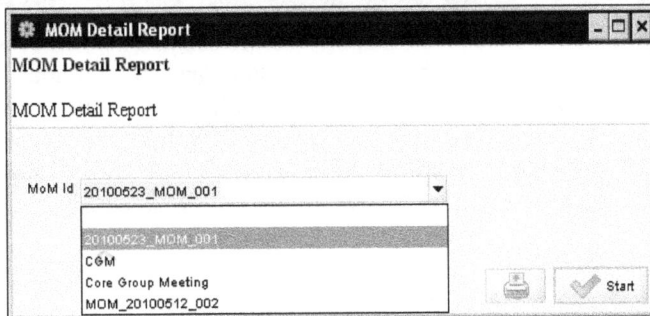

17. Select a MOM from the drop-down menu and click on the **Start** button to run the report. Upon success, you shall see the well formatted MOM details presented to you by the report.

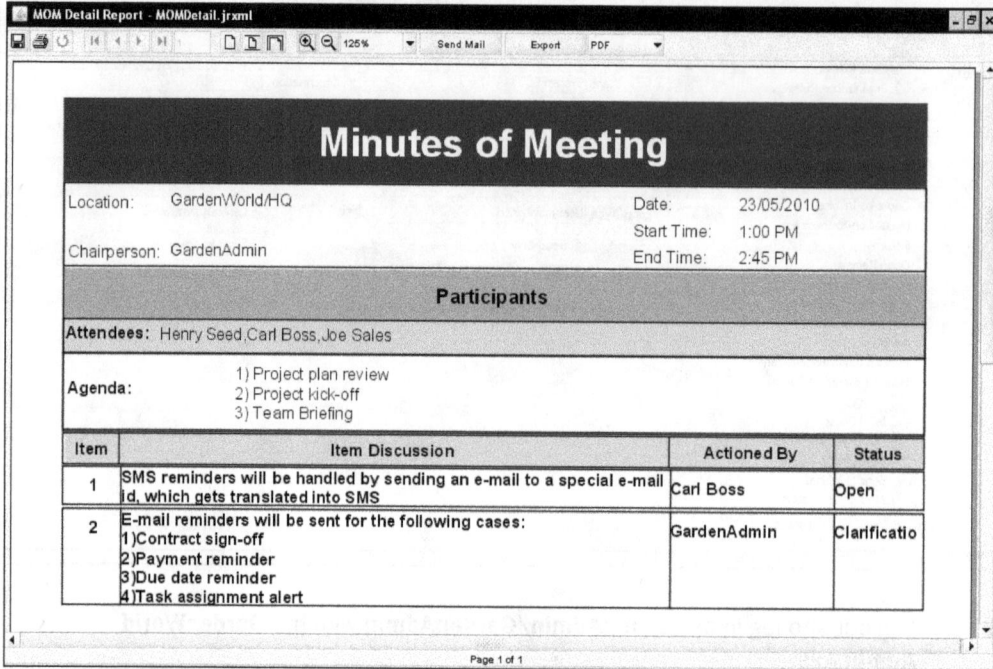

```
MOM Detail Report - MOMDetail.jrxml                                    _ 8 x
```

Minutes of Meeting

Location:	GardenWorld/HQ		Date:	23/05/2010
			Start Time:	1:00 PM
Chairperson:	GardenAdmin		End Time:	2:45 PM

Participants

Attendees: Henry Seed,Carl Boss,Joe Sales

Agenda:	1) Project plan review 2) Project kick-off 3) Team Briefing

Item	Item Discussion	Actioned By	Status
1	SMS reminders will be handled by sending an e-mail to a special e-mail id, which gets translated into SMS	Carl Boss	Open
2	E-mail reminders will be sent for the following cases: 1)Contract sign-off 2)Payment reminder 3)Due date reminder 4)Task assignment alert	GardenAdmin	Clarificatio

Page 1 of 1

Using custom report for printing

When a **Print Format** is not defined for a tab, or when we click on the **Print Preview** or **Print** toolbar button, by default, ADempiere picks up the default layout and renders the report using it. However, there may be situations where we may have to produce a nice looking document, (for example, a quotation) which can be shared with the customers or suppliers. To accomplish this, in this recipe, we will see what steps we have to go through to use the report that we designed in the previous recipe for the **Print Preview**.

How to do it...

1. Go to the **Menu | System Admin | General Rules | Printing | Print Format** window and create a new print format, c_mom_v_2 – MOM Print Format, with the Form checked and MOM Detail Report selected as the **Jasper Process**.

2. Open the `Minutes Of Meeting` window detail on the **Application Dictionary |
   Window**, **Tab**, and **Field** window.

3. Go to the **Tab** tab, elect `MOM Detail Report` in the **Process** drop-down, and save
   the record.

4. Log out and log in as **GardenAdmin/GardenAdmin** with the **GardenWorld Admin** role and click on the **Print Preview** toolbar button. This will prompt you to select the MOM.

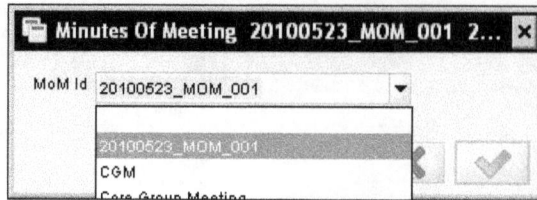

5. Select a MOM and click on the tick button. You shall see the output generated as per the designed report.

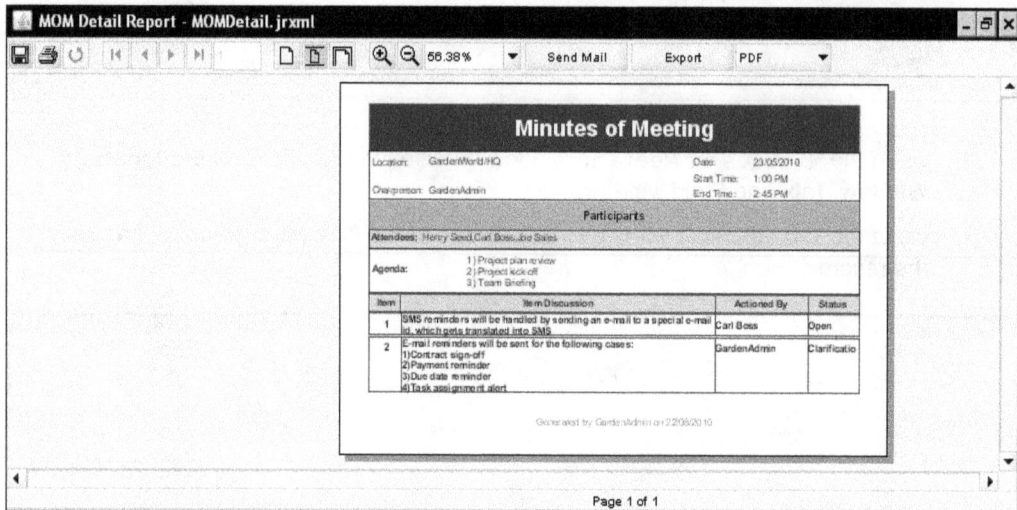

7
PayPal Integration

In this chapter, we will cover:

- ▸ Preparing the ground
- ▸ Working with PayPal APIs
- ▸ Making payment to a PayPal account
- ▸ Receiving payment from a PayPal account
- ▸ Integrating PayPal **Instant Payment Notification** (**IPN**)

Introduction

PayPal is one of the most popular and convenient ways to make a payment to someone who owns a PayPal account. PayPal provides the integration with the shopping cart (using their different checkout mechanisms) as well as the integration with the back-office (using their APIs and IPN). In *Chapter 6, VirtueMart Integration*, we looked at the integration of ADempiere with the Joomla! VirtueMart shopping cart, which provides integration with the PayPal checkout. In this chapter, we will focus on the back-office integration of PayPal with ADempiere to process payments online.

As we all may know that, in order to transact with PayPal, one needs to have a PayPal account. PayPal offers different types of accounts which serve a specific purpose like a buyer account or a seller account, and so on. While we are building the integration layer, we will have to go through many cycles of testing and verification. Doing this in the production environment is next to impossible to imagine, as it involves real accounts and real transactions (and hence charges). To overcome this stumbling block, we will be using PayPal's Sandbox infrastructure, which is intended for developer use. This infrastructure facilitates the building and the testing of the integration code and once it is tested, thoroughly, then all it requires is a couple of changes, like, replacing the sandbox access detail with the production access detail, and the same code will work in the production environment as well.

In this chapter, we will start with setting up the PayPal accounts and its API SDKs so that it can be used in the integration code and testing of the same. Later, we will build the PayPal payment processor in ADempiere to post payments directly to the PayPal accounts.

Preparing the ground

This recipe describes the things required to prepare ourselves for the PayPal integration including the PayPal account setup and preparing the environment for integration using the PayPal APIs.

Getting ready

Install soapUI, which we will be using to test PayPal APIs.

How to do it...

1. Sign up for a PayPal Sandbox account on `https://developer.paypal.com/`.

2. Log in using the newly created account detail.

3. Follow the instructions mentioned in the **PayPal Sandbox User Guide** (`https://developer.paypal.com/en_US/pdf/PP_Sandbox_UserGuide.pdf`) and create the **Preconfigured Test Accounts** with PayPal providing the following default types

   ▸ Buyer

   ▸ Seller

   ▸ Website Payments Pro

4. Select the **Website Payments Pro** account and click on **Enter Sandbox Test Site**. Enter the login and password details for the selected account, when prompted.

5. Go to the **Merchant Services** tab.

6. Click on the **Website Payments Pro** link on the left-hand side of the page.

7. Click on the **GET STARTED** button.

8. Click on the **View API Signature** link under the **Request API** credentials to create your own API username and password option and save the details for further use.

9. Now, select the seller account on the **Test Accounts** page and click on the **Enter Sandbox Test Site** button.

10. Click on **API Access** link under the **Account information** section on the **My Account | Profile** tab.

11. Click on the **View API Certificate** link in the **Option 2** section and make note of the credentials.

12. Set up a project in **soapUI** using PayPal's WSDL: `https://www.paypalobjects.com/wsdl/PayPalSvc.wsdl`.

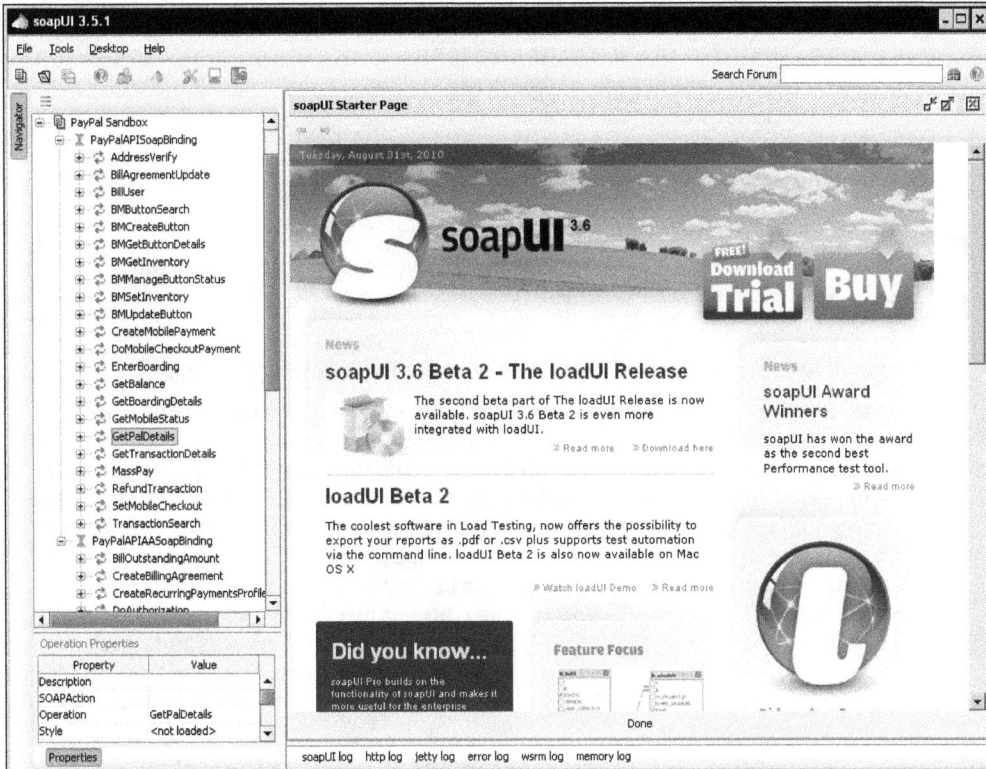

13. From the WSDL file, note down the version value. At the time of writing this chapter, the version was 64.

14. Run the following SOAP request in **soapUI**:

```
<soapenv:Envelope xmlns:soapenv="http://schemas.xmlsoap.org/soap/
envelope/" xmlns:urn="urn:ebay:api:PayPalAPI" xmlns:urn1="urn:ebay
:apis:eBLBaseComponents">
  <soapenv:Header>
      <urn:RequesterCredentials>
        <urn1:Credentials>
            <urn1:Username>ajitku_1282880134_biz_api1.gmail.com</
urn1:Username>
            <urn1:Password>1282880141</urn1:Password>
        <urn1:Signature>AXTsSMU3tr.t2l4lsPvBiX3G34zMAk2bw8FZpxAUBE
K2ymQHTMc-VZdS</urn1:Signature>
        </urn1:Credentials>
      </urn:RequesterCredentials>
```

```
    </soapenv:Header>
    <soapenv:Body>
        <urn:GetPalDetailsReq>
          <urn:GetPalDetailsRequest>
      <urn1:Version>64.0</urn1:Version>
          </urn:GetPalDetailsRequest>
        </urn:GetPalDetailsReq>
    </soapenv:Body>
</soapenv:Envelope>
```

[You must replace the Username, Password, and Signature with
   your account-specific details.]

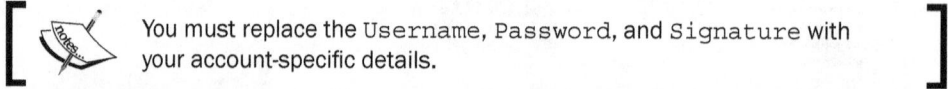

15. If everything was set up correctly, you would get the following response:

```
<SOAP-ENV:Envelope xmlns:SOAP-ENV="http://schemas.xmlsoap.org/
soap/envelope/" xmlns:SOAP-ENC="http://schemas.xmlsoap.org/soap/
encoding/" xmlns:xsi="http://www.w3.org/2001/XMLSchema-instance"
xmlns:xsd="http://www.w3.org/2001/XMLSchema" xmlns:xs="http://www.
w3.org/2001/XMLSchema" xmlns:cc="urn:ebay:apis:CoreComponentTyp
es" xmlns:ed="urn:ebay:apis:EnhancedDataTypes" xmlns:wsu="http://
schemas.xmlsoap.org/ws/2002/07/utility" xmlns:saml="urn:oasis:na
mes:tc:SAML:1.0:assertion" xmlns:ds="http://www.w3.org/2000/09/
xmldsig#" xmlns:wsse="http://schemas.xmlsoap.org/ws/2002/12/
secext" xmlns:ebl="urn:ebay:apis:eBLBaseComponents" xmlns:ns="urn:
ebay:api:PayPalAPI">
    <SOAP-ENV:Header>
        <Security xsi:type="wsse:SecurityType" xmlns="http://
schemas.xmlsoap.org/ws/2002/12/secext"/>
        <RequesterCredentials xsi:type="ebl:CustomSecurityHeaderTy
pe" xmlns="urn:ebay:api:PayPalAPI">
            <Credentials xsi:type="ebl:UserIdPasswordType" xmlns="urn
:ebay:apis:eBLBaseComponents">
                <Username xsi:type="xs:string"/>
                <Password xsi:type="xs:string"/>
                <Signature xsi:type="xs:string">AXTsSMU3tr.t214lsPvBiX
3G34zMAk2bw8FZpxAUBEK2ymQHTMc-VZdS</Signature>
                <Subject xsi:type="xs:string"/>
            </Credentials>
        </RequesterCredentials>
    </SOAP-ENV:Header>
    <SOAP-ENV:Body id="_0">
        <GetPalDetailsResponse xmlns="urn:ebay:api:PayPalAPI">
            <Timestamp xmlns="urn:ebay:apis:eBLBaseComponents">2010-
08-31T06:16:06Z</Timestamp>
            <Ack xmlns="urn:ebay:apis:eBLBaseComponents">Success</
```

```
Ack>
        <CorrelationID xmlns="urn:ebay:apis:eBLBaseComponents">d7
3baa14924be</CorrelationID>
        <Version xmlns="urn:ebay:apis:eBLBaseComponents">64.0</
Version>
        <Build xmlns="urn:ebay:apis:eBLBaseComponents">1421734</
Build>
        <Pal xsi:type="xs:string">AK6REQJW3RMQY</Pal>
        <Locale xsi:type="xs:string">en_US</Locale>
      </GetPalDetailsResponse>
    </SOAP-ENV:Body>
  </SOAP-ENV:Envelope>
```

The response returns the **Account ID** of the PayPal account, which you can see on the **My Account | Profile** tab of the **Sandbox Test Site**. Similarly, you can test this out with the **Website Payments Pro** account credentials to ensure that the **Account ID** is returned as part of the response. With this, we have successfully set up the PayPal accounts and also verified that the SOAP APIs are accessible. We will use this backbone in the subsequent recipes to build the integration between ADempiere and PayPal.

How it works...

PayPal Sandbox provides interfaces and supports processes, which are similar to the production version of PayPal. This is a great playground for developers, like us, who are integrating their solutions with PayPal. The **Website Payments Pro** account provides API access to the account and provides the required API credentials to call them in a secure way. Those credentials are used in all the PayPal API calls so that the request is authorized and served by PayPal.

There's more...

Alternately, we can get a certificate file generated from PayPal Sandbox and use it in place of the API signature as many times as we want. In the production setup, it may not be a good idea to use the API signature.

Working with PayPal APIs

PayPal provides the following types of APIs:

▶ **NAV**: Name and Value pair based
▶ **SOAP**: Web services API

NAV APIs are very useful for website integration with PayPal services. For back-office integration, SOAP APIs are useful. PayPal provides SDK to speed up the integration. In this recipe, we will look at the steps involved in using the Java SDK and we will use it to test an API to check the API call.

Getting ready

Make sure that the following is installed and set up:

- Install JDK 1.6
- Install Eclipse

How to do it...

1. Download SOAP SDK for Java from `https://www.paypal.com/sdk`. I have downloaded the Windows version of the SDK.

PayPal API: SOAP Interface

PayPal recommends that you use the PayPal NVP interface to the PayPal API unless you are already familiar with using SOAP web services.

Supported Platforms: Windows Server 2000, 2003; Red Hat Linux 9.0; Sun Solaris 9.0; .NET 1.1 Service Pack 1; NET 2.0; JDK 1.6.x; PHP 4.3 or later; Tomcat 5.0 or later; ColdFusion MX 7.

SOAP SDKs

	Windows 2000	Linux	Solaris
Java	.zip	.sh | tar.gz	.sh | .tar
ASP.NET*	.msi		
PHP	.zip	.tar.gz	.tar

---

2. Extract the downloaded zipped file (to, say, `c:\paypal_java_sdk`).
3. Create a new Java project in **Eclipse**.
4. Create a `PayPalInterfaceImpl.java` class file and save the following code in it:

```java
import com.paypal.sdk.profiles.APIProfile;
import com.paypal.sdk.profiles.ProfileFactory;
import com.paypal.sdk.services.CallerServices;
import com.paypal.soap.api.GetPalDetailsRequestType;
import com.paypal.soap.api.GetPalDetailsResponseType;

public class PayPalInterfaceImpl {
  private static final String API_USER_NAME = "ajitkumar601_api1.
gmail.com";
  private static final String API_PASSWORD = "ZUGQSLQ86GDFJKRG";
```

```
  private static final String API_SIGNATURE =
"AFcWxV21C7fd0v3bYYYRCpSSRl31AtxOKtyfBGWmYb9j7h4PVs9C5J90";
  private static final String API_ENVIRONMENT = "sandbox";
  private static final String API_SUCCESS = "SUCCESS";

  public String getPalDetails()
  {
    String responseValue = null;
    String returnVal = null;
    CallerServices caller = new CallerServices();

    try
    {
      APIProfile profile = ProfileFactory.
createSignatureAPIProfile();

      // Set up your API credentials, PayPal end point, and API
version.
      profile.setAPIUsername(PayPalInterfaceImpl.API_USER_NAME);
      profile.setAPIPassword(PayPalInterfaceImpl.API_PASSWORD);
      profile.setSignature(PayPalInterfaceImpl.API_SIGNATURE);
      profile.setEnvironment(PayPalInterfaceImpl.API_ENVIRONMENT);
      caller.setAPIProfile(profile);

      GetPalDetailsRequestType pprequest = new
GetPalDetailsRequestType();
      pprequest.setVersion("64.0");

      // Execute the API operation and obtain the response.
      GetPalDetailsResponseType ppresponse =
(GetPalDetailsResponseType)
        caller.call("GetPalDetails", pprequest);
      responseValue = ppresponse.getAck().toString();

      if (responseValue.equalsIgnoreCase(PayPalInterfaceImpl.API_
SUCCESS)) {
        returnVal = ppresponse.getPal();
      }

    }catch(Exception ex)
    {
      ex.printStackTrace();
    }

    return returnVal;
  }

}
```

5. Add all the JAR files from the `c:\paypal_java_sdk\lib` folder to the project **Build Path**.

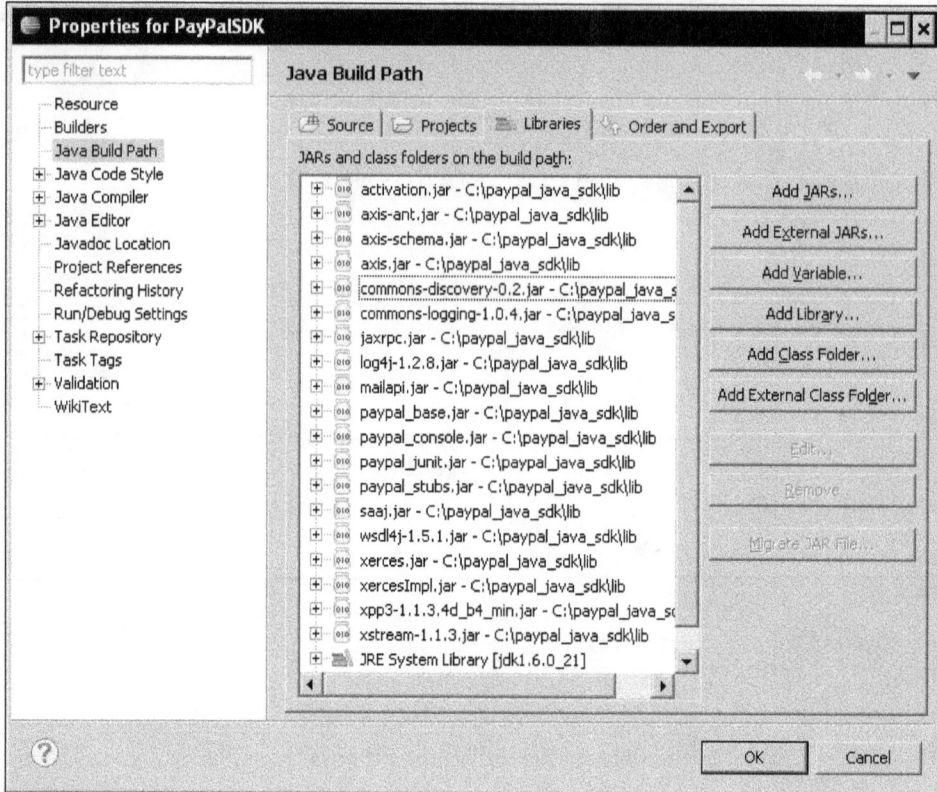

6. Set the JDK version to 1.6.x.

7. Write the following JUnit test case:

```
public void testGetPalDetails() {
    PayPalInterfaceImpl ppImpl = new PayPalInterfaceImpl();
    String responseVal = ppImpl.getPalDetails();
    assertFalse(responseVal == null);
    System.out.println("Pal Id: " + responseVal);
}
```

8. The following shall be the console output when the test case passes:

- Proxy configuration file not found. Looks like proxy not being used.

- getPalDetails sent

- getPalDetails Ack : Success Elapsed Time : 4,157 ms

Pal Id: VKDGKJ5DPWFJQ

How it works...

The following diagram depicts the pieces involved in the API integration:

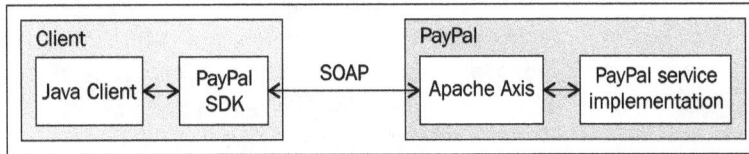

The Java client uses the data types and methods provided by PayPal SDK, which internally connect to the PayPal services. Which PayPal services will be invoked? The SDK takes this decision based on the environment set on the `APIProfile`. Since, we are working with the PayPal Sandbox environment, we set the environment to `sandbox`. Every API call returns `Success` or `Failure` as the acknowledgement (for example, `ppresponse.getAck()`). So, the further processing of the response object shall be based on this.

There's more...

Rather than using the PayPal-provided SOAP SDK for Java, we can also generate the Web services client by taking the bottom-up approach using the Sandbox WSDL file.

Making payment to a PayPal account

In this recipe, we will look at the steps we shall follow in order to post a payment to a PayPal account from ADempiere's Payment window.

Getting ready

Make sure that the **adempiere360lts** project is set up. You may follow the steps mentioned in *Chapter 1* to set up the project and the related database.

How to do it...

1. Create the `PP_PayPal.java` file in the `<ADEMPIERE_SVN>\tags\adempiere360lts\base\src\org\compiere\model` folder and save the following code in it:

```
package org.compiere.model;

import java.io.Serializable;

import com.paypal.sdk.exceptions.PayPalException;
```

```java
import com.paypal.sdk.profiles.APIProfile;
import com.paypal.sdk.profiles.ProfileFactory;
import com.paypal.sdk.services.CallerServices;
import com.paypal.soap.api.AddressType;
import com.paypal.soap.api.BasicAmountType;
import com.paypal.soap.api.CountryCodeType;
import com.paypal.soap.api.CreditCardDetailsType;
import com.paypal.soap.api.CreditCardTypeType;
import com.paypal.soap.api.CurrencyCodeType;
import com.paypal.soap.api.DoDirectPaymentRequestDetailsType;
import com.paypal.soap.api.DoDirectPaymentRequestType;
import com.paypal.soap.api.DoDirectPaymentResponseType;
import com.paypal.soap.api.PayerInfoType;
import com.paypal.soap.api.PaymentActionCodeType;
import com.paypal.soap.api.PaymentDetailsType;
import com.paypal.soap.api.PersonNameType;
import com.paypal.soap.api.SellerDetailsType;

/**
 *    PayPal Payment Processor Services Interface
 *
 *    @author Ajit Kumar
 */
public class PP_PayPal extends PaymentProcessor
  implements Serializable
{
  /**   Status          */
  private boolean       m_ok = false;
  private APIProfile    m_pp = null;

  /** PayPal Caller Service  */
  private CallerServices   m_caller;

//  private static final String API_USER_NAME = "ajitkumar601_
api1.gmail.com";
//  private static final String API_PASSWORD = "ZUGQSLQ86GDFJKRG";
  private static final String API_SIGNATURE =
"AFcWxV21C7fd0v3bYYYRCpSSRl31AtxOKtyfBGWmYb9j7h4PVs9C5J90";
  private static final String API_ENVIRONMENT = "sandbox";
  private static final String API_SUCCESS = "SUCCESS";
//  private static final String SELLER_ACCOUNT_ID =
"AK6REQJW3RMQY";

  public PP_PayPal()
```

```
    {
        super();
        m_caller = new CallerServices();
        try {

            m_pp = ProfileFactory.createSignatureAPIProfile();
        } catch (PayPalException e) {
            e.printStackTrace();
            log.severe("Failed to initialize signature API profile for
PayPal : " + e.getMessage());
        }
    }


    public boolean processCC () throws IllegalArgumentException
    {
        DoDirectPaymentRequestType request = new
DoDirectPaymentRequestType();
        DoDirectPaymentRequestDetailsType details = new
DoDirectPaymentRequestDetailsType();
        CreditCardDetailsType creditCard = new
CreditCardDetailsType();

        m_pp.setAPIUsername(p_mpp.getUserID());
        m_pp.setAPIPassword(p_mpp.getPassword());

        //using signature rather than API certificate, which is
suitable for production usage
        try {
            m_pp.setSignature(API_SIGNATURE);
            m_pp.setEnvironment(API_ENVIRONMENT);
            m_caller.setAPIProfile(m_pp);
        } catch (PayPalException e) {
            e.printStackTrace();
            log.severe("Failed to initialize signature API profile for
PayPal : " + e.getMessage());
            throw new IllegalArgumentException("PP_PayPal : Invalid
credentials");
        }

        //  Transaction Type
        if (p_mp.getTrxType().equals(MPayment.TRXTYPE_Sales))
            details.setPaymentAction(PaymentActionCodeType.Sale);
        else
            throw new IllegalArgumentException("PP_PayPal TrxType not
supported - " + p_mp.getTrxType());
```

```
      //  Card Type
      if (p_mp.getCreditCardType().equals("V"))
        creditCard.setCreditCardType(CreditCardTypeType.Visa);
      else
        throw new IllegalArgumentException("PP_PayPal CardType not
supported - Visa - " + p_mp.getTrxType());

      creditCard.setCreditCardNumber(MPaymentValidate.
checkNumeric(p_mp.getCreditCardNumber()));

      creditCard.setCVV2(p_mp.getCreditCardVV());
      creditCard.setExpMonth(p_mp.getCreditCardExpMM());
      creditCard.setExpYear(p_mp.getCreditCardExpYY());

      PayerInfoType cardOwner = new PayerInfoType();
      cardOwner.setPayerCountry(CountryCodeType.US);

      AddressType address = new AddressType();
      address.setPostalCode(p_mp.getA_Zip());
      address.setStateOrProvince(p_mp.getA_State());
      address.setStreet1(p_mp.getA_Street());
      address.setCountryName(p_mp.getA_Country());
      address.setCountry(CountryCodeType.US);
      address.setCityName(p_mp.getA_City());
      cardOwner.setAddress(address);

      PersonNameType payerName = new PersonNameType();
      payerName.setFirstName("Ajit");
      payerName.setLastName("Kumar");
      cardOwner.setPayerName(payerName);

      creditCard.setCardOwner(cardOwner);
      details.setCreditCard(creditCard);

      details.setIPAddress("192.168.1.3");

      SellerDetailsType seller = new SellerDetailsType();
      seller.setPayPalAccountID(p_mpp.getVendorID());

      PaymentDetailsType pymtDetail = new PaymentDetailsType();
      pymtDetail.setInvoiceID(String.valueOf(p_mp.getC_Invoice_
ID()));
```

```java
BasicAmountType orderTotal = new BasicAmountType();
orderTotal.setCurrencyID(CurrencyCodeType.USD);
orderTotal.set_value(p_mp.getPayAmt().toString());
pymtDetail.setOrderTotal(orderTotal);

BasicAmountType itemTotal = new BasicAmountType();
itemTotal.setCurrencyID(CurrencyCodeType.USD);
itemTotal.set_value(p_mp.getPayAmt().toString());
pymtDetail.setItemTotal(itemTotal);

if (p_mp.getTaxAmt().doubleValue() > 0.0) {
  BasicAmountType taxTotal = new BasicAmountType();
  taxTotal.setCurrencyID(CurrencyCodeType.USD);
  taxTotal.set_value(p_mp.getTaxAmt().toString());
  pymtDetail.setTaxTotal(taxTotal);
}

if (p_mp.getChargeAmt().doubleValue() > 0.0) {
  BasicAmountType handlingTotal = new BasicAmountType();
  handlingTotal.setCurrencyID(CurrencyCodeType.USD);
  handlingTotal.set_value(p_mp.getChargeAmt().toString());
  pymtDetail.setHandlingTotal(handlingTotal);
}

pymtDetail.setSellerDetails(seller);
details.setPaymentDetails(pymtDetail);

request.setVersion("64.0");
request.setDoDirectPaymentRequestDetails(details);

// Execute the API operation and obtain the response.
DoDirectPaymentResponseType ppresponse;
try {
  ppresponse = (DoDirectPaymentResponseType)m_caller.
call("DoDirectPayment", request);
  String responseValue = ppresponse.getAck().toString();

  p_mp.setR_Result(ppresponse.getAmount().toString());
  m_ok = API_SUCCESS.equalsIgnoreCase(responseValue);
} catch (PayPalException e) {
  e.printStackTrace();

  p_mp.setR_Result("");
  m_ok = false;
```

```
      }

      return m_ok;
   }

   public boolean isProcessedOK ()
   {
      return m_ok;
   }
}
```

2. Build the project and launch the desktop version of ADempiere.

3. Log in as **GardenAdmin/GardenAdmin** with the **GardenWorld Admin** role.

4. Go to the **Menu | System Admin | Organization Rules | Bank** window.

5. Add a new bank detail for PayPal usage on the **Bank** tab.

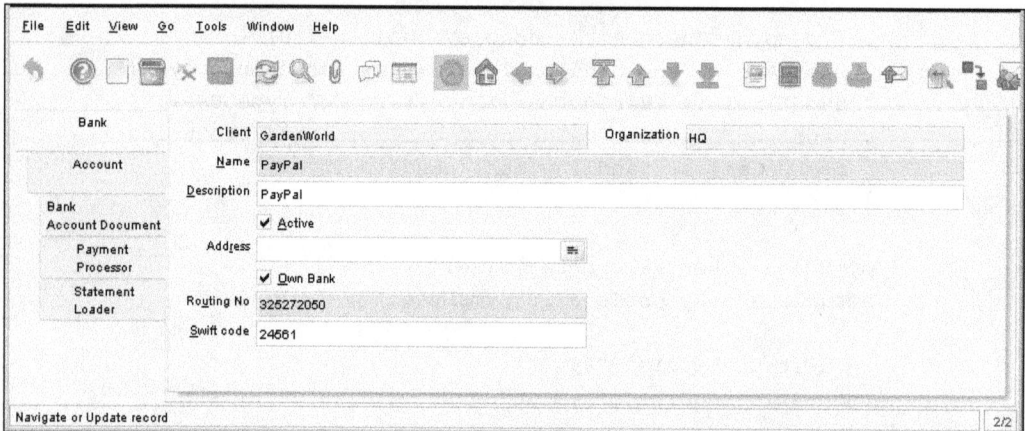

6. Add an account detail on the **Account** tab.

7. The values here are not being used, so you may default the mandatory fields to a sensible value. The only important field is **Currency**. Set it to USD.

8. Go to the **Payment Processor** tab and mention the following PayPal-related details:

▸ **Vendor ID**: <your PayPal account ID (for example, AK6REQJW3RMQY)>

▸ **User ID**: <your PayPal API username (for example, ajitkumar601_api1.gmail.com)>

▸ **Password**: <your PayPal API password (for example, ZUGQSLQ86GDFJKRG)>

▸ **Accept Visa**: Check

▸ **Only Currency**: USD

► **Payment Processor Class**: `org.compiere.model. PP_PayPal`

9. Go to the **Open Items | Payment** window and enter the payment details using the following PayPal-specific details:

► **Bank Account**: <the bank account we created in the previous step>

► **Document**

- **Tender Type**: `Credit Card`

- **Online Access**: check

- **Credit Card**: <buyer credit card number (for example, `4536523073948644`)>

- **Verification Code**: <buyer credit card's CVV number (for example, `456`)>

- **Exp. Month**: <buyer credit card exp. Month (for example, `8`)>

- **Exp. Year**: <buyer credit card exp. Year (for example, `2015`)>

- **Account Name**: <buyer name on credit card (for example, `Ajit Kumar`)>

- **Account Street**: <buyer credit card street address (for example, `"1 Main St"`)>

- **Account City**: <buyer credit card city in address (for example, `San Jose`)>

- **Account Zip/Postal**: <buyer credit card postal code in address (for example, 95131)>

- **Account State**: <buyer credit card state in address (for example, CA)>

- **Account Country**: <buyer credit card country in address (for example, United States)>

10. Click on the **Online Process** button to process the PayPal payment. After successful processing, the payment amount will appear in the **Result** section under the **Status** field group and the **Document** section will become read-only.

11. Verify that you have received a payment notification in your **Test Email** section of the **PayPal Sandbox**.

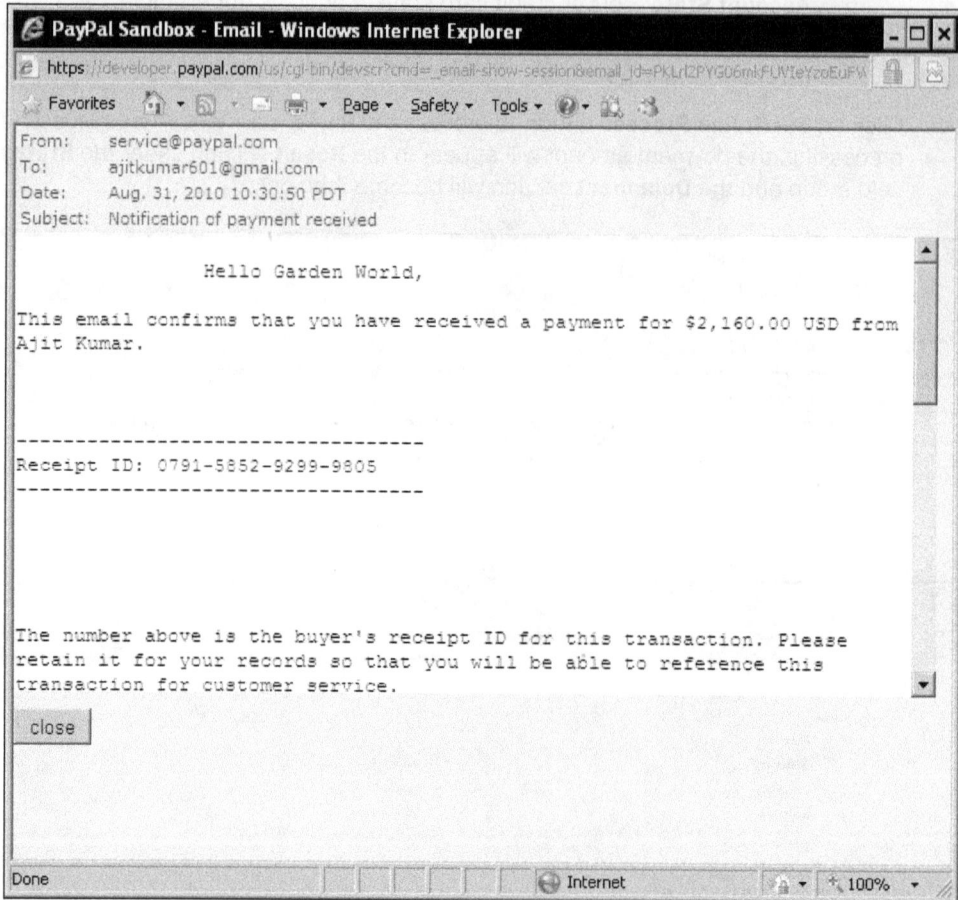

12. Go to the **My Account | History** tab of the Website Payments Pro account. You will see the recently posted payment details in your payment history.

How it works...

ADempiere provides the `PaymentProcessor` abstract class, which facilitates the online payment processing. ADempiere already has the integration with VeriSign's Payflow Pro, which extends the `PaymentProcessor` class. The heart of the class is the `processCC` method, which is expected to process the credit card payments. Our `PP_PayPal` class also extends the `PaymentProcessor` class. In the `processCC` method of `PP_PayPal`, we have currently provided support only for the `Visa` type of credit card if the payment transaction is of the type `Sale`. We have used the `DoDirectPayment` API to post payments to a PayPal account whose credentials are set up on the **Payment Processor** tab of the **Bank** window. Currently, the API signature is hardcoded in the code, which I expect it will be replaced with the usage of the API certificate file in the live environment.

There's more...

PayPal provides other APIs to capture a payment, authorize a payment, and so on, which can be used to support the different transaction types listed by ADempiere.

Integrating PayPal Instant Payment Notification (IPN)

If you are interested in receiving asynchronous notification from PayPal about the payments made to a PayPal account, then this recipe intends to cover that. This is a very useful feature provided by PayPal to integrate and automate our back-office operation (for example, initiate shipping as soon as the payment is confirmed).

Getting ready

Make sure your machine is accessible on the internet, as it is a must to implement IPN.

How to do it...

1. Install XAMPP, which provides the Apache Web server, on the machine. You may refer to *Chapter 5*, *VirtueMart Integration*, for the steps. Say, we have installed the XAMPP in `c:\xampp`

2. Create an IPN listener by referring to PayPal's IPN guide: `https://cms.paypal.com/cms_content/US/en_US/files/developer/IPNGuide.pdf`.

   This guide provides a PHP implementation of the listener, which you can use to follow this recipe. Say, we have named the listener `IPNListener.php`.

3. Keep the `IPNListener.php` in your Web server folder, which is accessible, say, in `c:\xampp\htdocs`. In this case, the URL that we will use with PayPal will be `http://<your host address>/IPNListener.php`.

4. On the **PayPal Sandbox** page, select the **Website Payments Pro** account and go to the **My Account | Profile** page of the same.

5. Click on the **Instant Payment Notification** preferences link under the **Selling preferences** section.

6. Click on **Choose IPN Settings** and enter the URL of your IPN listener and select the **Receive IPN messages** radio before saving the setting.

7. Go to the **Test Tools** page on your **PayPal Sandbox** page and click on the **IPN Simulator** to launch the simulator.

8. Fill in the **IPN Handler URL** and payment-related values and click on the **Send IPN** button.

If your listener URL is valid and the listener is running, you will see the IPN successfully sent message on the top.

How it works...

There are various PayPal APIs, which send the payment notification to a designated URL, for example, DoDirectPayment. For development and testing, we have used the IPN simulator provided by PayPal so that we can generate any notification without waiting for API integration and then posting a transaction using that. Our IPNListener receives the request from the IPN simulator, which POSTs the list of name-value pairs containing the payment-related information (for example, buyer information, seller information, item detail, and so on). The listener then sends the request back to PayPal for verification. PayPal may return either VERIFIED or INVALID. In the case of VERIFIED, we are okay to proceed with further processing—for example, we may store the complete IPN request (name-value pair details) in a database and provide a view for the user to look at those notifications, create a shipment request in ADempiere, and so on.

8
Equifax Integration

In this chapter, we will cover:

1. Equifax session service
2. Equifax address matching service
3. Equifax bank validation service
4. Equifax company matching service
5. Equifax consumer bureau service
6. Equifax password change service

Introduction

Say, you are a loan provider company and you would like to have a check on the customer's credit score to figure out whether a loan can be given to the customer, and if so, how much loan can be granted. You may also like to avoid or detect a potential fraud to minimize losses. All these are needed to basically cover the risk in the business. Equifax Inc. is one such credit reporting agency, besides, Experian and TransUnion. Each one of them provides APIs and mechanisms to report credit detail, programmatically. In this chapter, we will understand the Equifax APIs and what it would take to integrate it in any application, in general, and ADempiere, in particular.

Equifax is used to find out the information pertaining to customers and to evaluate their credit statuses and the validity of the information provided by the customers. It provides consumer data taken from a wide range of sources to enable its users to make informed decisions. To the user, Equifax provides the following types of services:

►   **Session service**: This provides a set of services related to the session management with Equifax. The logon request provides the session token, which is used in all the subsequent requests.

- ▸ **Address matching service**: This is useful in address matching (current as well as previous) to find the relevant individual.

- ▸ **Bank validation service**: It is useful to validate the bank details based on the bank account number and sort code provided during the request.

- ▸ **Company matching service**: Useful for correctly targeting any companies used in a commercial application.

- ▸ **Consumer bureau service**: Useful in finding out the address, credit score, and fraud scan details of a customer.

For the purpose of simplicity, we will not cover any details of Equifax as it is already explained in the Equifax documents. You shall get access to the documents after you have registered yourself with Equifax on `http://www.equifax.com`. Also, there are various scenarios where Equifax can be used in a business. So, without getting into the specifics of the scenarios, chapter shows how to work with the Equifax APIs.

Upon registration, you shall get the following information, which is required to execute the APIs:

- ▸ Client reference
- ▸ Domain ID
- ▸ User ID
- ▸ Password

Also, note that Equifax is not applicable to all countries. You may have to look at their website in order to find out whether the country, for which you are planning to implement the Equifax integration, is supported by Equifax. For this chapter, I have considered the UK.

In this chapter, we will understand the different Equifax APIs, which are available for integration and also learn what the typical requests and responses of each of the APIs are.

Equifax session service

Upon a successful logon, Equifax provides a session token which needs to be used on the subsequent API calls. While the token is useful to the application developer, Equifax uses this to keep track of the API usage and managing the connections.

Session service has the following requests:

- ▸ **Ping**: This is used to determine whether the Equifax XML interface is available
- ▸ **Logon**: This is used to logon the user to the Equifax NTG application architecture. The success response contains the session token
- ▸ **Log off**: This is used to log off the session identified by the supplied session token
- ▸ **Change password**: It is used to change the password

In this recipe, we will see the steps and code required to invoke an Equifax session service API. Ping is kept outside this recipe due to its simplicity, whereas, **Change password** is covered in a separate recipe, as it needs some more attention besides just changing the password.

Getting ready

1. Make sure you have the `adempiere_360` project set up in Eclipse. You may refer to _Chapter 1, Preparing the Ground_ if it is not already done.

2. Download the latest stable version of Apache HttpComponents from http://hc.apache.org/ and extract it into a folder, say, **C:\apache\ httpcomponents-client-4.0.3**.

3. Add the JAR files to the `adempiere_360` project's **Build Path** from **C:\apache\ httpcomponents-client-4.0.3\lib**.

How to do it...

1. Create the `EquifaxImpl.java` class file.

2. Using Apache HttpComponent, create a method `sendHttpRequest` to send a HTTP POST request to Equifax URL, and save it in the file:

```
private String sendHttpRequest(String url, List <NameValuePair>
nvps) throws Exception {
  HttpClient httpclient = new DefaultHttpClient();

  HttpPost httppost = new HttpPost(url);
  httppost.setEntity(new UrlEncodedFormEntity(nvps, HTTP.UTF_8));


  HttpResponse response = httpclient.execute(httppost);
  HttpEntity resEntity = response.getEntity();

  ByteArrayOutputStream baos = new ByteArrayOutputStream();
  if (resEntity != null) {
    resEntity.writeTo(baos);
  }
  if (resEntity != null) {
    resEntity.consumeContent();
  }

  httpclient.getConnectionManager().shutdown();
  return baos.toString();
}
```

3. Create a method `executeEquifaxRequest` to form the HTTP POST request for Equifax, and save it in the file.

```
private String executeEquifaxRequest(String xmlRequest) throws
Exception {
   final String EQUIFAX_URL = "https://www.uat.uk.equifax.com/
xmlcpulink/XMLServlet";
   List <NameValuePair> nvps = new ArrayList <NameValuePair>();
   nvps.add(new BasicNameValuePair("xml_request", xmlRequest));

   String response = sendHttpRequest(EQUIFAX_URL, nvps);
   return response;
}
```

4. Create a method `getLogonSessionServiceXml`, which shall form the logon XML and return the same to the caller.

```
private String getLogonSessionServiceXml() {
   String xml = "<?xml version=\"1.0\" standalone=\"yes\"?>"
      + "<request>"
      + "<request_header interface_version_no= \"1.0\"  dtd_
version_no=\"1.0\">"
      + "<client_reference>XXXX</client_reference>"
      + "</request_header>"
      + "<service_request id=\"1\">"
      + "<session_service>"
      + "<logon_request domain_id=\"XXXX\" user_id=\"XXXX\"
password=\"XXXX\" />"
      + "</session_service>"
      + "</service_request>"
      + "</request>";
   return xml;
}
```

Replace the XXXX with the values that you receive from Equifax.

5. Now, using the following code, run the following logon request:

```
public static void main(String args[]) {
   EquifaxImpl eqfaxImpl = new EquifaxImpl();
   try {
      String xml = eqfaxImpl. getLogonSessionServiceXml();
      String response = eqfaxImpl.executeEquifaxRequest(xml);
      System.out.println(response);
   } catch (Exception e) {
      e.printStackTrace();
   }
}
```

You shall see the following output:

```
<?xml version="1.0" standalone="yes"?>
<response>
<response_header>
<client_reference>XXXX</client_reference>
</response_header>
<service_response id="1" success_flag="1">
<session_response>
<logon_response grace_logon="0" session_token="22c06cf0-cfb4-11df-
87da-0a884fe6aa77-76"></logon_response>
</session_response>
</service_response>
</response>
```

6. Create a method `getLogoffSessionServiceXml`, which shall form the logon XML and return the same to the caller:

```
private String getLogoffSessionServiceXml() {
    String xml = "<?xml version=\"1.0\" standalone=\"yes\"?>"
        + "<request>"
        + "<request_header session_token=\"22c06cf0-cfb4-11df-87da-
0a884fe6aa77-76\" interface_version_no= \"1.0\"  dtd_version_
no=\"1.0\">"
        + "<client_reference>WTC001</client_reference>"
        + "</request_header>"
        + "<service_request id=\"1\">"
        + "<session_service>"
        + "<log_off_request/>"
        + "</session_service>"
        + "</service_request>"
        + "</request>";
    return xml;
}
```

Though, for brevity, I have hardcoded the session token. However, you shall parse the logon response XML to get the session token from it and use the same in the subsequent requests.

7. You shall see the following output:

```
<?xml version="1.0" standalone="yes"?>
<response>
<response_header session_token="22c06cf0-cfb4-11df-87da-
0a884fe6aa77-76">
<client_reference>XXXX</client_reference>
</response_header>
<service_response id="1" success_flag="1">
```

```
<session_response>
<log_off_response>
</log_off_response>
</session_response>
</service_response>
</response>
```

How it works...

Before any other service APIs are called, logon API must be called, as the successful execution of it returns the `session_token`, which must be included in the `request_header`.

At the end, the user shall call the logoff API to close the session. The `session_token` mentioned in the logoff API must match with the one returned in the logon response.

There's more...

While executing the API, there are a few important error responses which we shall be aware of and shall handle them in our code, if needed. The following are the two important such error responses:

Invalid Session

If the `session_token` passed in the request header of the API call is not a valid one, the response to that API call returns an error with the error code `03020007 - Invalid Session`.

```
<?xml version="1.0" standalone="yes"?><response><response_
header><client_reference>XXXX</client_reference></response_
header><service_response id="1" success_flag="0"><error
message="Internal Error." code="03020007"></error></service_
response></response>
```

Session Timeout

If the `session_token` passed in the request header of the API call has expired, the response to that API call returns an error with the error code `03020008 -Session Timeout`.

```
<?xml version="1.0" standalone="yes"?><response><response_
header><client_reference>XXXX</client_reference></response_
header><service_response id="1" success_flag="0"><error
message="Internal Error." code="03020008"></error></service_
response></response>
```

Equifax address matching service

Address matching is a very important aspect in finding the right individual for whom the credit report needs to be fetched. Equifax provides the current as well as previous addresses of the individual. This can be used to take decisions in the business logic code. This recipe describes the code required to integrate this service.

How to do it...

1. Create an XML for the address matching service.

```
String xml = "<?xml version=\"1.0\" standalone=\"yes\"?>"
    + "<request>"
    + "<request_header session_token=\"e47acafa-cef8-11df-a869-
0a884fe6aa77-73\" interface_version_no= \"1.0\"  dtd_version_
no=\"1.0\">"
    + "<client_reference>XXXX</client_reference>"
    + "</request_header>"
    + "<service_request id=\"1\">"
    + "<address_matching_service>"
    + "<address_match_request>"
    + "<input_address max_matches=\"3\" forename=\"\"
middlename=\"\" surname=\"\"\">"
    + "<fixed_format_address house_name=\"\" house_
number=\"00077\" street_1=\"\" street_2=\"\" district=\"\"
posttown=\"\" country=\"\" postcode=\"BA133BN\" />"
    + "</input_address>"
    + "</address_match_request>"
    + "</address_matching_service>"
    + "</service_request>"
    + "</request>";
Following shall be a typical response
<?xml version="1.0" standalone="yes"?>
<response>
<response_header session_token="aedf823c-cfb6-11df-a869-
0a884fe6aa77-24"><client_reference>XXXX</client_reference>
</response_header>
<service_response id="1" success_flag="1">
<address_matching_response>
<match_address_response>
<return_address request_id="0" district="" county="WILTS" ptc_abs_
code="58150004506" house_no="BLENLEY LODGE" post_town="WESTBURY"
match_status="5" house_name="" postcode="BA133BN" surname=""
street_2="" street_1="HIGH ST"></return_address><return_
address request_id="0" district="" county="WILTS" ptc_abs_
```

```
code="58150004256" house_no="BRIARFIELD" post_town="WESTBURY"
match_status="5" house_name="" postcode="BA133BN" surname=""
street_2="" street_1="HIGH ST"></return_address><return_
address request_id="0" district="" county="WILTS" ptc_abs_
code="58150004409" house_no="BRONALLT" post_town="WESTBURY" match_
status="5" house_name="" postcode="BA133BN" surname="" street_2=""
street_1="HIGH ST"></return_address>
</match_address_response></address_matching_response></service_
response></response>
```

How it works...

Based on the values of the attributes of `input_address` and `fixed_format_address` elements, the response is returned. If there are multiple matching addresses returned, the response will have multiple `return_address` nodes. The `match_status` attribute value determines the kind of address match, for example, 0—No match, 1—single match, 2—multiple matches, and so on. The details about each of the statuses can be found in Equifax's NTG XML Interface Specification document.

There's more...

During the integration if the need is that every address we capture in ADempiere must comply with Equifax address, then we will have to modify the **Location** dialog, so that it has the field specific to the Equifax. To modify the **Location** dialog, you will have to review and modify the following:

▶ `C_LOCATION`: This table contains the fields that are captured on the **Location** dialog. The table has the following fields where Equifax-related fields can be directly mapped, except the `District`, as shown in the following table:

Equifax field	C_LOCATION column
House Name	address1
House Number	address2
Street 1	address3
Street 2	address4
Post Town	city/c_city_id
Post Code	postal
Country	c_country_id
County	Regionname/c_region_id
District	▶ -

Add a new column, `districtname`, of the type `character varying(40)` to the `C_LOCATION` table.

- ▸ For the Swing version of the GUI, modify the `org.compiere.grid.ed.VLocationDialog.java` file, which contains the complete code for creating the Location dialog and the event handlers. You will have to change the labels and add a new field for `District`.

- ▸ For the **webui** version, you will have to modify the `WLocationDialog.java` file.

The next screenshot shows the modified dialog, which allows us to capture the address detail as per the Equifax specification. Once captured, further decision logic can be built in the system.

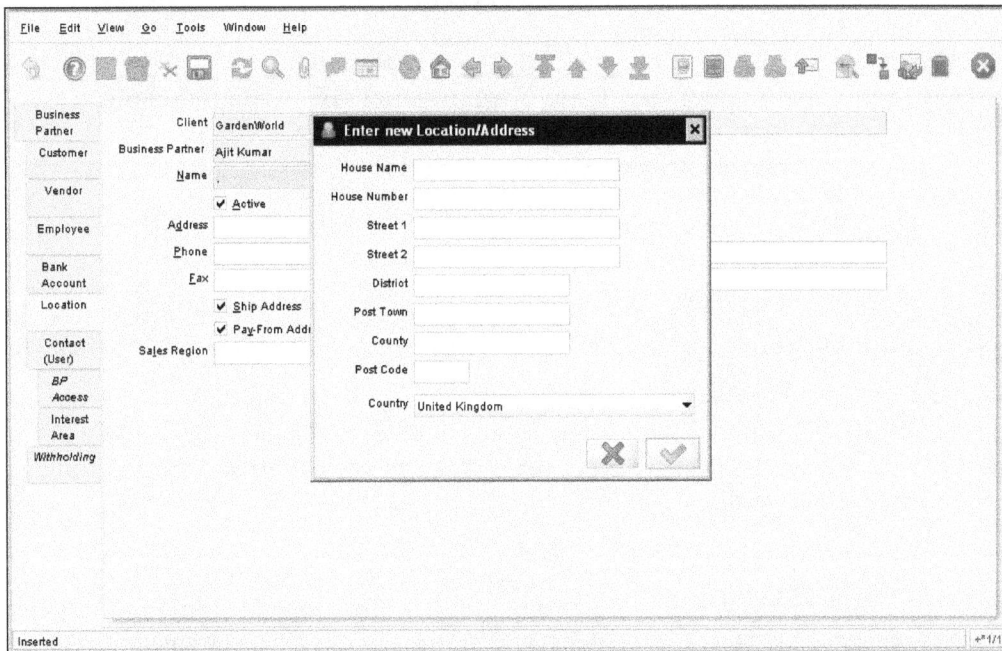

Equifax bank validation service

This recipe describes the bank validation service of Equifax, which is useful in validating the bank account details of the concerned individual.

How to do it...

▶ The following XML shall be created and sent to Equifax NTG XML interface for a typical bank validation service:

```
String xml = "<?xml version=\"1.0\" standalone=\"yes\"?>"
    + "<request>"
    + "<request_header session_token=\"22c06cf0-cfb4-11df-87da-
0a884fe6aa77-76\" interface_version_no= \"1.0\"  dtd_version_
no=\"1.0\">"
    + "<client_reference>XXXX</client_reference>"
    + "</request_header>"
    + "<service_request id=\"1\">"
    + "<bank_validation_service>"
    + "<bank_details_request>"
    + "<bank_details sort_code=\"21-43-34\" account_
number=\"12345678\">"
    + "</bank_details>"
    + "</bank_details_request>"
    + "</bank_validation_service>"
    + "</service_request>"
    + "</request>";
```

How it works...

For a bank account, the bank sort code and account number is required for the validation. The response will have the `result_code`, which indicates whether the sort code and account number were valid.

There's more...

In order to integrate this service with ADempiere, you may have to make the change to the **Bank Account** tab of the **Business Partner** window to include the sort code. To accomplish this, you will have to do the following:

▶ Add a new column—sortcode—of the type character varying (20) to the `c_bp_bankaccount` table

▶ Refer to the recipes mentioned in *Chapter 2, ADempiere Customization – Part I* to make the **Sort Code** field appear on the **Bank Account** tab of the **Business Partner** window

After this is stored in the database, further validation logic can be based on top of it.

Equifax company matching service

This service is useful for matching company details against the Equifax Commercial databases. This may be used to figure out whether the company detail provided by the applicant is valid or not.

How to do it...

1. The following XML shall be created and sent to the Equifax NTG XML interface for a typical company matching service:

```
String xml = "<?xml version=\"1.0\" standalone=\"yes\"?>"
    + "<request>"
    + "<request_header session_token=\"62da97aa-cefd-11df-a869-
0a884fe6aa77-22\" interface_version_no= \"1.0\"  dtd_version_
no=\"1.0\">"
    + "<client_reference>XXXX</client_reference>"
    + "</request_header>"
    + "<service_request id=\"1\">"
    + "<company_matching_service>"
    + "<company_match_request>"
    + "<company_details company_id=\"12345\" databases=\"L\"
country=\"GB\"/>"
    + "</company_match_request>"
    + "</company_matching_service>"
    + "</service_request>"
    + "</request>";
```

How it works...

Based on the company details, the API returns zero or more matching company details. The results are returned in the form of pages, if too many matches are found.

Equifax consumer bureau service

This service is used to find out the address, credit score, and fraud scan details of a customer. All input application data within the consumer bureau request should be in capital letters.

How to do it...

1. The following XML shall be created and sent to the Equifax NTG XML interface for a typical company-matching service:

```
String xml = "<?xml version=\"1.0\" standalone=\"yes\"?>"
    + "<request>"
    + "<request_header interface_version_no= \"1.0\"  dtd_
version_no=\"1.0\">"
    + "<client_reference>XXXX</client_reference>"
    + "</request_header>"
    + "<service_request id=\"3\">"
    + "<consumer_bureau_service>"
    + "<consumer_bureau_request domain=\"XXXX\"
usercode=\"XXXX\" password=\"XXXX\" operator_id=\"XXXX\" >"
    + "<consumer_search search_type=\"SE\" opt_in_out_
flag=\"I\" associate_jointapp_flag=\"\">"
    + "<scoring qcb_option=\"1\" same_company_insight=\"\">"
    + "<score_product code=\"RNILF01\"/>"
    + "</scoring >"
    + "<data_types>"
    + "<data_type id=\"ADO\" maximum=\"00\" />"
    + "<data_type id=\"ELR\" maximum=\"00\" />"
    + "<data_type id=\"CJR\" maximum=\"00\" />"
    + "<data_type id=\"INR\" maximum=\"00\" />"
    + "<data_type id=\"NCR\" maximum=\"00\" />"
    + "<data_type id=\"ASR\" maximum=\"00\" />"
    + "<data_type id=\"RRR\" maximum=\"00\" />"
    + "<data_type id=\"QCB\" maximum=\"00\" />"
    + "</data_types>"
    + "<display_requirements applicant_data=\"Y\" associate_
data=\"Y\" attributable_data=\"N\" potential_associate_data=\"N\"
family_data=\"N\" />"
    + "<applicant_details title=\"\" forename=\"Marc\"
second_name=\"\" surname=\"Brookes\"  >"
    + "<address_details time_at_address=\"\" address_match_
flag=\"\" address=\"77  High Street , Wiltshire,Westbury , BA13
3BN\" >"
    + "</address_details>" + "</applicant_details>"
    + "</consumer_search>" + "</consumer_bureau_request>"
    + "</consumer_bureau_service>" + "</service_request>"
    + "</request>";
```

2. The following shall be a typical response:

```
<?xml version="1.0" encoding="ISO-8859-1"?>
<response>
```

```xml
<response_header>
  <client_reference>XXXX</client_reference>
</response_header>
<service_response id="3" success_flag="1">
  <consumer_bureau_service>
    <consumer_bureau_response>
      <header error_code="00" error_message="" reference=""/>
      <non_address>
        <supplied_address id="ADS" sequence_number="1" noc_
indicator="N"/>
        <score id="SCO" label="RNILF01" sign="+" score="394"/>
        <bespoke_characteristics id="QCB" qcb_
field="M M M  M        M M                        M M M
M        M M              _____01_M __M M __00020100C
000002____M M M ____M M M M M MM_M MM_0001C        C
0048C C   C C C   C   0101C C C   C  SSSSSS01C 01C C
C         000000275C        C        C        0048SC01C 01C C C C C
_____M M M        M M   M M   M M
M   M   M M M M M  M  MMMMMM M M M M M        M        M
M        M        M   MM M M M M M M M M        M        M
M        M        M        M        M        M        M
_____M M M M M M M M M M  __M M M M M M M M
M M M __M  M  M  M  M  M  M  M YC        C        C C        C
C        M        M        M M        M        M        C
C        C        M        M        M        C CC        C CC
_____M MM M____C        C        C        M
M        M        C        C        C        M        M        M
CC        C        C        C        C C CC        C        C
C        C C MM        M        M        M        M M MM        M
M        M        M M C        C        C        M        M        M
C C01S_____M        M MM        M M_____
XXNNNNNNNNM "/>
      </non_address>
      <address_details sequence_number="1" match_indicator="L">
        <address_matched id="ADO" address_key="58150004076"
house_name="" house_number="00077" street_1="HIGH ST" street_2=""
district="" posttown="WESTBURY" county="WILTS" postcode="BA133BN"
address_type=""/>
        <electoral_roll id="ELR" name_match_indicator="A"
title="" forename="MARC" second_name="J" surname="BROOKES" date_
of_birth="" period="07-10" junior_senior=""/>
        <insight id="INR" name_match_indicator="C" title="MRS"
forename="HARRIET" second_name="L" surname="BROOKES" date_of_
birth="1971-01-01" company_class="FN" account_type="03" account_
number="" start_date="2006-11-01" end_date="2008-03-01" update_
date="2009-11-01" credit_limit="0" current_balance_sign="+"
current_balance="0" start_balance="0" default_balance="0" credit_
terms="275" repayment_period="300" payment_frequency="M" payment_
```

```
history="S" delinquent_date="" client_number="" quality_flags=""
quality_indicator_1="" quality_indicator_2="" credit_card_
payment_amount_sign="" credit_card_payment_amount="" credit_card_
previous_statement_balance_sign="" credit_card_previous_statement_
balance="" credit_card_cash_advance_value="" credit_card_cash_
advance_count="" credit_card_limit_change_flag="" credit_card_
minimum_payment_flag="" credit_card_promotional_rate_flag=""/>
        </address_details>
      </consumer_bureau_response>
    </consumer_bureau_service>
  </service_response>
</response>
```

3. Apply the bureau rules to the QCB characteristics (`bespoke_characteristics`).

How it works...

For your company, you will receive the bureau rules file. There is one more file which is used to get the condition variable positions from the QCB raw data. Based on the positions, you will have to compare the bureau rules variable values (from Equifax) with the bureau conditions.

In the bureau rules, there are three types of rules mentioned:

- ▸ Credit decision logic
- ▸ AML logic (Anti-Money Laundering logic)
- ▸ Risk navigator score

Your business can use various combinations of the preceding data to build further logic.

Equifax password change service

Equifax security forces its users to change their passwords every month. If that is the case, then as part of your application logic, you need to ensure that you keep track of this date and change the password, as per the expectation of Equifax. This recipe talks about the password change service of Session Service to change a user password.

Getting ready

Note down your current password.

How to do it...

1. Create the `change_password_request` XML using the old password and the new
   password.

```
String xml = "<?xml version=\"1.0\" standalone=\"yes\"?>"
        + "<request>"
        + "<request_header session_token=\"22c06cf0-cfb4-11df-87da-
0a884fe6aa77-76\" interface_version_no= \"1.0\"  dtd_version_
no=\"1.0\">"
        + "<client_reference>XXXX</client_reference>"
        + "</request_header>"
        + "<service_request id=\"1\">"
        + "<session_service>"
        + "<change_password_request domain_id=\"XXXX\" user_
id=\"XXXX\" current_password=\"XXXX\" new_password=\"YYYY\" />"
        + "</session_service>"
        + "</service_request>"
        + "</request>";
```

How it works...

For the `session_token`, the password gets changed if the new password follows Equifax's
password rules, which is detailed in the Equifax documents.

9
Mondrian Integration for Analysis

In this chapter, we will cover:

- ▶ Setting up the environment
- ▶ Defining analysis cubes
- ▶ Analyzing data using Mondrian and JPivot
- ▶ Slicing and dicing operations
- ▶ Producing charts and graphs
- ▶ Creating reports from the analyzed data set

Introduction

In an enterprise application, data analysis is an important aspect, which provides crucial insight into the data the enterprise has. This insight into the existing data can provide invaluable information about the overall business health and the areas where further improvement is needed or possible—leading to effective decision-making. Reports are a static way of analyzing the data and getting the information out of it. However, reports require a pre-defined data analysis pattern—for example, a sales person will only look at the past year product-wise sale performance to come up with the forecast for this year. In today's dynamic world, it may not always be possible to come up with all the possible analysis patterns and provide reports based on that to the users. Hence the need of a good analytic framework becomes the need of the hour for an enterprise.

Traditionally, it is advisable not to load the transaction database with the analysis. Rather, create a data warehouse with the transactional data sources (for example, ADempiere database) using **ETL (Extract-Transform-Load)** tools, which are the foundations of Data Warehousing. The next diagram depicts the typical steps involved in using the transactional database (data source) for the presentation of analytical data:

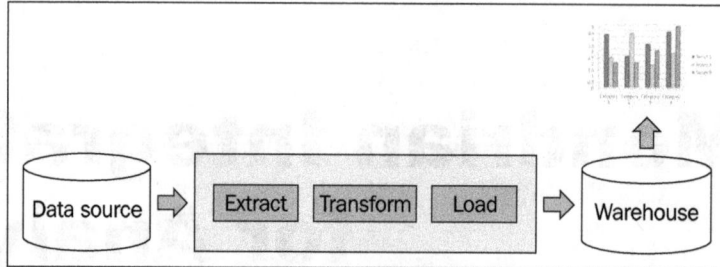

Having mentioned the Data Warehouse, for the **small and medium businesses (SMBs)**, this may be of too much overhead. Rather, it would be useful if the analytic capability can be built on top of the existing transactional data source. In this chapter, we will look at Mondrian, which is a popular OLAP engine, for integration with ADempiere to provide the analytic capability on top of the ADempiere transactional database. Mondrian provides Java APIs for integration. Though it is possible to build a complete and impressive presentation layer on top of Mondrian using its APIs, for simplicity, we will use the JPivot interface. This interface provides the presentation layer in the form of a Web interface and uses the pivot table to present the data. The following diagram depicts the complete eco-system for our ADempiere analytic, which we will be building using Mondrian:

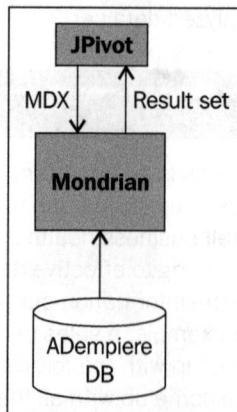

JPivot uses the Mondrian OLAP APIs to present the data using OLAP cubes. The APIs take the **MDX (multi-dimensional expressions)** queries and gives the matching result back to the caller. You may read more about Mondrian at `http://mondrian.pentaho.com/documentation/`.

In this chapter, we will be using the following software:

▶ **Apache Tomcat**: `http://tomcat.apache.org`

▶ **Mondrian**: `http://mondrian.pentaho.com`

I will assume that you have Apache Tomcat already installed on your system. If not, you may refer to the Apache Tomcat website for the complete installation steps.

Setting up the environment

Before we can do anything, it is important to have the right setup in place. In this recipe, I will describe the steps required to set up the environment for implementing analytics on top of ADempiere using Mondrian.

Getting ready

Verify that Apache Tomcat is installed and is running fine on your system. Note down the path where it is installed (we'll refer to this as `TOMCAT_HOME`) and also the port number, say `8080`, on which it will be listening for client connections.

How to do it...

1. Download Mondrian.
2. Extract it to a folder of your choice, say, `c:\mondrian`. Going forward, we will refer to this path as `MONDRIAN_INSTALL_DIR`.

3. Create a database in PostgreSQL with the following detail:

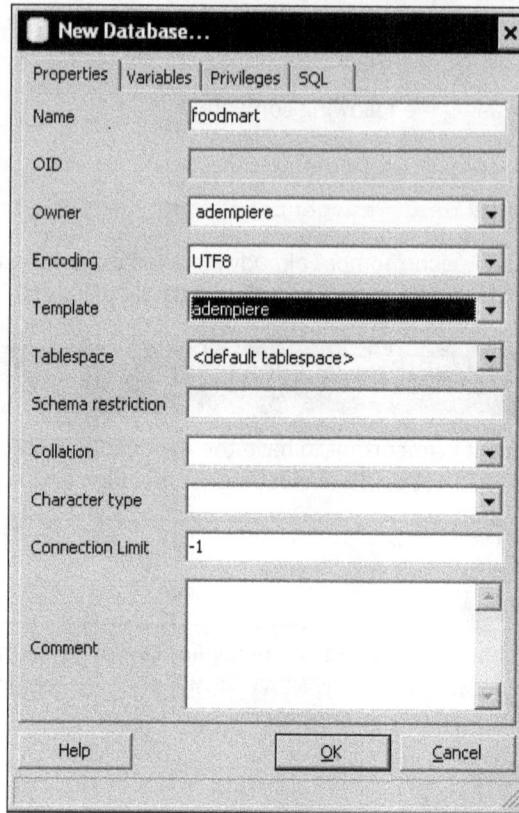

4. Go to the MONDRIAN_INSTALL_DIR folder.

5. Verify that the lib folder under it has the following JARs:

If you don't find these JAR files in the `lib` folder, you shall be able to find them in the `WEB-INF\lib` folder after extracting the downloaded zipped file, the `mondrian.war` file, which can be found in the `lib` folder. You may have to copy the PostgreSQL JAR file from its website or from the `<ADEMPIERE_SVN>\tags\ adempiere360lts\ tools\lib` folder.

6. Add the above mentioned JAR files in the `CLASSPATH`.

7. Run the following command:

```
java mondrian.test.loader.MondrianFoodMartLoader -verbose -tables
-data -indexes -jdbcDrivers="org.postgresql.Driver,sun.jdbc.odbc.
JdbcOdbcDriver" -inputFile=C:\mondrian\demo\FoodMartCreateData.
sql -outputJdbcURL="jdbc:postgresql://localhost/foodmart"
-outputJdbcUser=adempiere360 -outputJdbcPassword=adempiere.
```

8. After the successful execution of the command, you shall see the following indicating everything went well:

```
Finished load at: Thu Oct 9 13:32:39 GMT+05:30 2010.
```

9. Extract `MONDRIAN_INSTALL_DIR\lib\mondrian.war` to `TOMCAT_HOME\ webapps\mondrian`.

10. Copy `postgresql.jar` from the `<ADEMPIERE_SVN>\tags\ adempiere360lts\ tools\lib` to `WEB-INF\lib` folder.

11. Open the `mondrian.properties` file in `TOMCAT_HOME\webapps\mondrian\ WEB-INF` and change the following properties:

   ❑ `Jdbc=jdbc:postgres://localhost/foodmart?user=adempiere&# 38;password=adempiere`

   ❑ `JdbcDrivers=org.postgresql.Driver`

12. Go to the `TOMCAT_HOME/webapps/mondrian/WEB-INF/queries` folder and change the following properties:

   ❑ `jdbcDriver="org.postgresql.Driver"`

   ❑ `jdbcUrl="jdbc:postgresql://localhost/foodmart?user=ademp iere&#38;password=adempiere"`

   ❑ `jdbcUser="adempiere"`

   ❑ `jdbcPassword="ipgplprod"`

13. In the following files:

   ❑ `mondrian.jsp`

   ❑ `arrows.jsp`

   ❑ `colors.jsp`

   ❑ `fourhier.jsp`

14. Start the PostgreSQL database, if it is not already running.

15. Start **Tomcat**.

16. Access the http://localhost:8080/mondrian URL in your browser. If all the steps were completed without an error, we shall see a screenshot similar to the following one:

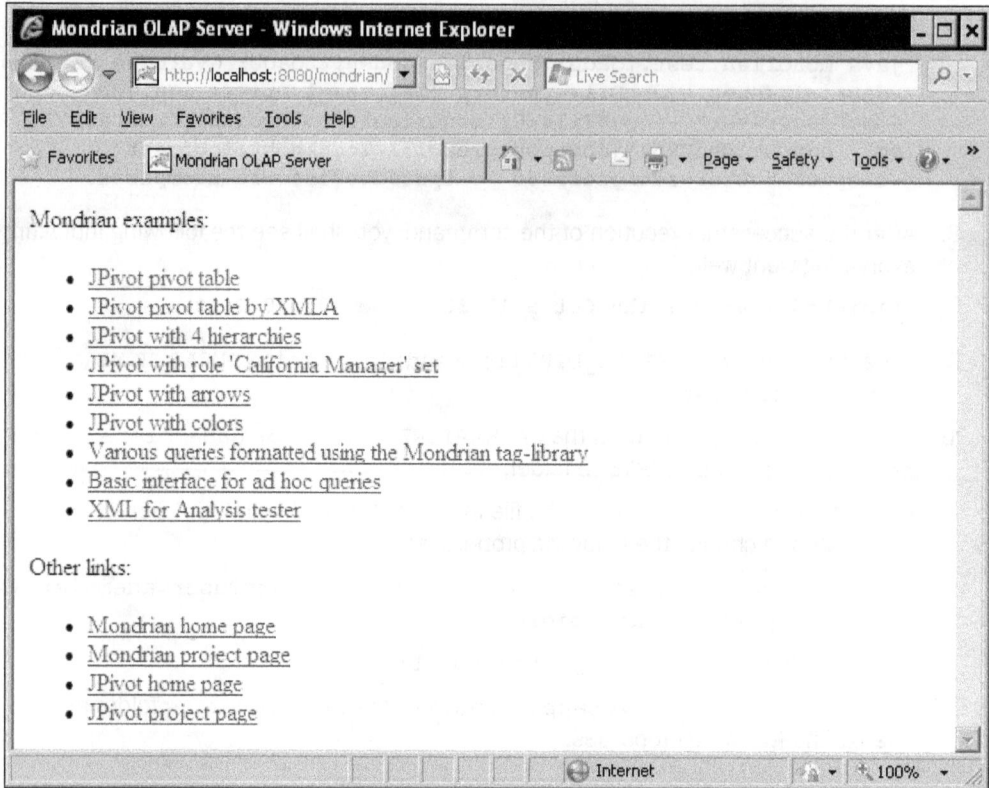

17. Click on the first line—**JPivot pivot table**. You shall see the following screenshot where the records are displayed after querying the food mart database:

18. This prepares us for the subsequent recipes in this chapter.

How it works...

MondrianFoodMartLoader creates the FoodMart schema and loads data in it using the FoodMartCreateData.sql file, which has all the SQL INSERT statements.

mondrian.war file comes with the pre-packaged Mondrian OLAP engine and JPivot-based Web application, which can be used to analyze the FoodMart database. The FoodMart. xml file in the TOMCAT_HOME\webapps\modrian\WEB-INF\queries folder contains the schema and the cube definition, which is used in the MDX queries in the .jsp files (for example, mondrian.jsp, colors.jsp, and so on.) These .jsp files are picked up by testpage.jsp in the TOMCAT_HOME\webapps\modrian folder based on the query parameter passed to it as part of the URL. The testpage.jsp is then used in the index. html file in the TOMCAT_HOME\webapps\modrian folder.

Defining analysis cube

Schema and cube is defined in the following way on Mondrian's documentation page—`http://mondrian.pentaho.com/documentation/schema.php`:

> *A schema defines a multi-dimensional database. It contains a logical model, consisting of cubes, hierarchies, and members, and a mapping of this model onto a physical model.*

> *The logical model consists of the constructs used to write queries in MDX language: cubes, dimensions, hierarchies, levels, and members.*

> *The physical model is the source of the data which is presented through the logical model.*

Cube is a basic construct of Data Warehousing discussion of which is out of this book's scope as there are numerous books existing on this topic and explaining it here may not be a good idea.

In a nutshell, the steps to perform data analysis in Mondrian require us to define a cube, use that cube to define the MDX query, and use the query in the analysis. In this chapter, we will learn how to define a cube using the ADempiere database. In order to understand the subject, I am going to take the following case study and use it throughout the chapter.

Say, in ADempiere, we have a way to capture the sales orders as well as the purchase orders. Now, to the business user for their analysis, say, they need to analyze the sales and purchase data with reference to the products, warehouses, and dates, some of the analysis they may be conducting are:

- ▸ Year-wise product-wise sales and purchase figures
- ▸ Month-wise product-wise warehouse-wise sales and purchase figures
- ▸ Sales and purchase data for a particular set of products
- ▸ Warehouse-wise sales, purchase figures, and more...

Let us see how we can define a cube and schema that can help us to analyze the data as per our need.

Getting ready

Verify that all the steps mentioned in the previous recipe are completed successfully to set up the environment.

How to do it...

1. Create the `kabota_date_dim` date dimension table in the ADempiere database (`adempiere360`) by running the following SQL:

```
CREATE TABLE kabota_date_dim (
    date_id numeric(11,0) NOT NULL,
    for_date date,
    day_of_year numeric(11,0) DEFAULT NULL::numeric,
    year numeric(11,0) DEFAULT NULL::numeric,
    month numeric(11,0) DEFAULT NULL::numeric,
    year_quarter numeric(11,0) DEFAULT NULL::numeric,
    year_and_month numeric(11,0) DEFAULT NULL::numeric,
    year_month_week numeric(11,0) DEFAULT NULL::numeric,
    year_month_date numeric(11,0) DEFAULT NULL::numeric,
    day_of_month numeric(11,0) DEFAULT NULL::numeric,
    week_nbr numeric(11,0) DEFAULT NULL::numeric,
    quarter_nbr numeric(11,0) DEFAULT NULL::numeric,
    day_name character(3) DEFAULT NULL::bpchar,
    month_name character(3) DEFAULT NULL::bpchar
);


ALTER TABLE adempiere.kabota_date_dim OWNER TO adempiere;
```

2. Insert records in the `kabota_date_dim` table. The following is an example for INSERT:

```
INSERT INTO kabota_date_dim VALUES (1, '2009-01-01', 1, 2009, 1,
20091, 200901, 2009011, 20090101, 1, 1, 1, 'THU', 'JAN');
```

3. Create the `va_ana_order_line` view in the ADempiere database by running the following SQL:

```
CREATE VIEW va_ana_order_line AS
SELECT line.c_orderline_id, line.c_order_id, c_order.issotrx,
CASE WHEN c_order.issotrx='Y' THEN 'Sales'
        ELSE 'Purchase'
    END as type
,
line.dateordered, order_dim.date_id AS dateordered_id, line.
datepromised, promised_dim.date_id AS datepromised_id, line.
datedelivered, delivered_dim.date_id AS datedelivered_id, line.m_
product_id, line.m_warehouse_id,line.pricecost,line.priceactual,
line.pricelist, line.pricelimit,line.discount, line.qtyordered,
line.qtyreserved, line.qtydelivered FROM (((c_orderline line
JOIN kabota_date_dim order_dim ON (((line.dateordered)::date
= order_dim.for_date)))JOIN c_order ON (line.c_order_id = c_
```

```
order.c_order_id) LEFT JOIN kabota_date_dim promised_dim ON
(((line.datepromised)::date = promised_dim.for_date))) LEFT JOIN
kabota_date_dim delivered_dim ON (((line.datedelivered)::date =
delivered_dim.for_date)));
```

4. Set the owner:

```
ALTER TABLE adempiere.va_ana_order_line  OWNER TO adempiere;
```

5. Create an `Adempiere.xml` file in the `TOMCAT_HOME\webapps\mondrian\WEB-INF\queries` folder and save the following cube definition in it:

```xml
<?xml version="1.0"?>
<Schema name="Adempiere">

<Cube name="orderline">
  <Table name="va_ana_order_line"/>

  <!--  Ordered Date -->
  <Dimension name="OrderDate" foreignKey="dateordered_id">
    <Hierarchy hasAll="true" allMemberName="All Dates"
primaryKey="date_id">
      <Table name="kabota_date_dim"/>
        <Level name="YEAR" column="year" type="Integer"
uniqueMembers="false"/>

   <!-- Here nameColumn is used to take date from "MONTH" column,
and month name from "MONTH_NAME" in this way we get MonthName in
sorted order -->
        <Level name="MONTH" column="month" nameColumn="month_name"
uniqueMembers="false"/>

        <Level name="DAY OF MONTH" column="day_of_month"
type="Integer" uniqueMembers="false"/>
    </Hierarchy>
  </Dimension>

  <Dimension name="Order Type" >
    <Hierarchy hasAll="true" allMemberName="All Types">
      <Level name="Order Type" column="type"
uniqueMembers="false"/>
    </Hierarchy>
  </Dimension>

  <!-- Product Dimension- some more product related attribute can
appear as Hierarchy-->
  <Dimension name="Product" foreignKey="m_product_id">
    <Hierarchy hasAll="true" allMemberName="All Products"
```

```
primaryKey="m_product_id">
  <Table name="m_product"/>

  <Level name="ProductName" column="m_product_id"
nameColumn="name" uniqueMembers="false"/>
  </Hierarchy>
  </Dimension>

  <!-- Warehouse and location -->
  <Dimension name="Warehouse" foreignKey="m_warehouse_id">
    <Hierarchy hasAll="true" allMemberName="All Warehouses"
primaryKey="m_warehouse_id">
  <Table name="m_warehouse"/>

  <Level name="WarehouseName" column="m_warehouse_id"
nameColumn="name" uniqueMembers="false"/>
  </Hierarchy>
  </Dimension>

  <Measure name="pricelist" column="pricelist" aggregator="sum"
></Measure>
  <Measure name="Actual Price" column="priceactual"
aggregator="sum" ></Measure>
  <Measure name="Quantity" column="qtyordered" aggregator="sum"
></Measure>
  <Measure name="qtyreserved" column="qtyreserved"
aggregator="sum" ></Measure>
  <Measure name="qtydelivered" column="qtydelivered"
aggregator="sum" ></Measure>
    <CalculatedMember
        name="Profit"
        dimension="Measures">
      <Formula>[Measures].[pricelist] - [Measures].[Actual
Price]</Formula>
    </CalculatedMember>
</Cube>
</Schema>
```

Analyzing data using Mondrian and JPivot

Now that we have defined the cube and schema for our analysis, we will hook that on to
the Mondrian and JPivot so that we can start seeing the action using the JPivot Web-based
interface. This recipe is all about knowing what it takes to write a query using the cube that
we defined in the earlier recipe and make the required changes to the Web application to use
JPivot-based presentation.

Getting ready

Verify that you have completed all the previous recipes of this chapter without any error.

How to do it...

1. Save the following code in `order.jsp` in the `TOMCAT_HOME\webapps\mondrian\WEB-INF\queries` folder:

```
<%@ page session="true" contentType="text/html;
charset=ISO-8859-1" %>
<%@ taglib uri="http://www.tonbeller.com/jpivot" prefix="jp" %>
<%@ taglib prefix="c" uri="http://java.sun.com/jstl/core" %>

<jp:mondrianQuery id="query01" jdbcDriver="org.postgresql.Driver"
jdbcUrl="jdbc:postgresql://localhost:5432/adempiere360?user=ademp
iere&password=adempiere"  catalogUri="/WEB-INF/queries/Adempiere.
xml">

select {[Measures].[Actual Price],[Measures].[Quantity]} ON
COLUMNS,
   {([Order Type].[All Types],[OrderDate].[All Dates],[Product].
[All Products],[Warehouse].[All Warehouses])} ON ROWS
from [orderline]

</jp:mondrianQuery>

<c:set var="title01" scope="session">Order Analysis</c:set>
Add the following code to <body> element in index.html in TOMCAT_
HOME\webapps\mondrian folder:
<p>ADempiere cubes:</p>
<ul>
<li><a href="testpage.jsp?query=order">Product wise date wise
sales and purchase</ul>
</ul>
```

2. Restart the Tomcat server.

3. Access the `http://localhost:8080/mondrian/` URL in the browser. You will see the following page:

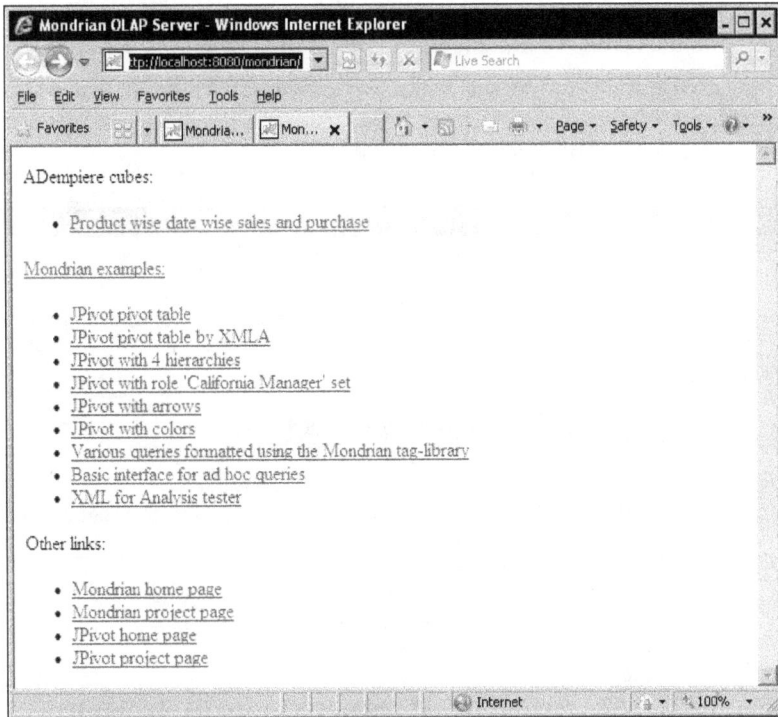

4. Click on the **Product wise date wise sales and purchase** link. You shall see the following page:

With this, you are now ready to analyze the data using the cube that we had defined earlier. The tooltip on the buttons tells us what functionality is driven by which button.

Clicking on the **+** sign shows the detail. For example, click on **All Types** and then expand the **All Dates** for each **Order Type** to see the year-wise sales and purchase details, as shown in the following screenshot:

Slicing and dicing

The query, by default, returns a data set on which the analysis is carried out. During the analysis, if you want to limit the data set to a smaller set and base your analysis on top of it, then you can create a slice of the data and use it. This is achieved using the filters in JPivot. This recipe describes the steps required to define and apply a filter and how to remove it.

For the recipe, we have taken the use case where the user only wants to look at the sales and purchase details pertaining to a particular product—Patio Table.

How to do it...

1. Click on the ⬚ toolbar button. The following section appears:

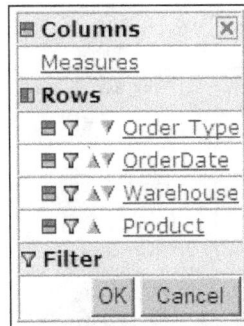

```
▣ Columns              ⊠
    Measures
▥ Rows
    ▤ ▽  ▽ Order Type
    ▤ ▽ ▲▽ OrderDate
    ▤ ▽ ▲▽ Warehouse
    ▤ ▽ ▲  Product
▽ Filter
              OK  Cancel
```

2. Click on the ▽ icon appearing before the **Product** under **Rows**. This will add the **Product** to the **Filter**.

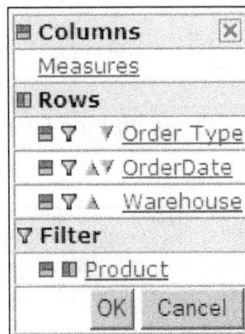

```
▣ Columns              ⊠
    Measures
▥ Rows
    ▤ ▽  ▽ Order Type
    ▤ ▽ ▲▽ OrderDate
    ▤ ▽ ▲  Warehouse
▽ Filter
    ▤ ▥ Product
              OK  Cancel
```

3. Click on the **Product** link and click on the red colored ✛ icon appearing before **All Products** and click again on the ✛ icon appearing before **Patio Table...**

4. Select **Patio Table**.

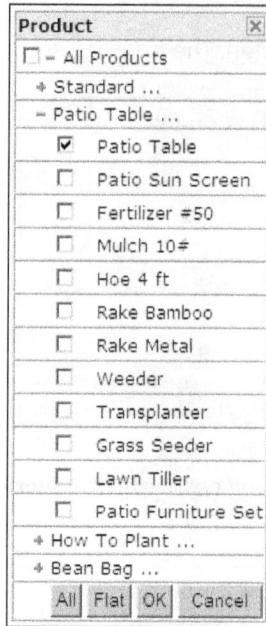

```
Product                                    [X]
[ ] - All Products
    + Standard ...
    - Patio Table ...
        [✓]   Patio Table
        [ ]   Patio Sun Screen
        [ ]   Fertilizer #50
        [ ]   Mulch 10#
        [ ]   Hoe 4 ft
        [ ]   Rake Bamboo
        [ ]   Rake Metal
        [ ]   Weeder
        [ ]   Transplanter
        [ ]   Grass Seeder
        [ ]   Lawn Tiller
        [ ]   Patio Furniture Set
    + How To Plant ...
    + Bean Bag ...
    [ All ][ Flat ][ OK ][ Cancel ]
```

5. Click on the **OK** button. You shall see that the filter detail has been mentioned as follows:

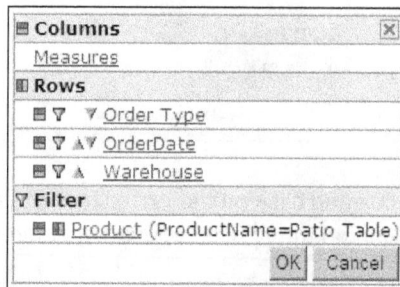

```
▣ Columns                                  [X]
    Measures
▣ Rows
    ▤ ▽ ▽ Order Type
    ▤ ▽ ▲▽ OrderDate
    ▤ ▽ ▲ Warehouse
▽ Filter
    ▤ ▣ Product (ProductName=Patio Table)
                              [ OK ][ Cancel ]
```

6. Click on the **OK** button. The filter is applied and the detail is displayed based on the slice of data filtered by the product name:

7. To remove the filter, click on the ▢ button. You shall see the **Product** under the **Filter** section.

8. Click on the **Product** link, uncheck the **Patio Table** and click on the **OK** button.

9. Click on the ▦ button. This shall take the **Product** back to the **Rows**. You may use the ⬆⬇ buttons to position the **Product** among **Rows**.

10. Click on the **OK** button. The result set will now include all the products.

Producing charts and graphs

Tabular data is great, but to give a quick idea or to quickly derive some information from the data set, a visual representation is helpful. The JPivot interface of Mondrian provides the support for charts and graphs. It produces charts based on the current data set and also allows a user to configure the chart type and its details. In this recipe, we'll see how to do it.

How to do it...

1. On the **Order Analysis** page, click on the 📊 button. This will present the current data set in the form of chart:

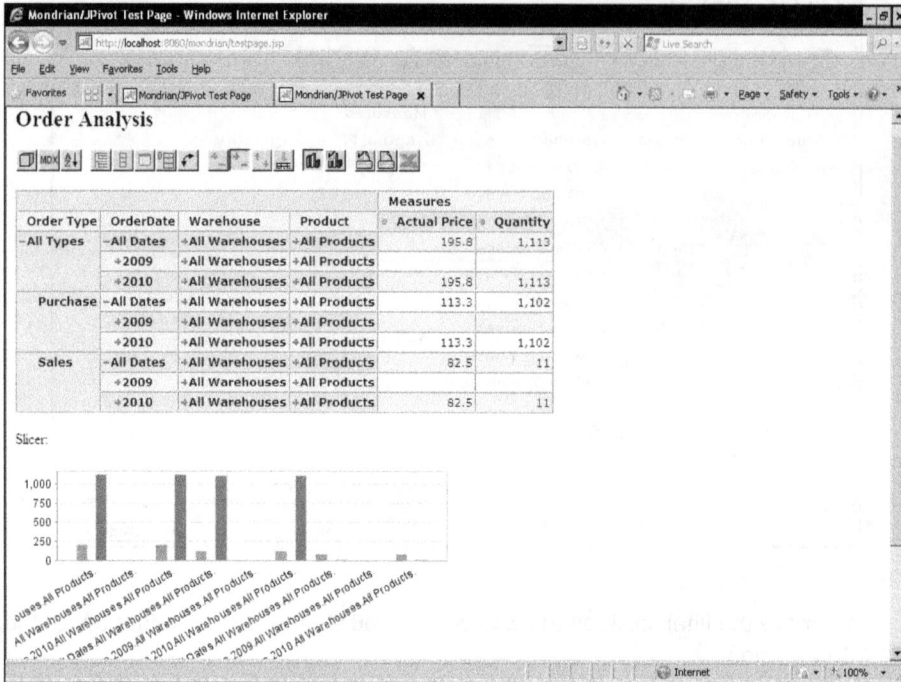

2. To change the chart type or to configure a chart, click on the 📊 button. This will present the following options:

3. Say, you change the **Chart Type** to **Stacked Vertical Bar 3D** and checked the **Enable Drill Through**. Click on the **OK** button after changing these values. This shall present the chart in the selected form, and clicking on the bar shall show you the drill through information.

4. Click on the ⊛ icon in the **Quantity** column header to drill through the quantity.

Creating reports from the analyzed data set

Apply filters, change column orders, apply sorting, and the like on the crosstab representation that represents your current analysis outcome at a given instance of time. Once you have got your data set, it may be required to print a report from it so that the same can be shared with others. The Web interface provides support for printing the reports in PDF and the MS-Excel format. This recipe describes the steps to print reports using Mondrian and JPivot.

How to do it...

1. Prepare your crosstab view after your analysis and click on the ⊟. button, which presents the data in PDF form.

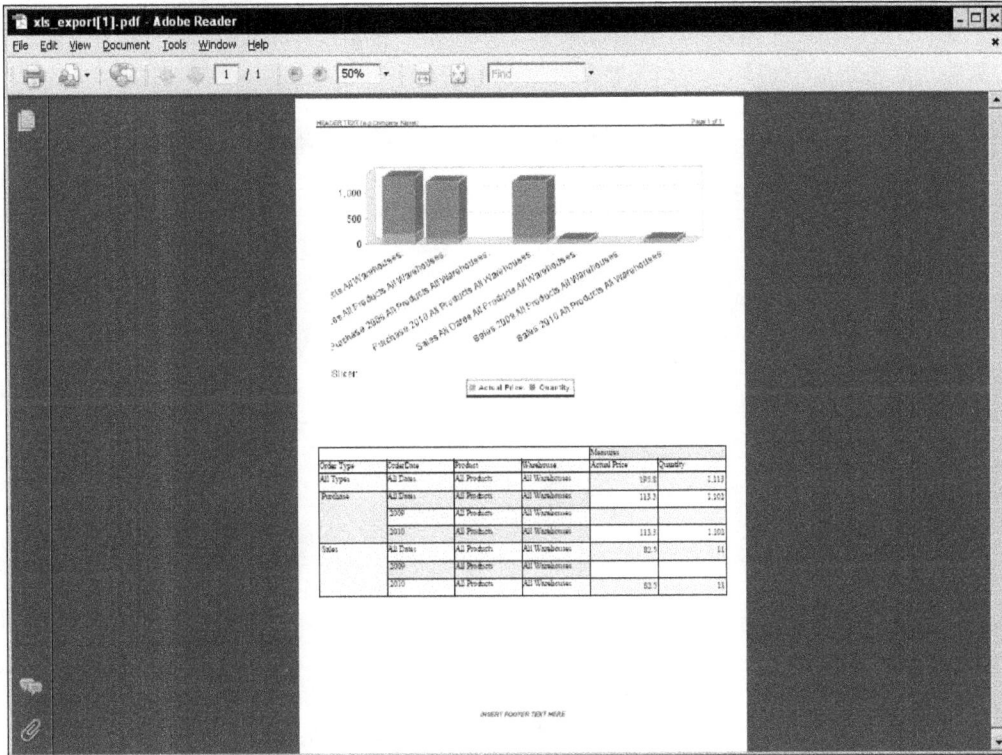

2. To produce an MS-Excel sheet, click on the ⊠ button.

3. To change the print settings, click on the ⊟ button.

10
E-mail Integration with Mozilla Thunderbird

In this chapter, we will cover:

- ▸ Setting up the environment
- ▸ Extending the Thunderbird toolbar
- ▸ Working with ADempiere contacts from Thunderbird

Introduction

Sending e-mail to the outside world is present in ADempiere and works great for the e-mail notification, alerts, and reminders. We already made use of it in our previous chapter to send mail to the users. However, many a time, it is very convenient to use the full-fledged mail clients like, Mozilla Thunderbird, MS Outlook, Evolution, and so on for two different reasons:

1. More people use these mail clients than ADempiere and there is almost certain probability that an ADempiere user might already be using (and still using) a mail client before and after he/she became an ADempiere user, as well.

2. They are more complex and more complete than ADempiere's Send Mail capability.

The bottom line is that we use them and it would be good if we can have a two-way integration with ADempiere so that things like outbound and inbound messages, tasks, and events can be in sync between both. This gives the user the access to the same data from two different places, depending upon which software he/she is using at a given instance.

In this chapter, we'll cover a few items related to the integration between a mail client and ADempiere. I have selected Mozilla Thunderbird because of its popularity, simplicity, and the extensibility support. We will see how we can pull out the users detail from ADempiere and use them in sending bulk messages. For example, if you want to send a mail to all your prospects, then you can pull out the prospects from the ADempiere database and use them to send e-mails.

To achieve the goal, we will be developing a Thunderbird add-on. The details about how to develop a Thunderbird add-on/extension can be found at `https://developer.mozilla.org/En/Building_an_Extension`https://developer.mozilla.org/En/Building_an_Extension.

Setting up the environment

As we are going to develop a Thunderbird plug-in and also work with the ADempiere database to pull out the contact detail, this recipe focuses on setting up the right environment for the work. We will install the development tools for Thunderbird and for ADempiere integration. This time, we'll keep it simple and straightforward by integrating it with a PHP backend, which directly queries the ADempiere database. Alternatively, you may integrate the add-on with the ADempiere Web services, which we saw in *Chapter 4*, *Web Services*.

How to do it...

1. Download and install Mozilla Thunderbird from the URL `http://www.mozillamessaging.com/en-US/thunderbird/`. This recipe uses the latest 3.1.4 version.

2. Set up your favorite e-mail account in it.

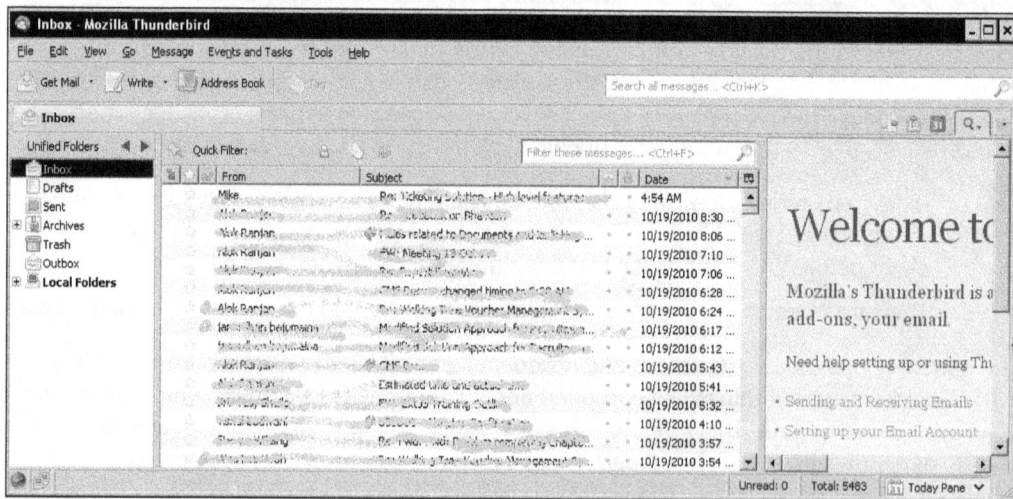

3. Click on the **Tools | Add-ons** menu and add the following add-ons:
    ▸ **DOM Inspector**
    ▸ **JavaScript Debugger**

On the Extensions(screentext style) tab, verify that the add-ons have been added, as shown in the following screenshot.

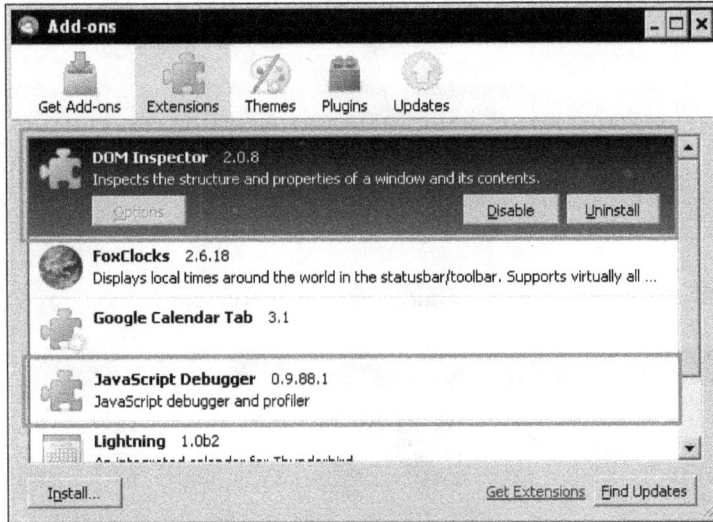

4. Verify that the entries are created in the **Tools** menu of Thunderbird for the newly installed add-ons.

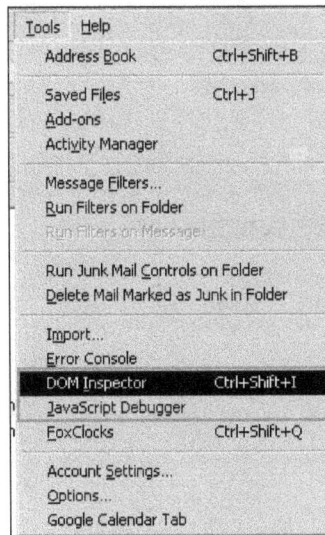

5. Click on the **Tools | DOM Inspector** menu. The **DOM Inspector** window comes up.

6. On the **DOM Inspector** window, click on **Inspect Chrome Document | Inbox | Mozilla Thunderbird**.

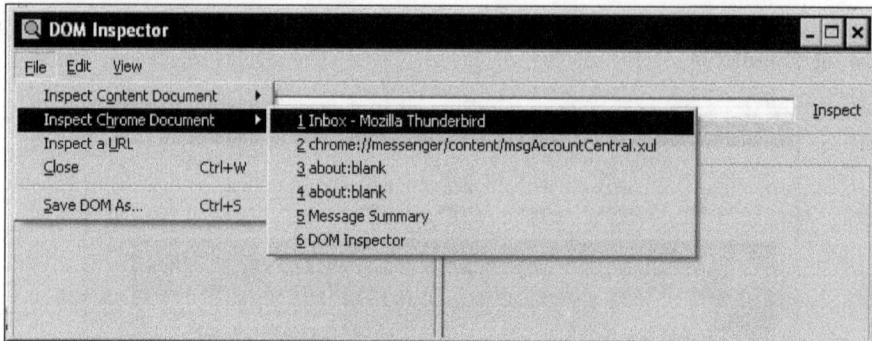

You shall see the DOM for the Thunderbird main window.

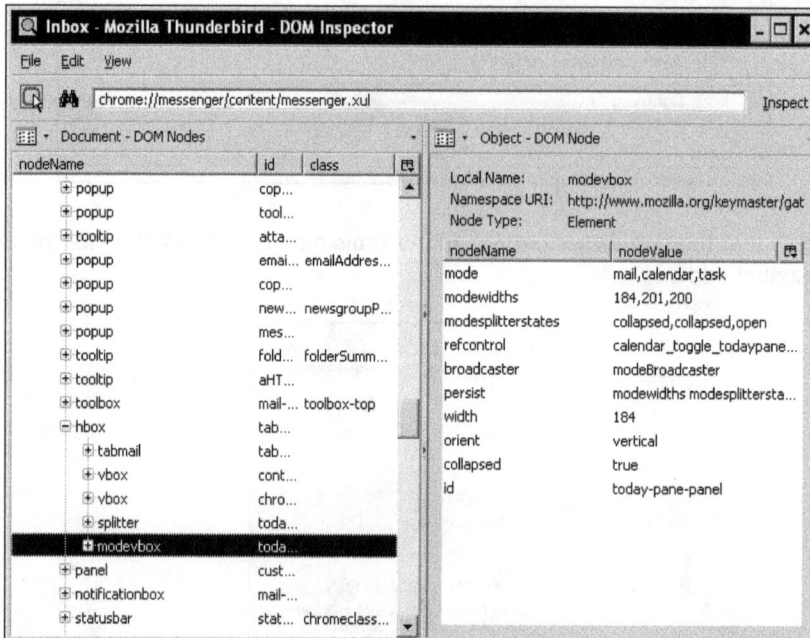

7. Click on the **Tools | JavaScript Debugger** menu. The **JavaScript Debugger** window comes up and you shall be able to open the source code of any file being shown in the **Loaded Scripts** tree.

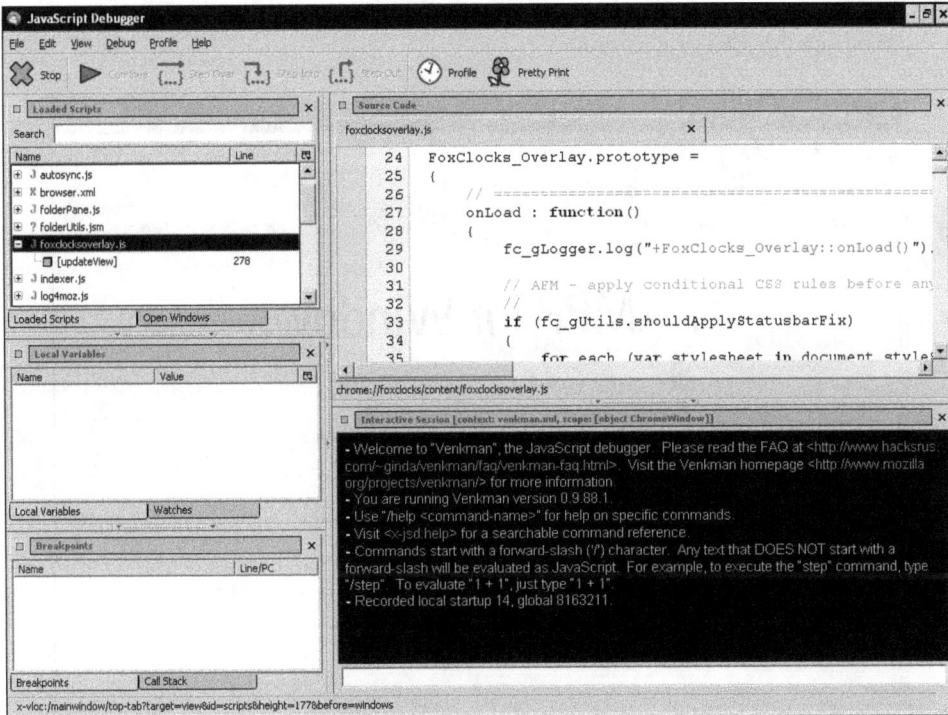

8. Install XAMPP from `http://www.apachefriends.org/en/xampp.html` URL in say, `c:\xampp` folder. We'll refer this folder as `XAMPP_HOME`. This recipe uses the latest version - 1.7.

9. Run `XAMPP_HOME\xampp-control.exe` and start **Apache**.

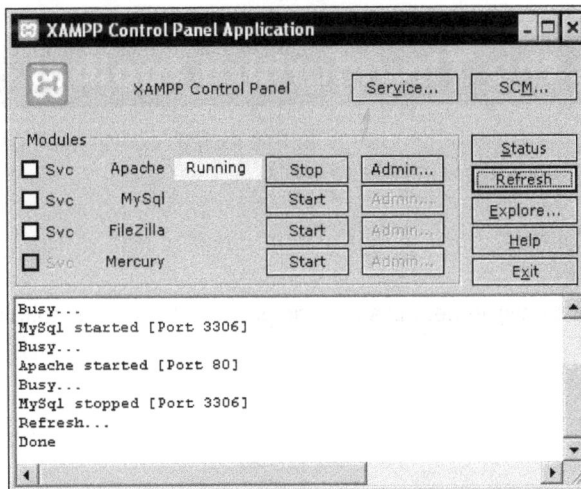

10. Open `http://localhost/` URL in the browser. If XAMPP was installed properly, you shall see the following screen:

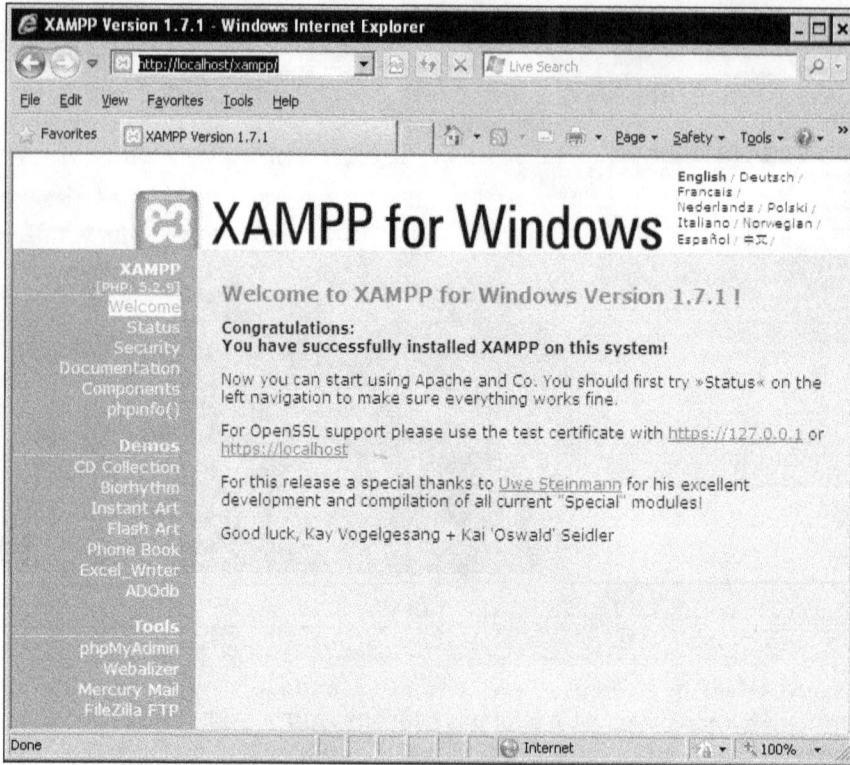

These steps pretty much set up the complete development environment for us.

Extending the Thunderbird toolbar

Now that we have got the environment ready, in this recipe, we will see how we can build a simple add-on for Thunderbird, install it, and use it.

Getting ready

Verify that the complete environment is set up as per the steps outlined in the previous recipe.

How to do it...

1. Create a folder by name, say, `ADempiere_TB_BasicAddOn` in `C:\`.

2. Create the following folders within it:

- ▶ `content`

- ▶ `locale`

- ▶ `en-US`

- ▶ `skin`

```
⊟ 🗀 ADempiere_TB_BasicAddOn
     🗀 content
  ⊟ 🗀 locale
       🗀 en-US
     🗀 skin
```

3. Create the `mail-bar3-overlay.xul` file in the `content` folder and save the following XUL code in it:

```xml
<?xml version="1.0" encoding="UTF-8"?>
<?xml-stylesheet href="chrome://adempiere/skin/overlay.css"
type="text/css"?>
<!DOCTYPE overlay SYSTEM "chrome://adempiere/locale/adempiere.
dtd">
<overlay id="adempiere-overlay"
         xmlns="http://www.mozilla.org/keymaster/gatekeeper/there.
is.only.xul">
  <toolbar id="mail-bar3"> <!-- Thunderbird (toolbar) -->
   <toolbarbutton id="adempiere-toolbar-button"
   label="&adempiereToolbar.label;"
   tooltiptext="&adempiereToolbar.tooltip;"
   oncommand="adempiere.onToolbarButtonCommand()"
   class="toolbarbutton-1">
   </toolbarbutton>
   </toolbar>
</overlay>
```

Overlay is a concept used to extend an existing component/control in Mozilla. In this code, we are extending the Thunderbird toolbar, which is referenced using the `id – mail-bar3`. You can get the `Id` using the DOM Inspector.

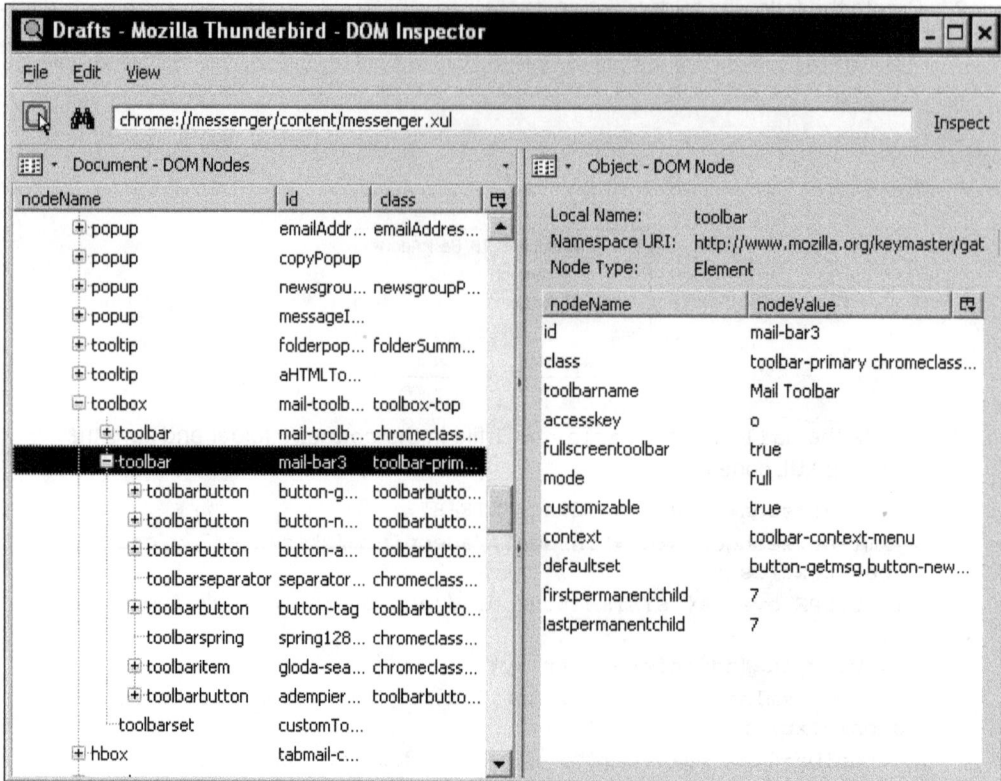

4. Copy an ADempiere logo file (say, `AdempiereLogoNew.png`) from the ADempiere project to the `content` folder, so that we can use the same as an image for the add-on as well as the toolbar image, which we will be adding shortly. You may have to resize the image to 32x32 dimensions if the image you have copied is larger.

5. Copy the same image to the `skin` folder.

6. Create the `overlay.css` file in the skin folder and save the following CSS detail to it:

```
#adempiere-toolbar-button
{
   list-style-image: url("chrome://adempiere/skin/
AdempiereLogoNew.png");
}
```

This file contains the CSS styles specific to our component.

7. Create the `adempiere.dtd` file in the `locale\en-US` folder and save the following code in it:

```
<!ENTITY adempiereToolbar.label "ADempiere">
<!ENTITY adempiereToolbar.tooltip "Provides integration points
with various ADempiere functionalities">
```

This file contains the messages and string literals used in our program

8. Create the `install.rdf` file in the `C:\ADempiere_TB_BasicAddOn` folder and save the following content in it:

```
<?xml version="1.0" encoding="UTF-8"?>
<RDF xmlns="http://www.w3.org/1999/02/22-rdf-syntax-ns#"
 xmlns:em="http://www.mozilla.org/2004/em-rdf#">
  <Description about="urn:mozilla:install-manifest">
    <em:id>adempiere.addon@walkingtree.in</em:id>
    <em:name>ADempiere</em:name>
    <em:version>0.1</em:version>
    <em:description>ADempiere add-on</em:description>
    <em:creator>Ajit Kumar</em:creator>
    <em:iconURL>chrome://adempiere/content/AdempiereLogoNew.png</
em:iconURL>
    <em:targetApplication>
      <Description>
        <em:id>{3550f703-e582-4d05-9a08-453d09bdfdc6}</em:id> <!--
thunderbird -->
        <em:minVersion>1.5</em:minVersion>
        <em:maxVersion>3.1.*</em:maxVersion>
      </Description>
    </em:targetApplication>
  </Description>
</RDF>
```

This file is required for Mozilla to be able to install the add-on. `3550f703-e582-4d05-9a08-453d09bdfdc6` is the unique application ID to identify Thunderbird.

9. Create the `chrome.manifest` file in the `C:\ADempiere_TB_BasicAddOn` folder and save the following content in it:

```
content    adempiere content/
locale     adempiere    en-US    locale/en-US/
skin       adempiere    classic/1.0    skin/
overlay    chrome://messenger/content/messenger.xul    chrome://
adempiere/content/mail-bar3-overlay.xul
style      chrome://global/content/customizeToolbar.xul    chrome://
adempiere/skin/overlay.css
```

10. Create a zipped file, say, `adempiere-tb-basicaddon.zip` using all the files and folders in `C:\ADempiere_TB_BasicAddOn`. When you look into the archive file, you shall see the following content:

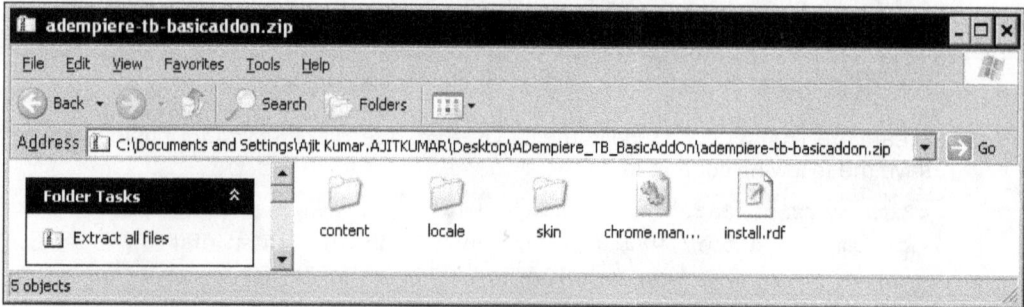

11. Rename `adempiere-tb-basicaddon.zip` to `adempiere-tb-basicaddon.xpi`.

12. Click on the **Tools** | **Add-ons** menu in Thunderbird. This will show the **Add-ons** window with the currently added add-ons listed.

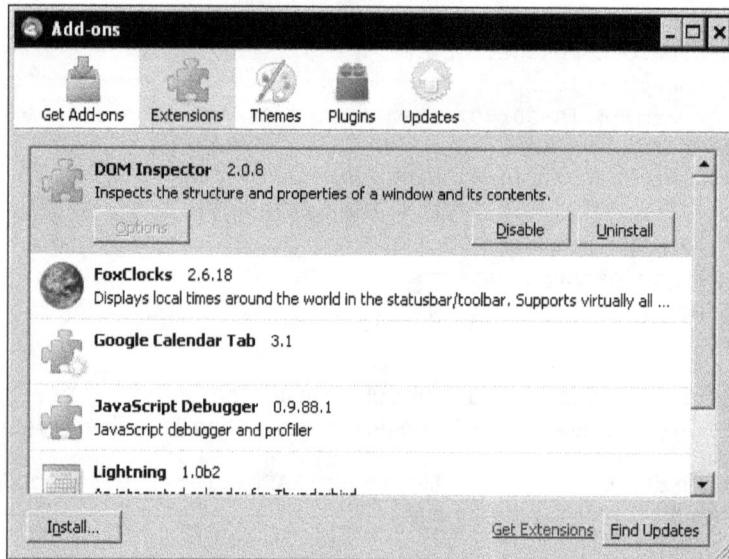

13. Click on the **Install...** button and select the `adempiere-tb-basicaddon.xpi` file. Thunderbird shall show the add-on detail in the **Software Installation** dialog.

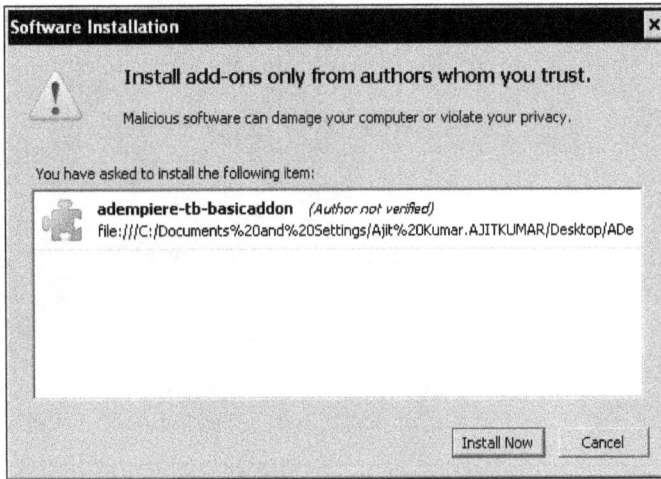

14. Click the **Install Now** button. This will install the new add-on in Thunderbird and prompt you to restart Thunderbird.

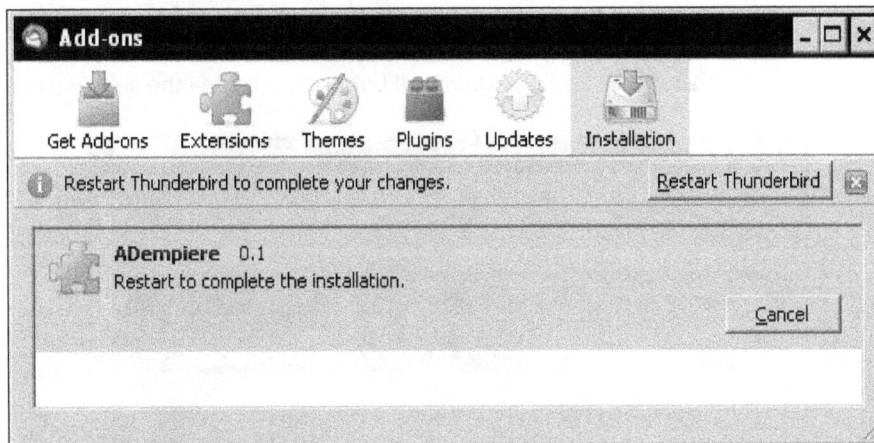

15. Click the **Restart Thunderbird** button. This will restart Thunderbird and it will show the newly-added **ADempiere** button in the toolbar.

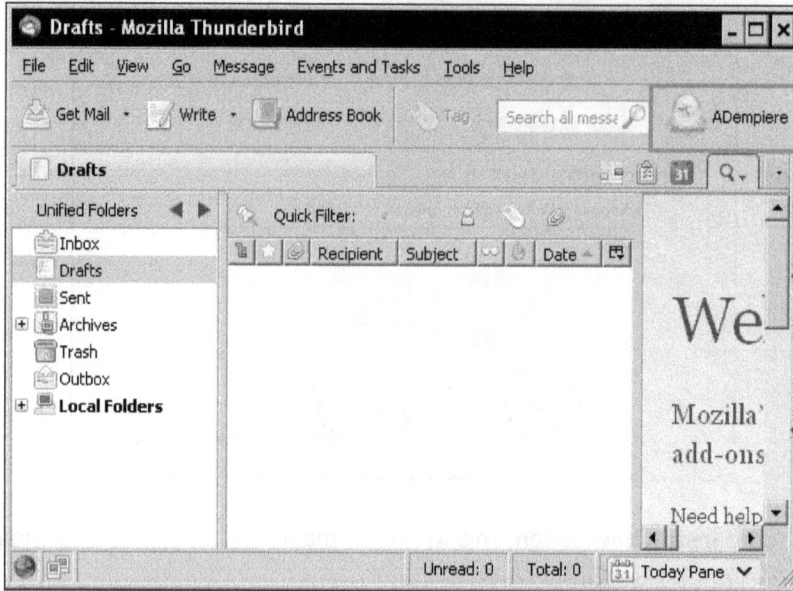

16. To uninstall the add-on, click on the **Tools | Add-ons** menu.

17. Select the extension and click the **Uninstall** button to uninstall the selected add-on.

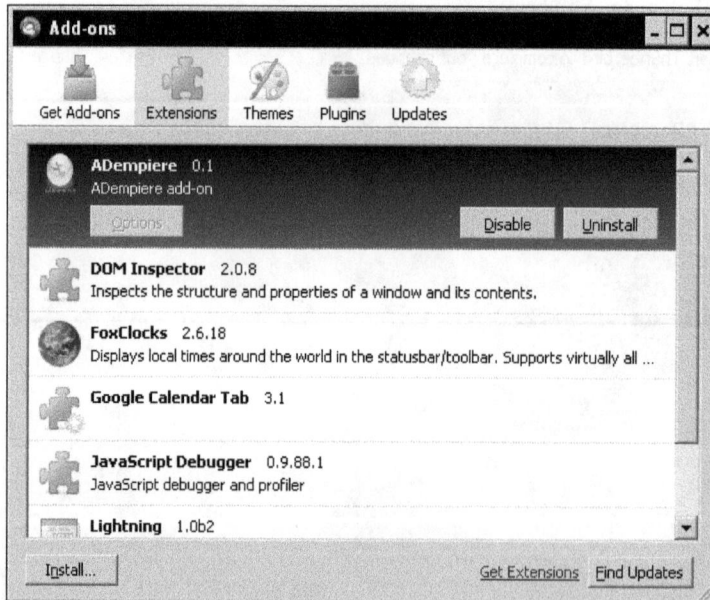

18. Restart Thunderbird to complete the uninstallation, which will remove the ADempiere button from the toolbar.

Working with ADempiere contacts from Thunderbird

In this recipe, we will further extend our basic add-on, which we developed in the previous recipe, so that we can pull out the contact detail from the ADempiere database and use the e-mail IDs in composing mail in Thunderbird. The following diagram depicts the setup, which is used in this recipe:

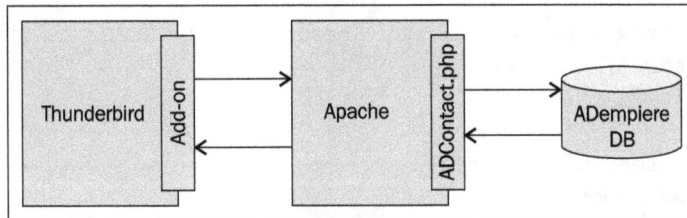

The add-on allows the user to select a business partner type (vendor/customer/employee/prospect/sales rep). Based on the selected type, it makes a call to the `ADContacts.php` to get the user contacts of the selected type from ADempiere. `ADContacts.php` reads the matching users detail (name and e-mail) and returns the list back to the add-on. Add-on then parses the list, gets all the e-mail IDs out from it and launches the compose mail window with the e-mails IDs already added in the **To** list. The add-on can be used to quickly send a mail to a category of users in ADempiere.

Getting ready

Verify that you have got the basic add-on ready after following the steps mentioned in the previous recipe.

How to do it...

1. Create the `ADContacts.php` file in the `XAMPP_HOME\htdocs` folder and save the following PHP code in it:

```php
<?php
$retArr = array();

$dbconn = pg_connect("host=localhost dbname=adempiere360
user=adempiere password=adempiere")
    or die('Could not connect: ' . pg_last_error());
```

```
$query = 'SELECT a.name,a.email FROM adempiere.ad_user a,
adempiere.c_bpartner b ' .
    ' WHERE a.c_bpartner_id=b.c_bpartner_id AND a.c_bpartner_id IS
NOT NULL' .
    ' AND a.email IS NOT NULL';

if (isset($_REQUEST['type']))
    $query .= " AND b." . $_REQUEST['type'] . "='Y'";

$result = pg_query($query) or die('Query failed: ' . pg_last_
error());

while ($row = pg_fetch_array($result, null, PGSQL_ASSOC)) {
    $retArr[] = $row;
}

pg_free_result($result);
pg_close($dbconn);

Echo '{users:'.json_encode($retArr).'}';

?>
```

2. Start **Apache** Web server in **XAMPP**

3. Create the `adempiereoverlay.js` file in the content folder and save the following JavaScript code in it:

```
var adempiere = {
    onLoad : function() {
    // initialization code
    this.initialized = true;
    },
    makeAjaxRequest : function(cmdParam) {
    var xhr;
    try {
        xhr = new ActiveXObject('Msxml2.XMLHTTP');
    } catch (e) {
        try {
        xhr = new ActiveXObject('Microsoft.XMLHTTP');
        } catch (e2) {
        try {
            xhr = new XMLHttpRequest();
        } catch (e3) {
            xhr = false;
```

```
        }
      }
    }

  xhr.onreadystatechange = function() {
    if (xhr.readyState == 4) {
    if (xhr.status == 200) {
      var obj = eval("(" + xhr.responseText + ')');
      var mailTos = "";
      for ( var i = 0; i < obj.users.length; i++) {
      if (mailTos == "")
        mailTos += obj.users[i].email;
      else
        mailTos += "," + obj.users[i].email;
      }

      var sURL = "mailto:" + mailTos + "?subject=";

      var msgComposeService = Components.classes["@mozilla.org/
messengercompose;1"]
        .getService(Components.interfaces.
nsIMsgComposeService);

      // make the URI
      var ioService = Components.classes["@mozilla.org/network/
io-service;1"]
        .getService(Components.interfaces.nsIIOService);

      aURI = ioService.newURI(sURL, null, null);

      // open new message
      msgComposeService.OpenComposeWindowWithURI(null, aURI);
    } else
      alert("Error code " + xhr.status);
    }
  };

  xhr.open("GET", "http://localhost/ADContacts.php"
    + (cmdParam != "" ? "?" + cmdParam : ""), true);
  xhr.send(null);
  },
  onEmployeeCommand : function(e) {
  adempiere.makeAjaxRequest("type=isemployee");
  },
```

```
onVendorCommand : function(e) {
adempiere.makeAjaxRequest("type=isvendor");
},
onProspectCommand : function(e) {
adempiere.makeAjaxRequest("type=isprospect");
},
onSalesRepCommand : function(e) {
adempiere.makeAjaxRequest("type=issalesrep");
},
onCustomerCommand : function(e) {
adempiere.makeAjaxRequest("type=iscustomer");
}
};


window.addEventListener("load", function(e) {
    adempiere.onLoad(e);
}, false);
```

4. Replace the content of `mail- bar3-overlay.xul` with the following code:

```
<?xml version="1.0" encoding="UTF-8"?>
<?xml-stylesheet href="chrome://adempiere/skin/overlay.css"
type="text/css"?>
<!DOCTYPE overlay SYSTEM "chrome://adempiere/locale/adempiere.
dtd">
<overlay id="adempiere-overlay"
         xmlns="http://www.mozilla.org/keymaster/gatekeeper/there.
is.only.xul">
  <script src="adempiereoverlay.js"/>
  <toolbar id="mail-bar3"> <!-- Thunderbird (toolbar) -->
   <toolbarbutton id="adempiere-toolbar-button"
   type="menu"
   label="&adempiereToolbar.label;"
   tooltiptext="&adempiereToolbar.tooltip;"
   oncommand="adempiere.onToolbarButtonCommand()"
   class="toolbarbutton-1">
     <menupopup>
       <menuitem label="Employees" oncommand="adempiere.
onEmployeeCommand()"/>
       <menuitem label="Vendors" oncommand="adempiere.
onVendorCommand()"/>
       <menuitem label="Prospects" oncommand="adempiere.
onProspectCommand()"/>
       <menuitem label="Customers" oncommand="adempiere.
onCustomerCommand()"/>
       <menuitem label="Sales Reps" oncommand="adempiere.
```

```
onSalesRepCommand()"/>
        </menupopup>
    </toolbarbutton>
    </toolbar>
</overlay>
```

❑   We have added a menu for the toolbar button

5.   Create the `adempiere-tab-basicaddon.xpi` file.

6.   Install the add-on in Thunderbird. Upon successful installation of the add-on, you shall see a menu appearing when you click on the **ADempiere** button.

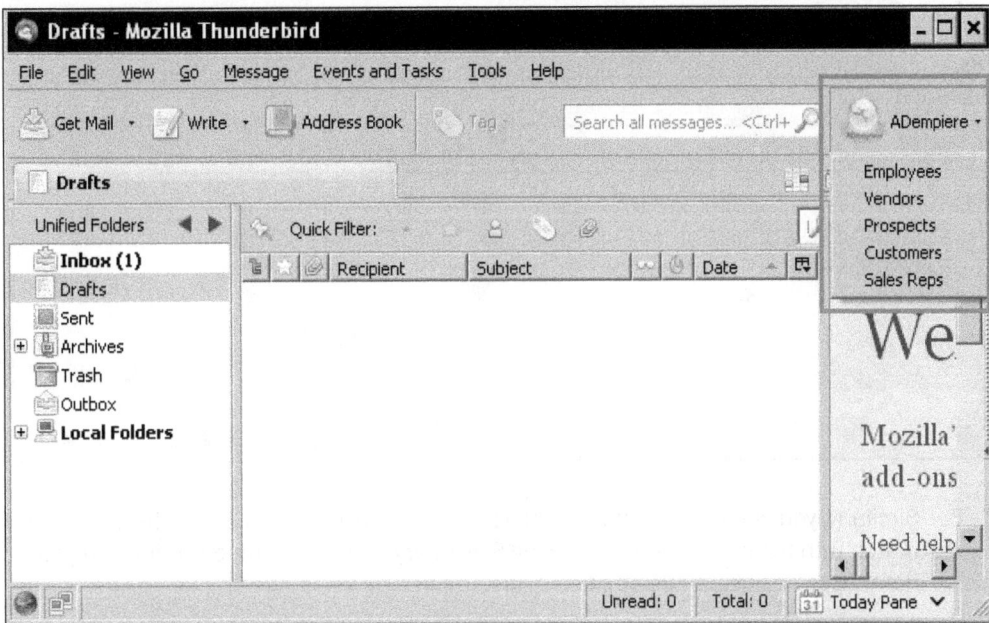

7. Click on the **ADempiere | Employees** menu. You will see the compose mail window with the e-mail IDs of all the employees set up in ADempiere.

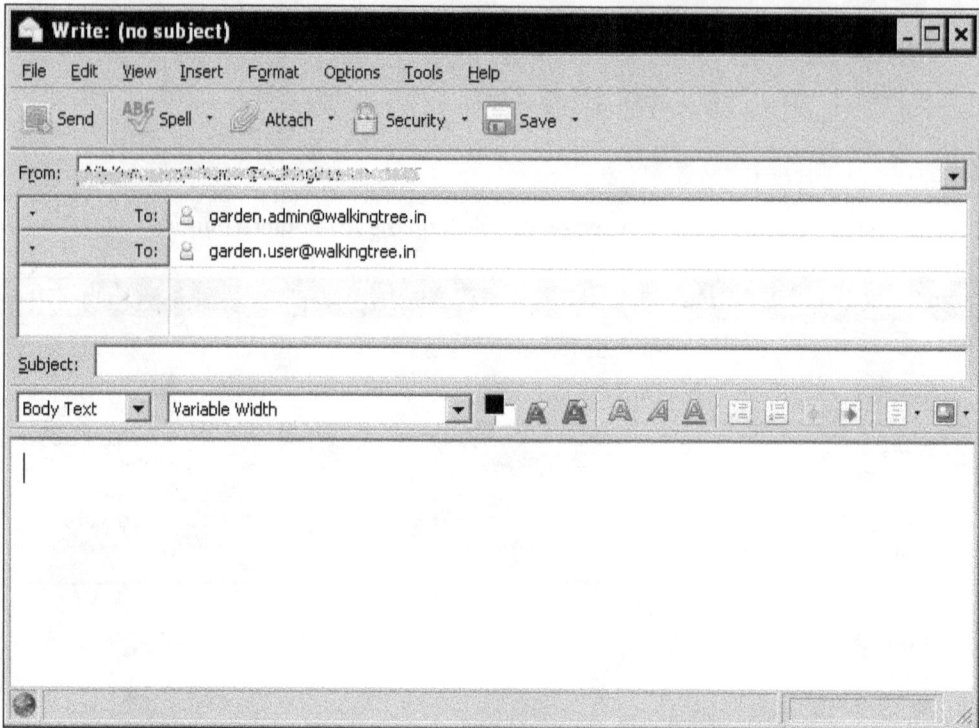

8. Similarly, you can try out other menu options. The results (mail IDs of the users) shall match with the output of the following SQL query (when you run on your ADempiere database – `adempiere360`):

```
SELECT a.name,a.email,b.isvendor,b.isemployee,b.isprospect,b.
iscustomer,b.issalesrep
FROM adempiere.ad_user a, adempiere.c_bpartner b
WHERE a.c_bpartner_id=b.c_bpartner_id
AND a.isactive='Y'
AND a.c_bpartner_id IS NOT NULL
AND a.email IS NOT NULL
```

	name character var	email character varying(60)	isvendor character(1)	isemployee character(1)	isprospect character(1)	iscustomer character(1)	issalesrep character(1)
1	GardenUser	garden.user@walkingtree.in	Y	Y	N	Y	Y
2	Henry Seed	henry.seed@walkingtree.in	Y	N	N	Y	N
3	GardenAdmin	garden.admin@walkingtree.in	Y	Y	Y	N	Y
4	Joe Sales	joe.sales@gmail.com	Y	N	N	N	N
5	Carl Boss	carl.boss@yahoo.com	N	N	Y	Y	N

Index

Symbols

3E_WebServices project 160

A

ActiveMQ adapters
building 196-199
working 200
ad_client_id 44
add() function 207
ADempiere
about 157
callout, creating 130-132
combo-box list, populating 76-80
customizing 37, 39
data display, defaulting to single/multi row
mode 95
data, filtering at tab level 102, 104
default logic, configuring 108, 109
default print format of window,
customizing 117-119
desktop version of toolbar, extending
146-149
display logic, configuring 104-108
dynamic validation 114-116
e-mail integration with Mozilla
Thunderbird 293
entity and line items, displaying on same tab
96-98
environment, developing 7
Equifax integration 255
existing window, customizing 55-57
hooks for model, modifying 133-136
info window, creating for desktop version 127
info window, creating for web version 128,
129

installing 13, 16
JasperReports integration 210
lookup record, configuring 111-113
menu tree, assigning to role 91-94
model, generating 123-126
MOM template 42
Mondrian integration 271
multiple instances, running on single server
34-36
multiple tabs adding to window 58-66
new menu tree, creating 89, 90
new print format for window, configuring
119-123
PayPal integration 235
process, creating 137-145
read-only fields, creating 87, 88
read-only tab, creating 84-86
read-only window, creating 83
role, setting up 91-94
search widget, creating 66-75
software requirement 8
tab fields, grouping 155
tab replica, creating 100, 101
VirtueMart integration 188
Web services, configuring 162, 163
Web services, configuring for record update
177-180
Web services, configuring to create record
164-168
Web services, configuring to read list of
records 171-174
Web services, configuring to read record
168-171
Web services, configuring to remove record
181-183
Web services, configuring to run process
183-186

createData, generic APIs 158
createdby 44
cube 278
customization
  ADempiere 37-39
custom report
  using, for printing 232, 234

D

data
  analyzing, Mondrian and JPivot used
    281-284
  filtering, at tab level 102-104
database view
  creating 214
data display
  defaulting, to single/multi row mode 95
debugging
  Adempiere client application 17-22
  Adempiere server application 23-33
default logic
  configuring 108, 109
default print format, window
  customizing 117-119
deleteData, generic APIs 158
desktop version, of toolbar
  extending 146-149
display logic
  configuring 104-108
dynamic validation
  about 114
  implementing 114-116

E

Eclipse Galileo 8
eCommerce Integration Web services 158
e-mail integration, with Mozilla Thunderbird
  about 293
  environment, setting up 294-298
  Thunderbird toolbar, extending 298-305
entities, VirtueMart. *See* VirtueMart
    entities
entity and line items
  displaying, on same tab 96-98

environment, ADempiere-JasperReports
    integration
  iReport, installing 210
  iReport, running 210
  PostgreSQL JDBC driver, downloading 210
  reports, generating using view 213-218
  reports, generating without view 218222
  setting up 210
environment, ADempiere-VirtueMart
    integration
  Apache ActiveMQ, installing 189
  setting up 188
  VirtueMart, installing 189
Equifax
  about 255
  services 255
Equifax address matching service
  about 261
  integrating 263
  working 262
  XML, creating 261
Equifax bank validation service
  about 263
  integrating 264
  working 264
Equifax company matching service
  about 265
  working 265
Equifax consumer bureau service
  about 265-267
  working 268
Equifax password change service
  about 268
  working 269
Equifax session service
  about 256
  error responses 260
  invoking 257-259
  requests 256
  working 260
error responses, Equifax session service
  invalid session 260
  session timeout 260
ETL (Extract-Transform-Load) tools 272
executeEquifaxRequest method 258
existing window
  customizing 55-57

F

fixed_format_address element 262

G

getList, generic APIs 158
getLogonSessionServiceXml method 258
getVersion Web service 161
getXmlRepresentation() function 207

H

hooks, for model
  modifying 133-136

I

information flow, from VirtueMart to ADempiere
  enabling 207, 208
info window
  creating, for desktop version 127
  creating, for web version 128, 129
  role-based access 128
input_address element 262
installation
  Adempiere 13, 16
installer
  creating, from source code 9-12
  creating, RUN_Build.bat used 13
  working 13
IPN
  about 253
  implementing 253, 254
iReport
  about 210
  installing 210
  running 210
isactive 44

J

JasperReports integration
  about 210
  environment, setting up 210

Java SDK
  using 240-242
  working 243
JBoss 4.2.3 GA 8
JDK 1.5 8
Joomla!
  downloading 189
Joomla! VirtueMart 187
JPivot interface 272
JPivot Web-based interface 281

L

list of records
  reading, getList used 175, 176
lookup record
  configuring 111-113

M

main method 22
match_status attribute 262
MBPartnerProduct.java class 205
MDX (multi-dimensional expressions) queries
  273
Minutes Of Meeting (MOM) 42
model
  generating 123-126
model oriented Web services 158
MOM template 42
Mondrian
  about 272
  cube 278
  reference link 273
  schema 278
  URL 273
Mondrian integration
  about 271
  filter, applying 284-287
  filter, defining 284-287
Mozilla Thunderbird
  ADempiere contacts, importing 305-310
  downloading 294
  e-mail account, setting up 294, 295
  installing 294
MProductPrice.java class 205
MQClient 201

multiple instances
running, on single server 34-36

N

NAV APIs 240
new menu tree
creating 89, 90

O

Openbravo POS integration Web services 158

P

payment
making, to PayPal account 243-252
posting, to PayPal account from ADempiere
Payment window 243-252
PaymentProcessor abstract class 252
PayPal
about 235
Java SDK, using 240-242
PayPal APIs
NAV APIs 240
SOAP APIs 240
working with 239
PayPal Instant Payment Notification. *See*
PayPal IPN
PayPal integration 235
PayPal IPN
about 253
reference link 256
working 254
PayPal Sandbox 239
Persistence Object class 201
PHP Stomp client library
downloading 195
PostgreSQL JDBC driver
downloading 210
PostgreSQL Database 8.x 8
PP_PayPal class 252
print format, window
configuring 119-123
process
creating 137-145
running, runProcess used 183

processCC method 252
products and prices
publishing, to VirtueMart 202-206

Q

queryData, generic APIs 158

R

readData, generic APIs 158
read-only fields
creating 87, 88
read-only tab
creating 84-86
read-only window
creating 83
record
creating, createData used 164
list of records, reading using getList 175, 176
list of records, reading using queryData 171
reading, readData used 168
removing, deleteData used 181
updating, updateData used 177
report
context, using 223-226
creating, from analyzed data set 290, 291
developing, with sub-report 226-232
generating, view used 213-218
generating, without view 218-222
request_header 260
requests, Equifax session service
change password 256
log off 256
logon 256
ping 256
role
menu tree, assigning 91-94
setting up 91-94
RUN_Build.bat 13
runProcess, generic APIs 158

S

schema 278
search widget
creating 66-75
sendHttpRequest method 257

sendMessage() function 208
SendMOMMail process 183
services, Equifax
  address matching service 256
  bank validation service 256
  company matching service 256
  consumer bureau service 256
  session service 255
session_token 260
setDocAction, generic APIs 158, 186
shopping cart applications
  Magento 187
  osCommerce 187
  VirtueMart 187
small and medium businesses (SMBs) 272
SOAP APIs 240
SOAP SDK
  downloading 240
soapUI
  installing 236
software requirement
  Eclipse Galileo 8
  installation steps, reference link 8
  JBoss 4.2.3 GA 8
  JDK 1.5 8
  PostgreSQL Database 8.x 8
  SVN client 8
Stomp 192

T

tab fields, grouping 154, 155
tab replica
  creating 100, 101
Thunderbird toolbar
  extending 298-305
toolbar 146

U

UI oriented Web services 157
updateData, generic APIs 158
utils_dev folder 13

V

VirtueMart
  about 201

downloading 189
download link 189
installing 189
VirtueMart entities
  about 202
  mappings 203
  setting up 202
VirtueMart integration 188
VMImport 201

W

Web services
  configuring 162, 163
  configuring, for record update 177-180
  configuring, to create a record 164-168
  configuring, to read a list of records 171-174
  configuring, to read a record 168-171
  configuring, to remove a record 181-183
  configuring, to run a process 183-186
Web services interfaces
  eCommerce Integration Web services 158
  Model oriented Web services 158
  Openbravo POS integration Web services 158
  UI oriented Web services 157
Web services support
  building 159, 161
web version, of toolbar
  extending 150-153
window
  creating 43-54
  discussion detail tab 58
  multiple tabs, adding 58-66
  participants tab 58
  replicating 109-111

X

XAMPP
  about 191
  installing 253
XML, Equifax address matching service
  creating 261

Z

zoom window
  configuring 80-82

[PACKT] open source *
PUBLISHING   community experience distilled

Thank you for buying
ADempiere 3.6 Cookbook

About Packt Publishing

Packt, pronounced 'packed', published its first book "*Mastering phpMyAdmin for Effective MySQL Management*" in April 2004 and subsequently continued to specialize in publishing highly focused books on specific technologies and solutions.

Our books and publications share the experiences of your fellow IT professionals in adapting and customizing today's systems, applications, and frameworks. Our solution based books give you the knowledge and power to customize the software and technologies you're using to get the job done. Packt books are more specific and less general than the IT books you have seen in the past. Our unique business model allows us to bring you more focused information, giving you more of what you need to know, and less of what you don't.

Packt is a modern, yet unique publishing company, which focuses on producing quality, cutting-edge books for communities of developers, administrators, and newbies alike. For more information, please visit our website: www.packtpub.com.

About Packt Open Source

In 2010, Packt launched two new brands, Packt Open Source and Packt Enterprise, in order to continue its focus on specialization. This book is part of the Packt Open Source brand, home to books published on software built around Open Source licenses, and offering information to anybody from advanced developers to budding web designers. The Open Source brand also runs Packt's Open Source Royalty Scheme, by which Packt gives a royalty to each Open Source project about whose software a book is sold.

Writing for Packt

We welcome all inquiries from people who are interested in authoring. Book proposals should be sent to author@packtpub.com. If your book idea is still at an early stage and you would like to discuss it first before writing a formal book proposal, contact us; one of our commissioning editors will get in touch with you.

We're not just looking for published authors; if you have strong technical skills but no writing experience, our experienced editors can help you develop a writing career, or simply get some additional reward for your expertise.

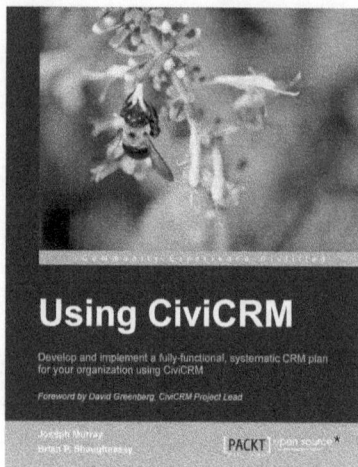

Using CiviCRM

ISBN: 978-1-84951-226-8   Paperback: 464 pages

Develop and implement a fully functional, systematic CRM plan for your organization Using CiviCRM

1. Build a CRM that conforms to your needs from the ground up with all of the features that you want

2. Develop an integrated online system that handles contacts, donations, event registration, bulk e-mailing, case management and other functions such as activity tracking, grants, reporting, and analytics

3. Integrate CiviCRM with Drupal and Joomla!

4. Build solutions from the ground up with the help of easy-to-understand steps from three practical use-case scenarios

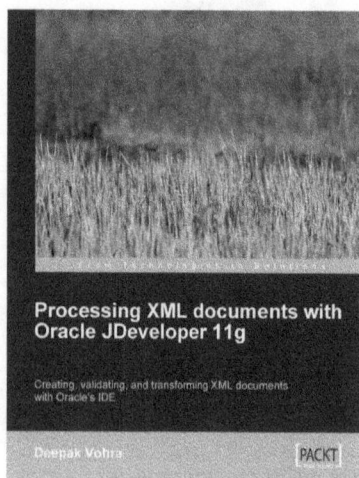

Processing XML documents with Oracle JDeveloper 11g

ISBN: 978-1-847196-66-8   Paperback: 384 pages

Creating, validating, and transforming XML documents with Oracle's IDE

1. Will get the reader developing applications for processing XML in JDeveloper 11g quickly and easily

2. Self-contained chapters provide thorough, comprehensive instructions on how to use JDeveloper to create, validate, parse, transform, and compare XML documents.

3. The only title to cover XML processing in Oracle JDeveloper 11g, this book includes information on the Oracle XDK 11g APIs.

Please check **www.PacktPub.com** for information on our titles

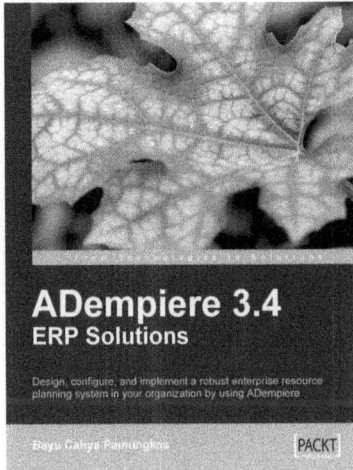

ADempiere 3.4 ERP Solutions

ISBN: 978-1-847197-26-9   Paperback: 460 pages

Design, configure, and implement a robust enterprise resource planning system in your organization using ADempiere

1. Successfully implement ADempiere—an open source, company-wide ERP solution—to manage and coordinate all the resources, information, and functions of a business

2. Master data management and centralize the functions of various business departments in an advanced ERP system

3. Efficiently manage business documents such as purchase/sales orders, material receipts/shipments, and invoices

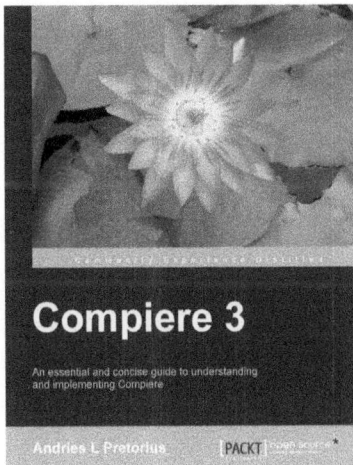

Compiere 3

ISBN: 978-1-849510-84-4   Paperback: 224 pages

An essential and concise guide to understanding and implementing Compiere.

1. Successfully implement Compiere, the leading open source ERP business solution, to manage and coordinate all the resources, information, and functions of a business

2. Efficiently manage business documents such as purchase/sales orders, material receipts/shipments, and invoices

3. A quick way to evaluate the Compiere software against your needs, or to get a prototype implementation to test with users or management

Please check **www.PacktPub.com** for information on our titles